A FRAMEWORK FOR MONETARY STABILITY

FINANCIAL AND MONETARY POLICY STUDIES

Volume 27

The titles published in this series are listed at the end of this volume.

A FRAMEWORK FOR MONETARY STABILITY

*Papers and Proceedings of an International Conference organised
by De Nederlandsche Bank and the CentER for Economic
Research at Amsterdam*

Edited by

J. ONNO DE BEAUFORT WIJNHOLDS
*De Nederlandsche Bank, Amsterdam and University of Groningen,
The Netherlands*

SYLVESTER C.W. EIJFFINGER
CentER for Economic Research and Tilburg University, The Netherlands

and

LEX H. HOOGDUIN
De Nederlandsche Bank, Amsterdam, The Netherlands

KLUWER ACADEMIC PUBLISHERS
DORDRECHT / BOSTON / LONDON

Library of Congress Cataloging-in-Publication Data

A framework for monetary stability : paper and proceedings of an international conference
    organised by De Nederlandsche Bank and the CentER for Economic Research at Amsterdam,
    The Netherlands, October 1993 / edited by J. Onno de Beaufort Wijnholds and Sylvester C.W.
    Eijffinger and Lex H. Hoogduin.
        p. cm. -- (Financial and monetary policy studies ; 27)
        ISBN 0-7923-2667-9 (HB : acid free paper)
        1. Monetary policy--Congresses.   2. Banks and banking, Central-
    -Congresses.   I. Beaufort Wijnholds, J. A. H. de.   II. Eijffinger,
    Sylvester C. W.   III. Hoogduin, Lex H.   IV. Nederlandsche Bank.
    V. Center for Economic Research at Amsterdam.   VI. Series.
    HG230.3.F72   1994
    332.4'6--dc20   93-45987

ISBN 0-7923-2667-9

Published by Kluwer Academic Publishers,
P.O. Box 17, 3300 AA Dordrecht, The Netherlands.

Kluwer Academic Publishers incorporates the publishing
programmes of D. Reidel, Martinus Nijhoff, Dr W. Junk and MTP Press.

Sold and distributed in the U.S.A. and Canada
by Kluwer Academic Publishers,
101 Philip Drive, Norwell, MA 02061, U.S.A.

In all other countries, sold and distributed
by Kluwer Academic Publishers Group,
P.O. Box 322, 3300 AH Dordrecht, The Netherlands.

Printed on acid-free paper

Printed in the Netherlands

TABLE OF CONTENTS

Foreword   ix
Introduction   xi

Part A – Thursday October 21, 1993

Wim F. Duisenberg
Opening Speech by the President of De Nederlandsche Bank   3
David Mullins Jr.
Keynote Speech by the Vice Chairman of the Federal Reserve Board: 5
A Framework for Monetary Stability – A Policy Maker's Perspective

Session I – The Final Objective of Monetary Policy

Charles Freedman
Formal Targets for Inflation Reduction: The Canadian Experience   17
Stanley Fischer
The Costs and Benefits of Disinflation   31
John Driffill
Comment on C. Freedman: Formal Targets for Inflation Reduction: 43
The Canadian Experience
José Luis Malo de Molina
Comment on S. Fischer: The Costs and Benefits of Disinflation   49

Session II – The Position of the Central Bank

Alex Cukierman
Commitment through Delegation, Political Influence and Central Bank   55
Independence
J. Onno de Beaufort Wijnholds and Lex Hoogduin
Central Bank Autonomy: Policy Issues   75
Eduard Bomhoff
Comment on A. Cukierman: Commitment through Delegation,   97
Political Influence and Central Bank Independence

Manfred J.M. Neumann
Comment on Onno de Beaufort Wijnholds and Lex Hoogduin: Central   103
Bank Autonomy: Policy Issues

Session III – The Design of Monetary Policy

Benjamin M. Friedman
Intermediate Targets versus Information Variables as Operating Guides   109
for Monetary Policy
Otmar Issing
Monetary Policy Strategy in the EMU   135
Alexandre Lamfalussy
Comment on B.M. Friedman: Intermediate Targets versus   149
Information Variables as Operating Guides for Monetary Policy
Paul de Grauwe
Comment on O. Issing: Monetary Policy Strategy in the EMU   153

Dinner Speech by *Wim F. Duisenberg*: To Cut or Not to Cut Interest   157
Rates: Some Remarks on the ERM

Part B – Friday October 22, 1993

Session IV – The Application of Monetary Policy

Andrew D. Crockett
Rules versus Discretion in Monetary Policy   165
Manuel Guitián
The Role of Monetary Policy in IMF Programs   185
Jacques J. Sijben
Comment on A.D. Crockett: Rules versus Discretion in Monetary Policy 211
Henk Jager
Comment on M. Guitián: The Role of Monetary Policy in IMF Programs   217

Session V – Monetary Policy and Exchange Rates

Marcello De Cecco and Francesco Giavazzi
Italy's Experience within and without the European Monetary System: 221
A Preliminary Appraisal
André Icard
Monetary Policy and Exchange Rates: The French Experience   239
Gunter D. Baer
Comment on M. De Cecco and F. Giavazzi: Italy's Experience within   257
and without the European Monetary System: A Preliminary Appraisal
Ralph C. Bryant
Comment on A. Icard: Monetary Policy and Exchange Rates: The   263
French Experience

Session VI – Monetary Policy in Eastern Europe and Latin America

Richard Layard
Can Russia Control Inflation?   269
Rudiger Dornbusch
Stabilization and Monetary Reform in Latin America   283
Oleh Havrylyshyn
Comment on R. Layard: Can Russia Control Inflation?   299
Guillermo Ortiz
Comment on R. Dornbusch: Stabilization and Monetary Reform in   305
Latin America

Sylvester Eijffinger
A Framework for Monetary Stability – General Report   309

List of Participants   331

Foreword

Recently, De Nederlandsche Bank in cooperation with the CentER for Economic Research of Tilburg University organised an international conference on monetary policy. This volume contains the papers, comments and speeches given on that occasion. The organisation of such a conference and the publication of this book were possible only through the efforts of a number of people. More in particular I would like to thank the organising committee (prof Onno de Beaufort Wijnholds, assoc prof Sylvester Eijffinger, dr Lex Hoogduin and Broos van der Werff), Hans Haan the conference manager, Imelda Drubbel and Nicolette Ligtenberg who constituted the conference secretariat, Bert Groothoff who acted as press officer and Eric Schaling for their assistance. A special word of appreciation is due to mrs Bodil Andersen (Denmarks National Bank) and mr Kumiharu Shigehara (Organisation of Economic Cooperation and Development) who accepted the difficult task of chairing the meetings which they did most admirably. Of course, a conference cannot even take place without participants and cannot be a success without good participants. I am very pleased that we could be the host of the eminent group of people who in my view made the conference such a success. Before the conference I thought it would be a one-time-event. After the event I am not so sure.

Amsterdam
November 1993

Wim F. Duisenberg
President of De Nederlandsche Bank

ix

Introduction

During October 20–23, 1993 an international conference took place at the Grand Hotel in Amsterdam under the theme "A Framework for Monetary Stability". This conference was organised by De Nederlandsche Bank and the CentER for Economic Research of Tilburg University. The aim was to discuss various aspects of monetary policy within a limited circle of high-ranking central bankers and prominent monetary economists from universities and research institutes from all over the world. In fact there were participants from all continents. It was felt that an interaction between central bankers and academics could be a fruitful exercise, not only in terms of an exchange of views, but also because it might contribute to a convergence of thinking on monetary policy.

In this volume the papers presented at the conference, the contributions of the discussants, the speeches given and the general report in which the conference was summarised are published. The outline of this book reflects the programme of the conference. After a short opening speech by President Duisenberg (De Nederlandsche Bank) clarifying the theme of monetary stability, Vice Chairman David Mullins Jr. (Federal Reserve Board) delivered the keynote speech in which he gave a policy maker's view of monetary stability.

The conference was further organised in six sessions, three sessions on each day. In each session two papers were presented by the authors. Subsequently, comments were given by a discussant followed by a general discussion with the participants of the conference. The subjects of the sessions were: the final objective of monetary policy, the position of the central bank, the design of monetary policy, the application of monetary policy, the consequences of participating in exchange rate regimes for monetary policy, and monetary and financial reform in Eastern Europe and Latin America. At the end of the first day, President Duisenberg gave a dinner speech on recent developments within and the future of the European exchange rate mechanism. Finally, the papers and discussions were summarised and personal conclusions were drawn in a general report by Sylvester Eijffinger (CentER and Tilburg University).

In our view, the material in this book covers a wide variety of issues presently discussed with respect to monetary policy. It also makes clear where opinions differ and on what grounds. Time will tell whether the conference promoted the hoped-for convergence of views among the participants. However, it certainly increased the degree of understanding of each others position. This was clearly facilitated by the lively discussions that took place in the agreeable environment in which the conference was held (the former council meeting hall of the city of Amsterdam). A list of authors, discussants and other participants is given at the end of this volume.

The editors wish to express their gratitude to all the contributors to this volume. They have made it possible that this book can be published relatively soon after the conference by submitting their papers in a timely fashion and by their general willingness to revise them already at the venue of the conference. The issues addressed are therefore still highly topical. We hope the readers will benefit as much from reading the papers, comments and speeches as we enjoyed organising the conference and editing this volume.

Amsterdam/Tilburg
November 1993

J. Onno de Beaufort Wijnholds
Sylvester C.W. Eijffinger
Lex H. Hoogduin

PART A

Thursday October 21, 1993

Opening Speech

WIM F. DUISENBERG

President of De Nederlandsche Bank

Ladies and gentlemen,

Good morning, and very welcome indeed to the heart of Amsterdam.

I would like to welcome you at this conference today, on behalf of De Nederlandsche Bank and the CentER for Economic Research of Tilburg University. Speaking for the Bank of course I am particularly pleased because of the subject you are going to discuss the next two days: I can hardly think of an item which should raise more the interest of a central banker than the issue of monetary stability.

I need hardly tell you how important a stable economic climate is. It is a prerequisite for the price mechanism to fulfill its allocative role, and thus for sustainable economic growth. A sufficiently stable price level also acts as a guarantee against arbitrary redistributions of income and wealth, which often threaten to destabilize whole societies. This danger has shown itself clearly in history, and is quite visible even today. Though the desirability of a stable price level is clear in general, actual conditions, alas, differ substantially between countries and regions. This gives room to different points of view. Under the general theme of monetary stability a rather wide variety of items can be identified.

The programme for the conference makes this visible. In my view it also reflects the number of issues which are currently being investigated by our profession. It may sound like a truism, but I am convinced that it is right to say that from a monetary perspective we live in a turbulent time. Let me mention as example some of the themes which you will be dealing with at this conference. I could for instance point to the preparation of a European Economic and Monetary Union, to the vast changes in our financial systems to which policy makers (this includes many of you) will have to adapt. Or to the struggle for stability in the transforming economies in Eastern Europe and elsewhere. Your discussions will therefore focus on highly topical areas.

I would like to express my sincere thanks to all of you for being present these days. Especially of course a word of welcome and thanks to Vice Chairman Mullins from the Federal Reserve Board, who has been so kind to come to

J.A.H. de Beaufort Wijnholds, S.C.W. Eijffinger and L.H. Hoogduin (eds.), A Framework for Monetary Stability, pp. 3–4.

Amsterdam in order to deliver what will be the real opening address to us this morning.

My special thanks also extend to the participants who have been willing to deliver a paper or to act as a discussant in one of the sessions, and of course also to those chairing the meetings.

Looking at the list of participants one gets the impression that a careful balance has been struck between the worlds of monetary policy makers on the one hand and, may I call them, monetary academics on the other hand. At the same time a large variety of countries is represented today. In fact somebody from every continent of the world is present here. This could bring fruitful discussions in which we all may benefit from your specific knowledge, background, and experience.

The ingredients for a stimulating and interesting conference seem to be in place. It is up to you to fulfill this promise.

Now, I am very pleased to give the floor to Mr Mullins who will speak on 'A framework for monetary stability : a policy maker's perspective'.

A Framework for Monetary Stability – A Policy Maker's Perspective

DAVID W. MULLINS, JR.

Vice Chairman, Board of Governors of the Federal Reserve System, Washington, D.C.

I am pleased to initiate this conference by exploring a number of the issues to be addressed more rigorously in later sessions. My focus will be that of a practitioner, one who attempts to deal with these issues on a daily basis.

I shall begin with the ultimate objective of monetary policy. From my perspective, that of a U.S. policymaker, the ultimate objective is not price stability. The ultimate objective of monetary policy is to maximize economic growth, to maximize economic well-being and to contribute to the advancement of living standards. Ultimately, the source of legitimacy for monetary policy is the extent to which policy contributes to economic welfare.

What can monetary policy do to contribute to maximum growth? Of course, this is where price stability enters the equation. Most central bankers are guided by the conviction that creating an environment of price stability is what monetary policy can do to contribute to the goal of maximizing economic growth. Thus, I do not view price stability as an end in itself, but as the means through which monetary policy can contribute to the ultimate objective of maximizing economic well-being. Central bankers are likely to be able to sustain and justify the objective of price stability within the political system and with the public only to the extent that a convincing case can be made that price stability contributes in a substantial way to increased economic well-being.

This linkage between price stability and economic growth may seem obvious and fully accepted in many countries. Indeed, it is now almost universally accepted that high rates of inflation – double digit inflation rates – are damaging to an economy and detrimental to economic welfare. This was the lesson of the 1970s – inflation is an impediment to growth, not an engine of growth.

Unfortunately, there is a less well established case against moderate, single digit levels of inflation on the order of a 4% annual inflation rate. I am aware of very little definitive, convincing evidence on the magnitude of the benefits and the costs associated with disinflation from moderate single digit levels of inflation. And, different countries reflect very different views on whether such inflation levels are acceptable or detrimental. For example, one suspects the Germans would judge 4%–5% inflation as unacceptably high, but in the United States the political system and the public seem reasonably content with

J.A.H. de Beaufort Wijnholds, S.C.W. Eijffinger and L.H. Hoogduin (eds.), A Framework for Monetary Stability, pp. 5–15.

U.S. inflation that has averaged 4%–5% over the last decade.

In my view, 4% inflation is unacceptably high. I do think there is a good case, a sound rationale to conclude that reducing inflation from the 4%–5% level to a *deminimis* level (taking into account measurement bias) is on balance beneficial, perhaps significantly beneficial. However, in some countries such as the United States, this case has yet to be persuasively made and widely accepted.

The case against moderate inflation centers on the elimination of economic distortions engendered by inflation even at the 4% level. For example, absent tax indexation, even low inflation rates produce substantial increases in the real effective tax rates for investors and businesses adversely affecting investment. Of course, indexation of taxes for inflation, rejected numerous times by the U.S. Congress, would eliminate this drag on investment and growth. A simpler solution is to essentially eliminate inflation. More generally, the elimination of inflation should minimize real interest rates across the maturity spectrum by minimizing risk or uncertainty premia. And, low real interest rates and low effective tax rates encourage investment-producing growth in productivity, the only reliable path to sustained growth in living standards. This is the chain of reasoning connecting price stability and enhanced economic well-being. I believe it provides a compelling case against complacency with moderate inflation; a strong argument for seeking to achieve truly deminimis inflation levels as the practical objective of monetary policy.

It is worth noting that, to achieve these benefits, it is not just actual, measured inflation that must be reduced. Inflationary expectations must be reduced. This is because it is expected that inflation is built into long-term bond rates and wage contracts, and inflation expectations guide long-term investment decisions by businesses and consumers. This makes the task more difficult because markets have long memories; so do consumers and business executives. It takes a long time to build inflationary expectations into markets and into the attitudes of decision makers, and at least as long to extinguish inflationary expectations. Reducing firmly entrenched inflationary expectations is far more difficult than dousing a temporary, cyclical runup of inflation above the mean expected level.

This is particularly relevant to the current prospects for inflation in the United States. Although U.S. inflation has averaged 4%–5% over the last decade, recent inflation trends and underlying inflation fundamentals suggest the possibility of a change in inflation regimes; specifically, a return to the deminimis levels of inflation experienced in the early 1960s. A commensurate reduction in inflationary expectations would logically lead to the establishment of a sustainable low interest rate and high stock price capital market environment similar to that prevailing in the early 1960s. The result would be enhanced growth.

Of course, if the recent U.S. inflation performance turns out to be simply the trough in a cyclical variation around an unchanged inflation mean of 4%, then the capital market environment is likely to revert to the less hospitable structure of the 1980s. If this occurs, this chance for a significant downward adjustment in inflationary expectations – an opportunity that appears only once every decade or so – will be lost. Thus, in the current U.S. environment, price stability and the enhanced economic growth it engenders seem within reach, but this achievement is by no means assured.

Another issue concerns the relationship between the objective of price stability and the economic stabilization objective assigned to many central banks. Some argue that there exists a trade-off between these two objectives. In an economic downturn, monetary authorities can be more stimulative only at a cost – the risk of higher inflation.

However, many central bankers disagree and instead argue that there is a supportive, symbiotic relationship between the objectives of price stability and economic stabilization. Credibility enhances the effectiveness of monetary policy as an economic stabilization tool. If markets are convinced that a central bank is committed to price stability, then in an economic downturn, short-term interest rates can decline markedly without engendering inflationary fears and counterproductive movements in long-term interest rates. Without credibility, the benefits of reduced short-term interest rates should be to some extent offset by the adverse impact of inflationary fears on the long-term end of the yield curve. Therefore, a credible commitment to price stability provides a fulcrum that amplifies and enhances a central bank's effectiveness in economic stabilization.

A similar line of reasoning applies to fiscal policy. But, it seems most fiscal policy makers have failed to establish a credible anchor that enhances effectiveness in stabilization. If markets are not confident that there is a long-term commitment to fiscal discipline, to low deficits, then the expansionary force of fiscal stimulus will be diminished by the contractionary force engendered by higher interest rates that reflect market concerns about higher deficits in the long term as well as near term.

Examination of the issue of stabilization leads to the next topic I would like to address – the recent economic cycle most industrialized countries have been struggling through. Within this cycle, the United States appears to be somewhat ahead of many countries. While there may exist significant differences in this economic cycle in different countries, it may, nonetheless, be useful to share some insights gained from the U.S. experience.

Some, but not all, elements of the U.S. experience of the last three years seem roughly consistent with what academic economists have called the "credit view" of monetary economies; others call it "debt deflation." The process has also been described as one of balance sheet adjustment and repair. The 1980s were characterized by asset price inflation as well as debt growth at unsustainable rates leading to an inevitable adjustment.

Why did this happen? Why did the 1980s see a decade-long borrowing binge? There were no doubt many components contributing to this phenomenon including changes in financial institution regulatory policies, tax policies and the like. But this was a worldwide phenomenon occurring in many countries. Thus it is not clear how much responsibility should be assigned to country specific, idiosyncratic factors. While there may be much left unexplained, it may be useful to sketch some of the significant broadly based underlying factors contributing to the leveraging behavior of the 1980s in the U.S.

In my view, the decade of the 1980s was characterized by an unprecedented degree and pace of financial innovation fueled by technological advances. This resulted in increased access to debt that challenged and undermined traditional norms of leverage.

Why the 1980s debt binge? A simple view is that before the 1980s, many economic agents could not get the debt. In the 1980s, for the first time, they could get the debt. And, in the context of a long economic expansion, they got a bit too much debt leading to the adjustment experienced in the early 1990s.

Who got the debt? First, consumer debt increased markedly. There have been two periods of discontinuously rapid consumer debt growth in the U.S. The first was in the 1950s with the introduction of the credit card, and the second was the 1980s when technology propelled the spread of credit more broadly within the U.S. population. For example, point of sale credit authorization systems made possible tight credit control and allowed banks to qualify people with incomes below the poverty line for credit cards. Later in the decade securitization reinforced credit availability at reasonable cost. Technology reduced the administrative cost of credit origination and administration.

Who else gained expanded access to credit in the 1980s? Business borrowers with bond ratings below investment grade gained access to the depth and cost efficiency of the public bond market for the first time with the development of the high yield (or "junk") bond market in the late 1970s. The rapid development of this market provided growing, accelerating access to a vast group of borrowers. Access to the high yield bond market played a pivotal role in fueling the boom in mergers and acquisitions and leveraged buyouts that in turn contributed to an upward spiral in asset values based, in part, on unrealizable expectations. The high yield bond market grew explosively in the 1980s, but possessed only a short history to gauge riskiness. For example, research suggests investors may have underassessed default risk, and pricing may have outrun fundamentals.

But it was not just below investment grade, junk bond issuers who expanded leverage. Why did investment grade companies substantially increase their use of debt in the 1980s? Before the development of the below investment grade bond market, many firms pursued low debt ratio, high bond rating capital structure policies for fear of losing access to debt in poor economic times. The development of the high yield bond market provided an apparently reliable source of funds for high debt ratio firms. Enticed by the advantages of leverage, such as the tax benefits of debt financing, many investment grade firms concluded that they could safely lower their target bond ratings, increase their target debt ratios without risking a loss of access to the market even under adverse circumstances. Many others were coerced into abandoning traditionally conservative debt ratios and increasing debt by the threat of a takeover financed by high yield bonds. As a result, during the decade of the 1980s large U.S. firms' average bond ratings fell from AA to B, their average debt to total capital ratio increased from about 25% to close to 50%.

Then in 1989, the high yield bond market disintegrated leaving firms with below investment grade bond ratings without access to the bond markets and threatening lower rated investment grade firms with loss of access in bad times. Firms were faced with the necessity of reducing their leverage ratios to ensure continuous financing for their business activities. Research documents that issuing equity is costly leading many firms to implement a process of restructuring designed to generate internal cash flows to work down high debt ratios.

There were, of course, many other components of this experience. Overbuilding and asset price inflation in commercial real estate; asset price inflation in agricultural and residential real estate; bank lending collateralized by reflated, market values of real estate and other assets such as leveraged buyouts. The subsequent collapse of these asset price spirals left banks with damaged capital bases igniting retrenchment within the banking system and tightened credit conditions throughout the economy – the so-called "credit crunch." Globalization and securitization helped transmit these forces of financial expansion and contraction.

Thus, in my view, financial innovation played an important role in fueling the leveraging in the 1980s. It increased access to debt, challenged and made obsolete time-honored leverage norms. And, in the context of a long period of expansion, the result was garden variety overshooting in some asset values and in leverage. This process went beyond sustainable levels; an adjustment was unavoidable. When the process collapsed, businesses, consumers and financial institutions were left with excess debt and impaired net worth.

The adjustment process is one of balance sheet adjustment, and it is fundamentally different from a cyclical episode, an overheated economy leading to an inventory adjustment. In the traditional cycle, faced with excess inventories, firms cut production sharply and lay off workers temporarily. The adjustment takes two or three quarters to bring inventories into line. Their laid off workers are recalled, and production is increased markedly. The result is the classic "V-shaped" recession and recovery; it is clear to all when the economy is in recession and when recovery is under way.

A balance sheet adjustment process is quite different. With a capital structure out of line, firms do not cut production sharply. Maximum cash flow is needed to pay down excess debt. The adjustment involves minimizing asset investment, cutting overhead, eliminating every nonessential worker and layoffs that appear permanent. The adjustment process goes beyond simple financial restructuring. Many firms viewed this as an opportunity to initiate a comprehensive restructuring to enhance cash flow. The process of restructuring and redressing an overly extended capital structure takes not two or three quarters, but perhaps two or three years or longer.

The result is a much different pattern from a traditional economic cycle; no sharp downturn, no sharp rebound; instead a protracted period of sluggishness. The inevitably slow pace of this adjustment process, the focus on painstakingly cleaning up old problems, rather than looking to the future, is, I think, quite damaging to public sentiment, to the attitudes of consumers and business people. Because the structural dynamics of this balance sheet adjustment process differ so fundamentally from a typical cyclical episode, simple comparisons with earlier cycles are not particularly useful nor insightful.

What are the primary policy implications of this analysis? This balance sheet adjustment process takes time to work through. I doubt that this sort of adjustment process is sharply and quickly responsive to macroeconomic policy actions. Nonetheless, the deleveraging process is inherently disinflationary, and monetary policy can play a useful role.

But, in the initial stages of adjustment, the role of monetary policy is one of facilitating and accelerating the adjustment process. As U.S. interest rates have been reduced in the early 1990s, the initial force of monetary ease was channeled not into new spending, but into the financial restructuring process to reduce debt burdens; firms issuing equity to pay down debt not for new spending; consumers refinancing mortgages rather than purchasing new homes; banks replenishing depleted capital bases rather than expanding lending. This is, of course, not wasted energy, but important work for monetary policy, for it advances the day that business and consumers can turn to renewed spending, banks to renewed lending.

This is the process of balance sheet repair under way in the United States; a process that is gradually turning the corner from repair to spending. Business capital spending is now growing. Consumers are spending now at a moderate pace; consumer installment debt is growing, no longer contracting; the housing market is picking up; and banks having replenished depleted capital bases are now in a position to expand lending. Thus, in this sort of adjustment process monetary policy is effective, but compared to a traditional recession, it takes longer to foster growth in spending.

Another consequence of these financial processes is distortion of the traditional relationships between monetary aggregates and economic activity. Financial innovation has altered monetary aggregates. The financial system is no longer simply the banking system with money on one side of the balance sheet and credit on the other side with the central bank in firm control of the whole system. With the complexity of the modern financial system, the vitality of financial innovation, the trends toward securitization and globalization, many wonder whether monetary authorities will ever again be able to depend upon one simple summary statistic as an intermediate monetary target to gauge the stance and progress of policy.

The current adjustment process has distorted the relationship of M_2 and nominal GDP in the U.S. With banks restructuring, borrowers deleveraging, and investors offered convenient access to higher yields in the capital markets, funds are flowing from banks to bond and stock mutual funds. Contrary to normal experience in a declining interest rate environment, M_2 velocity is increasing, and M_2 has lost, perhaps temporarily, its traditional usefulness foreshadowing nominal growth. While it might be possible to define a new, broader monetary aggregate incorporating flows to mutual funds, recent experience raises doubts concerning how long it would retain its usefulness.

In my view, the loss of a simple, mechanical relationship between monetary aggregates and economic activity is not debilitating to policy makers. It does require policy makers to examine a wide range of indicators, information variables as guides to policy. And, ample guides exist. There is still ample information within money and credit flows, price data and forward-looking indicators of real economic activity. As always, a process of judgment is required in weighing and assessing a wide variety of indicators coalescing these inputs into a policy conclusion. Some central banks have turned to targeting inflation rates directly. In view of the long time lags between monetary policy actions and the impact on inflation, one has to be wary of policy induced amplification of cycles from inflation rate targeting.

While in my view there is no loss of efficacy from the de-emphasis of the monetary aggregates, policymakers have lost, perhaps only temporarily, a useful tool for communicating the process and progress of policy to the markets, the political system, and the public.

There is a broader issue for policy suggested by our recent experience. When one surveys the experience of the 1980s and the adjustment of the 1990s, it is clear that this process of asset price inflation and leverage overshooting and retrenchment is at least as damaging to the economy as a traditional economic cycle, at least painful and costly as a traditional recession.

It is useful to reflect upon the role monetary policy might have played in creating these problems and attempt to identify policy actions that might avoid a recurrence of this sort of cycle. What can be done to attenuate asset price misalignments, excessive debt growth and thus avoid the costly consequences for the real economy? Indeed, one might suspect a monetary dimension in debt growth and asset price inflation. The complex, rapidly evolving global financial system underscores the need to examine rigorously our recent experience in search of lessons useful in avoiding or reducing the severity of similar episodes in the future. For example, in view of recent experience, is a focus on consumer price stability alone sufficient?

While I shall defer a full discussion of policy implications to be derived from those experiences, it is worth noting one clear implication. The complexity of our recent economic and financial environment raises serious new doubts concerning the feasibility of a monetary policy based upon simple rules, as opposed to a policy guided by the exercise of discretion by monetary authorities.

The final topic I would like to address briefly is the issue of central bank independence or autonomy, a topical issue in a number of countries.

The concept of an independent central bank in a democratic society is not an obvious one. One is reminded of this in discussions with officials of emerging democracies. Such officials are instructed that government should be run by the elected representatives of the people, with relatively short terms for elected government officials for tight political control by the populace – except for control over money and the economy which is to be ceded to unelected economists. This approach seems not obviously derived from democratic principles.

As a practical matter the argument in favor of an independent central bank is empirical. Central banks with some measure of independence from direct political control simply perform better in terms of keeping inflation under control. The empirical evidence supporting this conclusion is compelling. One would expect that independent central banks perform better in terms of contributing to higher economic growth because of this better inflationary performance, but the evidence is less illuminating on this point.

It is especially important to articulate the persuasive empirical case for central bank independence in the current political climate. In the past these issues seemed less prominent, in part because central banks were less publicized. Now central banks are highly visible. In view of protracted, sluggish economic conditions, high unemployment, the sense by some that inflation seems "under control," central banks' performance, structure, and the objective of price stability may well come under increased public and political scrutiny.

Of course, an independent central bank is legitimately derived from democratic principles because this independence is granted by statute through the democratically elected political process. For this reason, the credibility of central bank performance and structure in the political and public arena is quite important. No central bank is truly independent. The independence granted by statute can be eliminated at any time by a vote of the legislature.

Such debates are not inappropriate in a democratic society. It is not unhealthy periodically to require institutions to defend their performance, to argue, to justify their existing structure or make the case for an improved structure.

And, an important point our host, President Duisenberg, often makes is that central bank independence is created not just by statute. Regardless of statute, independence is earned through performance; the painstaking process of creating credibility with markets, the political system, and the public, through doing what is right and necessary and exercising the political sensitivity to do this. This earned independence exists almost independent of statute. It is difficult to create and easy to lose and, I might add, quite difficult to capture in traditional research methodologies on central bank independence.

Nonetheless, central banking statutes are important in defining the nature of the selection process for monetary policymakers. This, I believe, is even more important than statutory objectives for monetary policy, because the nature of the selection process helps determine whether central banks are able to attract policymakers capable of creating credibility and true independence.

There are currently several proposals in the U.S. to alter the structure of the Federal Reserve. I shall not provide a detailed analysis of these proposals nor a defense of the existing structure. I would, however, note characteristics of these proposals.

The proposals to change the Federal Reserve do not focus primarily on the Board of Governors nor on the structure of the district Federal Reserve banks. The focus of these structural proposals is squarely on the FOMC, the Federal Open Market Committee, the monetary policy-making body of the Federal Reserve System. The target of these proposals is the determination of monetary policy.

In general, these proposals seek to change the selection process for FOMC members, the composition of the monetary policy-making body. There are many aspects of these proposals with potentially far-reaching implications for the structure and performance of the Federal Reserve. But, the simplest result would be to increase substantially the voting percentage of the FOMC selected by an incumbent administration and Congress. In contrast to the existing structure in which a U.S. President in a four-year term has very little chance of appointing a majority of the FOMC, in the proposed structures, a U.S. President in a four-year term would seem almost assured of appointing a voting majority of the FOMC. Of course, this may also alter the type of people appointed to policymaking positions.

A concern is whether such a change in the selection process for the FOMC would result in a monetary policy more attuned to short-term political pressures, rather than longer-term economic needs. Indeed, some have observed that, in view of the performance of U.S. fiscal policy compared with U.S. monetary policy, it is not obvious that it would be wise to put those responsible for fiscal policy in charge of monetary policy as well.

Nonetheless, this is a legitimate debate in a democratic society. A central bank must be prepared to participate effectively in these debates because despite a measure of independence in the formulation and implementation of monetary policy, all central banks are extensions of the political system. And, it is encouraging that in many countries, despite difficult economic conditions, the debate concerns granting additional autonomy to central banks.

Before concluding, I should acknowledge that I have omitted many important monetary policy issues including the interaction of different countries' monetary policies. This is an increasingly important issue in an increasingly interdependent world bound together not only by world trade but by global capital markets. The issue of policy coordination is also deeply imbedded in a set of political issues, especially those associated with national sovereignty. These issues are sufficiently complex and important to warrant extensive analysis.

Let me sum up with reference to a longer-term time frame. In many ways, monetary policy has been very successful during the past decade. Motivated by the inflation of the 1970s and its consequences, a remarkable consensus has emerged concerning the wisdom of pursuing a monetary policy predicated on price stability. Much progress has been made in implementing sound monetary policies around the world.

Nonetheless, I do not think this is a time for complacency. Memories of the inflation of the 1970s are receding replaced by new problems. The difficult economic environment of the 1990s – high unemployment and sour public sentiment – has already taken an impressive toll through the political system resulting in the rejection of numerous incumbent governments and the dimming of some of the bright promise of substantially liberalized world trade regimes. One must be particularly vigilant that our notable progress on instituting sound monetary policies does not fall victim to this climate of political disaffection.

I have sought to provide a policy practitioner's viewpoint on several monetary policy issues. In this environment, central bankers need to make a convincing case that price stability enhances economic welfare, that even moderate single digit inflation is damaging. Central bankers need to understand and help others understand the nature of the economic and financial adjustments underway in the current environment. And, central bankers need to make a persuasive case as to the efficacy of autonomy in controlling inflation and in enhancing economic growth. In all of this, I have stressed the importance of building a rigorous case on these issues and communicating and articulating that case within the political system and with the public.

This is why central bankers take economic research very seriously. Economic research provides the foundation for our work, the basis for the positions we articulate in the political system and with the public. And, this is why a conference such as this one is so useful.

SESSION I: THE FINAL OBJECTIVE OF MONETARY POLICY

Formal Targets for Inflation Reduction: The Canadian Experience

CHARLES FREEDMAN[1]
Bank of Canada

In early 1991 the Bank of Canada and the Government of Canada jointly announced targets for reducing the rate of inflation. Canada thus joined New Zealand in employing a formal target path for inflation reduction as an important tactical element to aid in the achievement of the objective of price stability.

In the first section of this paper I set out the background situation leading up to the introduction of the targets. I then turn to the objectives that the targets were intended to achieve and to some of the issues that had to be resolved in developing the targeting framework. Finally, I assess our experience to date with the targets and draw some tentative conclusions from this experience.

1. THE BACKGROUND LEADING UP TO THE ANNOUNCEMENT OF THE TARGETS

Monetary policy in Canada, as in many other countries, has as its goal the achievement and maintenance of price stability. By fostering confidence in the value of money, monetary policy makes its contribution to the ultimate objective of public policy – a well-functioning economy[2].

Even though the achievement and maintenance of price stability is the longer-term goal of monetary policy, central banks have found it useful to have an intermediate nominal target to help them guide monetary policy over the short and medium term. Such a target acts as an anchor to help the monetary authorities avoid cumulative errors. For countries on a fixed exchange rate regime, the exchange rate can serve as a nominal anchor to the system, provided that the partner country has a domestic nominal anchor. For countries on a flexible exchange rate regime, monetary aggregates, credit aggregates and nominal spending are all potentially useful intermediate targets for monetary policy. The ability of such variables to function effectively as intermediate targets is based both on the stability of their empirical relationship to the goal variable and on their relationship to the instrument of monetary policy.

17

J.A.H. de Beaufort Wijnholds, S.C.W. Eijffinger and L.H. Hoogduin (eds.), A Framework for Monetary Stability, pp. 17–29.
© 1994 *Kluwer Academic Publishers. Printed in the Netherlands.*

In Canada, the narrow monetary aggregate M1 was used as the intermediate target of monetary policy between 1975 and 1982. It was dropped as a target in 1982 primarily because innovations by Canadian financial institutions resulted in the introduction of new financial instruments which significantly weakened the linkage of M1 to nominal spending[3]. With the demise of M1 as a target, the Bank embarked on a protracted empirical search for an alternative monetary aggregate target, but no aggregate was able to bear the weight of being a formal target. Instead, the Bank used both monetary and credit aggregates in the lesser role of information variables or guides to policy. Although nominal spending was considered as a possible intermediate target, there were a number of practical reasons for not choosing to make nominal spending the formal target of policy[4]. Thus, from 1982 to 1991 monetary policy in Canada was carried out with price stability as the longer-term goal but without intermediate targets or any specified time path to the longer-term goal.

2. THE OBJECTIVES OF THE INFLATION-REDUCTION TARGETS

The inflation-reduction targets were jointly announced by the Bank and the government on February 26, 1991. The government's announcement came as part of its annual budget, while the Bank issued a press release[5] and a background note[6] setting out practical details regarding the operation of the targets.

The targets set out an explicit path towards price stability. The first guidepost was set for the end of 1992 (22 months after the announcement) and provided for a 12-month rate of increase in the CPI of 3% (more precisely a band of 2 to 4%), to be followed by a band of 1 1/2 to 3 1/2% for mid-1994 and 1 to 3% by the end of 1995 (See Figure 1.) It was specified that after 1995 there would be further reductions of inflation until price stability was achieved[7].

The targets were intended to achieve both near-term and longer-term objectives. In the near term they were intended to prevent the price shocks that were then buffeting the economy from leading to a further wage-price spiral and to help reduce the prevailing inflation expectations. In the longer term they were designed to make more concrete the commitment of the authorities to the goal of achieving and maintaining price stability and to add to the credibility of that goal.

(i) Near-term objective

Although the rate of inflation had remained relatively flat in the 3 to 4% range in the mid-1980s (following a period of double digit inflation in the late 1970s and early 1980s), from 1987 on inflationary pressures heated up as spending

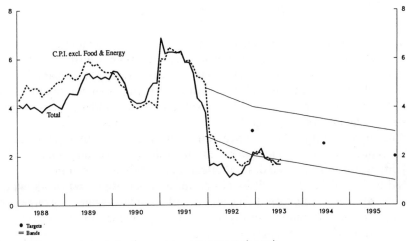

Figure 1 Consumer price index (year-over-year percent change).

pressed against the productive capacity of the economy. Even though the goal of price stability was re-iterated in very clear fashion in 1988[8] and monetary conditions were progressively tightened over the period between 1987 and mid-1990 (with the exception of a short period following the 1987 stock market crash) there was a clear intensification of inflationary pressures and inflation expectations were further entrenched. Even after the economy slowed and a gap began to open in output and labour markets, price and, especially, wage inflation were slow to decline. Moreover, the sharp rise in oil prices following the invasion of Kuwait and the anticipated rise in the price level resulting from the replacement of the existing federal sales tax at the manufacturers' level by a broader VAT-type goods and services tax (GST) at the beginning of 1991 raised concerns about a deterioration of inflation expectations and the possibility of additional upward pressure on inflation. In the background note setting out the operational framework for the targets, the Bank noted that "the outlook for inflation seems at present to be unduly pessimistic in a number of quarters in Canada" (Bank of Canada [1991c], (page 11). By providing a clear indication of the downward path for inflation over the medium term the key near-term aim of the targets was to help firms and individuals see beyond the shocks to the level of prices to the underlying downward trend of inflation at which monetary policy was aiming and to take this into account in their economic decision making.

(ii) Longer-term objective

By making explicit the path to price stability, the announcement of the targets was aimed at facilitating the achievement of the longer-term goal of price stability. To quote from the background note once again, "if Canadians begin to base their economic decisions on this declining path for inflation, the objectives can be readily achieved and will contribute to lower interest rates" (Bank of Canada [1991c], page 11).

Although the Bank had long been on record regarding the ultimate goal of price stability, it was becoming apparent that this general commitment to price stability was not having the desired effect on inflation expectations and that it would be useful to buttress it by either an intermediate target or an explicit downward path for inflation. In the absence of a viable intermediate target, this argued for inflation-reduction targets as a way of making more concrete and more credible the nature of the commitment.

Moreover, since the targets were presented as a joint commitment of the Bank and the government to inflation reduction and price stability, it was made clear that the government was supportive of the price stability goal[9]. It had earlier been argued that the credibility of this goal and the willingness of individuals and companies to act on it was lessened by the concern that the government was not fully committed to it and that such a goal would therefore not be achievable. This concern was heightened by the fact that the longer-term inflation projections in the budgets of preceding years did not seem to be consistent with the Bank's announced goal of price stability[10]. The projections in the 1991 budget, in contrast, were entirely compatible with the inflation-reduction targets[11].

To the extent that the credibility of the inflation-reduction objective was enhanced by the targets, the adjustment of inflation expectations could be accelerated. The costs of adjustment to lower inflation could thus be reduced and monetary conditions could be easier than otherwise would have been the case. Although it was not clear that the announcement of the targets would have any such short-run effect on expectations, it was anticipated that, at a minimum, the achievement of the first milestone at the end of 1992 would enhance the credibility of the subsequent targets and hence facilitate the achievement of these targets as well as the movement to price stability thereafter.

Finally, by providing information on the specific objectives to which the monetary policy actions of the Bank would be directed, the targets were intended to make the Bank's actions more readily understandable to financial market participants and to the general public. They would thus provide a better basis than before for judging the performance of monetary policy and would further improve the accountability of the Bank.

3. ISSUES REQUIRING RESOLUTION DEVELOPING THE TARGETING FRAMEWORK

In establishing targets for inflation reduction, there were a large number of decisions that had to be made, some technical and some of a more substantive nature. In this section I examine a number of the issues that arose in the course of planning the framework for the targets.

(a) How fast should the decline of the target path for inflation be?

This issue is, of course, simply a variant of the long-standing debate in the economics literature on gradualism versus "cold shower" policies[12]. In that literature, the existence of long-term contracts, lags in adjustment of behaviour, and lags in the adjustment of inflation expectations all argue for more gradual disinflation. On the other hand, credibility notions and, in particular, the possibility that a more rapid disinflation could break entrenched expectations could argue for a more rapid disinflation.

In the consideration of various target paths for inflation reduction, similar factors came into play. The lags in the response of the Canadian rate of inflation to changes in monetary policy have traditionally been long, both as a result of institutional characteristics (such as the widespread use of two and three year contracts in labour markets) and expectational sluggishness[13]. At the same time, the path had to depict a clear downward trend in inflation if there was to be any gain in credibility. In the event, it was decided to opt for a rather gradual path, in which the rate of inflation fell by 1 percentage point in total over 3 years after the initial 3% target at the end of 1992. The gradualism of the targeted pace of disinflation was related to the fact that we were moving down into ranges of price inflation not seen for almost three decades. There was therefore considerable uncertainty about how the economy would react and how feasible a more rapid pace of disinflation would be.

(b) What measure of inflation should be used?

The two principal contenders for this role were the CPI, or one of its variants, and the GDP deflator. The CPI was chosen, in large part because it is the most commonly used measure of inflation and it is the most relevant measure for most Canadians. The widespread acceptance and understanding of the CPI by Canadians was particularly important given the role of the targets as a means of communicating the aim of monetary policy. There were also more technical reasons for preferring the CPI: it is available on a monthly basis and hence can be tracked regularly; it is published in timely fashion without long delays; and it is almost never revised.

In order to emphasize trend movements in inflation and not short-term fluctuations, the targets focussed on the 12-month rate of increase of the CPI. Although the targets are specified in terms of the total CPI, the Bank in practice uses the CPI measure which excludes food and energy as the basis for its policy actions since it is a better measure of underlying inflation. Since, over time, the CPI and the CPI excluding food and energy have tended to move together, achieving the target path for the latter would also achieve it for the former. Nonetheless, if there were a divergence in the trend movements of the two series, it is the overall CPI that would provide the basis for targeting over the longer term[14].

(c) What is the response to changes in indirect taxes?

In designing the targets, an approach to large once-off price changes arising from increases in indirect taxes had to be developed. It was decided that the first-round or direct effects on the CPI resulting from large and unexpected increases in indirect taxes would be accommodated, but not their second-round effects. Thus, "tax-induced drift" from unexpected changes in indirect taxes would be permitted in the price level but not in the ongoing rate of inflation. However, since this approach was adopted to deal with unusually large or unpredictable tax changes, it was decided (consistent with the treatment of trends in food and energy prices) that if indirect tax increases came to occur with such frequency and predictability that they constituted a trend, that trend would not be permitted to impinge on the targets[15].

(d) What should be done in response to very large price shocks?

Certain major price shocks would justify a change to the entire target path but this should be done only in very unusual circumstances. For example, a very large increase in oil prices that could not be prevented from spilling over into a broad range of other prices or a widespread natural disaster would be situations that might call for a reconsideration of the entire target path to see whether it remained feasible, and perhaps for the establishment of a revised target path to price stability[16]. This provision is not intended to deal with the more typical demand and supply shocks that buffet the economy.

(e) The relationship between the targets and monetary policy

The way in which the target path was framed and explained is importantly related to the nature of monetary policy in a number of ways.

(i) Choice of the first target date
Monetary policy, as is well known, operates with long and variable lags. Hence, an attempt to achieve targets for the rate of inflation (or, equivalently, the price level) in the very near term would be either impossible or totally inappropriate[17]. Indeed, earlier work at the Bank of Canada had ruled out the near-term price level or rate of inflation as a target for monetary policy because it would result in large swings in the economy as well as potential instrument instability. It seemed appropriate to set the first target almost two years away, at the end of 1992, and to focus on rates on inflation in the future, not the present, in taking policy actions.

(ii) The use of bands
The difficulty in forecasting inflation and the lack of precision in predicting the effects of monetary policy actions on inflation also suggested that bands be set around the targets. Thus, bands of plus and minus 1% were established around the target path for inflation. These ranges were in fact smaller than called for by empirical work done at the Bank[18].

There is a trade-off in such circumstances between the probability of successful achievement of the targets and the usefulness of the targets as a communications device designed to influence expectations. The wider are the bands, the higher is the probability of successful achievement of the targets but the less useful are the targets in changing behaviour. In the event, it was decided to use somewhat narrower bands to avoid the problem that overly wide bands might leave the impression that the authorities were not serious about bringing inflation down.

(iii) Deviations from the target
Unexpected price shocks, for example a substantial increase in the prices of raw materials, can result in temporary deviations from the target band. Although monetary policy actions cannot be expected to reverse such effects in the very short run, actions can be taken to put in train adjustments needed to return the trend rate of inflation to the target path. If such shocks were large enough or occurred close to the target date, they might push the rate of inflation above the band at the announced target date. In such circumstances, policy actions would have to be directed to ensuring that the target rate of inflation announced for the following period was met[19].

The target path for inflation reduction does not in itself give direct guidance on how the instrument of monetary policy should be set. In making judgements on the necessary actions to achieve the target path, it is helpful to monitor a variety of indicators that stand between the policy instrument and the rate of inflation. The Bank of Canada has focussed on such variables as the rate of expansion of money (especially the broader aggregates M2 and M2+, which are the best indicators of future rates of inflation), the growth of credit and the rate of increase of total spending as guides to policy action. Also, estimates of excess demand or supply (or "gaps") in goods and labour markets are followed closely, as are leading indicators of costs, such as wage settlements[20].

4. THE EXPERIENCE TO DATE

The announcement of the targets in early 1991 was initially met with considerable scepticism. Business economists and forecasters expressed doubt that the target of 3% at the end of 1992 (2 to 4% band) would be met. In the event, the 12-month rate of increase in the CPI at the end of 1992 was 2.1% (2.0% for the CPI excluding food and energy), just above the bottom end of the band.

The underlying rate of price inflation was low from early 1991 on although this was not widely recognized by the general public for some time because the "headline" 12-month rate of increase of the CPI included the various major indirect tax increases introduced in the early months of 1991[21]. The cyclical weakness of the economy and the major restructuring of Canadian industry in response to increased globalization were key factors putting downward pressure on the rate of inflation, initially on prices and subsequently on wages[22].

Changes in expectations regarding future rates of inflation appeared to become widespread in the latter part of 1991. In part they were related to the very slow rate of increase of prices through most of 1991 and the continuing decline in the 12-month rate of increase in the CPI. In part, they were linked to the perceived sluggishness of the recovery from the 1990–91 recession. As it became apparent that this cyclical recovery would be much weaker than past recoveries[23], some of those who had been sceptical about the likelihood of achieving the targets began to change their views. And there was a change in the backdrop within which labour negotiations were taking place as it was increasingly recognized that the inflationary environment, which had been a central part of past negotiations, was quickly receding[24]. Another sign of changing views was the appearance of more and more articles in financial advice columns in the newspapers on how to invest in a world of low inflation[25].

As noted earlier, there were both near-term and longer-term objectives that the targets were expected to achieve. The near-term objective, to avoid a resurgence of inflation pressures following the once-off price increases related to the oil price increase and the introduction of the GST, was clearly achieved. Of course, the oil price increase was fortuitously reversed in early 1991 but, on the other hand, unexpected increases in excise taxes, especially on tobacco, put added upward pressure on price levels. Moreover, the substantial depreciation of the Canadian dollar beginning in late 1991 and continuing through most of 1992 (13% on an effective basis) provided a further price level shock to the system. The absorption of the large shocks to prices from indirect taxes and the currency depreciation without a wage-price spiral can be considered a major accomplishment of policy over the period. The clear statement by the Bank in the context of the targets that the first-round effects of such shocks would be accommodated but not the second-round effects probably contributed, along with the sluggishness of the economy, to the avoidance of a wage-price spiral in response to the shocks.

As for the longer-run objective of the targets – to facilitate the achievement and maintenance of price stability – it is obviously too early to draw firm conclusions. Most notably, at this stage of the process it is not possible to be definitive about the relative importance of the sluggishness of the economy (i.e., gaps in the output and labour markets) and changes in expectations in the achievement of the first target at the end of 1992[26]. On the one hand, it appears that the typical augmented Phillips curve equation for price inflation is able to track the broad downward movement of inflation. This suggests that there is no need to resort to explanations involving credibility and changes in expectations to explain the pace of disinflation in Canada. On the other hand, one can be somewhat sceptical about such projections in the uncharted territory of low inflation on the basis of an equation estimated over a period in which inflation was rarely below 4%[27]. One should therefore be cautious about using such equations for price inflation to infer that expectational changes have played little or no role in the disinflation.

Of course, it was far from certain that the initial announcement of the targets would, in and of itself, have a major effect on expectations. It is evident that words without actions are not particularly helpful. However, there is a distinct possibility that actions with words can have a stronger effect than actions without words. Moreover, even if the announcement of the targets did not have much direct effect on the achievement of the first milestone at the end of 1992, there is a greater likelihood that with the achievement of the first target the credibility of the policy has been enhanced and expectations of inflation weakened such that the subsequent targets can be achieved more easily.

5. SOME TENTATIVE CONCLUSIONS

Although it is too early to draw definitive conclusions, there are a number of points worth noting on the basis of the Canadian experience thus far and I would also like to offer some reflections on future developments.
(i) The targets have played a useful role in communicating and making more concrete the Bank's policy of moving to price stability. The publicity attached to the original announcement was very helpful in this regard[28].

(ii)   The original announcement of the targets included an undertaking to provide a definition for price stability and to fix a target path for the period after 1995. Work has been going on in a number of areas relating to price stability and the targets, including the extent of bias, if any, in the CPI measure[29], the different implications of a target based on a price level and one based on zero inflation, whether or not there are non-linearities associated with price stability[30] and the kinds of changes in economic behaviour that will likely emerge as the economy moves from inflation to price stability.

(iii)   The usefulness of the bands was apparent in the outcome of the first target. With the unexpected sluggishness of the economy, the rate of inflation fell faster and further than initially anticipated, and this in spite of the fact that monetary conditions were easing for most of the period between the announcement of the targets and the first target date, the end of 1992.

(iv)   The targets were expected to aid the credibility of the price stability policy, especially after the first target was achieved. The importance of achieving the first target suggests that such targets should not be introduced at a time of upward pressure on underlying inflation, but rather at a time when there is a realistic chance of getting inflation down. Furthermore, one should fix a downward path for the targets that is not so steep that it appears impossible to achieve, but sufficiently steep that it shows a clear downward trend for inflation.

(v)   In the face of the decline in the rate of inflation to the lower band of the first target (about 2%), the question of how to deal with the next target (1 1/2% to 3 1/2% in mid-1994) came to the fore. The Bank noted in its most recent Annual Report (issued at the end of February 1993) that the trend to lower inflation appeared to be "on track" to an outcome in the lower part of the band. Underlying this statement was a view that it would be inappropriate to take action deliberately to push up the rate of inflation once it had reached the lower band of the target range, given that the longer-term goal was to achieve price stability.

(vi)   Although the near-term expectations of inflation remain very subdued in Canada there does remain a lingering uncertainty about the longer term. This shows up in long-term bond yields which, although down appreciably from their peaks, remain high relative both to recent rates of Canadian inflation and to their U.S. counterparts[31]. These relatively high rates are partly attributable to fiscal problems in Canada as well as political uncertainties[32].

(vii)   Inflation-reduction targets can be thought of as allowing for a form of automatic stabilization in response to demand shocks and hence for partial stabilization of output fluctuations. Thus, when inflation is above the targets monetary conditions will tighten, and the demand pressures will thereby be mitigated. Conversely, in a weak economic situation with inflation declining in line with the targets there is scope for easing in monetary conditions and hence providing support for the economy. Thus, as inflation has declined in Canada, monetary conditions have eased, with both interest rates and the external value of the Canadian dollar down significantly from their peaks. And with wage and price inflation under control, the nominal depreciation has been translated into a real depreciation.

In conclusion, I would note that although inflation-reduction targets are neither necessary nor sufficient to achieve price stability, it appears on the basis of the Canadian experience thus far that they can be very helpful in the attainment of this goal. As a form of pre-commitment by the authorities to the reduction of inflation, they can perhaps be considered as a way of dealing with the time-inconsistency problem[33]. A comparison of inflationary developments in Canada and New Zealand, which used inflation-reduction targets, and those in other countries without such targets will provide interesting material for future researchers about the role of formally-announced targets in affecting expectations and helping to achieve price stability. However, it will be necessary to await the inflation results over a whole business cycle before drawing firmer conclusions about the role of the targets on the basis of the experience of these countries.

NOTES

1. The views expressed are those of the author and do not necessarily represent those of the Bank of Canada.
2. See Bank of Canada (1991a), chapter 2 and Selody (1990) for a detailed discussion of the costs of inflation and the benefits of price stability. Lipsey (1990) and York (1990) contain contributions to the debate over price stability in Canada and Freedman (1991) provides an overview of the debate.
3. Freedman (1983), Thiessen (1983).
4. These included concerns about the quality and timeliness of nominal spending data, the inability of the authorities to achieve such a target with any precision in the short to medium run, and the potential for misunderstanding of the actual reach of monetary policy when the central bank appears to take responsibility for overall spending in the economy. See Ando et al (1985), pp. 6–9.
5. Bank of Canada (1991b).
6. Bank of Canada (1991c).
7. Although a precise definition of price stability was not specified when the targets were introduced, the work that had already been done on the meaning of price stability indicated a rate of increase in the consumer price index that was "clearly below 2%".
8. Crow (1988).
9. Having a joint announcement with government at the time of the budget also had significant publicity value for the price stability goal.
10. Parkin (1982), Johnson (1990).
11. This has also been the case in subsequent budgets.
12. Ball (1993).
13. The latter may of course have been related to a lack of credibility after more than two decades of inflation.

14. In such circumstances, the operating path for the CPI excluding food and energy would be different from the target path for total CPI.

15. Thus, for example, if the trend increase in indirect taxes contributed ½ percentage point to the CPI, an increase in indirect taxes that resulted in a 1¼ percentage point increase in the CPI would be accommodated to the extent of ¾%, not the full 1¼%. See Bank of Canada (1991d).

16. A similar provision can be found in the New Zealand framework for achieving price stability.

17. In a small open economy operating in a flexible exchange rate regime, sufficiently large exchange rate movements could affect the price level in a very short period of time, provided the pass-through from the exchange rate to prices was very rapid. Although the authorities could in principle try to use exchange rate movements to hit a near-term inflation target, it is far from clear that they could influence the exchange rate in such a way as to succeed in achieving such a target, nor would it be economically sensible to do so even if it were possible.

18. The standard error of estimate of equations explaining the rate of inflation is on the order of 1½% to 2%.

19. In other words, along the path to price stability base drift would be accepted for the price level but not for the rate of inflation.

20. For details of the way in which such information is incorporated into the policy process, see Duguay and Poloz (1993).

21. By mid-1991 these various tax changes are estimated to have increased the 12-month CPI growth rate by about 2½%.

22. The wage restraint policy introduced by the federal government at the same time as the targets were announced may also have sped up the decline in wage inflation by setting an example for wage setting in other sectors, most notably the provincial government sector.

23. This can be attributed to a number of factors, including the continuing effects of the debt overhang and oversupply of commercial real estate, the weak U.S. recovery and the slowdown overseas, low raw materials prices, and the restructuring of Canadian industry.

24. In an article in the Financial Post of February 13, 1992 dealing with the decline in strikes in Canada the chief economist of the Canadian Labour Congress was cited as saying that low inflation may be another reason that some unions have not felt the need to strike over wage issues.

25. This was spurred on no doubt by the associated declines in interest rates offered on deposits at banks and other financial institutions.

26. Bank of Canada (1993).

27. There are two aspects to this scepticism. Would the simple autoregressive lag continue to capture expectations of inflation or would some weight be placed on the target itself? Are there previously ignored non-linearities, such as floors on wage changes, that begin to operate as the economy approaches price stability but which are not relevant at moderate rates of inflation?

28. The Reserve Bank of New Zealand has also issued semi-annual reports on its targets, which have served to focus the attention of the public on the targets periodically.

29. Crawford (1993a) and Crawford (1993b).

30. Summers (1991), Lebow, Roberts and Stockton (1992).

31. The differential fell to 55 basis points at one point in the fall of 1992 but subsequently rose to more than 100 basis points again.

32. The constitutional referendum in the fall of 1992 played an important role in this regard.

33. See Barro and Gordon (1983), and Persson and Tabellini (1993). Having an explicit mandate in legislation could also be helpful in this regard.

References

Ando, Albert et al (eds.) (1985) *Monetary Policy in Our Times*, Cambridge, Mass., MIT Press.

Ball, Lawrence (1993) "What Determines the Sacrifice Ratio?" in N.G. Mankiw (ed.), *Monetary Policy*, Chicago, University of Chicago Press.

Bank of Canada (1991a) *Annual Report of the Governor* for 1990.

Bank of Canada (1991b) "Targets for Reducing Inflation", *Bank of Canada Review* (March), 3.

Bank of Canada (1991c) "Background Note on the Targets", *Bank of Canada Review* (March), 9–15.

Bank of Canada (1991d) "Targets for Reducing Inflation: Further Operational and Measurement Considerations", *Bank of Canada Review* (September), 3–23.

Bank of Canada (1993) *Annual Report of the Governor* for 1992.

Barro, Robert J., and Gordon, David B (1983) "A Positive Theory of Monetary Policy in a Natural Rate Model", *Journal of Political Economy*, 91 (August), 589–610.

Crawford, Allan (1993a) "Measurement Biases in the Canadian CPI: A Technical Note", *Bank of Canada Review* (Summer), 21–36.

Crawford, Allan (1993b) "Measurement Biases in the Canadian CPI", *Bank of Canada Technical Report*, 64.

Crow, John W (1988) "The Work of Canadian Monetary Policy", *Bank of Canada Review* (February), 3–17.

Duguay, Pierre and Poloz, Stephen (1993) "The Role of Economic Projections in Canadian Monetary Policy Formulation", *Canadian Public Policy*.

Freedman, C. (1983) "Financial Innovation in Canada: Causes and Consequences", *American Economic Review*, 73 (May), 101–106.

Freedman, Charles (1991) "The Goal of Price Stability: The Debate in Canada", *Journal of Money, Credit and Banking*, 23 (August), 613–618.

Johnson, David R. (1990) "An Evaluation of the Bank of Canada Zero Inflation Target: Do Michael Wilson and John Crow Agree?", *Canadian Public Policy*, 16 (September), 308–325.

Lebow, David E., Roberts, John M., and Stockton, David J. (1992) "Economic Performance Under Price Stability." Board of Governors of the Federal Reserve System, Economic Activity Section, *Working Paper Series*, Number 25.

Lipsey, Richard G. (ed.) (1990) *Zero Inflation: The Goal of Price Stability*, Toronto, C.D. Howe Institute.

Parkin, Michael (1982) "Canadian Monetary Policy and Fiscal Planning: Two Fundamental Inconsistencies", Paper Presented at the May 1982 Meetings of the Canadian Economics Association, held at the University of Ottawa.

Persson, Torsten and Tabellini, Guido (1993) "Designing Institutions for Monetary Stability." *Carnegie-Rochester Conference Series on Public Policy*, 39.

Selody, Jack (1990) "The Goal of Price Stability: A Review of the Issues", *Bank of Canada Technical Report*, 54.

Summers, Lawrence (1991) "How Should Long-term Monetary Policy be Determined?", *Journal of Money, Credit and Banking*, 23 (August), 625–631.

Thiessen, Gordon G. (1983) "The Canadian Experience with Monetary Targeting." in Paul Meek (ed.), *Central Bank Views on Monetary Targeting*, New York, Federal Reserve Bank of New York, 100–104.

York, Robert C. (ed.) (1990) *Taking Aim: The Debate on Zero Inflation*, Toronto, C.D. Howe Institute.

The Costs and Benefits of Disinflation

STANLEY FISCHER

Massachusetts Institute of Technology and NBER

In the G-7 as in almost all the industrialized countries, inflation is now as low as it was during the golden age of 1960–73 (Table 1)[1]. Thus for many industrialized countries, the inflation policy question in 1993 is not whether to disinflate, but rather how and how far to preserve the gains of the disinflation of recent years. Some OECD countries, including Germany, Italy, and Spain, still face the challenge of further disinflation, as do formerly medium inflation countries such as Chile, Israel and Mexico.

Table 1. Inflation rates, 1960–93 (CPI, % p.a.).

	1960–73	1973–79	1979–90	1991	1992	1993
G-7	3.9	9.7	5.5	4.3	3.0	2.8
United States	3.2	8.5	5.5	4.2	3.0	3.1
Japan	6.2	9.9	2.5	3.3	1.7	1.3
Germany	3.4	4.7	2.9	3.5	4.0	4.2
France	4.6	10.7	6.9	3.2	2.4	2.3
Italy	4.7	16.1	10.6	6.4	5.3	4.4
United Kingdom	5.1	15.6	7.5	5.9	3.7	1.5
Canada	3.6	9.7	5.6	5.6	1.5	2.0
Australia	3.5	12.1	8.3	3.2	1.0	2.2
New Zealand	4.9	13.8	11.3	2.6	1.0	1.4

Sources: *OECD Historical Statistics; OECD Economic Outlook*, June 1993; forecasts for 1993 from Goldman Sachs, *International Economics Analyst*, September 1993, except for New Zealand which is form *OECD Economic Outlook*, June 1993.

Despite the many rational expectations and game-theoretic related advances in the understanding of policy in the last twenty years, the basic analysis of the decision of whether to disinflate has not changed much since Phelps (1972) set out the cost-benefit approach to monetary planning. At the margin, the tradeoff is between the short-run costs of lower output and recession associated with the reduction of inflation, and the longer-run benefits of a lower inflation rate.

Although the basic analysis is the same, the last two decades have produced

J.A.H. de Beaufort Wijnholds, S.C.W. Eijffinger and L.H. Hoogduin (eds.), A Framework for Monetary Stability, pp. 31–42.

many refinements. The non-vertical long-run Phillips curve, which was on the way out in 1973, has long since disappeared. In its place is the powerful counterargument that higher inflation may reduce the long-run growth rate. Understanding of the role of policy credibility, the interactions between credibility and the speed of disinflation, the institutional design of the central bank, and the institutional structure of the economy in determining the costs of disinflation and the benefits of low inflation has greatly increased.

In section 1, I discuss the optimal steady state inflation rate. The costs of disinflation and the question of how to keep inflation low are taken up in section 2. In section 3 I discuss the potential for indexation and other institutional changes to reduce the costs of inflation.

1. THE OPTIMAL INFLATION RATE

The standard account of the costs of inflation[2] starts by assuming that all institutions in the economy are perfectly adjusted for the existence of inflation, equivalently that the economy is indexed to the maximum possible extent. The costs of inflation are then the shoe-leather costs, measured by the area under the demand curve for non-interest bearing money, and the menu costs of changing prices.

The shoe-leather costs appear to be very small at low inflation rates, with Fischer (1981) estimating that a reduction in the inflation rate from 10 to 0% in the United States would produce a welfare gain of 0.3% of GNP. Even the shoe-leather cost could be reduced by paying interest on bank reserves. There is in addition the proposition due to Friedman (1969), that a negative inflation rate, implying a zero nominal interest rate (presumably on the closest substitute for money in a multi-asset world) would be optimal, since it would reduce the marginal cost of holding real balances to zero. Of course, a negative inflation rate would incur menu costs of price change, though costs of wage change would be reduced since nominal wages would in a world of rising productivity be changed less frequently if prices were declining at a rate close to that of productivity growth.

At the theoretical level, the Friedman proposition has been re-examined in a variety of models, and appears to be generally robust. The main exception, due to Phelps (1972), is that, given costs of raising taxes, real balances should generally be taxed (through inflation), thereby raising the inflation rate above the Friedman level. However, as Faig (1985) has shown, real balances should not be taxed if they serve as an intermediate good.

These arguments point to zero as the optimal or target inflation rate in a world whose institutions are perfectly adapted to inflation. Institutional nonadaptation, for instance the failure to index the tax system, and the tilting of real payment streams in long-term nominal mortgages, typically reinforce the zero target. Evidence that the inflation rate and price level uncertainty are positively associated further supports the view that the optimal inflation rate is zero[3].

Zero inflation and price stability targets

Once uncertainty is taken into account, it becomes important to make the distinction between a *zero inflation target* and a *target of price stability*, meaning that the goal is to keep the price level constant and predictable in the long run. Suppose that policy succeeds each period in setting the inflation rate $(p_t - p_{t-1})$, at zero, up to an identically independently distributed error term, ϵ_t, with variance σ^2:

$$(p_t - p_{t-1}) = \epsilon_t \tag{1}$$

Suppose further that the target of policy is a zero inflation rate. Then the variance of the price level T periods hence is $T\sigma^2$. This means that uncertainty over price levels that are distant in time can be very large, even though expected inflation over the period is zero.

If the goal of policy is instead to attain a target-price level, p^*, each period, and ϵ_t is the error, then each period:

$$\begin{aligned} p_t &= p^* + \epsilon_t \\ &= p_{t-1} + \epsilon_t - \epsilon_{t-1} \end{aligned} \tag{2}$$

Period-to-period price level variability is greater under the price level rule, but the variance of the price level T periods hence is only σ^2: price level targeting increases short-term price variability in order to reduce long-term price level uncertainty[4].

There is thus an important distinction between a zero inflation target and a price stability target. Period-to-period price level variability (short-run inflation variability) will generally be larger with a price stability target than with a zero (or any constant level) inflation target.

Many of the arguments in favor of a zero or low inflation target point in fact to the desirability of low long-run *price level* uncertainty. For instance, the view that low inflation encourages long-term nominal contracting[5] must be based on the assumption that price level uncertainty is lower at low inflation rates. It is, but uncertainty about future price levels can differ greatly even for a given average rate of inflation.

A central bank that credibly proclaims a zero inflation target is increasing certainty about the price level in the short-run; a central bank that has a credible long-term price level target is increasing certainty about the price level in the long run. The difference is whether the central bank intends to remove the effects of past disturbances on the price level. For instance, a central bank with a price level target would after a supply shock aim for a period of deflation, whereas a zero inflation central bank would aim to disinflate.

The welfare benefits of long-term nominal contracting have not yet been analyzed in any serious way. The importance of being able to contract in nominal terms for 100 years, as was done in the nineteenth century, is probably very small. Of course, the financially unsophisticated who suffer from money illusion would benefit from having more certainty about the real value of their retirement savings if they saved in nominal form, but the United States historical record, in which equities have far outperformed bonds over long periods, suggests that such a strategy is in any case a bad one[6]. We return to the topic of the welfare benefits of price stability in section 3.

Inflation and growth

The early theoretical articles on the link between inflation and growth generally predicted a positive relationship, resulting from the portfolio shift towards real capital brought about by a lower real return on money[7]. Subsequent contributions suggested mechanisms through which higher inflation might reduces output and growth, most importantly that: real balances serve as a factor of production; higher inflation is less certain inflation and price level uncertainty decreases the efficiency of the price system; and distortions in the tax system, for instance the failure to index taxation of capital income, adversely affect capital accumulation.

Cross-sectional empirical work that includes developing countries finds a clear negative *ceteris paribus* association between inflation and growth. It is especially clear that inflation that exceeds 50% per annum is bad for growth. But surprisingly, Fischer (1993) shows in linear equations that the statistical significance of the negative association between inflation and growth is stronger for inflation below 15% than for higher inflation rates[8]. Evidence in the same paper suggests that higher inflation reduces growth by reducing both capital accumulation and productivity growth. There is not yet empirical evidence on which of the many potential routes through which inflation negatively affects capital accumulation and productivity are most important.

The negative effects of inflation on growth greatly reinforce the argument for a low target inflation rate. The present value of higher future output (and therefore consumption) levels implied by lower inflation would offset and, depending on the magnitude of the growth effect, could exceed the present value of the output losses implied by the need to disinflate – even without taking into account the other benefits of lower inflation.

For the industrialized countries, the key question is the nature of the inflation-growth relationship at inflation rates of 5% or less. The Canadian debate over a zero inflation (later a price stability) target was influenced by a remarkable finding by Jarrett and Selody (1982) that an increase in the inflation rate by 1 percentage point would reduce the rate of productivity growth by 0.3

percentage points. Some variants of unpublished regressions along similar lines for the United States show a significant but smaller negative association between productivity growth and inflation, but the result is not robust. One obvious explanation, that such a relationship results from business cycle phenomena in which productivity growth is highest in the early stages of a recovery, when inflation is low, does not receive strong support from the data.

The low-inflation relationship between inflation and growth is clearly an area where further research is needed[9]. However, such research will be impeded by the absence of many observations of the behavior of economies at inflation rates below 3%. It is simply not known at present what would be the growth rate effects of a reduction in inflation from a low level of, say, 3% to 1 or 0%. Further, in this range, inaccuracies in the measurement of prices and inflation come into play: it is difficult to know whether a 2% rate of increase in the CPI is significantly different from zero.

I would advance the hypothesis that, as a result of output costs of deflation, there is a tradeoff between inflation and the level of output at very low inflation rates. If the average inflation rate is low, there will have to be periods of deflation to balance inflationary episodes. If there are asymmetries in the short-term Phillips curve relationship, the output costs of the deflation periods are greater than the output gains during the inflationary periods[10].

In addition, there should be no mistaking the fact that there is an inflation-output tradeoff over periods long enough to be politically relevant. At particular times, for instance in Germany in 1990, macroeconomic decisions are made that affect the inflation and growth outlooks for periods of five to ten years. The German decision in 1990 to finance the costs of unification by borrowing meant that the Bundesbank would be fighting inflation (and helping create a recession) for at least three to four years. A tighter fiscal stance would quite likely have permitted both lower inflation and higher growth over the first half of the 1990s, a significantly long period in anyone's life.

Credibility and inflation targets

It has long been argued that the only credible inflation target is zero – that at any other inflation rate, the public will always believe that a little more inflation can be accepted. If this is the case, no central bank has any credibility on inflation, since there is no post-war experience of zero inflation over any sustained period.

It could be that a central bank that succeeded in producing zero inflation over long periods would be far more credible than any existing central bank. Based on recent experience, though, central banks that succeed in producing low inflation (2–4%) succeed in building reputations as defenders of the value of the currency.

I conclude from this discussion of the optimal inflation rate that there is no case for targetting an inflation rate that exceeds 4%, that anyone should be comfortable with a 1–3% target, and that we simply do not know whether there is any good reason to aim lower. Because of price level measurement errors, because I am dubious about the magnitude of economic gains from facilitating very long-term nominal contracting, and because of the possibility that there is a Phillips curve tradeoff at very low inflation rates, I doubt that the inflation target needs to be below 2%.

The analysis of the benefits of price level stability versus low inflation remains to be developed. Note, however, that if it is true that the only credible inflation target is zero, and if economic agents form expectations on the basis of experience, then central banks need a goal of price level stability rather than zero inflation – for with the latter goal, they are very unlikely to produce a zero inflation rate *ex post*[11].

2. THE COSTS OF DISINFLATION

Amidst the debris created by the rational expectations and econometric evaluation critique earthquakes, the short-run Phillips curve stands essentially intact. Whether because of the lack of credibility of anti-inflationary policies, or because of inflationary inertia due to long-term or overlapping nominal contracts, contractionary policy to reduce the inflation rate tends to create a recession. There is a long list of recent examples.

The sacrifice ratio, the ratio of percentage points of GNP (at an annual rate) lost, to the decline in inflation, is generally estimated to be about 5 in the United States[12]. At the theoretical level[13], it is well understood that the sacrifice ratio should depend on the credibility of policy, on the contract structure (which is itself affected by economic policy, but that can be taken as predetermined from the viewpoint of a given business cycle), on the time path of the policy change, and on the exchange rate regime. There is considerable evidence for the United States that the exchange rate played an important role in the disinflation process of the early 1980s.

It is quite easy to build models in which costless disinflation is possible. All it takes is contracts in which wages and prices react to expected policies (because expected policies affect expected inflation), and either or both sufficient forewarning of the change in policy or a sufficiently clever path for the money stock that just offsets the effects of the contract structure on inflation.

However we do not have examples of costless disinflation in the industrialized economies. There *are* examples from other countries of substantial declines in inflation that have not been accompanied by recession. Between

1990 and 1993 both Chile and Israel have seen inflation move from more than 15% to below 10% per annum during periods of rapid growth. To a considerable extent these countries are reaping the rewards of lower international inflation, which has enabled them to reduce the nominal rate of devaluation without producing a real appreciation. In the Israeli case, an increase in labor supply helped the disinflation by putting downward pressure on real wages; indeed the Israeli disinflation was accompanied by high unemployment as well as high growth.

These examples suggest a low output-cost gradualist and opportunistic strategy for reducing inflation: take advantage of favorable cost shocks to ratchet inflation down, while seeking merely to prevent the inflation rate from rising in the absence of favorable shocks. Such a strategy implies a lower average level of output than would be attained if the goal were merely to keep average inflation constant, but it does present the possibility of low or zero cost disinflation if shocks are favorable.

This strategy takes a singularly determined and consistent monetary policy – one that surrenders neither to the temptation to inflate in normal or adverse circumstances, nor to the temptation to increase output when circumstances are favorable. The strategy has been carried out by central banks and governments of some countries, and is therefore not inherently impossible.

Once inflation has been brought down, the big question is how to keep it low, say within the range of 1–4%, with 2–3% as the target range. The recent literature on central bank independence[14] suggests that at least in the industrialized countries, an independent central bank is part of the solution. However, the fact that there is no clear relationship between central bank independence and inflation in developing countries makes it clear that something more than the statutes of the central bank are needed to make a central bank into an effective inflation fighter. Debelle (1993) shows that the inflation performance of the central bank is typically affected by the preferences of the fiscal authority; more generally, the effective independence of the central bank reflects the underlying inflationary preferences of the society.

The success of the Bundesbank in keeping inflation low (though certainly not in maintaining a constant price level) has caused it to be viewed as the model of a low-inflation central bank. In the academic literature, independence is measured by such characteristics as the clarity of the goals of the bank (in the case of the Bundesbank, to preserve the value of the currency) and the independence of the board from the government. While the Bundesbank's goal is stated unambiguously, it does not single-mindedly pursue anti-inflationary policies without regard to their impacts on output. If it did, the inflation rate in Germany would not have exceeded 4% in 1993. Indeed, I believe the statement of an unqualified goal, when the goal is in practice qualified, is likely to detract from the credibility of policy. Perhaps the appointments process of the president and the board are more important. But most important is the strong support of the German public for the goal of low inflation: if that were not the case, inflation in Germany would be higher than it has been, and the Bundesbank would look like the central bank of Iceland, which has high inflation along with a good measure of formal independence.

The accountability of the central bank has not received much attention in the recent academic literature. There are two senses of accountability. First, an agency may have to explain its actions and subject itself to cross-examination from relevant sources, for instance a parliamentary committee. Second, an agency may be held responsible for not achieving its goals, and have to pay a penalty for failing to do so. Accountability in the first sense is surely desirable in any society that values democracy, the belief that it is possible to learn from experience, and the view that the need to explain one's actions tends to lead to a due regard for their consequences. While many central banks have this accountability, some – such as the Bundesbank – do not. This lack of accountability will ultimately weaken its authority.

Accountability in the second sense – of being held responsible for achievement of the goals of policy – is the distinguishing feature of the new central bank law of New Zealand, as well as to a lesser extent the Canadian law. In New Zealand, the governor of the central bank reaches an agreement with the government on the target inflation rate for the coming year. This rate may change to reflect the state of the business cycle, or economic shocks. For instance, the target inflation rate could be higher following a supply shock. The tradeoff between inflation and output is thus agreed upon between the government and the central bank, and the law does not imply that there is no such tradeoff. Then the governor of the central bank is held responsible for achieving the inflation goal. If he does not, the government has the right to fire him.

Persson and Tabellini (1993) have shown that the problem of dynamic inconsistency that is at the root of most of the theoretical literature on precommitment and central bank independence can be solved by adding to the central bank's loss function a term that is linear in inflation. The trick then is to find an institutional structure that corresponds to this loss function. That seems to be the structure that has been created in New Zealand. Note though, that once again the preferences of the society ultimately determine the outcome of policy: if the government does not want to keep inflation low, the central bank governor will not be charged with that task.

We do not in this paper discuss alternative operating or intermediate targets of monetary policy. In a small country, it may make sense to fix the exchange rate, as has Argentina, as a way of precommiting monetary policy. Or a simple monetary rule could conceivably help the central bank stay on its anti-inflationary tracks. Whichever rule is chosen, the central bank is more likely to achieve it, the more effective the rule is in helping the central bank attain the ultimate goals of policy, the more independent the bank, and the more accountable it is.

So, how is inflation to be kept low? The prime requirement is that the society wants to maintain low inflation. It will reach that determination only through a thorough understanding – typically gained through adverse experience – of the consequences of failing to keep inflation low. Given that determination, an independent central bank or better an accountable central bank can help attain the goal.

3. REDUCING THE COSTS OF INFLATION AND PRICE LEVEL UNCERTAINTY

Given the inevitability of at least occasional inflationary episodes, and given the failure of any government in the postwar period to maintain a stable price level, the question arises whether it is possible to mitigate the costs of inflation and price level uncertainty. The costs of inflation could be mitigated by reducing the distortions that arise, for instance, from non-indexation of the tax system. The consequences of price level uncertainty could be mitigated by providing hedges against unanticipated price level changes, for instance by introducing indexed bonds.

The welfare analysis of such changes is complicated by the general theory of the second best. For a given inflation rate and in the absence of other distortions, the removal of distortions due to inflation would increase welfare. Similarly, if asset markets were complete except for the absence of an indexed bond market, and there were no other distortions in the economy, the introduction of an indexed bond would either increase or not reduce welfare.[15]

At a less formal level, it appears likely that the introduction of long-term indexed bonds, as in the United Kingdom, would increase economic welfare. Such bonds make it possible for individuals to purchase – at a market price – secure long-term real income streams, and thereby to avoid the costs of price level uncertainty. Many of the fears that were expressed before the introduction of such bonds, for example, that they would drive nominal bonds out of existence, have not materialized.

Fischer and Summers (1989) show that under some circumstances, the introduction of policies to reduce the costs of inflation can reduce economic welfare. The problem arises because the initial equilibrium is not a Pareto optimum. However, a change of this type that increases the costs of inflation to the government would not reduce welfare. And the introduction of indexed bonds would make inflation more costly at the margin for the government.

4. Concluding comments

The costs of disinflation are the transitional output loss that should be expected during a disinflationary program; the gains are the lower inflation and better economic performance associated with it. The evidence points to an inflation range of 1–3% as being optimal, with more work being needed to answer the question of whether lower inflation within this range is associated with higher productivity growth. Once lower inflation is attained, the challenge for policy is to preserve those gains. Central bank independence and central bank accountability are likely to help keep inflation low, but formal independence and accountability will not help unless the society fundamentally supports the goal of low inflation.

There is an important distinction between a long-run inflation target and a long-run price stability target. A policy that targets the price level increases short-run price variability while reducing long-run price variability. No central bank has succeeded in producing long-run price stability in the postwar period, and it is not clear that the goal justifies the likely costs. These costs could be mitigated by reducing the costs of price level uncertainty, for instance through the introduction of indexed bonds, in ways that increase the costs of inflation for the government.

Notes

1. Worldwide inflation was accelerating during the 1960's, but the same statement applies to the comparison between 1993 and 1960–68.
2. For example, Dornbusch and Fischer (1994), Chapter 17, Fischer and Modigliani (1978), Fischer (1981), Howitt (1990), and Selody (1990).
3. However, the direction of causation between the inflation rate and price level uncertainty is not self-evident.
4. Of course, the period-to-period variability of the inflation rate can be reduced by slowing the return to the target price level, but it will still remain true that period-to-period price level variability is greater with a price level target.
5. Proponents of low-inflation targets often point to the existence of 100-year railroad bonds and 99-year nominal leases in the nineteenth century. In the United States, Sears has recently successfully sold a 100-year nominal bond.
6. In a lead article on the benefits of low inflation, the *Economist* explained that it would again become sensible to write 99-year leases at a fixed nominal rent. There would in any case be enormous real uncertainty about the short-term market-clearing rent over a 99-year period, and it is hard to believe that optimal risk-sharing in this case would take the form of a fixed-nominal price contract.
7. See Fischer (1983) for a review of the theory, along with some Latin American evidence finding a strong negative relation in practice.
8. The explanation may be that the basic relationship between inflation and growth is non-linear.
9. Research on the association between central bank independence (CBI) and inflation, growth, and the variance of output and inflation (reviewed and extended in Eijffinger and Schaling,

1993) suggests a weak inflation-growth relationship for the industrialized countries. For these countries, the data show a negative association between inflation and CBI, but no significant association between CBI and growth.

10. See Tobin (1972).
11. With a zero inflation target, we would expect though to find significant periods during which the average inflation rate is negative.
12. Gordon (1990) calculates a sacrifice ratio of 6 for the United States; for any given episode, there is always some uncertainty about the baseline from which the output loss should be measured. Gordon suggests that 6 is also the ratio that should have been expected on the basis of evidence available before 1980.
13. See Ball (1993).
14. For instance, Cukierman *et al* (1993), and Eijffinger and Schaling (1993).
15. Fischer (1986, Chapter 12) presents a complete model in which the introduction of indexed bonds increases welfare; in general it is difficult to explain the non-existence of indexed bonds, as is shown in Fischer (1986, Chapter 9).

REFERENCES

Ball, Lawrence (1993), "What Determines the Sacrifice Ratio?", in N. Gregory Mankin (ed.), *Monetary Policy*, Chicago, University of Chicago Press.

Cukierman, Alex, Pantelis Kalaitzidakis, Lawrence H. Summers and Steven B. Webb (1993). "Central Bank Independence, Growth, Investment, and Real Rates", mimeo, World Bank (February).

Debelle, Guy (1993). "Central Bank Independence: A Free Lunch?", mimeo, MIT (September).

Dornbusch, Rudiger and Stanley Fischer (1994), *Macroeconomics*, sixth edition, New York, McGraw-Hill.

Eijffinger, Sylvester and Eric Schaling (1993), "Central Bank Independence: Theory and Evidence", *CentER Discussion Papers* number 9325 (May), Center for Economic Research, Tilburg.

Faig, Miguel (1985), "Optimal Taxation of Money Balances", unpublished, Stanford University.

Fischer, Stanley (1981), "Toward an Understanding of the Costs of Inflation: II", in Karl Brunner and Allan H. Meltzer (eds.), *The Costs and Consequences of Inflation*, Carnegie-Rochester Conference Series on Public Policy, Vol. 15, Amsterdam: North-Holland, 5–42 (reprinted in Fischer (1986, *loc.cit.*))

—— (1983), "Inflacion y Crecimiento," (Inflation and Growth), *Cuadernos de Economia*, 20, (Dec), 267–278. (Sidrauski Memorial Lecture, in English as NBER Working Paper, No. 1235.)

—— (1986), *Indexing, Inflation, and Economic Policy*, Cambridge, MA, MIT Press.

—— (1993), "The Role of Macroeconomic Factors in Growth", *Journal of Monetary Economics* (October).

—— and Franco Modigliani (1978), "Toward an Understanding of the Real Effects and Costs of Inflation", *Weltwirtschaftliches Archiv*, 810–832 (reprinted in Fischer (1986, *loc.cit.*))

—— and Lawrence Summers (1989), "Should Governments Learn to Live with Inflation?", *American Economic Review, Papers and Proceedings*, 79, 2 (May), 382–387.

Friedman, Milton (1969), "The Optimum Quantity of Money", in *The Optimum Quantity of Money and Other Essays*. Chicago: Aldine.

Gordon, Robert J. (1990), "The Phillips Curve Now and Then", in Peter Diamond (ed.), *Growth/Productivity/Unemployment*, Cambridge, MA, MIT Press, 207–217.

Howitt, Peter (1990), "Zero Inflation as a Long-Run Target for Monetary Policy", in Richard G. Lipsey (ed.), *Zero Inflation: The Goal of Price Stability*, Toronto, C.D. Howe Institute.

Jarrett, Peter and Jack Selody (1982), "The Productivity-Inflation Nexus in Canada, 1963–79", *Review of Economics and Statistics*, 64, (August), 361–367.

Persson, Torsten and Guido Tabellini (1993), "Designing Institutions for Monetary Stability", mimeo, Institute for International Economic Studies, Stockholm (March).

Phelps, Edmund S. (1972), *Inflation Policy and Unemployment Theory*, New York, Norton.

Selody, Jack (1990), "The Goal of Price Stability: A Review of the Issues", Technical Report No.54, Bank of Canada.

Tobin, James (1972), "Inflation and the Phillips Curve Tradeoff", *American Economic Review*, 62, 1 (March), 1–18.

Comment on Charles Freedman: Formal Targets for Inflation Reduction: The Canadian Experience

JOHN DRIFFILL

University of Southampton

Mr Freedman has described the effects of introducing inflation targets in Canada in 1991. The targets provide for a band for inflation, 2 percentage points wide, gradually falling over time, with a target of 3% at the end of 1992, 2.5% in mid-1994, and 2% at the end of 1995. The formulation of a direct target for inflation was chosen in the absence of a viable intermediate target for monetary policy. The targets were announced in a joint statement by the Central Bank and the Government to demonstrate that they enjoyed wide support and to give them credibility. The record on inflation in Canada has been that it (the year on year increase in the CPI) fell rapidly in 1991 from around 7% to around 2%, where it has remained throughout 1992 and for the first half of 1993. (Indeed, it stood at 1.7% per annum at the end of August 1993.) While the policy has clearly got off to a good start, in that inflation has been below and within the bottom end of the target band since the targets came into effect, it is clear that the policy has been operating in favourable conditions. Unemployment has remained very high in Canada. It was 11.6% a year ago and in August 1993 it was 11.3% (according to The Economist). Inflation in the US has been 2.8% over the last year, and unemployment in the US was 6.7% in August 1993 (as against 7.6% a year ago). So it appears that labour demand has been very weak in Canada, and inflation in Canada's main trading partner has been low. Wage growth in Canada has been low as well (2.7% in the year to June 1993), unsurprisingly, and this presumably suggests that price increases will remain low over the coming year. The only unfavourable condition has been the recent depreciation of the Canadian dollar, but that appears to have had no effect on the price level. In these conditions, it is perhaps little surprise that it has been possible to maintain low inflation in Canada.

What role are the inflation target zones intended to serve? One is to help private sector agents form inflation forecasts. In an economy where people are making decisions about savings and investments the results of which depend on future inflation (among other things), they tend to want to have some sort of forecast of future inflation, and government statements about its future policy provide one source of information on which forecasts can be based. It helps of

43

J.A.H. de Beaufort Wijnholds, S.C.W. Eijffinger and L.H. Hoogduin (eds.), A Framework for Monetary Stability, pp. 43–47.
© 1994 *Kluwer Academic Publishers. Printed in the Netherlands.*

course if government policy plans are internally consistent, and plausible, given the government's record. Financial market operators have developed a need for some framework for monetary policy. While in the 1970s they may have muddled through without there being anything clear, in the 1980s they seem to have become more and more dependent on some such model. In the UK, the MTFS provided it for a while, with planned growth rates of the money stock. More recently the policy of shadowing the Deutschemark, and subsequently actual membership of the ERM, provided a point of reference. Sterling's exit from which September 1992 left the financial markets adrift and desperate for some government statement of policy that would enable them to forecast inflation. They were eventually placated when the British government, somewhat like the Canadian, announced a target range for inflation.

Another intended role for the targets is to influence private sector inflation expectations downwards and "make more concrete the commitment of the authorities to the goal of achieving and maintaining price stability and to add to the credibility of that goal." It is be hoped that if the targets are met, they will become more "credible". The argument underlying this is presumably that if the government were seen to be doing the things it said it would do, then people might come to believe with more confidence that the government would continue in the future to do the things that it says it would do. If such a process were at work, the targets would gradually acquire importance as they are given greater weight by people in forming expectations about future inflation. The targets might be seen as a way for the government to commit itself to the announced path of inflation. It might be thought that the effects of the government's not honouring the target range for the inflation rate would be so bad that it was effectively constrained by its announcements, and this would provide an escape from the time inconsistency problem. This is clearly the way in which the government of Canada would like to see them.

The test of the policy would occur in the future when the conditions for low inflation were less good. The value to a government of keeping to its planned inflation rate may depend on its remaining term of office and the prospects for re-election, and the effects that alternative policies would have on the prospects of re-election. Would a pre-election spending boost improve its prospects or not? Would the electorate be more likely to vote for the party that has kept to its low inflation promises at the expense of higher taxes, lower spending, and higher unemployment? Or would it be taken in by claims that high taxes etc. were the reflection not of honesty but incompetence. These considerations suggest that as elections approach, the discipline imposed by being a government that has stuck to its low inflation plans might falter. If this process were understood in financial markets, you would expect that the "credibility" of the policy would last only as long as did the economic and political conditions that made sticking to the original plans attractive to the government, and you might see signs of that, such as increasing interest rates, as elections approach.

It might be asked whether the introduction of inflation targets has in fact done anything to make the maintenance of low inflation more likely to persist further into the future? Has this policy provided a framework for price stability? It does not seem to have done so. These statements do not do anything to commit the government to sticking to a low inflation policy in the future when circumstances change, despite the arguments made above. They have not taken monetary policy out of the hands of the politicians and put it into the hands of an independent central bank like the Bundesbank. (How independent is the Bank of Canada? Mr Freedman's paper was silent on this question. In this respect Canada seems to be different from New Zealand, another adherent of inflation targets.) They have not abolished the Canadian dollar and put monetary policy into the hands of the US Federal Reserve. There is no mechanism in place which will prevent the Canadian government at some time in the future expanding demand and allowing inflation to rise, in response to some shock or some overwhelming political imperative.

Therefore it seems to me unlikely that the inflation targets would produce a "credibility effect". And indeed the Canadian financial markets do not appear to have been completely convinced that this marks a shift to permanent low inflation. Mr Freedman remarked that although long term interest rates have fallen somewhat, they remain high relative to recent Canadian inflation and relative to US interest rates. This suggests that long term inflation expectations have not been reduced very much by the new policy.

The foregoing comments are based on the presumption that there is or has been a "credibility problem" afflicting monetary policy in Canada, and that without some concrete sign, financial markets and others are not convinced by statements that Canadian monetary policy has as its goal "the maintenance and achievement of price stability." They presumably feel that any government, whatever its attitudes to inflation and unemployment, would wish to make such statements and attempt thereby to lower inflation expectations. Nevertheless, Mr Freedman reports that the inflation targets have been useful in Canada. The puzzle is to understand why that should be so when simple analysis suggests that they should have had no effect.

One way that the inflation targets announced by the Canadian government might be understood, in the context of economic theory, is in relation to the concept which is rather disparagingly called *cheap talk* in game theory. Cheap talk is a signal sent from one player in a game (typically one who has some private information) to the other player(s), before the players take the actions which affect their payoffs. The cheap talk itself does not affect any payoffs and it does not restrict the subsequent choices of actions made by the players. The talk is cheap because the messages cost nothing to send.

This distinguishes it from costly signalling mechanisms, which are useful because the costs of sending signals gives players incentives to send true and often revealing signals, in situations when, in the absence of the cost of sending the signal, all players would like to send the same signals: educational attainments signal ability because more able people find the acquisition of educational attainments less costly or difficult than do less able people; a signal of a strong preference for low inflation, like the pursuit of a very low inflation policy even in the face of high unemployment, acts as a signal because it is less costly for a government with a strong preference for low inflation than it is for a government with only a weak preference for low inflation. Signals work where, taking into account the cost, one type of player would not want to emit the same kind of signal as the other. In these cases, the signal sent by a player can serve to communicate information about that player's "type", and provide useful information to other players in the game which might affect the actions they take. If inflation targets were a signal in this sense, they might affect the inflation expectations of the private sector. Presumably, the Canadian authorities would like to influence inflation expectations downwards.

Cheap talk cannot be used as a signal in as wide a set of conditions as can costly signals, however. And the inflation targets seem to be more like "cheap talk" than costly signals. That is because the targets *per se* impose no restrictions on the future actions of the authorities, and there is no cost involved in the announcement *per se* of one target rather than another. Therefore, a statement that inflation will be in the range 1–3% is unlikely to influence expectations of inflation in a downward direction, since all kinds of governments are likely to want to announce that inflation will be low, regardless of what they will ultimately do about inflation.

The targets, viewed as "cheap talk", can nevertheless make a number of contributions, in certain circumstances. One possibility is that they focus attention on one particular outcome which would have been one of many possible equilibrium outcomes of the game without announcements. For example, in the monetary policy game analyzed by Barro and Gordon there are many equilibria with different inflation rates. (In these the authorities stick to a low inflation rate because they believe correctly that, if they were to switch to a more inflationary policy, they would find themselves subsequently imprisoned by high inflation expectations in a high unemployment/high inflation trap.) In this kind of a world, inflation targets might focus attention on one outcome, and solve a coordination problem. Perhaps this is what has been going on in Canada.

Another situation in which they can play a role is when the private sector is unsure about the government's objectives, and different kinds of governments would like to send out different messages and influence expectations in *different* ways. Such a model was developed by Jeremy C. Stein ("Cheap Talk and the Fed: A Theory of Imprecise Policy Announcements," *American*

Economic Review, vol. 79, no. 1, March 1989, 32–42) drawing on an idea of Vincent P. Crawford and Joel Sobel ("Strategic Information Transmission," *Econometrica*, vol. 50, no. 6, November 1982, 1431–1451). He models governments of different types as having different exchange rate targets which are private information, and having the same target for interest rates. All governments would give misleading messages if they gave a precise message about their exchange rate target. (It turns out in his example that they would signal a larger money supply than they actually would implement.) Precise messages would therefore be incredible and of no value. But different governments would like to give out different messages. It proves possible for vague messages – of the kind "inflation will be between 1% and 3%" – to be both credible and informative. In this situation, the "cheap talk" conveys some useful information about the preferences of the government. Perhaps the inflation targets are serving this kind of function: informative, but sufficiently diffuse that the government would not want to deviate from the announced actions. The difficulty of rationalizing them this way is that it requires a reason as to why different types of governments would like to send different signals of future inflation, whereas there seems to have developed a consensus in which all governments seem to want to achieve inflation at or around zero.

Turning from the question of how inflation targets might be rationalized theoretically to a narrower and more technical issue, I noted that Mr Freedman commented that the width of the target zone – 2% – might be on narrow side given the standard errors of one-year ahead inflation forecasts produced by econometric equations. I wonder if he need be so cautious on this issue. It may be possible to control inflation with greater accuracy than the equations suggest. The government and the central bank have tools that they can use within the year to affect inflation fairly quickly, and have more tools available and can respond to more factors than are represented in econometric forecasts. A change in interest rates that affects the exchange rate, for example, presumably has a rapid effect on the CPI. A change in indirect tax rates also has rapid effects. Moreover, the econometric forecasts were based on equations estimated over a period in which inflation targets were not in force, and consequently the behaviour of inflation relative to the explanatory variables might be quite different than when inflation is a target. Doesn't this issue recall the discussion in the 1960s about the effectiveness of monetary versus fiscal policy: if fiscal policy were able to stabilize output perfectly in the face of various shocks, there would appear to be no effect of fiscal policy on output. And the predictive power of equations which were unable to model the principal sources of shocks would be low.

Comment on Stanley Fischer: The Costs and Benefits of Disinflation

JOSÉ LUIS MALO DE MOLINA

Banco de España

First, I should like to thank the organisers for my last-minute opportunity to discuss Stanley Fischer's paper "The costs and benefits of disinflation". Despite such short notice I was, in view of the great relevance of the subject and the author's authority, unable to resist accepting the role of discussant. My only regret is not to have had greater time in which to prepare my comments to the extent the subject and the author merit. Unquestionably, the costs and benefits of attaining price stability are pivotal to the macroeconomic debate of recent decades. They likewise have major and serious implications for the definition and pursuit of economic policies, in particular monetary policy. My comments will focus on those issues most related to the design and implementation of monetary policy from the standpoint of the problems and dilemmas facing policy-makers.

As befits a central bank representative, I should first voice my thorough agreement with the basic analysis advocating the necessary anti-inflationary priority of monetary policy. This priority is based on the conviction that the complementarity of price stability and economic growth is predominant in the medium and long term. Such complementarity advises against resorting to loose monetary and financial policies aimed at obtaining stimulatory effects on activity and employment. Indeed, these effects may prove ephemeral and yet harmful for macroeconomic stability. The arguments stressing the adverse effects of inflation on growth are robust and forceful. Recent literature has generated a large variety of models, from very diverse analytical standpoints, which have firmed the broad consensus (although there is no unanimity) existing on this approach. Professor Fischer has drawn these brilliantly together, so it is meaningless to insist on the defence of this issue before listeners who I presume are already convinced.

The predominant approach at central banks towards establishing an explicit commitment to price stability ultimately rests on the intellectual conviction that long-term growth is determined by real factors. Under the same belief, inflation is seen as a predominantly monetary phenomenon which entails high costs in terms of distortions in saver and investor decisions, in resource allocation and in income distribution (the redistributive effects of inflation

J.A.H. de Beaufort Wijnholds, S.C.W. Eijffinger and L.H. Hoogduin (eds.), A Framework for Monetary Stability, pp. 49–53.
© 1994 *Kluwer Academic Publishers. Printed in the Netherlands.*

adversely affect the incomes of the worst-off or those with less bargaining power). However, according priority to price stability says little about the most suitable monetary policy stance in different economic situations. The goal of price stability cannot mean that monetary policy measures may be adopted irrespectively of what the initial situation of the economy is. Tuning the tone of monetary policy to cyclical developments without loss of credibility is a complex matter that cannot be resolved via the mere resort to principles or to final goals. Insistence on price stability as a priority goal should not be cause for disregarding the complexity of situations which may arise and which may require the pursuance of strategies which are also relatively complex.

This is an area where central bank officials tend to shun explicitness, so as not to stir the ghosts of fine-tuning and prompt an erosion of the credibility they have built up. When this question arises, the reply usually given is that the application in each circumstance of the final goal of price stability is something pertaining to the central banker's craft, where no specific, explicit recommendations can be established.

The main contribution of the Fischer paper is its attempt to step beyond the definition of the final goals and place analysis where the concrete facts and practical difficulties facing stability-geared monetary policy can be confronted. Two possible economic policy recommendations with an appropriate analytical grounding may be deduced from Fischer's paper:

1. Departing from inflationary situations, the goal of price stability should be pursued with a certain – although ambitious – gradualism. Or, tantamount to this, the inflation goal assumed by monetary policy cannot be independent of the initial inflation rate. That is a consequence of the irrefutable existence of costs in the disinflation process, even though the complementarity of economic growth and price stability is predominant in the long run. This approach blends fairly well with what has been the virtually habitual practice of central banks facing inflationary processes and, moreover, it is the rationale underpinning the European Community's convergence plans. But the fact is that the acceptance of possible gradualism which minimises the costs of disinflation may give rise to major complications in monetary policy management which run the risk of generating situations of temporary inconsistency and credibility loss. In this area, then, the empirical evidence is perhaps not very favourable to excessive gradualism. According to recent research by Lawrence Ball, the results appear favourable to rapid disinflation processes. For the OECD countries, Ball found that disinflations that were concentrated in a short period of time (say five quarters) implied an output loss that was less than half of that resulting from an equivalent disinflation spread out over twice the time. It appears that successful cases of a "gradualist" strategy – Professor Fischer cites Chile and Israel in the 1990s as examples – appear to be the exception rather than the rule.

2. For countries that have moved onto a path of stability, an inflation target of 1–3% seems sufficient. Regarding this range, it is not clear whether being closer to zero inflation is necessarily better than accepting moderate rates within said range.

There is no reason that, at low rates of inflation, the latter should be prevented from reflecting the course of the variable constraints of supply and demand. It should be remembered that the proper functioning of the economic system implies constant changes in relative prices and that the existence of information costs and of uncertainty determines asymmetric behaviour whereunder reductions in the level of prices are more costly than rises; accordingly, a positive rate of inflation – albeit minor – is unavoidable. This argument tends to reinforce Fischer's pragmatic approach and may explain why no central bank has succeeded in sustaining absolute price stability or why, in the major monetary unions, inflation shows persistent and even systematic regional disparities.

Here, it appears that Fischer's conclusions can but with difficulty be refuted, though the logical fears of the risks inherent to complex situations may be evoked. Indeed, it is very difficult to know whether a 2% rate of increase in the CPI is really different from zero inflation, but that also entails the difficulty of diagnosing the threshold above which persistent inflationary processes may be activated.

Having accepted this approach, criticism of the non-existence of a treatment of other situations that are closely connected with the problem at hand can, nonetheless, be raised. Given the existence of costs associated with disinflation, what should the most appropriate response be in the face of a sudden adverse supply or demand shock such as the oil crises or German unification? The paper's approach appears to advocate a certain degree of accommodation; but how then can the loss of credibility be avoided?

Along this same line, another more complex but not thereby less frequent situation is that where monetary policy confronts the inflationary consequences of the pursuance of inappropriate policies in other economic policy areas. This is particularly the case regarding budgetary, labour-market or incomes policies. The conventional view is that the stabilising function of monetary policy should act as an offsetting or disciplinary factor to these other economic policy components.

However, this approach ignores the fact that monetary policy has a limited capacity to offset inflationary effects stemming from other distortions and that the rigid upholding of medium- and long-term targets may in turn generate some costs and loss of credibility.

Thus, for example, certain episodes of the recent ERM crisis have revealed that attempts to maintain the credibility of the stabilising commitments of monetary policy via the exchange rate, through interest rate increases without sufficient adjustment of the other economic policy components, tended to erode credibility and foreign exchange stability rather than improve them.

Clearly, against the problems posed by the specific application of the price-stability target, it is most difficult to define a monetary policy implementation framework that determines, in each particular circumstance, how the authorities should react.

The reputation models appear to demonstrate the superiority of pre-set rules versus discretionary action regarding the behaviour of the authorities. However, the experience of the various attempts to design monetary policies based on the automatic observance of certain rigid rules of conduct cannot be said to have been fully satisfactory. Many countries have, in certain periods, attempted to pursue relatively strict rules for the growth of the monetary or credit aggregates or for the behaviour of the exchange rate. But it has not been possible to pursue such rules with the automatism originally sought. Although monetary or exchange-rate targets have played and play an important role in monetary policy conduct, central banks have had to resort to certain extent to interpretation and discretionary action in pursuing them.

Numerous factors of instability or volatility mark current financial markets, which are heavily deregulated, open to free international capital movements and undergoing rapid innovation. If regard is had to such factors, adherence to rigid rules for a certain financial variable proves difficult and may have a distorting effect. A degree of interpretation or discretionary action is inevitable.

However, if it is not possible to set automatic rules which translate mechanically the explicit commitment to price stability, how can the authorities ensure that, in the use of their margin of discretion, they do not deviate from the set target? The institutional provisions governing the central bank and its decision-making bodies thus become a matter of great importance. Who holds this discretionary power, and under what rules and guidelines? How is the exercise of such power controlled? Such questions are at the heart of the current debate on monetary policy and its relationship to the other realms of economic policy.

The elimination of macroeconomic instability is the main mission of a central bank. Most of the time this mission is not a straightforward one. A suitable institutional structure offering the necessary independence can be very useful, but this should not be seen as the solution to all the problems of anti-inflationary policy effectiveness. Indeed, the autonomy of a central bank does not depend only on its legal structure; it is also closely linked to its actual margin for manoeuvre, which is determined not by legal provisions alone but – mainly – by a set of rules of conduct which tacitly or expressly establish its relationship to other social and governing bodies. Indeed, a central bank can only behave relatively independently, even if its formal independence is provided for, when there is sufficient social consensus about the importance of preserving the goal of economic stability, as indicated by Professor Fischer. It is not a logical follow-on, therefore, that central bank independence is a panacea for complex problems rooted in the culture of economic agents and in the structural deficiencies of the economy.

The credibility of anti-inflationary policies is undoubtedly a key element for cutting the costs of disinflation and of maintaining stability. Unfortunately, there are no institutional formulae or rules of conduct that can ensure it. The ERM experience has been most illustrative in this respect. The mere undertaking of foreign exchange stability commitments did not by itself ensure the expected credibility benefits in all cases. These were only obtained by the countries which acted persistently and consistently with this commitment.

Further, the contribution of monetary policy to such credibility is limited and cannot always offset the indiscipline or inconsistencies stemming from other economic policy areas. The anti-inflationary credibility of monetary policy hinges crucially on the credibility of the overall macroeconomic policy which, in turn, reflects the attitudes of elected governments towards inflation.

It is thus perhaps best not to address the costs and benefits of disinflation confining oneself to the credibility of monetary policy. Reference should be made to other economic policy areas – particularly supply-side policies and structural reform – which can and should contribute decisively when it comes to reducing the costs of disinflation.

For countries yet to converge towards the moderate inflation rates within Fischer's 1–3% range, and which evidence deep-seated and persistent inflationary biases, convergence is a priority task as regards reducing the costs of inflation, which no doubt diminishes in relevance once a firm path of stability is achieved. Most important in this area, perhaps, is the elimination of the fiscal drag via an appropriate correction of tax rates according to the course of inflation.

Lastly, Mr. Chairman, I should like to close my address highlighting the contribution that the Treaty of Maastricht has made to clarifying the social debate on the final goals of monetary policy and to overcoming the legal and constitutional obstacles to central bank independence in many European countries. At a time of certain pessimism about the application of the Treaty, it is only fair that this contribution be acknowledged.

SESSION II: THE POSITION OF THE CENTRAL BANK

Commitment through Delegation, Political Influence and Central Bank Independence

ALEX CUKIERMAN*

Tel Aviv University and CentER

1. INTRODUCTION

Politicians in office often delegate authority over some areas of policy to partly independent institutions within the public sector. This paper takes the view that delegation is used as a partial commitment device. By specifying the objectives of an institution more or less tightly and by giving it broader or narrower powers, politicians determine the extent of commitment to a policy rule. The wider the set of contingencies over which the rule is binding, the stronger the commitment. This set is wider and an institution more independent the more politically costly it is, for the political principals, to override the decisions of the institution. Hence a public institution with broader power in a particular area of policy corresponds to a stronger commitment to given restrictions on policy in this area.

A main objective of this paper is to identify economic and political factors that induce politicians to delegate more or less authority to semi-independent public institutions. Although some of the ideas in the paper probably have wider applicability they are illustrated by means of delegation in the area of monetary policy. More delegation of authority in this area usually means that the central bank has a stronger mandate, as well as a sufficient degree of independence from government, to conduct monetary policy so as to achieve price stability.

Besides price stability monetary policy can be directed at achieving other objectives such as a high level of economic activity and stabilization policy. In addition, inflationary finance can be used to reduce the real value of existing government debt. The temptation to use monetary policy to achieve such objectives is stronger the more depressed is the economy and the larger the size of the public debt. It is well-known that these temptations lead to equilibria in which those objectives are not achieved (or only partially achieved), and in which the rate of inflation is suboptimally high[1]. Politicians in office can precommit monetary policy by delegating some or all of the authority to

* I have benefited from the comments of Eddie Dekel and Matthias Raith.

J.A.H. de Beaufort Wijnholds, S.C.W. Eijffinger and L.H. Hoogduin (eds.), A Framework for Monetary Stability, pp. 55–74.

conduct monetary policy to the central bank (CB) and by directing it through law or convention to give high priority to price stability. Recent evidence reveals that there are substantial cross-country variations in the degree of CB independence[2]. The main objective of this paper is to develop a conceptual framework that makes it possible to formulate hypotheses that can account for at least some of this variation in CB independence.

Politicians in office obviously do not have to delegate authority. When they decide to do that it is because such delegation serves their purposes. More independence to the CB entails both a benefit and a cost. The benefit is that by reducing inflationary expectations a higher level of CB independence reduces interest charges on new government debt and moderates wage increases. This moderation ultimately makes it possible to stimulate the economy with lower inflation. The cost involves a loss in flexibility for the party in office. This foregone flexibility could have been useful since its presence would have made it possible to engage in stabilization policy and to tax away some of the national debt via inflation. There is consequently a tradeoff between the credibility of low inflation and flexibility[3]. In extreme situations government can override the decisions of the CB, but such a course of action entails a political cost for the party (or parties) in office.

The above considerations are complicated further when the different parties competing for office disagree about the structure of government expenditures. In the presence of such disagreements the party currently in office may grant some independence to the CB also in order to restrict the ability of the opposition (if and when it accedes to office) to spend on public goods which are in low priority for the incumbent party[4]. When it decides how much independence to grant to the CB, the party in office weigh these various elements, taking into consideration the likelihood that it will not be re-elected.

The paper presents a precise analysis of the effect of these different factors on the tendency to delegate authority to the CB within a framework in which government is uncertain about the future state of the economy as well as about how long it will survive in office. The analysis suggests that the delegation of authority to the CB is used as a device to reduce interest charges on new government debt. The higher the importance attached by government to this objective, the larger the level of independence accorded to the CB.

The analysis also reveals that CB independence is higher the larger the average, employment motivated inflationary bias, the larger political polarization and political instability[5] and (under reasonable conditions) the larger the amount of funds that government plans to borrow on the capital market.

After having delegated some authority to the CB, the executive or legislative branches of government can redirect monetary policy either by overriding the bank openly or by exerting more subtle political pressure on it[6]. Sections 2 and 3 focus on the first channel and section 4 on the second one. The extent of political pressure is usually private information and the public learns about it gradually, but optimally. The main lesson from the analysis of this case is that, while in office, CB governors with lower survival probabilities display less resistance to expansionary political pressures than governors with higher survival probabilities. Recent evidence supports this implication[7].

Section 2 presents a model of delegation of authority and characterizes its equilibrium level. Comparative static results are presented and interpreted in section 3. Section 4 illustrates the effect of instability at the CB on the response of the latter to informal political pressures. This is followed by concluding remarks.

2. A MODEL OF ENDOGENOUS DELEGATION

a. An intuitive overview

This section illustrates some of the ideas in the paper by means of a precise model. There are two parties that randomly alternate in office. Both parties like a high level of employment and dislike inflation. Due to the existence of nominal wage contracts the party in office can affect employment by creating unanticipated inflation. Natural employment is affected by real economic shocks but is always below desired employment[8]. Because of the fluctuations in the natural level of employment, the value of unanticipated inflation to policymakers varies depending on the realization of these shocks. In periods of low natural employment, monetary surprises are more valuable than in periods with high levels of natural employment. Although they value high employment and price stability to the same extent, the two parties have different preferences with respect to the *composition* of government expenditures[9].

The government in office also wants to issue a fixed amount of bonds in order to finance the current budget deficit. All bonds are discount bonds. Hence the interest charge is paid up front. Other things the same, policymakers like to keep financing costs as low as possible. These costs depend in turn on what the public believes about the rate of inflation that will occur until the bonds are redeemed. If the public believes that inflation will be high, the nominal rate it demands is high and the finance charge is large. If the public believes that inflation will be low, the nominal rate that needs to be paid in order to place the bonds is low and the discount is small. Hence, other things the same, incumbent policymakers prefer lower inflationary expectations since they are associated with lower costs of financing the national debt.

But once bonds have been issued, nominal wage contracts concluded and real shocks to employment have realized the government in office is tempted to inflate. This temptation arises for two reasons. One is that once it is held by the public at a fixed nominal rate the real value of debt can be inflated away, thus alleviating the fiscal burden. The other is that given fixed nominal wage contracts the divergence between actual and desired employment can be reduced by unanticipated inflation. Since the public is aware of these temptations it requires a nominal interest that would compensate it for the average value of expected inflation. Obviously this raises the cost of financing the government debt. As is well known, government can reduce these costs by credibly committing its policy to a zero or low inflation at the outset[10].

I focus here on partial commitment through the delegation of authority to the CB. In the presence of delegation the bank is directed to focus first on the maintenance of price stability. But the political authorities can override its decisions at a cost. The larger the level of independence granted to the bank at the outset the larger the (political) cost of overriding its decisions and the stronger the commitment to price stability. But, given the level of independence, the price stability objective is abandoned if the realization of shocks is extreme enough to make the option to renege on it sufficiently attractive[11]. The stronger the commitment the lower inflationary expectations and the smaller is the discount on government bonds. This is a benefit for government objectives. But a stronger commitment also entails costs since it reduces government's ability to stabilize employment and to utilize the inflation levy on government debt. The level of CB independence is determined by weighing those opposing considerations optimally *before* nominal contracts are concluded and *before* the realization of shocks to natural employment.

To capture these elements I consider the following six-stage sequence of events. In the first stage the incumbent government decides how much authority to delegate to the CB. In the second stage it floats a fixed amount of discount bonds whose discount is determined by the real rate required by the public and by its inflationary expectation. Elections take place in the third stage and either the incumbent or the challenging party is voted into office and remains there until the end of the game. Nominal wage contracts are concluded in the fourth stage and shocks to the natural level of employment realize in the fifth stage. In the sixth and final stage the party in office decides whether or not to exert pressure on the CB to inflate and if it does – at what rate. Immediately after that bonds are redeemed. (A schematic representation of the sequence of events appears in Figure 1).

The benefit of a more independent CB is that higher independence reduces inflationary expectations. A cost of higher CB independence is that it restricts the ability of politicians to inflate the debt away making it more difficult to spend on the type of public good that they like. But, from the perspective of the incumbent party in stage 1, this cost differs depending on whether it is re-elected or not. If not re-elected, the incumbent party does not value the ability to inflate the debt away as much as it values this ability when it is reelected. The reason is that in the second case, this ability enables it to spend more on the public goods it likes, whereas in the first case this enables the other party to spend more on public goods which the incumbent party does not particularly care about. In different words, the incumbent party prefers a stronger level of commitment and therefore a more independent CB when it is certain of not being re-elected than when it is certain of being elected.

b. The formal structure

Viewed from the perspective of the first period, the incumbent party's objective is to maximize

$$as(1 - n) + \beta E_x[x(\pi - \pi^e) + \lambda Bs\pi + (1 - \lambda)bs\pi - \frac{d}{2}\pi^2 - \lambda c(x)], \quad (1)$$

$$B > b \geq 0, 1 \geq \beta, \lambda \geq 0, x > 0$$

where

$$c(x) = \begin{pmatrix} 0 - \text{if the political authorities respect the CB authority in stage 6} \\ c - \text{if the political authorities override the CB decisions in stage 6} \end{pmatrix}.$$

s is the (exogenous) amount of bonds that the incumbent government desires to sell (in stage 2), n is the nominal rate of interest necessary to induce the public to buy this quantity of bonds. Since government debt takes the form of discount bonds the government actually raises funds of size $s(1 - n)$ when it places an amount with a face value of s on the market. The parameter a measures how much the incumbent government values the ability to raise funds and n is the nominal rate of interest.

The remaining costs and benefits all materialize in the last period. They are therefore discounted by the political discount factor of the incumbent – β. π and π^e are actual and expected inflation respectively. The difference $\pi - \pi^e$ measures the amount of period 6's inflation which was not anticipated by individuals when nominal contracts that are based on π^e were concluded. It is well-known that unanticipated inflation has positive effects on employment and output[12]. The stochastic parameter x measures how valuable are the effects of stimulatory inflationary surprises to the incumbent government. It can be thought of as an index of the natural level of employment. The lower natural employment, the more valuable are positive surprises and the larger, therefore, x[13]. The important feature of x is that it is not known with certainty prior to its realization in the fifth stage. Thus, from the perspective of the first stage, in which the level of CBI is chosen, x̂ is a stochastic variable. This is the reason for the appearance of the expected value operator, E, in equation (1).

λ is the probability that the incumbent party is re-elected, πs measures the inflation-induced reduction in the real value of the debt. The terms $Bs\pi$ and bsπ respectively measure the benefit to period one's incumbent of this reduction when he remains and when he does not remain in office. The constraint B > b reflects the view that the reduction in the real value of debt is more valuable to either party when it is in office. This presumption originates from the notion that when it is not in office, either party prefers a more independent CB since such a bank makes it more difficult for the other party to spend on a public good that is not desired by the first party. The term $(d/2)\pi^2$ measures the costs of inflation and d is a positive parameter which determines how seriously these costs are taken by either party.

Finally c is the political cost incurred by policymakers if they decide to override the commitment of the CB to price stability in period 6. The size of this (fixed) cost is larger the higher the degree of independence that was conferred on the bank in the first period. This cost is multiplied by λ (the probability of remaining in office) since the political blame for overriding the CB is directed only at the party in office at the time.

The following figure summarizes the sequence of events and moves.

1	2	3	4	5	6
CB independence is chosen by incumbent party	An amount s of bonds is sold to public	Elections take place	Nominal wage contracts (based on π^e) are concluded	x realizes	Incumbent party decides whether to override the CB. If it does it also picks inflation, π

Figure 1 Sequence of events and timing of moves

The figure is largely self-explanatory, but the following additional facts are worth noting:

1. The extent of delegation of authority as embodied in c, is chosen before the results of the elections, and the state of the economy as proxied by x are known. As a consequence, in choosing CB independence, the incumbent government has to weigh the benefits of commitment against the loss in flexibility associated with more independence to the CB.
2. Although they are influenced by events from all stages, the components of the objective function in equation (1) (or payoffs) are located in only two of the six stages. The component as$(1 - n)$ is located in stage 2 and all the other components in stage 6. Correspondingly β should be thought of as the discount factor between stage 2 and stage 6.
3. The incumbent government makes decisions in stages 1 and 6. The public makes decisions in stages 3 and 4, and nature moves in stage 5.
4. Government bonds are redeemed in stage 6 *after* the realization of inflation.

c. When does government override the CB?

I now turn to the derivation of equilibrium strategies. It is natural and convenient to start from the last period and to go backwards. In the last stage, uncertainty about the election result and the state of the economy (x) has been resolved and CB independence (c) and government debt (s) are taken as given. Hence the incumbent's party problem is given by

$$\text{Max}_{\pi} \; x(\pi - \pi^e) + Bs\pi - \frac{d}{2} \pi^2 \equiv \text{Max}_{\pi} \; V(\pi,x) \tag{2}$$

if it decides to override the authority of the CB. In the other case the CB is free to focus on price stability and $\pi = 0$. The solution to the problem in equation (2) is

$$\pi_D(x) = \frac{1}{d}(x + Bs) \tag{3}$$

where the index D that is attached to π stands for "discretionary" since when it overrides the CB, government acts in a discretionary manner.

When does government override the CB? To answer this question we calculate the value of government's objectives when π_D is chosen by using (3) in (2). This yields

$$V(\pi_D,x) = -x\pi^e + \frac{1}{2d}(x + Bs)^2 . \tag{4}$$

Government decides to override the CB and to inflate at rate π_D if and only if[14]

$$V(\pi_D,x) - V(0,x) > c \tag{5}$$

where, from (2), $V(0,x) = -x\pi^e$. Using this and (4) in (5) and rearranging, government overrides the CB if and only if

$$x > \sqrt{2dc} - Bs \equiv x_c . \tag{6}$$

Equation (6) states that, given x_c, government overrides the CB when the level of employment is sufficiently depressed – x is sufficiently high. But the larger CB independence (the larger c), the larger the value of x above which government overrides the CB. I assume $x_c > 0$ since otherwise there is no commitment at all and the problem becomes trivial.

d. Equilibrium expectations and wage contracts

Nominal wage contracts are agreed upon in stage 4 and are in effect until the end of the game. The level of the contract wage is higher the higher are inflationary expectations π^e. For simplicity and without loss of generality we proxy the contract nominal wage by π^e. In stage 4 individuals do not know x with certainty. But since they understand government's decision rule contingent on x they can use it to calculate the (statistical) expected value of inflation. This expected value is

$$\pi^e \equiv \mathop{E}_{x} [\pi \, x_c] = \int_0^{x_c} 0 \cdot dF(x) + \int_{x_c}^{\infty} \pi_D(x) dF(x) = \tag{7}$$

$$= \frac{1}{d} \{ \int_{x_c}^{\infty} x dF(x) + Bs \int_{x_c}^{\infty} dF(x) \}$$

where $F(x)$ is the distribution function of x.

Since, from equation (6), x_c is an increasing function of CB independence, equation (7) implies that inflationary expectations are lower the higher is CB independence.

e. Determination of the discount on government bonds

Let

$$s^d(r) = K + \alpha r, \quad \alpha > 0 \tag{8}$$

be the demand for government bonds in period 2 where r is the ex-ante real rate of interest. Since government insists on selling a quantity s of (in terms of face value) bonds, the real rate of interest is determined from

$$r = \frac{1}{\alpha} (s - K) . \tag{9}$$

When elected, both parties use the same decision rule in period 6. As a consequence, inflationary expectations are the same before and after elections. To obtain the real rate in equation (9), individuals have to be compensated for the expected rate of inflation π^e. Hence, the nominal rate, n, is

$$n = r + \pi^e = \frac{1}{\alpha} (s - K) + \pi^e . \tag{10}$$

Since bonds are of the discount type, a higher nominal rate implies that government raises less funds for the budget given the size of s.

f. Determination of CB independence

CB independence (c) is chosen by the party in office in period 1 before it knows whether it will be re-elected and before it knows what will be the state of the economy (x) after the elections. A higher level of CB independence reduces π^e. Such a reduction is beneficial for two reasons as can be seen from equations (1) and (10). First, it reduces the discount on government bonds. Second, a lower

π^e implies lower nominal wages and therefore, given x and π, a higher level of economic activity in period 6. But a higher level of CB independence also has costs since in some states of nature it prevents government from conducting anticyclical monetary policy and in the remaining states a political cost has to be paid for engaging in such policy. In addition, a higher level of CB independence reduces the scope for inflating away the national debt. Thus, by delegating more authority to the CB, government gains credibility, but loses flexibility. The level of CB independence is determined by optimally trading off these two elements in period 1.

Formally the government in office in period 1 chooses c so as to maximize the objective function in equation (1) subject to the relations given in equations (3), (6), (7) and (10). Substituting equations (7) and (10) into equation (1), rearranging, and dropping terms which do not depend on c the government's problem in period 1 can be expressed as

$$\text{Max } J(\cdot) \equiv \text{Max } \frac{as + \beta Ex}{d} \left[\int_{x_c}^{\infty} x dF(x) + Bs \int_{x_c}^{\infty} dF(x) \right] \quad (11)$$
$$c \qquad\qquad c$$

$$+ \beta \int_{x_c}^{\infty} \left[\frac{1}{d} (x + Bs) \{ \frac{x}{2} + [(1 - \lambda)b + (\lambda - \frac{1}{2})B]s\} - \lambda c(x) \right] dF(x)$$

where x_c is given in equation (6). After some rearrangement, the first-order condition for an internal maximization of this problem is

$$J_c(\cdot) = [as + \beta \{ Ex + (1 - \lambda) [(B - b)s - \sqrt{\frac{dc}{2}}] \}] f(x_c) \quad (12)$$

$$- \beta\lambda \int_{x_c}^{\infty} dF(x) = 0$$

where f(x) is the probability density of x. Equation (12) determines the level of CB independence, c, as a function of various parameters. The second-order condition for an internal maximum is

$$J_{cc}(\cdot) = \sqrt{\frac{d}{2c}} \left\{ [as + \beta\{Ex + (1 - \lambda) [(B - b)s - \sqrt{\frac{dc}{2}}]\}]f'(x_c) \quad (13) \right.$$

$$\left. + \frac{\beta}{2} (3\lambda - 1)f(x_c) \right\} < 0$$

where $f'(\cdot)$ is the derivative of $f(\cdot)$ with respect to x. Jointly sufficient, but not necessary conditions for the fulfillment of the second-order condition are $(B - b)s > \sqrt{dc/2}$, $f'(x_c) < 0$ and $\lambda < \frac{1}{3}$. The second condition states that the probability density is decreasing at the critical value x_c and the third requires that the probability of re-election is smaller than $\frac{1}{3}$. When $\lambda \geq \frac{1}{3}$, the second-order condition implies that if $(B - b)s > \sqrt{dc/2}$, then $f'(x_c)$ must be negative.

3. POLITICAL AND ECONOMIC DETERMINANTS OF THE LEVEL OF CENTRAL BANK INDEPENDENCE

This section uses the results of the previous section in order to characterize the political and economic factors that induce political authorities to delegate more authority to the CB. The results are derived by performing comparative static experiments with respect to various parameters on the first-order condition in equation (12). Derivations appear in the appendix. The section summarizes the main results in a series of propositions and discusses the intuition that underlies them. In all the propositions "other factors" that are not mentioned explicitly are held fixed.

PROPOSITION 1: The CB is granted more independence (c is larger) the larger Ex and "a".

The intuition underlying the proposition can be understood by noting from equation (3), that the average inflationary bias in the absence of any form of commitment by political authorities is

$$E\pi_D(x) = \frac{1}{d}(Ex + Bs) .$$

Hence, given s, the average inflationary bias is larger the larger Ex and the benefits of a partial commitment are therefore larger. As a consequence c is larger the larger is Ex as stated in the first part of the proposition.

A larger "a" means that the importance attached by political authorities to the reduction of the discount on government debt is larger. With a higher level of CB independence, expectations are lower, the nominal rate is lower and the discount on new government debt therefore lower. Hence the larger the importance attributed to decreasing the discount on bonds the larger the level of CB independence. I turn next to political factors.

LEMMA 2: The CB is granted more independence the smaller is b.

The meaning of the lemma can be understood by recalling that the term B − b measures the difference in the value of the option to inflate the debt away between a state in which a party is in office and a state in which it is not in office. The more polarized are the parties with respect to the structure of public expenditures, the larger the (positive) difference B − b. Hence a smaller b means that the level of polarization is larger. The lemma implies therefore

PROPOSITION 2: The CB is granted more independence the larger the degree of polarization about the structure of government expenditures.

The intuition is that the party in office likes a stronger constraint on the other party's ability to spend the larger the disagreement about the structure of public spending. This is achieved by imposing a stronger limit on the other party's ability to inflate the debt away through a higher level of CB independence.

PROPOSITION 3: The higher the level of political instability (the lower λ) the larger the level of independence that is granted to the CB provided political polarization is sufficiently large.

The precise meaning of "sufficiently large" is elaborated in the appendix. In any case the condition is only sufficient and not necessary. There are many other configurations of parameters, some of which are discussed in the appendix, for which proposition 3 holds. The intuition underlying the proposition is similar to the intuition underlying proposition 2. Given the level of polarization the party in office prefers a more independent CB the smaller are its re-election prospects. The party in office in period 1 obviously likes to have more flexibility for itself than for the other party. The smaller its chances of re-election the larger the benefits of CB independence in terms of restricting the other party's ability to spend in comparison to the cost of being similarly constrained. In addition the smaller the chances of re-election the smaller the likelihood that the incumbent party will incur the political blame for overriding the CB if future circumstances make such a course of action optimal.

The effect of the amount of bonds that government wishes to sell on CB independence is generally ambiguous. But there is a presumption that this effect is positive. Alternative sufficient conditions for a positive effect are summarized in the following proposition.

PROPOSITION 4: If either of the following conditions holds:
(i) $\lambda \geq \frac{1}{3}$ and β is relatively small, or
(ii) λ is near to either 0 or 1
(iii) $f(x_c)$ is very small,
then CB independence is higher the larger is the amount of funds s, that government wishes to borrow from the public.

A larger s triggers two opposing effects on the tendency to delegate authority to the CB. On the one hand the reduction in the up-front discount on government bonds induced by higher independence is more valuable when government needs to raise more funds. But, by the same token, the value of ultimately retaining the option to inflate the debt away is also more valuable when s is larger. This tends to reduce the attractiveness of CB independence and operates, therefore, in the opposite direction. The proposition presents conditions under which the first effect dominates.

The effect of the parameter d on CB independence is unambiguous. Proposition 5 summarizes the result.

PROPOSITION 5: The CB is granted less independence the larger the relative concern of political autoritities for price stability (the higher d).

The intuition underlying proposition 5 follows. When d is high, the discretionary rate of inflation is lower for any given values of x and of s (see equation (3)) even in the absence of a commitment. As a result the benefits of any commitment level are smaller. This induces the executive and legislative branches of government to delegate less authority to the CB. An illustration of such a case is the U.K. In comparison to other central banks within industrial countries, the Bank of England is relatively dependent. But there is concurrently an anti-inflationary stance within the British civil service. Proposition 5 suggests that the conjunction of those facts may not be accidental.

4. INSTABILITY AT THE CENTRAL BANK AND INFLATION

Recent evidence shows that (within the group of less developed countries (LDC's)) there is a positive association between the turnover rate of central bank governors and average inflation across countries[15]. This section briefly describes a conceptual framework in which the policy chosen by the CB governor is influenced by the probability of his removal even when he remains in office and the CB is not formally overridden.

To this point the analysis has presumed that, if not officially overridden, the CB always sticks to a zero inflation policy. But governments often manage to influence CB policy through more subtle channels and pressures[16]. This section uses a framework in which the timing and extent of these pressures is the private information of the governor to show that the higher the probability that the governor will be removed from office, the higher inflation even when the governor remains in office.

The formal model is an extension of the model of a policymaker with an (extended) information advantage as presented in chapter 10 of Cukierman (1992). As long as he is in office the governor possesses an objective function with a *changing* but persistent relative emphasis on the creation of surprises versus price stability. In the present context this shifting weight can be thought of as originating in changes in the extent of political pressures on the CB. The public never gets to observe these pressures directly but can draw noisy inferences about their current and future state from past inflation rates. These inferences are noisy because the CB does not have perfect control over the rate of inflation.

Let s be the probability of survival of the governor in office in period t given that he has remained in office until period $t - 1$[17]. In states of nature in which he is not in office the governor does not care about either price stability or surprise creation[18]. The relevant part of the governor's objective function is

$$E_0\left\{[\pi_0 - \pi_0^e]x_0 - \frac{\pi_0^2}{2} + \sum_{i=1}^{\infty}(s\beta)^i[[\pi_i - \pi_i^e]x_i - \frac{\pi_i^2}{2}]\right\} \tag{14}$$

$$+ \sum_{i=1}^{\infty}s^{i-1}(1-s)K$$

where $x_i = A + p_i$, $p_i = \rho p_{i-1} + v_i$, $A > 0$ and $0 < \rho < 1$. v_i is a normal variate with zero mean and variance σ_v^2. Here π_i is actual inflation in period i and π_i^e the rate of inflation expected for that period at the beginning of the period. β is the discount factor and x_i is a stochastic variable whose realizations are restricted to the positive orthant[19]. It reflects the potency of political pressures on the CB. The larger x_i the stronger are the pressures of the political establishment on the governor to expand the money supply. x_i is private information. Its positive serial correlation reflects the presumption that when pressures are above their mean level they tend to remain above it for some time. K is the *constant* level of utility experienced by the governor when not in office. s^i is the probability that the governor survives in office until the end of period i and $s^{i-1}(1-s)$ is the probability that he terminates at the beginning of that period after having survived until the end of the previous period. Equilibrium is of the Nash variety; taking the (rational) process of expectation formation by the public as given, the governor plans rates of monetary expansion and inflation so as to maximize the objective function in equation (14); taking the behavioral rule of the governor as given, the public forms expectations so as to minimize the mean (square) forecast error.

Application of the results in chapter 10 of Cukierman (1992) to this case reveals that equilibrium inflation is given by

$$\pi_i = \frac{1 - s\beta\rho}{1 - s\beta\lambda}A + \frac{1 - s\beta\rho^2}{1 - s\beta\rho\lambda}p_i + \psi_i \tag{15}$$

where ψ_i is a normal variate with zero mean and variance σ_ψ^2. ψ_i characterizes the (lack of) precision of monetary policy in controlling inflation. λ is a known function of ρ, σ_v^2 and σ_ψ^2 and satisfies the following inequality

$$\lambda \leq \rho. \tag{16}$$

Note that since s, β, ρ and λ are all smaller than one, the coefficients of A and of p_i are positive. How does an increase in the governor's survival probability affect equilibrium inflation? The following proposition provides an answer to this question.

PROPOSITION 6: For any given realization of the political pressure shock (p_i) and of the control error (ψ_i) the rate of inflation is higher the lower is the survival probability, s, of the central bank governor.

PROOF: In part 2 of the Appendix.

Proposition 6 provides precise underpinning for the intuitively plausible notion that a governor with a low probability of survival in office will inflate at a higher rate than a governor with a higher probability of survival. The reason is that part of the cost of *currently* more expansionary monetary policy takes the form of higher *future* inflationary expectations. A governor who is less sure of being in office in the future is obviously less sensitive to this cost. He therefore inflates at a higher rate.

Two facts are worth noting. First, due to the dynamic nature of his optimization problem, the governor's policy while in office is influenced by what he perceives to be his future survival probability. Second, a lower survival probability raises the CB inflationary response to any given level of political pressure.

For LDC's proposition 6 is supported by evidence presented in chapter 20 of Cukierman (1992) and in Cukierman and Webb (1993).

5. CONCLUDING REMARKS

Preliminary empirical evidence suggests that legal CB independence is larger when party instability is larger and lower when regime instability is higher[20]. The first type of instability is usually relevant for constitutional democracies while the second is characteristic of non-democratic regimes in which changes in government occur through coups or other non-constitutional means. Part of this evidence is consistent with the implications of this paper. In particular the implication that a higher level of political instability is conducive to more independence for the CB is supported by the finding that legal CB independence is higher when party political instability is larger. The reason is that party instability occurs mainly in democratic countries and that in such countries legal independence is an important determinant of actual CB independence[21]. Hence in such countries legal independence is a reasonable proxy for the *actual* level of independence that political authorities *meant* to confer on the CB. This observation, in conjunction with the positive empirical relationship found between legal independence and party political instability are consistent with proposition 3.

Since the framework of the paper is appropriate mostly for constitutional regimes, the observed negative relationship between regime instability and legal independence is not directly explainable by it. It is possible, however, that it arises because in non-democratic regimes the structure of the regime makes it unlikely that a serious commitment can be upheld by constitutional means.

This reduces the effect of legal CB independence on expectations and with it the tendency of the regime to use legal CB as a commitment device. This effect is stronger the more unstable the regime since it is widely known that a new regime does not necessarily respect the institutions erected by the previous one. Those remarks should be viewed as conjectures to be tested in future work.

Some of the lessons to be learned from this paper are that:

1. A certain degree of CB independence is granted in order to reduce interest charges on government debt.
2. In many cases the tendency to delegate authority to the CB is stronger the larger the national debt. The 1986 "divorce" between the Italian CB and the Italian Treasury can be understood in these terms[22].
3. When capital markets are wide (α in equation (8) is small) it is likely that government will try to raise more funds through the capital market. In conjunction with the second conclusion this implies that, other things the same, governments of countries with wider capital markets will delegate more authority to the CB. This conclusion is supported by the observation that some of the most independent central banks are found in countries with well developed capital markets. Germany and the U.S. are examples.

But, on the other hand, proposition 5 suggests that if there is a strong preference for price stability within the executive branch of government, the tendency to delegate authority to the CB is likely to be lower. An example is the U.K. in which the traditional anti-inflation stance of the British civil service reduces the need for a highly independent CB.

The paper suggests that the need to rely on CB independence is greater the stronger is the inflationary bias under discretion. Furthermore this statement is independent of whether this bias arises because of employment considerations or because of a strong desire to reduce the real value of government debt. More generally, any factor that increases the tendency to inflate under discretion, such as a higher degree of polarization, also raises the tendency to delegate authority to the CB.

In order to influence monetary policy after having delegated some authority to the CB, political authorities do not always have to override the Bank openly. Instead they can exert more subtle political pressure (Havrilesky, 1992). The paper shows that CB governors who are less likely to survive in office find it more difficult to resist inflationary pressures. This conclusion is particularly relevant for LDC's.

What are the insights from the discussion of commitment through delegation in the area of monetary policy to other areas of policy? This is a largely open question. My feeling is that, at least for democracies with a certain minimal level of concensus, higher levels of political instability are likely to lead to more delegation of authority to semi-independent public institutions.

APPENDIX

1. *Proof of the propositions in section 3*

By the implicit function theorem

$$\frac{dc}{dD} = -\frac{1}{J_{cc}}\frac{\partial J_c}{\partial D} \tag{A1}$$

where D is a dummy parameter. Since J_{cc} is negative by the second-order condition in equation (13) the signs of dc/dD and of $\partial J_c/\partial D$ are identical. It is therefore enough to find the sign of the second term in order to determine that of the first one.

PROPOSITION 1: From equation (12)

$$\frac{\partial J_c(\cdot)}{\partial Ex} = \beta f(x_c); \quad \frac{\partial J_c(\cdot)}{\partial a} = sf(x_c). \tag{A2}$$

The proof is completed by noting that both expressions are positive and by letting D = Ex, a.

LEMMA 2: From equation (12)

$$\frac{\partial J_c(\cdot)}{\partial b} = -\beta(1-\lambda)sf(x_c) . \tag{A3}$$

The proof is completed by letting D = b and by noting that (A3) is negative.

PROPOSITION 3: From equation (12)

$$\frac{\partial J_c(\cdot)}{\partial \lambda} = -\beta[f(x_c)\{(B-b)s - \sqrt{\frac{dc}{2}}\} + \int_{x_c}^{\infty} dF(x)] . \tag{A4}$$

This expression is negative if

$$B - b \geq \frac{1}{s}\sqrt{\frac{dc}{2}} \tag{A5}$$

or, equivalently, if the level of political polarization is sufficiently high. Letting D = λ it follows that if (A5) is satisfied

$$\frac{dc}{d\lambda} < 0 . \tag{A6}$$

For a given level of polarization the result in (A6) is more likely to obtain the higher s and the lower d.

PROPOSITION 4: From equation (12)

$$\frac{\partial J_c(\cdot)}{\partial s} = \beta(1 - \lambda)(B - b)f(x_c) - [Hf'(x_c) + \beta\lambda f(x_c)]B \tag{A7}$$

where H is the coefficient of $f(x_c)$ in equation (12). This equation implies that H is positive. Note that H is also the coefficient of $f'(x_c)$ in equation (13). When $\lambda \geq \frac{1}{3}$ the second-order condition in equation (13) implies that $Hf'(x_c) < 0$. Hence, if in addition β is sufficiently small the expression in (A7) is positive. This establishes part (i).

The second-order condition is equivalent to the condition

$$Hf'(x_c) + \beta\lambda f(x_c) - \frac{1}{2}\beta(1 - \lambda)f(x_c) < 0 . \tag{A8}$$

When $\lambda \to 1$ this condition reduces to

$$Hf'(x_c) + \beta f(x_c) < 0$$

which implies that the expression in (A7) is positive. When $\lambda \to 0$ the first-order condition in equation (12) implies that

$$c = \frac{2}{d}\left[[\frac{1}{\beta} + B - b]s + Ex\right]^2$$

from which it follows that c is an increasing function of s. This establishes part (ii).

If $f(x_c)$ is very small the second-order condition implies again $Hf'(x_c) < 0$. Since $f(x_c)$ is small, this implies that the expression in (17) is positive which establishes part (iii).

PROPOSITION 5: From equation (12)

$$\frac{\partial J_c(\cdot)}{\partial d} = \frac{1}{2}[-\beta(1 - \lambda)f(x_c)\sqrt{\frac{c}{2d}} + \{Hf'(x_c) + \beta\lambda f(x_c)\}\sqrt{\frac{2c}{d}}]$$

$$= \left[Hf'(x_c) + \beta\lambda f(x_c) - \frac{1}{2}\beta(1 - \lambda)f(x_c)\right]\sqrt{\frac{c}{2d}} . \tag{A9}$$

The modified form of the second-order condition in (A8) implies that the expression in (A9) is negative. Hence, higher values of d are associated with lower levels of central bank independence.

2. *Proof of proposition 6*

Totally differentiating equation (15) with respect to s and rearranging

$$\frac{d\pi_i}{ds} = -K[(1 - s\beta\lambda\rho)^2 A + (1 - s\beta\lambda)^2 \rho p_i] \tag{A10}$$

where

$$K \equiv \frac{\beta(\rho - \lambda)}{(1 - s\beta\lambda)^2 (1 - s\beta\lambda\rho)^2}. \tag{A11}$$

Since $\rho - \lambda > 0$, K is positive. Since $A \geq p_i$ and $(1 - s\beta\lambda\rho)^2 > (1 - s\beta\lambda)^2\rho$ it follows that the expression in square brackets on the right-hand side of (A10) is positive. Hence

$$\frac{d\pi_i}{ds} < 0$$

which establishes proposition 6.

NOTES

1. See, for example, chapters 3 and 4 of Cukierman (1992).
2. Evidence for developed economies appears in Grilli, Masciandaro and Tabellini (1991) and for both developed and less developed economies in chapters 19 and 21 of Cukierman (1992) or in Cukierman, Webb and Neyapti (1992). The evidence in the first reference is based on CB charters and in the last two on CB charters as well as on the rate of turnover of CB governors.
3. Recent discussions of this tradeoff in the context of the employment motive for monetary expansion appear in Lohmann (1992) and in Cukierman, Kiguel and Liviatan (1992).
4. Alesina and Tabellini (1990) and Tabellini and Alesina (1990) have shown that such a conflict induces the incumbent to use public debt as a device for restricting the ability of the opposition to spend. In their framework the debt cannot be inflated away. Implicitly they assume therefore a fully independent CB. Here the degree of independence of the CB and therefore the extent to which government debt is inflated away are determined endogenously for a given level of debt. Hence this paper and theirs complement each other.
5. For reasons that are elaborated in the conclusion these results are restricted to democratic regimes.
6. Recent evidence on this kind of political pressure in the U.S. appears in Havrilesky (1992).
7. Details appear in chapter 20 of Cukierman (1992) and in Cukierman, Webb and Neyapti (1992).
8. Natural employment is the level of employment that prevails in the economy in the absence of monetary surprises. The assumption that it is below desired employment reflects the view that due to union power or minimum wage legislation the natural real wage is above its market clearing level. This point of view is developed explicitly in chapter 3, section 3.6 of Cukierman (1992).
9. Alesina and Tabellini (1990) and Tabellini and Alesina (1990) investigate the consequence of this conflict for the level of government debt. Cukierman, Edwards and Tabellini (1992) analyze its consequences for the efficiency of the tax system.

10. See chapter 6, section 6.4 of Persson and Tabellini (1990) or chapter 4, section 4.4 of Cukierman (1992).
11. A similar conception of CB independence appears in Lohmann (1992).
12. A precise mechanism that produces this relation is discussed in chapter 3, section 3.6 of Cukierman (1992). It is based on the interaction of nominal wage contracts with a natural real wage that is higher than that which would clear the market.
13. The positivity of x reflects the presumption that due to market power in the labor market, there always is an inflationary bias. Details appear in chapter 3 of Cukierman (1992). Variations in x may also reflect changes in the relative strength of price stability and of pro stimulation advocates within a given party.
14. I assume that when indifferent government respects the independence of the CB.
15. See chapter 20 of Cukierman (1992) or Cukierman, Webb and Neyapti (1992).
16. A recent documentation of some of these channels for the U.S. Fed appears in Havrilesky (1992).
17. I assume for simplicity that this probability is constant and independent from events in other periods.
18. This somewhat extreme assumption is used for simplicity. The main result would go through even if he cared but less than in periods in which he is in office.
19. More precisely the probability that p_i is negative and exceeds A in absolute value is negligible. Details appear in appendix A to chapter 9 of Cukierman (1992).
20. Details appear in chapter 23 of Cukierman (1992).
21. Evidence and a discussion appear in Cukierman, Webb and Neyapti (1992) and in chapters 20 and 23 of Cukierman (1992).
22. For details see Epstein and Schor (1986).

References

Alesina, Alberto and Guido Tabellini (1990), "A Political Theory of Fiscal Deficits and Government Debt in a Democracy", *Review of Economic Studies*, 57, 403–414, (June).

Barro, Robert and David Gordon (1983), "A Positive Theory of Monetary Policy in a Natural Rate Model", *Journal of Political Economy*, 91, 589–610, (August).

Cukierman, Alex (1992), *Central Bank Strategy, Credibility and Independence; Theory and Evidence*, MIT Press, Cambridge, MA.

Cukierman, Alex, Sebastian Edwards and Guido Tabellini (1992), "Seigniorage and Political Instability", *American Economic Review*, 82, 537–555, (June).

Cukierman, Alex, Miguel Kiguel and Nissan Liviatan (1992), "To Commit or Not to Commit to an Exchange Rate Rule: Is Dollarization the Answer?" *Revista de Analisis Economico*, 7, 73–90, (June).

Cukierman, Alex, Steven Webb and Bilin Neyapti (1992), "Measuring the Independence of Central Banks and its Effect on Policy Outcomes", *World Bank Economic Review*, 6, 353–398, (September).

Cukierman, Alex and Steven Webb (1993), "Political Influence on the Central Bank – International Evidence" manuscript, (May).

Epstein, Gerald and Juliet Schor (1986), "The Divorce of the Banca d'Italia and the Italian Treasury: A Case Study of Central Bank Independence", *Harvard Institute of Economic Research Discussion Papers*, No.1269, (September).

Grilli, Vittorio, Donato Masciandaro and Guido Tabellini (1991), "Political and Monetary Institutions and Public Financial Policies in the Industrialized Countries", *Economic Policy*, 13, 341–392.

74

Havrilesky, Thomas (1992), *The Pressures on American Monetary Policy*, Kluwer Academic Publishers, Norwell, MA.

Lohmann, Susanne (1992), "Optimal Commitment in Monetary Policy: Credibility versus Flexibility" *American Economic Review*, 82, 273–286, (March).

Persson, Torsten and Guido Tabellini (1990), *Macroeconomic Policy, Credibility and Politics*, Harwood Academic Publishers, London, Paris and New York.

Tabellini, Guido and Alberto Alesina (1990), "Voting on the Budget Deficit", *American Economic Review*, 80, 37–49, (March).

Central Bank Autonomy: Policy Issues

J. ONNO DE BEAUFORT WIJNHOLDS AND LEX HOOGDUIN*

De Nederlandsche Bank

1. Introduction

This paper is based on the presumption that central banks should have or be given a high degree of autonomy from the political authorities in their countries. The case for such autonomy or independence has been made convincingly[1].

Central bank autonomy (CBA) is a relatively new concept. It is, for instance, not discussed as such in De Kock's pre-war treatise on central banking[2]. Part of the explanation of the late appearence of CBA in the literature seems to be that independence has in many instances been an evolutionary process[3], which in a gradual manner has over time brought about important changes in the position of various central banks vis-à-vis the government. The extent to which such de facto enhanced CBA was enshrined in laws and statutes varies considerably. In other cases far-reaching discrete changes in central bank legislation were made possible by a drastic rupture of a constitutional nature; an obvious example is that of the Federal Republic of Germany. One of the most debated central bank statutes is that of the future European Central Bank, which has been modelled to a considerable degree on that of the Deutsche Bundesbank.

The case for CBA has been made with considerable success during the past ten years or so. In fact, we have been witnessing a world wide movement toward greater autonomy[4]. In Europe, the future European System of Central Banks (ESCB) casts its shadow forward in requiring the national central banks that will be part of the system to become autonomous before the start of the third stage of European Economic and Monetary Union. In part as a result of the recent crisis in the European Exchange Rate Mechanism, the status of a number of European central banks has recently been strengthened. A few years earlier, far-ranging reforms granting a high degree of CBA were already adopted in countries as diverse as Chile and New Zealand. The movement

* This paper reflects our own views and not necessarily those of De Nederlandsche Bank. Thanks are due to several of our colleagues for comments on an earlier version of this paper.

J.A.H. de Beaufort Wijnholds, S.C.W. Eijffinger and L.H. Hoogduin (eds.), A Framework for Monetary Stability, pp. 75–95.
© 1994 *Kluwer Academic Publishers. Printed in the Netherlands.*

towards greater CBA is still underway, also in developing countries where there is increasing recognition that stubborn high inflation is detrimental to sustainable economic growth. In the countries of Central and Eastern Europe undergoing the difficult transformation of planned to market economies, the issue of CBA is clearly an important one, as is the case in a country like China where – as part of the move toward a 'socialist market economy' – new banking legislation is imminent.

It is against this background that we discuss a number of policy issues with respect to CBA. The treatment does not purport to be exhaustive; our aim is to focus on what we consider to be the most important and/or contentious issues. In section 2 the relationship between monetary policy and supervision of the banking system is discussed. In section 3 we look at the question of democratic legitimacy and accountability for an autonomous central bank. The relationship between monetary policy and CBA is addressed in section 4. This is followed by some views on the relationship between monetary policy, exchange rate policy and CBA (section 5). Conclusions are presented in the final section.

2. MONETARY POLICY AND SUPERVISION OF THE BANKING SYSTEM

At present, prudential supervision is conducted solely or largely by the central bank in roughly half of the industrial countries; in the other half a separate government agency (sometimes more than one) is (largely) responsible for supervision. The statute of the ESCB foresees only a limited role for the European Central Bank (ECB) in the area of prudential control. The national authorities are to remain the main players in this area, with a certain coordinating role envisaged for the ECB.

Furthermore, there is no explicit mention of financial stability as an objective for the ECB. With respect to the European Monetary Institute, prudential control is not mentioned in its statute, although a primary task will be to '. . . hold consultations concerning issues falling within the competence of the national central banks and affecting the stability of financial institutions and markets' (article 4 of the statute). Of course, the statutory framework leaves room for closer interpretation and later evolution. It is, for instance, not explicitly stated that the ECB will be able to act as a lender of last resort, a function that is often seen as an important link between monetary policy and supervision of the banking system[5].

Since actual practice provides little guidance as to the desirability of combining monetary policy and prudential control within central banks, a closer examination of the arguments pro and contra is called for. In the recent literature the case for keeping prudential control outside the central bank has been forcefully made by Heller (1991), a view that is clearly shared by the Deutsche Bundesbank[6]. However, Goodhart and Schoenmaker (1993, p. 25, hereafter GS), who have extensively examined the matter, find that '. . . there are no overwhelming arguments for either model'. Furthermore, the central banks that combine the functions of monetary policy and prudential control generally are satisfied with the arrangement and do not appear to consider it a threat to their present or future (actual or hoped for) autonomy.

2.1. Arguments in favour of separating the functions

The first and main argument for not combining monetary policy and prudential supervision within a central bank is that of a possible contamination of monetary policy by supervisory considerations. In its simplest form, it is based on the fear that the central bank's anti-inflationary stance would be undermined by a large injection of liquidity aimed at keeping one or more important financial institutions from going under. A more sophisticated version of this conflict of interest argument is couched in terms of a willingness of the central bank to maintain lower interest rates than would be desirable on the basis of purely monetary considerations for the sake of counteracting fragility in the financial system[7]. Obviously, a receptiveness on the part of the central bank to outside pressures for easing monetary conditions in order to lessen potential risks of bank failures implies an impairment of CBA.

An attempt to provide empirical evidence for this argument has been made by Heller (1991). Using a limited sample, he compares the average rate of inflation of countries in which central banks have no supervisory authority, shared authority, or full supervisory authority. He finds that inflation is lowest in the first category and highest in the latter (which includes such hyperinflation countries with a history of lax budgetary policies as Argentina and Brazil). Heller admits that this result could also be caused by other factors. He also notes that there are exceptions '. . . like the highly independent Netherlands Bank', which also exercises the supervisory function but has maintained a good inflation record. Indeed, it seems clear that the quantitative evidence that Heller provides is too flimsy to serve as a basis for firm conclusions.

Another argument in favour of not combining monetary policy and prudential control, concerns the matter of ultimate responsibility and the role of paymaster. It can be argued that in cases involving serious rescue efforts of troubled banks, the government is bound to play some role. This is certainly the case when government (i.e. taxpayer) money is involved. Indeed, there is a case to be made for giving ultimate responsibility for bank supervision to the entity that pays when a mishap occurs[8]. Government influence through the channel of supervision or regulation will tend to reduce CBA.

A third reason for keeping prudential supervision out of the central bank, is the experience that bank failures or rescue operations can be messy and thereby damaging to the central bank's reputation and thus affect its autonomy. GS (p. 10) suggest in this context that '. . . the mood within the Bank of England appeared to change under the baneful influence of the BCCI affair.'

2.2. Arguments in favour of combining the functions

Three main arguments can be put forward here, and can be summarized under the headings: enhanced coordination, protection of the payments system and protection against systemic risk.

The first argument is the general preposition that if brought together under one roof[9], the coordination of monetary policy and prudential control will be strenghtened. Such coordination tends to increase efficiency, particularly by avoiding working at cross-purposes, but also includes matters such as dessimination of general information on the monetary and financial system which is of importance for both functions. Avoiding working at cross-purposes does not imply that those in charge of monetary policy or prudential control should always refrain from actions that might make life more difficult for the other. In fact it will clearly be unavoidable in some instances. But the negative impact of action in one field for the other may be lessened by means of early warning and explanation, which is achieved more readily within the board of a central bank than between separate entities. Not working at cross-purposes in practice comes down to avoiding unnecessary conflicts or undesirable outcomes caused by a lack of adequate communication or competence rivalries[10].

The second argument is based on central banks' involvement in the payments system and the credit and liquidity risks that are associated with it. These are particularly related to settlement schemes with uncollateralized overdrafts. As long as these risks are not greatly reduced by improvements in the safety of the payments systems, which can be expected to take time, there is a clear case for central banks closely following the financial situation of the participants in the payments system.

The final argument holds that combining monetary policy and prudential control can help to avoid systemic problems. Central banks generally act as lenders of last resort to the banking system. Apart from the provision of immediate liquidity, the central bank is often the pivot in organizing rescue operations for troubled banks that are deemed worth saving (i.e., that are considered basically solvent)[11]. The lender of last resort and rescue functions clearly make supervision of the banking system very important for central banks. Exercising such supervision itself has obvious advantages for the central bank when dealing with systemic problems, such as assured timeliness of information and decision-making.

2.3. Evaluation

Our first point is that in the debate on whether or not to separate prudential supervision from monetary policy, a useful distinction as to types of supervision appears to have been generally overlooked. It seems to us that the difference between general supervisory or macro prudential control on the one hand and specific or micro prudential control on the other can help to clarify the issue. Indeed, some central banks that are not involved with micro prudential control do play a role in shaping general supervisory policies. The distinction between central banks that do or do not exercise prudential supervision is therefore not as clear-cut as is often (implicitly) suggested. In our view the arguments pro and contra should focus on the exercise of specific or micro prudential control in combination with monetary policy. It is only in the case of micro prudential control that examinations and other close regulatory contacts with individual banks are involved, and where the conflict of interest argument could apply. We do not see any arguments against central banks being involved in macro prudential matters, whereas some of the advantages of combining the functions as discussed in 2.2 appear to apply.

Secondly, having reviewed the arguments, we – like GS – conclude that absolute judgements on the separation or combination of monetary policy and (micro) prudential supervision are not warranted. It appears possible to maintain CBA in both cases. GS suggest that the question needs to be looked at against the particular structure of the banking system in each country. What may also be relevant is the way in which a country conducts its monetary policy, which in turn may be correlated to the relative size of the country's economy. In a smaller industrial country such as the Netherlands, the risk of a conflict between monetary policy aims and supervisory considerations seems considerably less than in, for instance, Germany. Monetary policy in the Netherlands is nowadays geared towards maintaining a strong exchange rate of the guilder within the European Monetary System. There is no official domestic money supply target, such as applied in Germany, the attainment of which could be endangered by supervisory considerations.

A further thought may by that if there is one area in the realm of bank supervision and regulation which could affect CBA, it is probably that of deposit insurance or guarantee schemes run by the central bank. The moral hazard involved in such schemes has in fact triggered a general discussion on their very existence.

3. DEMOCRATIC LEGITIMACY AND ACCOUNTABILITY

When discussing democratic legitimacy and accountability in the framework of CBA, one is led rather far away from purely economic arguments. Economists need therefore be wary when treating this issue. Nevertheless, we feel justified in setting out the arguments and drawing certain conclusions, if only because constitutional specialists have so far not contributed much to this subject.

3.1. Democratic legitimacy

Within a parliamentary democracy the position of the central bank in relation to the political power structure constitutes the very essence of the question of autonomy. While a finely worded legal text granting central bank independence from the government and parliament is not enough to guarantee CBA, it is also true that there are probably very few, if any, instances of central banks which have a de facto high degree of independence despite a legally weak position vis-à-vis the government. CBA therefore requires a codified legal basis. There are various models for this. The most explicit and recent one is the statute of the future ESCB/ECB. The independence to be granted to it is spelled out in some detail, and is based on such matters as a prohibition from taking instructions from governments, a clear commitment to price stability and a fixed, non-renewable, term of duty for directors.

In our view such a high degree of CBA could have constitutional implications. At least this raises the question as to the position of a truly independent central bank within the government power structure[12]. The central bank's position is sometimes compared to that of the judiciary power which protects the integrity of the country's legal system. According to this train of thought the central bank has a special duty to protect the integrity of the country's monetary system. Like supreme court judges, central bank directors should be appointed by the government (or the European Council in the case of the ECB), but should be guaranteed an independent position and protected against politically inspired dismissal by securing their terms of office and other regulations[13].

In the discussion on the position of the ECB the question of democratic legitimacy has been a contentious matter. It has often been argued that the treaty of Maastricht is not sufficiently balanced between its monetary and its political component. While a high degree of supranationality and autonomy is to be conferred to the European Economic and Monetary Union (EMU) and the ESCB, it is felt that a 'democratic deficit' is likely to be created on account of a lagging behind of political integration. In this regard it is specifically considered a problem that the ECB would not have an obvious (political) counterpart under EMU, since a European minister of finance is not to be expected for a long time, if ever. On the other hand, some degree of monitoring will be exercised over the ECB by the European Parliament (EP), whose powers will be somewhat increased under the treaty of Maastricht. The President of the ECB will testify before the EP periodically, whereas the EP will also be consulted in case of appointments to the Executive Board of the ECB. At the next intergovernmental conference of the European Community, scheduled for 1996, the political side of European Union will again be addressed, and could lead to further modifications in the relationship between the ECB and the political branch.

3.2. Accountability

The foregoing has brought us to the subject of accountability, or the degree to which central banks explain or make visible their policies to parliament and/or the public. Here there are clear differences in tradition and in views. Rather few central banks have a legal obligation to establish strong accountability or monitoring mechanisms[14]. In some cases, that of New Zealand being the most outspoken, legal accountability is strongly linked to CBA. For the Reserve Bank of New Zealand accountability is based on four key elements, namely the object of price stability, a clear policy targets agreement, personal responsibility of the governor and publication of a regular monetary statement[15]. Political accountability of the central bank is, however, sometimes criticized as it is felt that it could affect CBA and therefore weaken the commitment to price stability. Neumann argues that since the central bank should not be required to make political decisions, and since an independent central bank should be committed only to achieving price stability, it is in fact taking only technical decisions and therefore need not defend its policies in parliament. This leads him to conclude with respect to the ESCB that '. . . the Maastricht provision according to which monetary policy has to be defended in the European Parliament has no justification'[16]. Neumann (1992, p. 25) also argues that since the Deutsche Bundesbank is not held politically accountable, its board members are more personally independent than ECB directors will be, and it is probably less prone to influence from the government on the exchange rate than the ECB would be, '. . . the Bundesbank is more independent than the ECB will become'[17].

3.3. Evaluation

If we try to narrow down the differences, it seems to us that these have to do with the way in which accountability is constructed. Formal political account-ability is complicated by the difficulty of developing good accountability arrangements, because as Governor Crow of the Bank of Canada notes: '. . . there is a 'tension' between the mechanisms needed to ensure the accountability of the central bank to government or parliament, and the ability of the central bank to carry out its responsibility as an institution apart from government'[18]. In practice, however, such highly independent central banks as those of Germany and Switzerland, while not subject to political accountability, make a considerable effort in explaining their policies to the public. They have also since long announced monetary targets, thus allowing close monitoring of their monetary policy performance by the public. This has contributed to the high credibility enjoyed by these institutions.

We conclude that accountability in the general sense of explaining and making visible a central bank's policies need not undermine CBA, and may actually enhance it by way of strengthening its credibility and the acceptance of its policies by the public. It may, however, be that political accountability, in the sense of reporting to and defending policies in parliament, could detract somewhat from CBA. This makes it all the more important for central banks, including the future ECB, to have able and committed directors. The selection of these individuals therefore needs to be based exclusively on central banking competence and not on their political skills[19].

4. THE RELATIONSHIP BETWEEN MONETARY POLICY AND CENTRAL BANK AUTONOMY

4.1. Introduction

We will look at the relationship between monetary policy and CBA from two perspectives. In the first place, the rationale for granting autonomy to the central bank affects monetary policy design. Secondly, different monetary policies have different consequences for the degree to which the central bank can be de facto independent. In this context monetary policy is defined broadly. It concerns the choice of a policy objective, a policy strategy, policy instruments and operational procedures. Policy strategy has to do with answers to questions like: are intermediate targets used in policy formulation and if so, which one(s)?; is monetary policy used for cyclical purposes?, etc.

4.2. The final objective and policy strategy

The rationale for CBA is that governments are tempted to undervalue the goal of price stability in the short run, while in the longer run no other economic policy objective benefits from this neglect. Giving governments too much responsibility for monetary policy would in the end only lead to higher inflation without higher employment. The consequence of this rationale for CBA is that price stability should be the sole objective of monetary policy. Other policy objectives can only be supported to the extent that they do not interfere with pursuing price stability. This objective should be stated in the bank law.

To strengthen CBA it is important that monetary policy is not over-ambitious and overburdened. The monetary policy framework should reflect that monetary policy cannot achieve price stability at short notice, but only in the longer run. Monetary policy should have a medium term orientation. It should also be stressed that price stability can only be achieved at reasonable costs if other policies, mainly fiscal policy, support monetary policy and if wage formation processes are in line with achieving price stability. Central banks should make this clear and express their views on budgetary policy and wage developments from the perspective of their impact on the goal of price stability.

There should be great restraint in actively using monetary policy to dampen the cycle in real economic activity. This does not only follow from the fact that monetary policy should be directed at price stability in a medium-term perspective, but also from the old insight that monetary policy works with long and variable lags[20]. Too much scope for countercyclical policy would make the central bank vulnerable to political pressure and would create expectations that cannot be met. Below we will argue that monetary policy can sometimes act as an automatic stabilizer. We do not favour an active role for monetary policy in cyclical policy.

In order to legitimize and maintain CBA, monetary policy should be conducted in a clear framework that is periodically explained to the public. The use of intermediate targets and/or indicators may be very helpful in this respect. They allow for a clear presentation of monetary policy intentions to the public and they also allow for an assessment by the public of the results of monetary policy. The question of which intermediate target(s) to choose cannot solely, or even primarily, be based on arguments with respect to CBA. Although in the following discussion we will focus on the relation between CBA and inter-mediate targets, also some other considerations not directly related to CBA, but essential for the choice of intermediate targets will be presented.

The presentation and explanation of monetary policy is clearest if only one intermediate target is used. This argues against a so-called eclectic approach in monetary policy in which as many indicators as possible are monitored and given variable weight according to prevailing circumstances. The advantage of the latter policy is that all available information is used. It is the more important, the less reliable intermediate target variables are available. This is to a large extent an empirical issue. Different conclusions may be reached for different countries and at different times. However, our strategy would be to attempt to find one appropriate intermediate target variable and consider an eclectic approach as a far less attractive alternative.

In choosing an intermediate target at least four criteria are important, also from the perspective of CBA. The target variable should as much as possible be controllable by the central bank. It should as little as possible be influenced by other factors. Variables with a bearing on other policy objectives have a special importance in this respect. The more important the target variable is from the perspective of other policies as well, the more the central bank is liable to political pressure. The target variable should have a sufficiently strong relation to the final objective of monetary policy, i.e. price stability. Finally, it should be clear how to arrive at a value for the target variable.

In our view, acceptance of these criteria leads to a ranking of potential intermediate targets which can be used in the search for the appropriate target variable. First in the ranking are quantitative monetary targets. They can be influenced (relatively) well by monetary policy instruments, are (relatively) immune to political pressure, while a value or interval for the target variable can be arrived at in a clear manner (about which more below). Under the influence of financial innovation, deregulation and increased capital mobility the stability of money demand and the controllability of the money stock have decreased in many countries. However, it is too early to conclude that monetary targeting should be placed at a lower place in our ranking, not only because of its relatively good score on the other criteria. There are countries and regions with a stable money demand. Germany is the most important example[21]. There are also some indications that the demand for money at a European level might be stable[22]. The case for stability can be increased by using a broad money concept that is defined in as general terms as possible (i.e. not by listing the specific assets that are included, but by stating that all assets with certain characteristics for instance with respect to maturity are incorporated)[23]. Many financial innovations are automatically included in money if this approach is taken and 'Goodhart's law' can be circumvented at least to a certain extent. It is also not clear how permanent the process of financial innovation will be[24]. The required stability of money demand is not a short run stability, but stability in a medium term context as monetary policy has a medium term orientation. The chances of longer term stability of money demand are higher than those of short run stability. Nevertheless, in some instances the longer run may be 'too long' for practical policy purposes.

The required stability is not an absolute one, but should be sufficient for policy purposes. The target for the development of money should be stated in terms of an interval or so-called target zone. Not only does this allow for some estimation errors, it also allows for a certain degree of automatic stabilization of the business cycle provided actual inflation is not too far removed from price stability.

Monetary targeting should not be a dogmatic affair. Rather, it should try to find a balance between the use of rules and discretion in the conduct of monetary policy. This will not always be easy, nor successful, but there are indications that the most successful central banks follow such an approach[25]. The element of rule following behaviour should be sought in clear procedures for arriving at the target zone, for instance by deriving it from the sum of the trend growth in productive capacity and trend changes in the velocity of income. The element of discretion has to be found in the way monetary policy is executed during the year. The development of money growth should be monitored continuously in the context of general economic developments. These overall developments can be assessed on the basis of a number of indicators. The central bank does not only look at money, but at other indicators as well. The latter are mainly used to arrive at a judgement of the monetary development. In some circumstances there may be good reasons to allow money growth temporarily to overshoot its target. The central bank should then not dogmatically try to push money growth back into the target zone, but should tolerate an overshooting. By making clear that it cannot always meet its target it can prevent unduly high expectations of its performance. However, in cases it cannot achieve its target the central bank has to come up with good arguments explaining why it was not able to meet its target. Otherwise, it would run the risk of losing its credibility, reputation and in the end its autonomy. Although this strategy heavily relies on monetary targets, it cannot be termed monetarist in a strict sence[26].

This is not to say that lack of stability of money demand can never hinder monetary policy. Our conclusion is rather that monetary targeting is the alternative that should be tried first and not be abandoned too soon. This conclusion especially applies to large countries. For smaller countries pegging its currency to that of a large country may offer an alternative even superior to targeting its own money growth. For this strategy to be advisable a number of conditions have to be met. Firstly, the peg should apply to a large country which pursues a credible anti-inflation policy and which has a good inflation record. Secondly, the pegging country should economically be highly integrated with this large country. The country should be prepared to give up its monetary policy autonomy. To prevent that pegging the exchange rate carries unacceptably high costs for the real economy, which would ultimately undermine this policy and thus CBA, it is necessary that wages are sufficiently flexible.

It is clear, however, that economic integration will never be perfect, nor does it need to be. This is demonstrated by the experience of the successful peg of the Dutch guilder to the German mark. Although both economies show a high degree of integration, the structure of both economies also displays non-negligible differences. The Dutch service sector for example is relatively large as compared to that in Germany, which is more specialized in industrial products with much emphasis on capital goods which are almost absent in the Netherlands' production package. Despite wage moderation in a number of years real wages in the Netherlands are not nearly as flexible as those in the US, although the degree of flexibility seems to be comparable to that in Germany which may be more important in this respect[27]. The guilder has already been tightly pegged to the D-mark for more than ten years and this peg was not put at risk by German unification. This policy has resulted in the same average inflation rate as in Germany and a marked reduction in the Dutch inflation rate[28]. It is important that the pegging country is prepared to accept that sometimes an exchange rate policy implies an interest rate level that is not optimal from its own domestic perspective. This should be seen as potential short run costs that are outweighed by the long(er) term benefits of this policy. This view should be held broadly, not only by the central bank but also by the government, politicians and the public at large.

The exchange rate is an attractive intermediate target. It can be monitored very precisely and almost continuously. Compared to money, it is much less subject to the potential distorting influence of financial innovation and of high capital mobility. Technically an exchange rate target can be observed easily. It requires the central bank to steer short-term interest rates to the appropriate level. Experience shows that technically the central bank is capable to do so. Apart from the above conditions one additional condition has to be met to make a pegging policy viable and sustainable: the central bank should be independent. If not, the perception may arise that when experiencing outside pressure the central bank will not be prepared to raise interest rates sufficiently high or for a sufficiently long period, especially if in prevailing circumstances domestic considerations would call for a lower interest rate.

Other intermediate targets are less attractive than monetary targeting or pegging the exchange rate. The next best alternative may be to target nominal income in a medium-term framework. Compared to monetary targeting drawbacks are that nominal income can less directly be influenced by monetary policy instruments and, more importantly, that targeting it may make the central bank more vulnerable to political pressure. The relation between the development of for instance income and employment is more visible than between money and employment. The risk of overshooting (and undershooting) the final objective of policy appears to be greater than with monetary targeting, because the impact of monetary instruments on nominal income is on average likely to involve a longer lag than their impact on money. A practical statistical problem is that data on income are available with a rather long lag. In our view targeting the inflation rate itself, as Canada and New Zealand have recently chosen to do, comes close to targeting nominal income. We rank it below nominal income as target variable, because inflation is the variable at the very end of the transmission chain. The risks of over- and undershooting the target appear to be considerable in this case. Nevertheless, we still prefer an inflation targeting strategy (completed with the monitoring of other indicators to assess whether the targeted path is observed) to a fully eclectic approach. This is not clear for other conceivable intermediate target variables. We would for instance be very hesitant to use the (long-term real) interest rate as an intermediate target, with a view to protecting the autonomy of the central bank in particular. The interest rate seems highly sensitive to political pressure. Moreover, the real rate of interest is not a directly observable variable. It can be calculated in a large number of ways with sometimes very different outcomes and implying very different developments. It is also not easy to determine at what level to target the real interest rate. The IS-curve is liable to shifts, among other things because of changes in the stance of fiscal policy. Finally, the long-term interest rate can be influenced by monetary policy, but there is not a straightforward and constant relation between monetary policy actions and changes in the long-term rate. Long-term rates are dependent on expectations (also about future policy moves) which as a result of policy actions may change in a way rather hard to predict.

4.3. Instruments and operational procedures

CBA appears to have some, but not many implications for the choice of monetary policy instruments and operating procedures. As to the choice of an operational target: almost all central banks in the industrialized world operate in a market environment. This calls for a (relatively) market oriented conduct of monetary policy. The choice is between the monetary base and a short-term interest rate. Given the usual interest inelasticity of the demand for base money, a fixed target for the monetary base would lead to undesirable fluctuations in short-term interest rates. Most central banks mainly look at short-term interest rates to assess the immediate impact of their actions. It is not necessary to adopt precise short-term target levels for short-term interest rates, nor is it always wise or even possible to do so. A consideration of strenghtening CBA may also be invoked here. A central bank comes under pressure sooner to change its interest rates the more it is viewed responsible for the level of short-term interest rates. Announcing target levels or zones for short-term interest rates may create or enhance that impression.

Avoiding being too visible in the money markets can also be realized by somewhat limiting the amount of open market operations. Relatively infrequent open market transactions by the central bank may be more conducive to CBA than a continuous presence in the market. This tactic of 'relative invisibility' can be completed with having available instruments that allow for some influence of market parties on the resulting interest rate. This approach of not always being too visible should not be overemphasized. Ultimately to achieve its intermediate target the central bank has to give a direction to the development of short-term interest rates. However, the normally longer term horizon of the intermediate target does not entail a very precise day to day management of short-term interest rates[29]. Thus, the medium-term character of the monetary strategy can be stressed.

It is important for CBA that the central bank has great freedom in designing and using its instruments. Some legal provisions are necessary. These may have a rather general character, for instance by stating that the policy instruments are designed by the central bank. It does not undermine CBA if some non-market conform instruments are explicitly prohibited (for example credit ceilings). In the same vein, it may be useful to explicitly state that some instruments are allowed. This applies to non-interest bearing cash-reserve requirements, because they imply a tax on the banking system. From the point of view of legal certainty the maximum reserve percentages could be defined by law, but the central bank should be given discretion in applying this instrument.

It is not sufficient that there is a legal basis for CBA. CBA should also be supported in practice. This especially applies to the use of the instruments, in particular if they lead to high(er) short-term interest rates. The government may be less tempted to put pressure on the central bank if its debt and deficit are relatively small and as small as possible a share of them is financed with securities of a short maturity. In the same context it is clear that the central bank should not be forced to finance the government. Generally, the central bank should only be willing to provide the government with finance for seasonal or incidental fluctuations in its cash position in the context of a well defined agreement that includes upper limits to this facility. Under EMU all central bank financing of the government will in fact be prohibited.

5. MONETARY POLICY, EXCHANGE RATE POLICY AND CENTRAL BANK AUTONOMY

Exchange rate policy and monetary policy are interdependent. In most countries the government is responsible for the choice of the exchange rate regime and for changes in parities in an adjustable peg system. The central bank is usually reponsible for executing exchange rate policy, because the instruments that are used for this policy are the same as those of monetary policy. This already indicates that a conflict may arise between the necessities of monetary policy and the obligations that follow from exchange rate agreements. This may put CBA at risk. Therefore, in this section we briefly elaborate on the division of responsibilities between the government and the central bank in exchange rate policy.

In principle at least five different exchange rate regimes are possible:
a) flexible exchange rates;
b) fixed exchange rates and no independent monetary policy;
c) fixed exchange rates and independent monetary policy;
d) fixed, but adjustable exchange rates;
e) flexible rates managed to a certain degree.

From the point of view of CBA a and b are in principle without problems. In regime a the central bank uses its instruments solely for monetary policy and in b solely for exchange rate policy. It should be noted that regime a in its pure form almost never occurs in practice. Regime c logically cannot exist in a world of free capital mobility and perfect international asset substitutability. In today's world capital restrictions have been removed to a large extent. International financial markets have become more integrated over time and therefore asset substitutability has increased and is likely to be rather high. The imperfections that still exist seem insufficient to allow for an independent monetary policy over more than a brief period. Regime c is therefore not a sustainable option.

Problems for CBA may arise in d and e. Experience shows (Bretton Woods and EMS) that an adjustable peg system normally evolves into a system with an anchor country that conducts a relatively independent monetary policy and with the other countries mainly directing their policies towards fixing their exchange rate against the currency of the anchor country. The non-anchor countries find themselves almost in b. The agreed fluctuation margins for their exchange rates usually do not allow sufficient scope for a really independent monetary policy[30]. The CBA of the central bank of the anchor country may be challenged from time to time, most likely in two ways. First, from abroad if partner countries would like to have another stance of monetary policy in the anchor country. Second, if the central bank of the anchor country is obliged to intervene in the foreign exchange market to an extent that its domestic intermediate targets (e.g. money supply) can no longer be met. To prevent, or at least contain, these pressures the conditions for tying one's currency to another, mentioned in section 4.2, are of paramount importance. An additional condition that may be added here is that unsustainable parities should be adjusted timely and in an orderly way. From the point of view of the anchor country it could be argued that its central bank should have the option to suspend intervention if its domestic monetary policy objectives are jeopardized. Partner countries may find this unacceptable. It may increase the chances of speculative attacks on their currencies and may be perceived as giving them an unbalanced share of the adjustment efforts. In practice, however, there is certainly a limit to the amount of interventions a central bank of the anchor country would be willing to conduct. In view of the importance of CBA this is perfectly understandable. Under regime e for central banks in all countries the same kind of problems may arise from time to time as for the central bank of the anchor country in d.

Viewed exclusively from the perspective of CBA, a flexible exchange rate system at first sight seems most attractive. (For non-anchor countries an adjustable peg system seems also relatively free of problems). But of course, the choice of an exchange rate system is not primarily based on considerations of CBA. Moreover, on closer inspection in a flexible rate system there can be considerable pressure on the central bank to adjust its policies, especially in relatively open economies. For these economies a system of fixed but adjustable parities may be the best option available. Consider the European case. Flexible rates between the open economies of Western Europe could easily lead to pressure on central banks to run a looser monetary policy than in other countries to bring about a competitive depreciation. When all countries would act in the same manner, the end result would be inflationary policies, possibly the imposition of trade restrictions and political strains. All this would imply a reversal of economic integration. Therefore, for Europe a system of fixed, but adjustable exchange rates seems the best option until a monetary union is established, also from the perspective of strenghtening CBA. However, if countries are not too strongly integrated a managed flexible rate system is preferable.

In our view it is nearly impossible to completely safeguard CBA by adopting rules or legal provisions in the context of the relation between exchange rate policy and monetary policy. Transferring the responsibility for the establishment of exchange rate regimes or for changes in parities to central banks could be considered. An important argument against it is that these decisions involve more than trying to achieve price stability. They should therefore be made in the context of a more general policy formulation which has to be done by government. Of course, central banks should be consulted by governments before concluding exchange rate agreements or before changing parities. Their advice should be published. This gives central banks a way to express their views and to influence decision making. In practice, the extent to which CBA can be impaired by exchange rate considerations seems to depend on the autonomy the central banks has in other fields (i.e. its overall autonomy), the reputation it has been able to establish and the importance attached to the goal of price stability and CBA by the government and the general public. The greater the overall independence of the central bank, the greater its reputation and the more importance attached to price stability as a goal of economic policy the less the risks seem to be[31]. The central bank has to protect its autonomy in the context of the consequences of exchange rate policy mainly through its own behaviour. It inevitably remains a field where central banks have to be alert, despite the fact that tensions between monetary policy and exchange rate policy may only emerge infrequently. This can be illustrated by looking at the arrangements envisaged for EMU. The division of the responsibilities for exchange rate policy between the ESCB and the political authorities is not clearly defined. The political authorities may give orientations related to exchange rate policy to the ECB. It is not clear, however, to what extent this diminishes the ECB's autonomy, because the statute adds that these orientations should not detract from the pursuit of price stability by the ECB. Therefore, the ESCB has to ensure largely in practice that its autonomy is not eroded by exchange rate policy. It cannot be denied that at times this may be a difficult, but also challenging job, because the ECB will be an institution without an established reputation to start with. On the other hand, no major tensions need arise in the foreseeable future. The EMU can be expected to operate a system of flexible exchange rates against the other large economic entities, i.e. the United States and Japan, given the relatively closed character of its economy.

6. CONCLUSIONS

In this paper a number of policy issues related to central bank autonomy (CBA) are analyzed on the presumption that central banks should be autonomous. The main conclusions can be summarized as follows:

1. The distinction between macro and micro prudential control can be useful to clarify the issue of whether to combine monetary policy and prudential supervision. The arguments against such a combination do not apply to macro prudential control. Absolute judgements on the separation or combination of monetary policy and (micro) prudential supervision are not warranted. It appears possible to maintain CBA in both cases. Besides the structure of the banking system, the way a country conducts its monetary policy may be a relevant factor in making the choice between the two alternatives.

2. CBA requires a codified legal basis. CBA may have constitutional implications. Accountability in the general sense of explaining and making visible a central bank's policies need not undermine CBA, and may actually enhance it by way of strengthening its credibility and the acceptance of its policies by the public. It may, however, be that political accountability, in the sense of reporting to and defending policies in parliament, could detract somewhat from CBA. This calls for able and committed directors of central banks to be selected exclusively on the basis of central banking competence and not on their political skills.

3. Given the rationale for CBA, price stability should be the final objective of monetary policy. Other policy objectives can only be supported as far as they do not interfere with the pursuit of price stability.

4. Monetary policy should be conducted in a medium term framework. Active anti-cyclical monetary policy is not to be recommended. If actual inflation does not deviate too much from price stability, monetary policy can contribute to automatic stabilization of the cycle in real economic activity. CBA can be strengthened by using intermediate targets in monetary policy. From the perspective of CBA intermediate targets can be ranked, with monetary targets as the most and interest rate targets as the least attractive. For an open economy, pegging its currency to that of a large country may be

best alternative under a number of conditions.

5. Central banks should be granted a large degree of freedom in designing and using their instruments. CBA may be enhanced by the central bank being not 'too visible' in the money markets. This argues for not too frequent open market operations and the availability of instruments which leave some scope for market participants' influence on the development of short-term interest rates. Otherwise, CBA has no strong implications for instruments and operational procedures.

6. To minimize potential political pressure on the central bank, governments should run only modest deficits, in principle to be financed in the capital market. Central banks should not be forced to finance the government directly.

7. There are reasons for making the political authorities responsible for decisions on exchange rate regimes and parity changes within an adjustable peg system. Inevitably, this entails that sometimes conflicts between monetary policy and exchange rate policy may arise which may impair CBA. This is even the case in a (managed) flexible exchange rate regime, for an open economy in particular. These conflicts cannot be fully prevented or resolved by regulations. The central bank should protect its autonomy in this respect mainly by its practical actions, among others by making public its advice on exchange rate matters. This is easier the higher the overall independence of the central bank, the greater its reputation and the greater the support among politicians and the general public for the goal of price stability.

NOTES

1. See, for instance, Alesina and Summers (1993), Cukierman (1992) and De Haan and Sturm (1992). For a recent ranking of central bank independence in industrial countries, see Eijffinger and Schaling (1993).
2. De Kock (1939). In fact De Kock (p. 328) mentions a '. . . recent trend towards state ownership and/or control of central banks . . . to be attributed primarily to the trend of public opinion in favour of direct state control of monetary and banking policy . . . .'.
3. See Goodhart (1988).
4. See, for instance, De Beaufort Wijnholds (1992).
5. See Baltensperger (1993) and Vives (1993).
6. See Tietmeyer (1991), p. 185. For the case for combining monetary policy and prudential supervision within the central bank, see Muller (1981).
7. See Goodhart and Schoenmaker (GS;1993), p. 8. They give some possible examples of this, such as the effect on US monetary policy of the savings and loan crisis.
8. GS, p. 4. This argument, however, extends only to the initial payer. Since central banks are nowadays all fully or partially government owned and transfer the bulk of their profits to the government, the ultimate payer tends to be the government, even if the central bank were to foot the bill initially.

9. Or rather kept together under one roof, as historically central banks tended to exercise both functions, albeit initially in a rudimentary fashion. Separate government agencies responsible for prudential supervision tended to be established much later than most central banks.

10. G and S (p. 10) cite the example of a Danish bank which a number of years ago received liquidity support from the central bank, but was subsequently closed by the supervisory agency without apparently having consulted with the central bank.

11. Whether the rescue of basically solvent banks experiencing acute liquidity problems is desirable, is from time to time challenged, mainly in academic circles. It has to be admitted that the distinction between liquidity and solvency problems is often difficult to make in practice (See Baltensperger (1993)). There is no straightforward solution for solving the moral hazard problem involved.

12. See De Beaufort Wijnholds (1992), pp. 13–14.

13. See for this argument former Nederlandsche Bank Governor Zijlstra (1992) p. 252, and *The Economist* (1991), pp. 19–20.

14. See Swinburne and Castello-Branco (1991), p. 27.

15. See Brash (1993).

16. Neumann (1992), p. 24. See also Neumann (1991).

17. For a different view, see Burdekin, Wihlborg and Willett (1992), who suggest that '. . . the institutional design of the new ESCB . . . scores high marks for likely effective independence' (p. 233).

18. Crow (1993), p. 8.

19. According to Article 11 of the statute of the ECB, directors will be chosen on the basis of a recognized reputation and professional expertise in the area of money and banking.

20. See Friedman (1959), pp. 87–88.

21. See BIS (1993), p. 141 and Deutsche Bundesbank (1993), pp. 19–20.

22. See for instance Kremers and Lane (1990). For a review and assessment of the literature on European money demand, see Van Riet (1992, 1993).

23. See also Duisenberg (1993) for the same view.

24. See De Beaufort Wijnholds (1991), p. 287.

25. See Bernanke and Mishkin (1992).

26. In the context of Dutch monetary policy the former governor of the Nederlandsche Bank, Zijlstra, has called an approach very akin to the one described: '*moderate* monetarism'.

27. See OECD (1989), p. 49.

28. See Berk and Winder (1994), who demonstrate this.

29. This is however necessary if the exchange rate is rather closely tied to that of another currency.

30. This may be different for the present ERM with fluctuation margins of 15%. One might argue, however, that this system has more characteristics of e than d as long as the exchange rates remain far removed from their intervention limits.

31. Politicians may foster CBA by not always being too directly involved in making decisions about exchange rate matters, even if they are formally responsible.

REFERENCES

Alesina, A. and L. Summers (1993), "Central Bank Independence and Macroeconomic Performance: Some Comparative Evidence", *Journal of Money, Credit and Banking*, vol. 25, no. 2, 151–162.

Baltensperger (1993), "Monetary Policy and the Lender of Last Resort Function", *Paper Presented at the Conference on Prudential Regulation, Supervision and Monetary Policy*, Bocconi University, Milan.

94

Beaufort Wijnholds, J.A.H. de (1991), "National and International Monetary Policy", in Frenkel, J.A. and M. Goldstein (eds.), *International Financial Policy: Essays in Honour of Jacques J. Polak*, International Monetary Fund, Washington D.C., 282–305.

Beaufort Wijnholds, J.A.H. de (1992), *Of Captains, Pilots and Judges. The World-wide Tendency Towards Central Bank Autonomy*, Inaugural lecture on the occasion of the assumption of the office of Professor of Money and Banking in the University of Groningen.

Berk, J.M. and C.C.A. Winder (1994), "Price Movements in the Netherlands and Germany and the guilder-Dmark Peg", *De Economist*, forthcoming.

Bernanke, B. and F. Mishkin (1992), "Central Bank Behaviour and The Strategy of Monetary Policy: Observations from Six Industrialized Countries", National Bureau of Economic Research, *Working Paper*, no 4082.

BIS (1993), *63rd Annual Report*, Basle.

Brash, D. (1993), *Speech given to the European Policy Forum*, London, (June).

Burdekin, R.C.K., C. Wihlborg and C.D. Willet (1992), "A Monetary Constitution Case for an Independent European Central Bank", *The World Economy*, vol. 15, no. 2, 231– 249.

Crow, J.W. (1993), "Monetary Policy, and the Responsibilities and Accountability of Central Banks", *Gerhard de Kock Memorial Lecture at the University of Pretoria, South Africa*, 10, (February).

Cukierman, A. (1992), *Central Bank Strategy, Credibility and Independence: Theory and Evidence*, MIT Press, Cambridge, Mass.

Deutsche Bundesbank (1993), "Ueberprüfung des Geldmengenziels 1993 und Senkung der Notenbankzinsen", *Monatsbericht*, vol. 45, no. 7, 19–26.

Duisenberg, W.F. (1993), "Monetary Policy in a Changing Financial Environment", De Nederlandsche Bank, *Quarterly Bulletin*, no. 1993/1, 9–14.

The Economist (1991), "As Independent as Judges", April 20, 19–20.

Eijffinger, S. and E. Schaling (1993), "Central Bank Independence in Twelve Industrial Countries", Banca Nazionale del Lavoro, *Quarterly Review*, no. 184, 49–89.

Friedman, M. (1959), *A Program for Monetary Stability*, Fordham University Press, New York.

Goodhart, C. (1988), *The Evolution of Central Banks*, MIT Press, Cambridge, Mass.

Goodhart, C. and D. Schoenmaker (1993), "Institutional Separation between Supervisory and Monetary Agencies", *Paper presented at the Conference on Prudential Regulation, Supervision and Monetary Policy*, Bocconi University, Milan.

Haan, J. de and J.E. Sturm (1992), "The Case for Central Bank Independence", Banca Nazionale del Lavoro, *Quarterly Review*, no. 182, 305–327.

Heller, H.R. (1991), "Prudential Supervision and Monetary Policy", in Frenkel, J.A. and M. Goldstein (eds.), *International Financial Policy: Essays in Honour of Jacques J. Polak*, International Monetary Fund, Washington D.C.

Kock, M.H. de (1939), *Central Banking*, King & Son, London.

Kremers, J.J.M. and T.D. Lane (1990), "Economic and Monetary Integration and the Aggregate Demand for Money in the EMS", *IMF Staff Papers*, vol. 37, no 4, 777–805.

Muller, H.J. (1981), "Macro- en microtoezicht in één huis?", in Den Dunnen, E., M.M.G. Fase and A. Szász (eds), *Zoeklicht op Beleid*, Leiden, 173–188.

Neumann, M.J.M. (1991), "Central Bank Independence as a Prerequisite of Price Stability", *European Economy*, Special Edition no. 1, 79–92.

Neumann, M.J.M. (1992), "Reflections on Europe's Monetary Constitution", *Central Banking*, vol. 3, no 3, 20–27.

OECD (1989), *Economies in Transition: Structural Adjustment in OECD Countries*, Paris.

Riet, A.G. van (1992), "European Integration and the Demand for Money in the EC", De Nederlandsche Bank, *Quarterly Bulletin*, no. 1992/3, 33–43.

Riet, A.G. van (1993), "Studies of EC Money Demand: Survey and Assessment", De Nederlandsche Bank, *Quarterly Bulletin*, no. 1992/4, 63–75.

Swinburne, M. and M. Castello-Branco (1991), "Central Bank Independence: Issues and Experience", International Monetary Fund, *Working Paper*, no. 58, Washington D.C.

Tietmeyer, H. (1991), "The Role of an Independent Central Bank in Europe", in Downes, P. and R. Vaez-Zadeh (eds.), *The Evolving Role of Central Banks*, International Monetary Fund, Washington D.C., 176–189.

Vives, X. (1993), "The Supervisory Function of the ESCB", *Paper Presented at the Conference on Prudential Regulation, Supervision and Monetary Policy*, Bocconi University, Milan.

Zijlstra, J. (1992), *Per Slot van Rekening*, Uitgeverij Contact, Amsterdam/Antwerpen.

Comment on Alex Cukierman:
Commitment through Delegation, Political Influence and Central Bank Independence

EDUARD J. BOMHOFF

Erasmus University Rotterdam

Alex Cukierman's paper is a welcome contribution to the new field of "constitutional economics". Cukierman analyses how much independence will be granted to a central bank, assuming that the degree of independence is chosen rationally by the politicians. The theoretical model in the paper shows how the answer depends on the politicians' assessment of what the central bank can do to mitigate business cycles, as well as on complicated dynamic calculations regarding the management of the national debt. On the one hand, an independent central bank makes it easier for the current government to sell national debt since the markets will impose a smaller risk premium as compensation for the risk that a politically-dominated central bank may inflate away the debt in the future. Conversely, if the government is hopeful of winning future elections and wishes to retain the option to eventually inflate its national debt, it may prefer a more compliant central bank to cooperate with an inflationary reduction of the real burden of the national debt.

We can now think about monetary stability on three different levels. Traditional neo-classical macroeconomics continues to be relevant for questions such as: "do high budget deficits lead to higher future inflation?"; "What exactly are the macroeconomic costs of high and unstable inflation?"; "Is it worth the temporary costs in terms of reduced output growth to force inflation in the range of 4–5% down further to 0–2%?" Macroeconomic answers to such questions can assume a transparent political process with a single national policy maker. The private sector incorporates the government sector in its own intertemporal optimizing model.

On a higher level, we can ask questions that belong to "political economy": "does a politically dependent central bank lead to higher inflation on average?" In modern political economy we use game theory to analyse outcomes that depend on (1) rational politicians; (2) an independent (or not so independent) central bank and (3) a representative economic agent in the private sector. The analysis can be performed for different political regimes such as fixed exchange rates, a currency board or any other type of institutional framework in which the central bank operates.

Cukierman explores the next higher level, that of constitutional economics.

J.A.H. de Beaufort Wijnholds, S.C.W. Eijffinger and L.H. Hoogduin (eds.), A Framework for Monetary Stability, pp. 97–102.

He attempts to determine the degree of independence of the central bank as a function of "deeper" institutional parameters, such as the degree of stability in the political process, the type of electoral law, and the desire of the politicians to have the national debt managed according to their interests. Economics, defined as the science of rational, optimizing behaviour under given constraints, is now extending its territorial ambitions even further into the area traditionally occupied by political science. Economic analysis will even deliver insights that are pertinent to the field of constitutional law if it can show correlations between the electoral system and the type of monetary policy preferred by the elected politicians.

There is one further rung on this ladder (not attempted by Alex Cukierman in this paper), namely a systematic attempt to apply economic analysis to historical questions. It is not a big step from constitutional economics: "which type of political process delivers the greatest amount of monetary stability?" to historical questions such as: "do extreme inflationary episodes lead on average to changes in the political system?" The great advantage of economics in having a clear methodology that lends itself well to formal mathematical and statistical analysis will than show up in its ability to not only test hypotheses in political science but even in the historical field.

In a political economy exercise, the interaction between the politicians, the central bank and the public is analyzed for each single period, for given political institutions. For instance, both the public and the politicians may realize that over the long term attempts to produce positive monetary surprises will not lead to higher employment, because the surprises cannot all be positive. But, even with full agreement about the way the economy works and the eventual futility of positive monetary stimulus, nevertheless the temptation to do so within the current period remains and the private sector may rightly suspect the central bank of giving in to political pressure to achieve a more favourable outcome within the current period (before the next elections!) if most of the benefits of positive monetary stimulus are felt immediately, whereas the costs in the form of higher inflation and a higher inflationary premium in long-term interest rates will become visible later. Cukierman's model in this paper incorporates all of these elements but he pushes the analysis further within the realm of constitutional economics by considering the self-interest of two political parties that alternate in power. Each party has to consider the optimal degree of independence for the central bank, not only in view of the central bank's potential contributions to stabilizing the business cycle or even producing an artificial boom just before the elections, but also from the point of view of the management of the national debt. According to Cukierman's model each political party would of course prefer to fund the current budget deficit at the lowest possible cost which requires a low inflationary premium in long-term interest rates, suggesting an independent central bank. Also, the political parties would not like to provide their political opponents with an option to choose an explosive path for the national debt whenever they return to power and subsequently inflate the debt away, but at the same time they prefer not to completely close the option of inflating away the national debt which might result from its own expansionary policies.

It is already clear from this description of the model in equation (1) in the paper, that some results with respect to the optimal degree of independence for the central bank from the point of view of the politicians will be ambiguous. Cukierman writes "if not re-elected, the encumbent party does not value the ability to inflate the debt away as much as it values this ability when it is re-elected". Since the probability of winning the next election is random in the model and does not depend on manipulation of the political business cycle or the chosen path for government expenditures, the model will be unable to deliver sharp results for the relationship between public debt management and political independence of the central bank. This indeed, proves to be the case (see propositions 3 and 4, both of which are conditional statements).

Cukierman is able to derive a number of interesting, positive results from his model, as follows:

1. The more desperate the current government is to fund a large deficit, the more they will value an independent central bank since this leads to a lower inflationary risk premium in long term interest rates (the central bank is not supposed to buy any part of the fresh national debt in the model).
2. Central bank independence is more helpful to the present government if the public has good reason to be suspicious about inappropriate monetary stimulus, again because an independent central bank delivers a smaller risk premium in interest rates.
3. Other things equal, the politicians will prefer an independent central bank more, the more they hate the political opponents, since the bank provides a more valuable constraint on these opponents' budgetary policies.

For the analysis Cukierman assumes that it is possible in principle for the politicians to override the central bank and impose their own preferred monetary policy, but that the cost of this goes up with the degree of independence bestowed on the central bank.

The formal model in the paper is limited to two political parties that alternate randomly in office, but in the final section Cukierman offers some speculations about the correlations between the type of political system and central bank independence. Referring to chapter 23 in his book "Central bank strategy, credibility and independence", he states: "preliminary empirical evidence suggests that legal central bank independence is larger when party instability is larger and lower when regime instability is higher". The regression results on page 447 of the 1992 book show, however, that the explanatory power of Cukierman's proxy variables for political instability and regime instability is minimal. The t-value on a variable measuring "party political instability" equals

1.1. That proxy variable is designed to capture the frequency of political change on the left-right dimension. The t-value on the index for "regime political instability" equals 1.4; in Cukierman's book that variable counts the number of changes in the type of regime (from authoritarian to democratic or vice versa).

However weak statistically, it is certainly worthwhile to try to analyze the effect of different types of constitutions and electoral laws on legal central bank independence. Rather stronger evidence in the same area has been provided by one of the papers cited by Cukierman, namely Grilli, Masciandaro and Tabellini (1991). Their Figure 2 (p. 352) shows a very strong correlation between the quality of fiscal policy as measured both by net government debt in 1979 and by primary deficits as a percentage of GNP (period average for 1950–89) when a large number of OECD economies are classified in three categories. Group 1, the representational parliamentary democracies (Austria, Belgium, Denmark, Greece, Italy, The Netherlands and Spain) exhibit multi-party democracy over most of or all of this period and have by far the largest primary deficits and the biggest national debt. Group 2 in the analysis of Grilli et al. covers the majoritarian parliamentary democracies (Australia, Canada, Germany, Ireland, Japan, New Zealand, Switzerland and the U.K.), countries in which two political parties alternate in office because of a political first-past-the-post-system, countries in this group show much smaller primary deficits on average and a ratio of net debt to GNP that is hardly more than half the ratio in the representational parliamentary democracies. Finally, the presidential democracies, France after 1958 and the U.S., show even smaller ratios of government debt to GNP and more modest primary deficits.

This evidence is quite suggestive of the hypothesis that multi-party systems with frequent elections and no realistic potential for a single party to obtain a clear majority in parliament lead to more instable or less time-consistent fiscal policies and thus to a more rapid growth in the real value of outstanding government debt. Grilli et al. also test for possible correlations between the type of constitution and electoral law on the one hand and average inflation on the other hand and find weaker results, corresponding to the evidence in Cukierman's 1992 book: "some countries with unsustainable debt paths have managed to maintain low inflation" Grilli et al. , p. 364) and: "the conclusion is that for most OECD countries fiscal policy has not been a major determinant of monetary stability in the post war period. Rather the evidence suggests that the often observed combination of large seigniorage and high public debt may reflect some other fundamental determinant, possibly linked to monetary institutions" (pp. 364–65).

Historical evidence from an earlier period also suggests a correlation between the type of electoral system and inflationary outcomes. In "Golden Fetters", Barry Eichengreen notes a preponderance of multi-party democracies in the set of countries that experienced high inflation in the aftermath of the first World War. The same countries remembered these inflationary episodes when faced with the choice whether to try to maintain or to devalue off the Gold Standard during the great depression of the 1930s. According to Eichengreen, the multi-party democracies of the 1920s were so influenced by memories of that episode, that they hesitated longest before abandoning the gold standard in the mid-1930s.[1]

The evidence from two historical periods suggests that there are useful issues to explore in constitutional economics in the area of relationships between choice of electoral system and resulting financial policies. The paper's formal analysis touches one of these questions, but the potential to derive rigorous results is limited since Cukierman has to assume a two party system and does not allow any feedback from government policy towards election outcomes. The speculations at the end of the paper make one hopeful that perhaps his next, more political, model will tackle these fascinating issues more directly.

An important feature of Cukierman's work, both in the present paper and in his 1992 book is the emphasis on well-understood macroeconomic trade-offs, somewhat at the expense of allowing a principal role for economic uncertainty. In Cukierman's world, if the central bank delivers a sub-optimal outcome, it does so on purpose because there is no better time-optimal policy. The formal analysis concentrates far more on avoiding inconsistent policies over time than on coping with uncertainty. Looking back at the 1980s, however, one could argue that inflationary episodes in the U.K. and Sweden as well as the "bubble" economy in Japan had much more to do with honest policy mistakes under conditions of great uncertainty regarding the income velocity of money and confusing signals of different macroeconomic indicators, than with a purposeful choice for a point on the short-term Phillips curve that generated somewhat higher economic growth over the short-term but delivered higher inflation later. The models in this paper as well as in the 1992 book assume full agreement and knowledge about the income velocity of money as well as of all relevant macroeconomic parameters. Hence, the emphasis on issues of time inconsistency at the expense of decision making under uncertainty.

I also do not believe that the claim made in passing in the paper that models with so little uncertainty are capable of analyzing the costs and benefits of different intermediate targets of monetary policy, especially the choice between interest rate smoothing or monetary aggregate targeting. Such issues require a richer menu of uncertain shocks, both temporary and permanent that may affect the economy. Modelling the problems that faced monetary policy makers in the 1980s also requires, in my view, taking into account the difficulties in forecasting medium-term inflation, and an answer to the question whether movements in asset prices or in the exchange rate provide information that can help us to improve upon a purely monetary reduced form forecasting equation for future inflation. Many important disputes about monetary policy

in the 1980s were related to uncertainty about velocity, to the correct interpretation of movements in asset markets and their potential implications for
monetary policy (Japan!), to the dynamics of house prices and real estates
prices in general as well as to the consequences for velocity of financial deregulation. Problems of time-inconsistent policies are far from trivial, but do
not capture all the features which would be necessary for a full analysis of the
difficulties of monetary policy making. I would have preferred (in Cukierman's
next paper?) richer stochastics somewhat along the lines of his paper with Allan
H. Meltzer "A theory of ambiguity, credibility, and inflation under discretion
and asymmetric information"[2].

NOTES

1. See Barry Eichengreen (1992), *Golden Fetters, The Gold Standard and the Great Depression
   1919–1939*, Oxford University Press, Oxford.
2. *Econometrica,* 54, pp. 1099–1128.

Comment on Onno de Beaufort Wijnholds and Lex Hoogduin: Central Bank Autonomy: Policy Issues

MANFRED J. M. NEUMANN

University of Bonn

De Beaufort Wijnholds and Hoogduin are to be complimented for an insightful paper on selected policy aspects of central bank autonomy. They carefully remind us of the various pros and cons of each issue before they draw conclusions. Naturally, their opinions are influenced by the impressive policy record of De Nederlandsche Bank.

In my comments I will briefly touch on the issues of banking supervision, central bank accountability, and monetary targeting but deal more extensively with the question what the merits might be of completing the status of central bank independence by taking away from government the authority over exchange rate matters.

1. BANKING SUPERVISION AND MONETARY POLICY

Is it advisable to make central banks responsible for banking supervision? The literature is split on the issue and the authors settle on the middleground which is, monetary policy in larger countries, aiming at money stock control, might be endangered by supervisory considerations, while such conflict is less likely in smaller countries where monetary policy takes the form of exchange rate pegging.

In my view, neither country size nor the specifics of the policy concept matter. The main issue to be considered is systemic risk. Any financial sector crisis, i.e. a run on banks or a crash of the stock or the bond market, requires that the central bank stands ready to satisfy the resulting excess demand for base money at the inherited interest rate level. Nobody disputes that the central bank has to act as the lender of last resort.

Accepting responsibility for banking supervision, in contrast, makes the central bank vulnerable to potential demand for offering emergency credit assistance, to help out an individual bank which is claimed to be temporarily illiquid but solvent (Goodfriend, 1993). The problem with accepting the micro-responsibility of providing emergency credit is to be seen in the danger that due to moral hazard the central bank becomes the lender of first resort. This leads

J.A.H. de Beaufort Wijnholds, S.C.W. Eijffinger and L.H. Hoogduin (eds.), A Framework for Monetary Stability, pp. 103–107.
© 1994 *Kluwer Academic Publishers. Printed in the Netherlands.*

me to prefer that the functions of monetary policy making and banking super-vision are kept institutionally separate, though the central bank might usefully assist in monitoring banks.

2. ACCOUNTABILITY

Democracy does not imply that any public institution is to be directly controlled by parliament. As the discussion by the authors indicates, the control of central bankers rests on three pillars: a legal status which defines the rights and obliga-tions of central bankers, the appointment of governors by government, and regular reporting about policy targets and implementation. The Bundesbank, for example, provides extensive economic and statistical information in monthly and annual reports, distributed free of charge, and in numerous public speeches. This way, the Bank permits democracy by public discussion. Intro-ducing the additional requirement of having the central bank's president testify in parliament – as provided for in the Maastricht-treaty – does nothing to enrich the public's information set but is likely to give rise to an undesirable politicisa-tion of monetary policy[1].

The authors rightly point to the need that central bankers are selected on competence rather than partisanship. However, this is part of the more complex problem of securing, what I call, the Thomas-Becket effect (Neumann, 1991), i.e. inducing central bankers upon appointment to adopt safeguarding the value of the currency as their personal *leitmotif* and to cut all former political ties. Personal independence presupposes an incentive-compatible status. Terms of office and reappointment as well as salaries are clearly important ingredients[2].

3. MONETARY TARGETING

Annual announcement of an intermediate target has become an accepted procedure of monetary policy making. Public targeting provides important information and can be used to shield monetary policy against political pressure. Moreover, it permits central bankers to gain some influence on wage bargaining and fiscal policy making. As regards choosing a target variable, I completely agree with the authors' evaluation of the alternative solutions.

Even if we disregard the problem of potential political pressure, variables like the inflation rate or nominal income are goal variables. They cannot credibly serve as target variables, because they cannot be controlled over the shorter run. Saving (1967) already pointed out that a target variable "must be readily observable with little or no lag and rapidly affected by the policy instruments."[3] Therefore, it seems that the current Canadian experiment with an inflation target will remain an experiment. Short-term interest rates, in contrast, can be controlled daily by monetary policy. However, any interest rate targeting invites the Wicksellian nightmare of cumulative inflation or deflation if the interest rate target or rule is not anchored by a money stock target (McCallum, 1981). In a nutshell, proponents of interest rate targeting are misled if they believe that a conjectured breakdown of money demand functions provides a valid argument in favour of replacing money supply targeting by interest rate targeting. With information about money demand lacking, it is impossible to determine the interest rate level compatible with price stability.

I conclude that there is no superior alternative to money supply targeting. Smaller countries, like Austria or the Netherlands, might prefer exchange rate pegging to money supply targeting. Clearly, this implies to accept the cost of importing the larger country's inflation as well as ideosyncratic shocks.

4. EXCHANGE RATE POLICY

De Beaufort Wijnholds and Hoogduin discuss the implications for central bank independence of alternative exchange rate regimes and settle with the traditional solution: The sovereignty of choosing the exchange rate regime and – in the case of a fixed rate system – of negotiating parity adjustments should remain in the hands of government because "these decisions involve more than trying to achieve price stability". It seems that the authors need to spell out what they have in mind. Since they do not support the attempt at competitive depreciation, there must be some hidden long-run consideration, possibly non-economic, which suggests that picking an exchange rate target that is in conflict with the objective of price stability might nevertheless be in the interest of the country. This is a rationalization of the status-quo. If we accept it, it will be difficult to hold central banks responsible for achieving price stability.

In general, price stability and exchange rate stability are non-compatible objectives. They require ranking. If primacy is given to exchange rate targeting, the adjustment of the price level is to be accepted and vice versa. Therefore, the ranking decision must rest with one authority, either the government or the central bank. The traditional solution assigns the decision to government and subordinates the central bank. This is a clean solution. Unfortunately, it has an inflation bias. For this reason a growing number of economists endorses providing the central bank with independence from government. However, in my view this alternative solution is seriously incomplete if the central bank remains subordinated to government with respect to exchange rate policy.

The authors acknowledge that splitting the authority over monetary and exchange rate policy invites conflict. To solve the problem they propose that the central bank makes public its advice on exchange rate matters, a few days, say, after a realignment. This is a surprising proposal. It amounts to presenting the conflict to foreign exchange markets and letting speculation be the judge on which authority is right. While this may have happened in the past by accident, inviting unnecessary upheaval in foreign exchange markets is hardly a defendable procedure. Moreover, I can think of no government that will accept as a regular procedure undermining open-mouth-policy by the central bank.

In conclusion, it seems preferable that we economists advertize the clean solution of providing central banks with the undivided power over monetary and exchange rate policies. Granting independence to the national central banks and completing independence by transferring the sovereignty over exchange rate matters to them, is likely to make an important contribution to resolving the present unclear status-quo of the European Monetary System (EMS). The recent extreme widening of the exchange rate bands has created a potentially unstable situation. It is open to interpretation whether governments continue considering some discipline as regards exchange rates an indispensable means towards reaching European Monetary Union (EMU) or whether they are longing for the unrestricted freedom of a free float. Foreign exchange markets will put governments to test, should they try exploiting the scope of the wider margins in the future.

As complete central bank independence implies binding the hands of government with respect to inflation and the exchange rate as well, it provides a credible signal that the exchange rate constraint will be honoured in the design of domestic policies. Granting complete independence would even permit reinstalling the EMS as a stable system of fixed, but adjustable exchange rates with more narrow bands. Independent bankers will be in a position of stabilizing the system by gradually eliminating inflation differentials, by precluding rekindling inflation and by responding to larger changes in real exchange rates much earlier than governments are prepared to. This flexibility will raise the credibility of the system and eliminate the incentive for large-scale speculation against any particular currency.

NOTES

1. The president of a smaller European central bank when invited by members of parliament to see them in parliament responded by inviting them to see him in the bank.
2. In passing we note that the provisions of the Maastricht treaty are seriously deficient in this respect. The members of the board of the European Central Bank will receive a single eight-years term, implying that they will look early for another position. For the national governors a minimum term of no more than five years is specified, the typical solution we know from

government-dependent central banks. Compare this with the Bundesbank. The members of the Central Bank Council receive an eight-years term with automatic reappointment.
3. See also Brunner (1969). It is like shooting into the fog if you reduce base money growth today in order to effect a desired level of inflation two years from now.

REFERENCES

Brunner, Karl (1969), *Targets and Indicators of Monetary Policy*, San Francisco, Chandler Pub.

Goodfriend, Marvin (1993), Financial Theory and Central Bank Policies, in: Stephen F. Frowen, (ed.), *Monetary Theory and Monetary Policy: New Tracks for the 1990s*, London, Macmillan, 105–118.

McCallum, Bennett T. (1981), "Price Level Determinacy with an Interest Rate Rule and Rational Expectations", *Journal of Monetary Economics, 8*, 319–329.

Neumann, Manfred J.M. (1991), "Precommitment to Central Bank Independence", *Open Economies Review, 2*, 95–112.

Saving, Thomas R. (1967), "Monetary-policy Targets and Indicators", *Journal of Political Economy, 75*, 446–456.

SESSION III: THE DESIGN OF MONETARY POLICY

Intermediate Targets versus Information Variables as Operating Guides for Monetary Policy

BENJAMIN M. FRIEDMAN*

Harvard University

The notion of 'a framework for monetary stability' – the title of this conference – immediately implies the desirability of maintaining steady growth, or under some circumstances even a steady level, of money however defined. This presumption is consistent with the recent practice of a number of central banks, and with the rhetoric of many more. For more than two decades, target growth rates for one or another measure of money have often played a key role in the formulation and implementation of monetary policy. European central banks, including in particular the Bundesbank, have been especially prominent in this regard.

In the United States, the country on whose experience this paper focuses, the Federal Reserve System first began to incorporate explicit money growth targets in its policymaking process in 1970, and since 1975 the Federal Reserve has been required under law to set such targets and to report regularly to Congress on its success or failure in meeting them. Since then the practical importance of money growth targets in U.S. monetary policymaking has varied over time. As is well known, these targets were especially important during the period of disinflationary monetary policy in 1979–82.

Stable money growth per se, of course, is not what monetary policy is all about. Explicitly or implicitly, most central banks' basic charge is to maintain price stability and/or full employment, and in many countries also to preserve a satisfactory equilibrium in the economy's international relationships and hence in the exchange value of the nation's currency. The presumption that monetary stability is a desirable objective for monetary policy is, in the end, a presumption that stable money growth is the most reliable way to achieve these more fundamental objectives.

At least in the United States, that presumption has foundered. The relationships that once connected money growth to the growth of either income or prices have utterly collapsed in the face of financial innovation, deregulation, and perhaps other influences as well. On the currently available

* I am grateful to Ben Broadbent for research assistance, and to the G.E. Foundation and the Harvard Program for Financial Research for research support. Parts of the paper draw on my recent work, including Friedman (1990, 1993) and Friedman and Kuttner (1992).

J.A.H. de Beaufort Wijnholds, S.C.W. Eijffinger and L.H. Hoogduin (eds.), A Framework for Monetary Stability, pp. 109–133.

evidence, money growth no longer reliably predicts any aspect of overall economic activity that is of interest for purposes of monetary policy. It is now unclear, therefore, what role – if any – monetary stability or even money growth targets at all can usefully play in the making of U.S. monetary policy. Instead, the Federal Reserve in the most recent period has relied ever more heavily on its influence over short-term interest rates, including in particular the federal funds rate.

While this change in the conduct of U.S. monetary policy has been taking place piecemeal for some time in response to the unraveling of money-based relationships, what was new most recently was the Federal Reserve's stark public admission that, at least for the foreseeable future, the era of its reliance on money growth targets is over. Rather than couching the matter in the usual central bankers' language describing a gradual shift in emphasis between one set of guidelines and another, Chairman Alan Greenspan's semi-annual report to Congress in July 1993 stated baldly that M2, the one aggregate that had figured importantly in monetary policymaking in recent years, 'has been downgraded as a reliable indicator of financial conditions in the economy, and no single variable has been identified to take its place'. Mr. Greenspan's testimony also pinpointed frankly the reason for the change: 'The historical relationships between money and income, and between money and the price level have largely broken down'[1].

The object of this paper is to lay out the considerations that determine whether money growth targets – or, for that matter, any other kind of targets that represent intermediate steps between a central bank's operations and its ultimate macroeconomic objectives – provide a useful focus for monetary policymaking. The paper instead makes the case for an alternative class of policymaking procedures relying on money and/or other indicators as information variables. In contrast to an intermediate target procedure, under which an aberrant movement of the designated target variable automatically requires corrective action, under an information variable procedure such movements merely create the presumption that a development has occurred that merits attention and that may warrant action depending upon circumstances. Hence the central bank must make a judgment of whether to respond at all, and if so then how.

Because of the need for such judgments, the information variable procedure clearly imposes more of an ongoing burden on a central bank than does the automatic pilot steered by an intermediate target. But the intermediate target procedure imposes burdens of another kind, in that it will lead to systematically good performance (measured by the ultimate objectives of monetary policy) only under stringent conditions. At least in the United States, there is currently no evidence that those conditions are satisfied.

Indeed, the paper's main conclusion is that, at least for the case of the

United States, the conditions that would warrant the elevation of 'monetary stability' to a central role in monetary policymaking neither exist now nor are likely to exist in the near future. The paper therefore concludes with some concrete suggestions not only for how to go about implementing an information variable procedure but also for what kinds of information variables might be useful. Whether these conclusions carry over to the case of central banks outside the United States, including those in Europe that in the past have relied heavily on money growth targets, is a question that this paper does not address. But the conceptual determinants of that question are, analytically, parallel to the ones illustrated here for the U.S. case.

Section 1 begins with basics by clarifying the distinction between an intermediate target and an information variable for monetary policy. Section 2 illustrates the collapse of the past decade's efforts to use intermediate targets in the United States by focusing on the behavior of three specific money or credit aggregates. Section 3 digresses to explore a particular problem that can arise in this regard under some institutional circumstances, using as an illustration the recent situation of M2 in the United States. Section 4 concludes with a discussion of how to implement an information variable procedure for monetary policy.

1. BASICS: INTERMEDIATE TARGETS AND INFORMATION VARIABLES

It is traditional to represent the use of any given intermediate target variable for monetary policy as a two-stage procedure. In the first stage, the central bank determines the value of the intermediate target that would be consistent with the desired ultimate policy objectives under a variety of ex ante assumptions – for example, zero values for all relevant disturbances. At the second stage, the central bank proceeds, in some ex post fashion, to treat achieving the value of the intermediate target that it has set ex ante as if doing so were the objective governing policy. The distinction between the 'ex ante' assumptions employed in the first stage of this process and whatever makes the second stage 'ex post' is clearly crucial. That distinction is, of course, largely a matter of the availability of new information as time passes. The key role of the intermediate target variable is to provide the central bank with a ready rule for processing and acting on this new information.

The context in which an intermediate target can be useful, therefore, is a dynamic economy in which the relevant behavior exhibits leads and lags distributed through time. For example, if people demand money for transactions purposes, and tend on average to accumulate money in advance of actual spending, then in general the observed value of the money stock at any time conveys information about the future strength of aggregate demand. Similarly, when individuals' or businesses' ability to spend depends in part on their ability to borrow, and loan transactions tend to precede actual spending, the observed volume of credit conveys information about the future state of aggregate demand. In either case, such information is at least potentially useful whenever monetary policy actions affect economic behavior with a lag.

Similarly, a variable like the money stock can also provide such useful information, even in the absence of behavioral economic lags, if there are lags in the availability of relevant data. For example, in a context in which disturbances to economic behavior are serially correlated, observations of the recent values of key variables convey information that is potentially useful for anticipating future outcomes. If observations of financial variables like money (or credit, or interest rates, or exchange rates) are available on a more timely basis than observations of variables like income and prices – as is the case in most countries – the information given by those financial variables in general has a role to play in setting the optimal value of the policy instrument. Equivalently, if observations of financial variables are available continuously throughout the 'period' of analysis but observations of variables like income and prices are not, and the central bank can adjust the value of its policy instrument as time passes within the period, then again these available observations in general have a role to play in the policymaking process.

Even so, finding that some variable like money conveys potentially useful information is not the same as establishing that the central bank should specifically use that variable as an intermediate target. Much of the literature of the intermediate target problem has focused on analyzing just this distinction. In an early paper on this subject, I analyzed this aspect of the intermediate target problem in the context of a 'bare bones' model consisting of an aggregate spending function

$$y_t = -\alpha_1 r_t + u_t \tag{1}$$

a money demand function

$$m_t = \beta_1 y_t - \beta_2 r_t + v_t \tag{2}$$

and a money supply (reserves demand) function

$$m_t = \delta_1 h_t + \delta_2 r_t + q_t \tag{3}$$

where y is nominal income, r is 'the interest rate,' m is the money stock, h is the reserve base, all constant terms are suppressed, all coefficients are positive, and u, v and q are disturbances exhibiting serial correlation.

For zero expectations of all three disturbances, the policy that delivers the minimum variance of income in such a model is to set either $r = 0$ or $h = 0$ (where the zero merely stands for the deterministic base value when the constant terms are suppressed), depending upon the comparison of variances along lines that are standard from the work of Poole (1970). The potential role then for money, an endogenous variable in either case, is to provice information indicating a likely non-zero realization of some relevant disturbance, and therefore – if this information is in hand in time to react to it – warranting a different value of the policy instrument. In particular, if the disturbances are serially correlated, knowing the values of each of the model's three endogenous variables at time $t - 1$ facilitates using (1)–(3) to discover the values of $u_{t-1}, v_{t-1},$ and q_{t-1} and then calculating 'informed' expectations of the three disturbances for period t as $\rho_u u_{t-1}, \rho_v v_{t-1}$ and $\rho_q q_{t-1}$, where the ρ_i are the respective autocorrelations. Given this information, the optimal value of the policy instrument for period t, is then not $r_t = 0$ but

$$r_t = \frac{\rho_u}{\alpha_1} u_{t-1} \tag{4}$$

under the interest rate instrument, and not $h_t = 0$ but

$$h_t = -\frac{1}{\alpha_1 \delta_1} \left[(\beta_2 + \delta_2) \rho_u u_{t-1} - \alpha_1 \rho_v v_{t-1} + \alpha_1 \rho_q q_{t-1} \right] \tag{5}$$

under the reserves instrument.

By contrast, using money as an intermediate target variable amounts to setting r or h so as to achieve $E_{t-1}(m_t) = 0$. This policy is either

$$r_t = \frac{1}{\alpha_1 \beta_1 + \beta_2} \left[\frac{\beta_1^2 \rho_u \sigma_u^2 + \rho_v \sigma_v^2 + \beta_1(\rho_u + \rho_v)\sigma_{uv}}{\beta_1^2 \sigma_u^2 + \sigma_v^2 + 2\beta_1 \sigma_{uv}} \ m_{t-1} \right] \tag{6}$$

under the interest rate instrument, or

$$h_t = -\frac{(\alpha_1 \beta_1 + \beta_2 + \delta_2)}{\delta_1(\alpha_1 \beta_1 + \beta_2)} \cdot \frac{\omega_1}{\omega_2} \cdot m_{t-1} \tag{7}$$

where ω_1 and ω_2 are appropriately weighted combinations of all three variances σ_u^2, σ_v^2 and σ_q^2 and all three corresponding covariances, under the reserves instrument[2].

The standard criticism of this procedure, then, is that in general neither (6) nor (7) is the policy that actually minimizes the variance of income, given the available information contained in the observations m_{t-1} and either r_{t-1} or h_{t-1}. The policy that minimizes $E_{t-1}(y_t^2)$ is instead either

$$r_t = \frac{1}{\alpha_1} \left[\frac{\beta_1 \rho_u \sigma_u^2 + \rho_u \sigma_{uv}}{\beta_1^2 \sigma_u^2 + \sigma_v^2 + 2\beta_1 \sigma_{uv}} \right] \cdot m_{t-1} \tag{8}$$

or

$$h_t = -\frac{(\alpha_1 \beta_1 + \beta_2 + \delta_2)}{\alpha_2 \delta_1} \cdot \frac{\omega_3}{\omega_4} \cdot m_{t-1} \tag{9}$$

where ω_3 and ω_4 are analogous (though not identical) to ω_1 and ω_2. Comparison of (6) to (8), or of (7) to (9), shows that treating money as an intermediate target of monetary policy does not in general deliver the instrument value consistent with minimizing the variance of income, given the information contained in lagged values of the endogenous financial variables, but under special conditions the two may be identical. Here, for example, if money demand is both interest inelastic and nonstochastic – that is, if $\beta_2 = \sigma_v^2 = 0$ – then both (6) and (8) trivially reduce to $r_t = (\frac{\rho_u}{\alpha_1 \beta_1}) m_{t-1}$. It is hardly surprising, therefore, that the normative debate over the use of money as an intermediate target for monetary policy has been inseparable (as it is in this paper as well) from the empirical debate over the properties of money demand.

Although the 'bare bones' model of (1)–(3) is far too simplified to be of direct practical import (it incorporates neither an exchange rate nor a distinction between real income and prices, to cite the two most obvious simplifications), the analytical issues illustrated here carry over to more sophisticated representations of economic behavior[3]. Whether movements in money do or do not reliably correspond to subsequent movements in income, or prices, or whatever aspects of economic activity are ultimately of concern to the central bank, is inevitably crucial to whether money can usefully serve as an intermediate target variable for monetary policy.

Once it is clear that using some endogenous variable like money as an intermediate target of monetary policy is tantamount to a way of reacting to incoming information, and perhaps not the best way at that, the question immediately arises whether it is possible to process such information in a superior way. The basic idea at work in the 'information variable approach' is again dynamic, therefore, arising in just the context discussed above of either behavioral lags or data lags as the motivation for the intermediate target strategy. Observations of a variable like the money stock are potentially useful for anticipating future stochastic movements of variables like income and prices that enter the central bank's objective, or for estimating contemporaneous stochastic movements of these variables before the relevant direct data become available. In either case, feedback rules analogous to those illustrated in (8) and (9) constitute the optimal way of exploiting that information, given the assumed behavioral model and policy objective.

One important implication of the information variable approach is that issues of behavioral causation, which have often been important in discussions of intermediate targets, become secondary. Whether the money stock does or does not 'cause' movements of future income or prices is not the issue. All that matters is whether observed values of the money stock provide information that helps predict future movements of these variables. More straightforwardly statistical analyses are therefore apt, despite questions about whether such tests are capable of saying anything about economic causation.

Another implication of the conceptual shift from an intermediate target approach to an information variable context that is especially important as a practical matter is that there is no longer any compelling reason to limit the focus of the central bank's policy setting rule to only one such endogenous variable. In principle, of course, it is always possible to employ some appropriately weighted combination of two or more endogenous variables as an intermediate target. In practice, however, the intermediate targets actually considered by most central banks have typically been univariate, like money or nominal income. By contrast, under an information variable approach there is no reason to restrict monetary policy to respond only to one endogenous variable, unless there is evidence suggesting that observations of that one variable contain all (or nearly all) of the available information relevant to achieving the central bank's objectives.

Perhaps most importantly, however, the information variable approach differs from an intermediate target procedure by explicitly framing the matter in terms of what the observed movements of one variable, like money, do or do not say about the likely future movements of other variables, like income and prices. If there is reason to believe that an unexpected surge or shortfall of money growth foretells a disturbance that will affect future income or prices, the central bank can decide to act so as to offset it either in whole or in part. More money (or a faster growth rate) than expected might mean that monetary policy is having a more stimulative effect on economic activity than anticipated. Or it could mean that, while monetary policy is having the anticipated effect, some independent influence – fiscal expansion, for example, or developments abroad – is more stimulative than anticipated. Either way, the indicated response would be to tighten monetary policy, exploiting the relationship of money to the ultimate policy objectives to make mid-course corrections as needed, rather than simply wait until the ultimate effect on income or prices has itself become fully evident.

But movements in money are not always a sign of movements in income and prices to come. More money (or a faster growth rate) than expected might instead mean that bank customers are simply choosing to hold larger deposits in place of alternative forms of wealth, for reasons unrelated to their spending or production decisions – for example, if changing exchange rate expectations lead them to favor domestic currency over foreign. Or it could mean that banks have decided that a smaller cushion of excess reserves is appropriate to newly prevailing market conditions. Whenever a central bank uses money (or any other observable quantity or price, for that matter) as an information variable to help guide monetary policy, it must inevitably make judgments about just such matters in order to decide whether, and if so by how much, to react when the chosen information variable behaves unexpectedly, rather than always reacting to unexpected movements in money as if they necessarily convey information about nonfinancial activity that warrant a policy change.

2. THE COLLAPSE OF INTERMEDIATE TARGET RELATIONSHIPS IN THE UNITED STATES

Which of the two approaches to monetary policymaking outlined in section 1 is preferable: the automatic pilot of the intermediate target procedure, or the inevitably judgmental information variable procedure? The answer is necessarily empirical, no doubt differing from one country to another and, within any one country, from one time to another. In the United States, recent statements and actions by the Federal Reserve System clearly reflect the view that – at least in that one country, and at the current time – conditions that would warrant pursuing an intermediate target procedure for monetary policy simply do not exist. To see why, it is useful to review the experience of three different money or credit aggregates that, at various times, the Federal Reserve has sought to designate as intermediate targets.

Narrow money

Two decades or so ago, the center of attention among economists and others who advocated a greater role for monetary aggregates in the making of U.S. monetary policy was the narrow money stock (M1), consisting essentially of currency and demand deposits. The reasons were theoretical, practical and empirical. The theory of the demand for money for transactions purposes seemed well worked out, especially in comparison to the more open-ended issues involved in demand for money as a means of wealth holding. As a practical matter, it was straight forward that currency and demand deposits were the two main ways of effecting transactions in the United States. By contrast, endless debate and ambiguity surrounded any attempt to draw a line separating what was 'money' from what wasn't for portfolio purposes. Finally, although Friedman and Schwartz's (1963) historical work had used a broader aggregate also including savings deposits at commercial banks (but not thrifts), widely publicized studies by Andersen and Jordan (1968), Goldfeld (1973) and others seemed to point to M1 as the measure exhibiting greatest stability in relation to income during the post World War II period.

As a result, M1 usually assumed pride of place in the Federal Reserve System's on-again off-again attempts, beginning in 1970, to incorporate monetary aggregate targets (or constraints, or provisos) in its regular decision making process. When the Federal Reserve dramatically adopted new operating procedures in October 1979, much of what the change was all about was a heightened emphasis on achieving targeted rates of money growth. Again M1 was the main focus of attention.

At the same time, it was well understood that the then existing structure of reserve requirements, under which banks held reserves against not only demand deposits but also savings deposits, weakened the Federal Reserve's potential control over M1. The Federal Reserve in 1978 had proposed a new system of reserve requirements focused more narrowly on 'transactions' balances, and also introducing reserves against such balances on account at nonmember banks and even at nonbank intermediaries[4]. Congress legislated approximately this system as part of the Monetary Control Act of 1980.

Ironically, just as the Federal Reserve was placing M1 at the center of its monetary policymaking framework and Congress was revamping reserve requirements to make M1 more closely controllable, the relationship between M1 and nonfinancial economic activity had already begun to break down. Following a widely debated episode at the end of the 1973–75 recession, in which business recovered sharply despite M1 growth that normally would have been consistent with a much slower advance of nominal income (to the evident consternation of the Federal Reserve's critics), Goldfeld (1976) added to his earlier paper a postscript wondering where the 'missing money' was. By the time the Federal Reserve formally abandoned its new M1-oriented operating procedures in October 1982, Judd and Scadding (1982) were already in print with a survey article citing more than eighty papers on the apparent demise of the money demand function and the ongoing effort to resuscitate it.

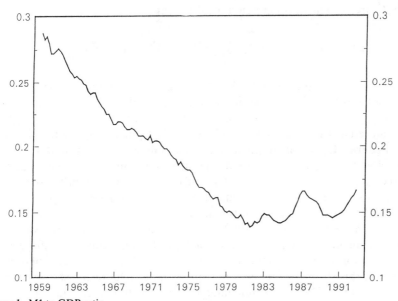

Figure 1. M1 to GDP ratio.

As Figure 1 shows, however, these events of the mid to late 1970s, troublesome as they were at the time, now appear as mere blips compared to what has happened since. The reason, presumably, is the revolution in ways of effecting transactions that began with the introduction of NOW accounts (at first in New England only) and money market mutual funds, assumed full force following the Depository Institutions Deregulation Act of 1980, and has since continued with the introduction of 'debit cards'.

Few people would have expected the demand for any transactions-centered monetary aggregate to remain unaffected by these developments (the Federal Reserve redefined M1, together with the other standard aggregates, in 1980), but many failed to anticipate the full extent of the collapse of M1's relationship to both income and prices. For example, well after the Federal Reserve had publicly abandoned its close adherence to money growth targets, Milton Friedman (1984) argued that the short-run relationship of M1 to nominal income remained as reliable as before but had merely accelerated the time lag involved, and moreover that the longer-run relationship of M1 to prices also remained predictive.

As the top row of Table 1 shows, however, there is no statistically significant relationship between M1 and nominal income in the post-1979 data. The table presents F-statistics for tests, across different time periods, of the null hypothesis that all of the coefficients on the lagged growth of M1 (that is, all of the β_i) are zero in autoregressions of the form

$$\Delta y_t = \alpha + \sum_{i=1}^{4} \beta_i \Delta m_{t-i} + \sum_{i=1}^{4} \gamma_i \Delta r_{t-i} + \sum_{i=1}^{4} \delta_i \Delta y_{t-i} + u_t \tag{10}$$

where y and m are, respectively, the logarithms of nominal gross domestic product and M1; r is the federal funds rate; u is a disturbance term; and α and the β_i, γ_i and δ_i are all coefficients to be estimated[5]. The first time period considered in Table 1 is 1960:2–1979:3, that is, from the earliest time for which the Federal Reserve provides data corresponding to its current definitions of the monetary aggregates until the point when it introduced new operating procedures for monetary policy. The end of the 1970s also marked the approximate onset, or the acceleration, of many of the changes in private-sector financial markets that have distinguished the more recent period. As the F-statistic makes clear, during 1960–79 M1 contained information about future nominal income movements that was statistically significant at the .01 level. By contrast, for the period since then (1979:4–1992:4) it simply has not done so. Further, this sharp difference is not simply an artifact of the shortness of the second sample. The same result emerges when the time period under consideration also includes the entirety of the 1970s (1970:1–1992:4).

The scope and import for monetary policy of changes like that documented in Table 1 should not be underestimated. For a central bank to use money even

Table 1. F-statistics for M1.

Dependent variable	1960:2-1979:3	1979:4-1992:4	1970:1-1992:4
Y	4.98***	.79	.56
X	.82	1.18	1.32
P	4.99***	1.06	.38

*** significant at the .01 level
** significant at the .05 level
* significant at the .10 level

as an information variable, much less as an intermediate target, it must know qualitatively that a relationship between money and nonfinancial economic activity exists *and* it must know at least something quantitatively about what that relationship is. If the F-statistic for 1979–92 (or even 1970–92) showed the existence of such a relationship, then the relevant questions for policy purposes would be whether it was the same as (or similar to) what had prevailed earlier on, and if not then whether (or how) the central bank can now have sufficient confidence in the relationship going forward to exploit it for policy purposes. But since there is no evidence of such a relationship in the first place, these questions do not arise. What could it mean to use an information variable that provides no information? Or to have an intermediate target that is not demonstrably intermediate?

It is always possible, of course, that M1 could bear a usefully informative relationship to the movement of either real income or prices separately, but that that relationship is obscured here by combining real income and prices into the single measure of nominal income. Traditionally, the most fundamental theory of 'money' in economics has emphasized the link to prices, leaving implications for real activity to more specific treatments embodying impediments to Walrasian equilibrium that may be realistic but rest on weaker foundations nonetheless. By contrast, much of the recent empirical literature of the subject has explicitly focused on whether fluctuations in money anticipate fluctuations in real output[6]. Either kind of relationship would potentially be useful for purposes of monetary policy, in that most central banks as a standard matter indicate their concern for both price inflation and real outcomes.

As the second and third rows of Table 1 show, however, such is not the case for M1. The second row presents F-statistics, analogous to those in the first row, for the β_1 coefficients in autoregressions of the form

$$\Delta x_t = \alpha + \sum_{i=1}^{4} \beta_i \Delta m_{t-i} + \sum_{i=1}^{4} \gamma_i \Delta r_{t-i} + \sum_{i=1}^{4} \delta_i \Delta x_{t-i} + \sum_{i=1}^{4} \phi_i \Delta p_{t-i} + u_t \quad (11)$$

where x and p are the logarithms of real gross domestic product and the corresponding price deflator, respectively, and all other variables are as in (10). The third row presents analogous F-statistics for a further set of autoregressions that are identical to (11) except that p replaces x as the dependent variable.

As is well known from the work of Sims (1980), M1 does not convey statistically significant information about subsequent movements of real income once the relationship allows for the effects of interest rates (here represented by the federal funds rate). That was true before 1980, and it has been true since. Before 1980 M1 did convey significant information about subsequent movements in prices, but it clearly no longer does so. Even the correlation between M1 growth and inflation, computed in the way Milton Friedman recommended to bring out the longer-run relationship (using two-year moving averages to smooth out transitory fluctuations, and a two-year lag to allow for sluggish price responses), dropped from .87 during 1959–78 to .10 during 1979–92.

Given these developments, the Federal Reserve in 1983 not only widened the M1 target range it reported to Congress but also stated explicitly that it was placing less emphasis on M1 than on broader aggregates. In 1986 the Federal Reserve widened the M1 target range to five percentage points. In 1987 the Federal Reserve gave up reporting any M1 target range at all.

Broad credit

In the late 1970s and early 1980s, I wrote a series of papers showing that the total outstanding debt of all nonfinancial U.S. obligors bore a relationship to nominal income that was comparable to that for any of the standard monetary aggregates[7]. At the most basic level, the motivation for this effort was the fact that in skeletal macroeconomic models like those of Tobin (1969) or Brunner and Meltzer (1972) there was no a priori presumption that one side of any sector's balance sheet be more intimately related than the other side to its nonfinancial activity. Liabilities could be just as relevant as assets. At a more substantive level, many of the disparate strands of what has since come to be called the 'credit view' of monetary policy at least had in common a focus on economic agents' ability to borrow.

Two aspects of this work were somewhat surprising, however, especially in the context of 'credit view' thinking. First, the debt aggregate that bore a statistically significant relationship to income – that is, the aggregate whose fluctuations tended to anticipate future movements of income – included both the debt of private-sector borrowers and government debt (unlike the private-sector-only measure, a form of which had for some time been an element of the standard index of leading indicators). Second, in contrast to the usual 'credit view' implication that there is something special about the debt of banks, or perhaps of banks together with other credit granting intermediaries, *total* credit consistently outperformed any bank-based measure in statistical tests of a relationship to income. While these specifics raised some puzzles to be explained, that did not take away from the fact that at least one measure of the economy's liabilities was as closely related to nonfinancial economic activity as any measure of its assets that could be labeled 'money'.

To recall from section 1, when a central bank uses an explicit intermediate target as the focus of monetary policy, there can be only one such target[8]. But when the central bank uses variables like money as information variables, there is no reason to limit the procedure to just one. Given the roughly equivalent performance of total credit with any of the standard M's in providing information about subsequent fluctuations of income, the conclusion I drew from these results was that if the Federal Reserve System were going to use a monetary aggregate to guide monetary policy it should *also* use total credit for this purpose. Not only were two sources of information likely to be better than one, but one monetary aggregate together with one credit aggregate also seemed preferable to using two different monetary aggregates in tandem (which some people at the time were suggesting). Using both a monetary aggregate and a credit aggregate would broaden the range of information thus brought to bear on the monetary policy process to encompass nonfinancial agents' liability-issuing behavior as well as their asset-holding behavior. In 1983 the Federal Reserve began to include in its reports to Congress a monitoring range for total credit (which it calls 'domestic nonfinancial debt'), and it has done so ever since.

As Table 2 shows, the collapse of the relationship between credit and nonfinancial economic activity has been just as dramatic as that for any measure of money. Figure 2 further illustrates the enormous break with prior debt-issuing patterns that began not long after the 1981–82 recession ended. Roughly one-third of the rise since then in total credit compared to income has reflected the federal government's by-now chronic fiscal imbalance. The dozen years since 1980 comprise the only sustained period since the establishment of the United States as an independent country in which the U.S. government's outstanding debt has risen faster than the national income. In 1980 the government's debt amounted to 26 cents for every dollar of U.S. gross domestic product. Today it is 53 cents.

The other two-thirds of the increase in total debt in relation to income reflects the borrowing of both businesses and households. While the government's rising debt is a matter of fiscal policy (at least in the first instance), the explosion of private-sector borrowing is very much the stuff of changing financial market structures and practices. The most dramatic changes in this regard have been in the business arena, where the wave of leveraged buy-outs, debt-financed acquisitions and stock repurchases that dominated corporate America during much of the 1980s clearly stands as an object of interest in its own right. So too does the development of the 'junk' bond market, which made

Table 2. F-statistics for credit.

Dependent variable	1960:2-1979:3	1979:4-1992:4	1970:1-1992:4
Y	4.70***	.71	.22
X	.55	.59	.78
P	4.32***	.55	.65

*** significant at the .01 level
** significant at the .05 level
* significant at the .10 level

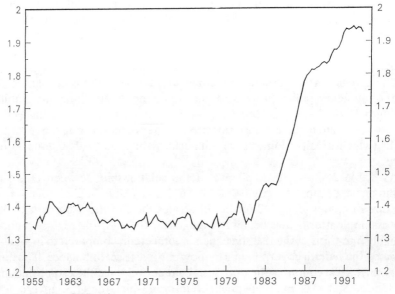

Figure 2. Credit to GDP ratio.

so many of these transactions possible. Between 1984 and 1989, U.S. nonfinancial corporations borrowed (net of repayments) over $1 trillion. Roughly $600 billion of that went into transactions that extinguished the equity either of the borrowing corporations themselves or of other companies they were acquiring.

Market structures and practices affecting household borrowing have changed as well. The most obvious and presumably the most important example here is the securitization of residential mortgages. The markets have also securitized other household sector liabilities, however, including automobile loans and credit card obligations. These changes have clearly increased households' *ability* to borrow. Examples of institutional change that plausibly increased households' *willingness* to borrow include the relaxation of bankruptcy requirements in various states.

In light of these pervasive changes affecting government, business and households, the collapse of the credit-to-income relationship documented in Table 2 and Figure 2 is hardly astonishing.

Broad money

To the extent that support exists today for the use of any of the conventional monetary aggregates as an intermediate target for monetary policy in the United States, the aggregate of choice seems to be the broad money stock (M2)[9]. Within the Federal Reserve System, Feinman and Porter (1992) have argued on empirical grounds not only that M2 demand is more stable than the demand for other standard M's but also that M2 outperforms other new candidate measures (for example, what others have called 'liquid M2,' consisting of currency plus all deposits in M2 that can be redeemed at par on demand). Outside the Federal Reserve, Ramey (1993) and Feldstein and Stock (1993) have argued that different forms of error correction procedures render stable the ratio of M2 to money (or, in reciprocal form, the mis-named M2 'velocity'). In recent years the Federal Reserve's semi-annual reports to Congress have also attached more importance to M2 than to other aggregates, at times suggesting that relationships based on M2 may now be settling into a new, more usefully exploitable stability after a period of disequilibrium due to changing market structures.

Interestingly enough, as Table 3 shows, M2 has never exhibited much predictive content in standard empirical exercises like the ones in which M1 or credit used to do well. Moreover, the performance of M2 during the most recent business cycle has also been anything but reassuring in this regard. As Figure 3 shows, M2 growth peaked in late 1986 and by yearend 1987 had slowed to rates that would normally represent a strong prediction of recession. Growth of M2 revived in 1988, faltered again in early 1989, but then revived even more strongly from mid 1989 onward, so that by the time the recession began at midyear 1990, M2 was giving the opposite signal. Throughout this period M2 gave false signals broadly similar to those given by other familiar business cycle indicators like the federal funds rate, the slope of the yield curve, and the spread between the commercial paper rate and the Treasury bill rate. As is evident in Figure 3, however, the difficulty with M2 has also persisted well into the recovery, with slow M2 growth more suggestive of renewed economic downturn than of even the modest recovery that has taken place.

Figure 4, updated from Feinman and Porter (1992), makes the M2 growth puzzle more specific by plotting M2 'velocity' against the Federal Reserve's standard measure of the opportunity cost of holding M2 – that is, the difference

Table 3. F-statistics for M2.

Dependent variable	1960:2-1979:3	1979:4-1992:4	1970:1-1992:4
Y	2.07*	1.47	1.14
X	.92	.65	.14
P	1.44	1.33	1.34

*** significant at the .01 level
** significant at the .05 level
* significant at the .10 level

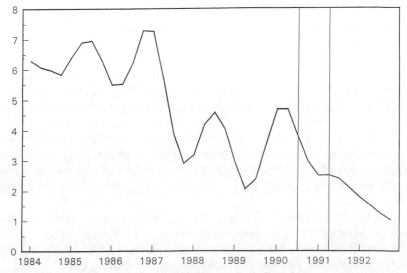

Figure 3. M2 growth (annual rate) with 1990–91 recession indicated.

between the weighted-average return paid on the various components of M2 and a weighted-average return on short-term market instruments not included in M2. Clearly something has changed since 1988. Feinman and Porter showed that expanding the set of market instruments considered to be alternatives to M2 (and, importantly, choosing weights on those instruments' returns that *retrospectively* maximized their explanatory power) reduced the magnitude of the recent discrepancy but did not eliminate it.

Put in the simplest way, the point of Feinman and Porter's suggested improvement in the analysis of M2 demand is that depositors may consider not just short-term money market instruments but bonds too, and perhaps even equities, as potential alternatives to the deposit components of M2. The conceptual point is hardly new, but there is reason to believe that market

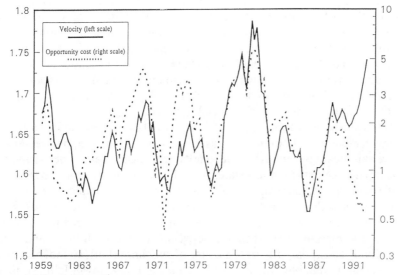

Figure 4. M2 velocity and opportunity cost.

conditions as well as the institutional response to those conditions have given it new practical relevance within just the past few years. The spread between long-term and short-term interest rates has been extraordinarily wide during the latest recession and recovery episode. Holders of maturing certificates of deposit therefore face a large gap between the rates at which they can renew their deposits and the current yields on bonds, and flows of household funds into bonds and stocks, and especially into bond and stock mutual funds, have been unusually large.

In its midyear report to Congress in July 1993, the Federal Reserve 'downgraded' the role of M2 in the monetary policymaking process, acknowledging that 'relationships between money and income, and between money and the price level have largely broken down.'

3. THE MATTER OF INFLUENCING THE TARGET

Implicit in the very concept of a target, intermediate or otherwise, is the presumption that the central bank's actions will affect the target in a way that is at least partly predictable. The whole idea of using money as an intermediate target for monetary policy is that when observed movements of money are inconsistent with the targeted growth rate, the central bank takes actions that it expects to restore money growth (or, under some arrangements, the level of the money stock) to the targeted value. This does not mean, of course, that the central bank can affect money in a perfectly predictable way (if it did, money would be the instrument of policy, not the intermediate target), and a large literature has examined the ability of central banks to influence money under stochastic conditions governing the public's money demand, banks' money supply, and so on[10]. But the relationship between how the central bank moves its instrument variable(s) and what happens to the intermediate target must be systematic and known to at least some degree. By contrast, no such requirement arises under the information variable approach.

It may seem to go without saying that a central bank knows how to affect its economy's money stock, in the stochastic sense intended here, but depending upon what is meant by money this need not always be the case. Once again, the recent experience of the United States provides an apt illustration. To recall, in recent years the measure of money that has been of greatest interest as a potential intermediate target of monetary policy in the United States is the broad money stock, M2. As the discussion in section 2 has already indicated, however, the margin of substitution between M2 and both bond and stock mutual funds has apparently become empirically important, so much so as to cause previously reliable M2 demand functions to break down. In brief, there is now a 'term structure' dimension to the demand for M2.

In addition to disrupting whatever relationships between M2 and nonfinancial economic activity may previously have existed (which in itself would have been damaging enough), this specific development has been especially subversive of any attempt by the Federal Reserve System to use M2 as an intermediate target for monetary policy because it has rendered ambiguous even the *sign* of the effect on M2 of the Federal Reserve's open market operations. Suppose, for example, that the Federal Reserve seeks to increase the rate of M2 growth (perhaps because, as in recent experience, actual growth has fallen below the targeted range). The presumptive action required is to buy securities, thereby adding to nonborrowed reserves and lowering the federal funds rate and, via the market's response, other short-term interest rates. The traditional expectation, based on the assumption of sluggish or even fixed deposit rates in contrast to quick-moving market rates, is an *increase* in money demand. But if M2 deposit rates decline roughly in step with short-term market rates, and if substitution between the short-term deposits that make up the bulk of M2 and longer-term assets is quantitatively important, the demand for M2 may actually *decline* unless (or until) the fall in short-term rates induces a matching fall in expected returns on the relevant long-term assets.

As a simple illustration, consider the following basic model of money demand, money supply, the term structure of interest rates, and aggregate spending:

$$m_t = \alpha_1 y_t + \alpha_2 r_{St} - \alpha_3 r_{Lt} \tag{12}$$

$$m_t = \beta_1 R_t + \beta_2 r_{St} \tag{13}$$

$$r_{Lt} = \gamma_1 r_{St} + \gamma_2 \sum_i r^e_{S, t+i} \tag{14}$$

$$y_t = -\delta_1 r_{St} - \delta_2 r_{Lt} \tag{15}$$

where m is the M2 money stock, y is income, R is the quantity of nonborrowed reserves, and r_S and r_L are short- and long-term interest rates, respectively. (In the term structure equation, $r^e_{S,t+i}$ indicates the expectation of short-term interest rates in the future.) All coefficients are assumed to be positive, and again all constant terms are suppressed.

If the impact on the short-term interest rate is seen as temporary, the effect on money of a change in nonborrowed reserves in this model is given by

$$\frac{dm}{dR} = \frac{\beta_1 Z}{\beta_2 + Z} \tag{16}$$

where

$$Z = \alpha_1\delta_1 + \gamma_1(\alpha_3 + \alpha_1\delta_2) - \alpha_2. \tag{17}$$

If the impact on the short-term interest rate is seen as permanent, the effect on money is

$$\frac{dm}{dR} = \frac{\beta_1 Z^*}{\beta_2 + Z^*} \tag{18}$$

where

$$Z^* = \alpha_1\delta_1 + (\gamma_1 + \gamma_2)(\alpha_3 + \alpha_1\delta_2) - \alpha_2. \tag{19}$$

In traditional models of money demand, in which money is assumed to bear a fixed (perhaps zero) return and both r_S and r_L represent competing returns on non-money market assets, α_2 would have the opposite sign (that is, α_2 as written would be negative), and so $\frac{dm}{dR} > 0$ unambiguously in either (16) or (18). But for the current situation of M2 in the United States, r_S is more plausibly the *own* return. In that case $\frac{dm}{dR} \lessgtr 0$ as $\alpha_1\delta_1 + \gamma_1(\alpha_3 + \alpha_1\delta_2) \lessgtr \alpha_2$ in the case of the temporary effect on the short-term interest rate (16, 17) or, analogously, $\frac{dm}{dR} \lessgtr 0$ as $\alpha_1\delta_1 + (\gamma_1 + \gamma_2)(\alpha_3 + \alpha_1\delta_2) \lessgtr \alpha_2$ in the case of the permanent effect (18, 19).

This ambiguity prevails even in a short run sufficiently short that open market operations do not yet affect nonfinancial economic activity, so that y is effectively predetermined with respect to m. Replacing (15) above by

$$y_t = -\delta_1 r_{S,t-1} - \delta_2 r_{L,t-1} \tag{15'}$$

simplifies (17) and (19) to

$$Z = \gamma_1\alpha_3 - \alpha_2 \tag{17'}$$

and

$$Z^* = (\gamma_1 + \gamma_2) \alpha_3 - \alpha_2. \tag{19'}$$

Here $\frac{dm}{dR} \lesseqgtr 0$ as $\gamma_1\alpha_3 \lesseqgtr \alpha_2$ or as $(\gamma_1 + \gamma_2) \alpha_3 \lesseqgtr \alpha_2$, respectively.

Needless to say, moving beyond the simple model in (12)–(15), either by making these four equations dynamic or by adding further equations, makes the sign condition on $\frac{dm}{dR}$ more complicated rather than simpler. However complex the Federal Reserve's model, though, in the end whether 'expansionary' open market operations expand or shrink M2 depends on relationships among parameters, importantly including interest elasticities, the estimation of which is typically difficult at best. How sharply the Federal Reserve staff has estimated those parameters (and, importantly, their variance-covariance structure) is an interesting matter about which to speculate. I conjecture that in the currently prevailing circumstances the Federal Reserve does not know with confidence even the *sign*, not to mention the magnitude, of the short-run response of M2 to open market operations.

These specific institutional circumstances affecting M2 are clearly particular to the United States. But there is no reason to think they could not arise in other countries as well. Nor is there reason for confidence that, under some exchange rate regimes, the margin of choice between domestic and foreign currencies might not create in some countries an ambiguity parallel to that analyzed here for the case of the term structure.

4. IMPLEMENTING AN INFORMATION VARIABLE APPROACH

What, then, is a central bank to do if conditions that would favor the use of money as an intermediate target do not exist? One possibility, of course, would be simply to fall back on whatever the central bank knows about the connections to income and prices of whatever instrument it sets directly – the reserve base, or the exchange rate, or a short-term interest rate – and make policy decisions on the basis of those ultimate relationships without drawing on any other direct inputs to the policy process. But because the lags between central bank actions and their ultimate economic consequences are so long (at least according to most estimates), such a bare-bones framework would inevitably be unsatisfying. Simply to wait it out until the full effects of any change in the instrument variable have worked their way through to nonfinancial activity, before determining whether the new instrument level is appropriate or not, is likely to be tantamount, in too many instances, to letting the damage accumulate. That is why so many central banks have sought to use at least some kind of intermediate target in the process that they follow for conducting monetary policy.

The central bank's fundamental need in this situation is information: information about the economy's current state and its future direction, as well as about the effects of the central bank's own actions. One implication of this basic description of the problem is that the monetary policymaking process needs to incorporate information *inclusively*, rather than focusing narrowly on any one variable (which would amount to discarding information from other sources). A parallel implication is that the policymaking process needs to exploit information *intensively*, through frequent re-examinations of just what the information provided by any one source is saying.

More specifically, the inclusive use of information presumably means using as information variables (in the sense of section 1 above) not just several financial aggregates, rather than only one as under an intermediate target procedure, but a broader range of measures with potential predictive content. For example, several researchers within the Federal Reserve System have analyzed the predictive properties of the term structure of interest rates with respect to real economic activity in the United States[11], and Mishkin (1990) has documented at least modest predictive content of some parts of the yield curve with respect to U.S. price inflation. Similarly, Kuttner and I have shown that the spread between the commercial paper rate and the Treasury bill rate contains substantial information about subsequent movements of real output in the United States, albeit not about inflation[12]. Indeed, as Table 4 shows, the paper-bill spread typically remains highly significant in equations like (11) above for real income even when other variables like money and credit are introduced, and those other variables usually lose their significance altogether in the presence of the paper-bill spread.

No one would suggest using either the term structure or the paper-bill spread as an *intermediate target* of monetary policy. But once the policymaking procedure is framed in terms of *information variables*, rather than an intermediate target, there is no reason why interest rate relationships are any less suitable for this purpose than monetary aggregates. Just as with a monetary aggregate, the central bank can think through in advance how the term structure and the paper-bill spread are likely to move over the coming months if its policy actions are having the intended effect and if nonfinancial activity is developing as expected. And just as with a monetary aggregate, a sufficiently large unanticipated movement of the term structure or the paper-bill spread could be the occasion for questioning whether economic activity, either as affected by monetary policy or in other regards, is in fact developing according to plan. That, in short, is what the information variable procedure for monetary policy is all about. In some countries, and under some exchange rate regimes, exchange rates can likewise play a parallel role.

There is also no *analytical* reason to restrict the central bank's set of formally exploited information variables to quantities or prices drawn exclusively from

Table 4 F-statistics for paper-bill spread and various aggregates.

Aggregate included	F-statistic on aggregate	F-statistic on spread
Monetary base	.87	6.33***
M1	.93	5.81***
M2	.76	6.16***
Credit	.47	6.65***
Bank Loans	1.02	6.58***

Note: Results are based on monthly data for 1973:6–1992:12.
The dependent variable is real output (industrial production). The equation includes lagged output, prices, the commercial paper rate, the paper-bill spread, and the aggregate indicated, with six lags on each variable. The equation also includes a linear time trend.

*** significant at the .01 level
** significant at the .05 level
* significant at the .10 level

the financial world. Many of the observable actions that are intermediate between what monetary policy does and what it hopes ultimately to achieve take place in the sphere of real activity. In the United States, conventional leading indicator indices have always exploited the fact that goods orders, building permits, ground breakings and the like typically precede the corresponding final sales and production that account for much of the economy's income and output (although less so as the share of services in total output rises). In contrast to the unstructured use of such variables as mere leading indicators, however, for purposes of monetary policy the relevant question is also what information they contain about how effects attributable to central bank actions themselves are spreading through the economy. As is true in the case of financial quantities and prices, therefore, there is room – indeed, there is need – to choose such variables in part according to how they fit into the central bank's conception of how monetary policy affects economic activity.

As a *practical* matter, however, it is likely that much of the substantive advantage to be gained from exploiting specific nonfinancial variables as explicit information variables for monetary policy is already implicit in many central banks' existing economic forecasting apparatus. If durable goods orders, or housing starts, or container shipments move in ways seriously at odds with the central bank's expectations for overall activity consistent with its policy stance, under current procedures that fact is unlikely to escape attention and, if warranted, close analysis. And, unless the central bank is binding its actions to the pursuit of a specific intermediate target – for example, monetary stability – after appropriate analysis it is likely to take whatever action it deems warranted. As a result, much of the concrete advantage of an explicit information variable procedure probably lies in a more inclusive exploitation of financial quantities and prices.

It is important to emphasize, however, that broadening the array of financial quantities and prices used as information variables does not guarantee superior ex post policy actions and outcomes. For example, in the period leading up to the 1990–91 recession in the United States, both the term structure and the paper-bill spread gave false signals quite similar to those given by M2 and other familiar aggregates. For purposes of the argument here, however, the demonstrable fallibility of such variables as predictors of economic activity just illustrates in yet another context the advantage of using any such measures as information variables, not intermediate targets. Unlike as with an intermediate target, an unexpected movement of an information variable does not automatically trigger a change in policy. It instead creates the presumption that there is an issue to be addressed. There remains, always, the need for a judgment.

Finally, it should also be clear that those judgments are best made frequently. Even the most reliable information variable can begin to give false signals, and changing exchange rate regimes, financial market structures and business practices can distort (compared to prior experience) the content of even those signals that continue to be informative. Is it possible to *know* in advance that any chosen variable will necessarily provide misleading information? Of course not. But that does not constitute grounds for proceeding under the immediate presumption that it will not, as is inherent either in an intermediate target procedure or in any procedure calling for automatic responses to unexpected movements of selected information variables. The appropriate presumption, instead, is that there are questions to be raised and responses to be undertaken or not in light of the best available answers. Precisely because the policy regimes and market structures and business practices that matter in this regard are as subject to change as they are, simply proceeding on the assumption that the answer implicit in an intermediate target derived from past experience is still right for today is an invitation to error.

NOTES

1. Alan Greenspan, Testimony before the U.S. House of Representatives, Committee on Banking, Finance and Urban Affairs, Subcommittee on Economic Growth and Credit Formation, July 20, 1993, pp. 9–10.
2. Under either instrument the model breaks down in such a way that targeting the money stock in this context requires responding only to the information contained in m_{t-1} but not whichever of h_{t-1} or r_{t-1} is endogenous.
3. See the extended discussion in Friedman (1990).
4. See *Federal Reserve Bulletin*, 64 (July, 1978), 605–610. The basic idea, however, was not new then. The Commission on Money and Credit, for example, made a similar proposal in its 1961 report.
5. See Friedman and Kuttner (1992, 1993b) for further details of the estimation and for the results of alternative specifications.

132

6. See, for example, the exchange between Stock and Watson (1989) and Friedman and Kuttner (1993a). Earlier on, see, for example, Sims (1980) and Eichenbaum and Singleton (1986).
7. See, for example, Friedman (1983).
8. The target can of course be an average, perhaps with unequal weights, of other variables. Even a single money growth target is, after all, an average of growth targets for the composite elements of whatever is defined as 'money', with weights on those elements in proportion to their size.
9. McCallum (1987, 1988) and others have advocated policy rules centered on the monetary base; but since the base is subject to direct Federal Reserve control (and that is a large part of McCallum's point), under such a procedure it would be the instrument of monetary policy, not an intermediate target.
10. See, for example, the discussion of this issue in Friedman (1990) and the references cited there.
11. See, for example, Laurent (1988), Strongin (1990) and Estrella and Hardouvelis (1991).
12. See again Friedman and Kuttner (1992, 1993b).

REFERENCES

Andersen, Leonall C., and Jordan, Jerry L. (1968), "Monetary and Fiscal Actions: A Test of Their Relative Importance in Economic Stabilization", Federal Reserve Bank of St. Louis, *Review*, 50 (November), 11–24.
Brunner, Karl, and Meltzer, Allan H. (1972), "Money, Debt, and Economic Activity", *Journal of Political Economy*, 80 (September–October), 951–977.
Eichenbaum, Martin, and Singleton, Kenneth J. (1986), "Do Equilibrium Real Business Cycle Theories Explain Postwar Business Cycles?", in: S. Fischer (ed.), *NBER Macroeconomics Annual*. Cambridge, MIT Press.
Estrella, Arturo, and Hardouvelis, Gikas A. (1991), "The Term Structure as a Predictor of Real Economic Activity", *Journal of Finance*, 46 (June), 555–576.
Feinman, Joshua N., and Porter, Richard D. (1992), "The Continuing Weakness of M2", Mimeo, Federal Reserve Board.
Feldstein, Martin, and Stock, James H. (1993), "The Use of A Monetary Aggregate to Target Nominal GDP", Mimeo, National Bureau of Economic Research.
Friedman, Benjamin M. (1983), "The Roles of Money and Credit in Macroeconomic Analysis", in: J. Tobin (ed.), *Macroeconomics, Prices and Quantities: Essays in Memory of Arthur M. Okun*. Washington: The Brookings Institution.
Friedman, Benjamin M. (1990), "Targets and Instruments of Monetary Policy." in: B. Friedman and F. Hahn (eds.), *Handbook of Monetary Economics*, Amsterdam, North-Holland Publishing Co.
Friedman, Benjamin M. (1993), "Ongoing Change in the U.S. Financial Markets: Implications for Monetary Policy." Federal Reserve Bank of Kansas City, *Changing Capital Markets: Implications for Monetary Policy*.
Friedman, Benjamin M., and Kuttner, Kenneth N. (1992), "Money, Income, Prices and Interest Rates", *American Economic Review*, 82 (June), 472–492.
Friedman, Benjamin M., and Kuttner, Kenneth N. (1993a), "Another Look at the Evidence on Money-Income Causality", *Journal of Econometrics*, 57 (May/June), 189–203.
Friedman, Benjamin M., and Kuttner, Kenneth N. (1993b), "Why Does the Paper-Bill Spread Predict Real Economic Activity?", in: J.H. Stock and M.W. Watson (eds.), *New Research on Business Cycle Indicators and Forecasting*, Chicago, University of Chicago Press.
Friedman, Milton (1984), "Lessons from the 1979–82 Monetary Policy Experiment", *American Economic Review*, 74 (May), 397–400.

Friedman, Milton, and Schwartz, Anna J. (1963), *A Monetary History of the United States 1867–1960*, Princeton, Princeton University Press.

Goldfeld, Stephen M. (1973), "The Demand for Money Revisited", *Brookings Papers on Economic Activity* (No. 3), 577–638.

Goldfeld, Stephen M. (1976), "The Case of the Missing money", *Brookings Papers on Economic Activity* (No. 3), 683–730.

Judd, John J., and Scadding, John L. (1982), "The Search for a Stable Money Demand Function: A Survey of the Post-1973 Literature", *Journal of Economic Literature*, 20 (September), 993–1023.

McCallum, Bennett T. (1987), "The Case for Rules in the Conduct of Monetary Policy: A Concrete Example", Federal Reserve Bank of Richmond, *Economic Review* (September/October), 10–18.

McCallum, Bennett T. (1988), "Robustness Properties of a Rule for Monetary Policy", *Carnegie-Rochester Conference Series on Public Policy*, 29 (Autumn), 173–204.

Mishkin, Frederic S. (1990), "Information in the Longer-Maturity Term Structure About Future Inflation", *Quarterly Journal of Economics*, 55 (August), 815–828.

Poole, William (1970), "Optimal Choice of Monetary Instrument in a Simple Stochastic Macro Model", *Quarterly Journal of Economics*, 84 (May), 197–216.

Ramey, Valerie (1993), "How Important Is the Credit Channel in the Transmission of Monetary Policy?", *Carnegie-Rochester Conference Series on Public Policy*.

Sims, Christopher A. (1980), "A Comparison of Interwar and Postwar Business Cycles: Monetarism Reconsidered", *American Economic Review*, 70 (May), 247–250.

Stock, James H., and Watson, Mark W. (1989), "Interpreting the Evidence on Money-Income Causality", *Journal of Econometrics*, 40 (January), 161–182.

Tobin, James (1969), "A General Equilibrium Approach to Monetary Theory", *Journal of Money, Credit and Banking*, 1 (February), 15–29.

Monetary Policy Strategy in the EMU

OTMAR ISSING[1]

Deutsche Bundesbank

1. THE TREATY OF MAASTRICHT

With the Treaty of Maastricht the European governments whose countries are members of the European Monetary System marked out their route to European Economic and Monetary Union. According to the provisions on monetary policy laid down in the treaty, the establishment of a European System of Central Banks and the "irrevocable fixing of exchange rates leading to the introduction of a single currency" are provided for in the final stage of this union. When this third stage is introduced, it will be the task of the ESCB to lay down and implement the monetary policy of the member states. The primary objective of the European Central Bank will be to ensure price stability. The ESCB has to support the general economic policies in the Community only as long as it is possible to do so without prejudice to this objective. In order to ensure that this mandate is observed the ESCB has a free hand in its monetary policy actions. The decision-making bodies of the European Central Bank and of the national central banks participating in the system are independent of all instructions.

Of course, independence implies responsibility. The ultimate objective of the European Central Bank is laid down in its commitment to price stability; how it achieves this goal with the help of the instruments which the Treaty of Maastricht has made available to it is something which the Bank must decide for itself. It is intended that the EMI carries out vital preliminary work in this sphere during stage two in the next few years. It would be a bad omen for the inauguration of the European Central Bank if a vacuum existed at the start of stage three, precisely at the time when a convincing strategy is expected.

2. ALTERNATIVE STRATEGIES

Both in theory and practice the right strategy for monetary policy has always been a point of contention during the past few decades. This is not simply

[1]The author wishes to thank Heinz Herrmann for his active assistance in the preparation of this paper.

J.A.H. de Beaufort Wijnholds, S.C.W. Eijffinger and L.H. Hoogduin (eds.), A Framework for Monetary Stability, pp. 135–148.

because there are so many economists in the world. The truth of the matter is that, time and again, new problems which require analysis in the light of current practice have emerged in both economic policy and in the conditions affecting monetary policy.

There is a wide range of proposals for the monetary policy strategy. These can be roughly categorised according to whether a central bank uses an inter-mediate target in pursuit of its ultimate objective or whether it tries to achieve its final objective in one move. Strategies which set about achieving monetary policy objectives direct were the rule until the end of the sixties or the beginning of the seventies. However, owing to the disappointing results of such a policy and the growing realisation of "the long and variable lags" in the effects of monetary policy – a synonym for our poor knowledge of the structure of our economies – there was subsequently an increasing number of people in favour of using intermediate targets in monetary policy[1]. Some countries, particularly Anglo-Saxon ones, have recently been returning more and more to a direct strategy while many in continental Europe have retained the idea of a two-step approach.

In view of the time lag before the impact of monetary policy measures is felt the idea of applying a strategy with intermediate target was, firstly, to enable the central bank to react early and, secondly, to make it easier to assess the appropriateness of the monetary policy chosen. However, the advantages of a strategy with intermediate targets were questioned fairly soon by those in favour of an optimal control approach[2]. On the other hand, it has become increasingly clear over the years that central banks which are convinced of the advantages of intermediate targets do not regard monetary policy as a simple technical problem of optimisation but rather as something involving politico-economic aspects in which the relationship between discussions on a one-tier versus a two-tier strategy and deliberations on rules versus discretion has played a major part[3]. Consequently, the performance of central banks can be more easily assessed, and the banks are continually under greater pressure to justify their actions. On the other hand, the success of this strategy has increased the banks' chances of building up a reputation. Another factor associated with this approach has been the attempt to make a clear distinction between the central bank's sphere of responsibility and that of the other decision makers involved in the economic process and therefore ultimately to assist in avoiding situations in which problems of credibility and inconsistency prevent an optimal solution[4].

The soundness of setting exact intermediate targets in advance has recently been questioned by monetarists, too, in other words, by those who were originally among the most ardent advocates of such an approach. Disappointed by the fact that it seems virtually impossible to realise intermediate targets at all costs, some have argued that granting the central bank independence may be a substitute for a simple strategy of intermediate targets[5]. Opinions of this kind are natural enough if one remembers the early years when a constant growth in the money stock was being discussed and one actually wanted to include it in the constitution[6].

The idea of institutionalised independence revives these basic ideas but avoids the practical weaknesses of a k-percent rule[7]. However, central bank independence does not actually free the central bank from submitting and pursuing a convincing self-contained strategy. Independence granted by the legislature is a complement to a clear concept rather than a substitute for it. After all, a strategy which makes the central bank's actions in pursuit of its targets understandable and assessible improves the acceptability of and support for the central bank's policy in the eyes of the public, and this should not be underestimated. The disciplinary effect which such a strategy has on the internal decision-making process of the central bank is just as important. The possibility of making a reputation and thus acquiring the freedom of greater flexibility is clearly more considerable under the conditions of institutionalised independence than in the case of a central bank which is subject to instructions.

Even if ever more sophisticated arguments are introduced into the theoretical discussion, it is no doubt safe to assume that in the last analysis it was the actual experience of the various countries and central banks that was decisive in adopting the one or the other approach to monetary policy. In contrast to the theoretical debate where strategies with intermediate targets are seen rather as second-best solutions which seem appropriate in the light of limited information, the absence of credibility or problems concerning time-inconsistency, the situation in the real world seems rather to be the other way round: central banks which try to achieve stability without an intermediate target appear to do so not so much because they consider such a strategy superior, in principle, but because they actually cannot identify any suitable intermediate target in their country or, at least, they think they cannot.

The English authorities are a typical example here. Following the failure of a policy based on money supply and exchange rate targets they are now pursuing one in which it is the direct realisation of an inflationary target that is their aim. Other countries which, on the other hand, have been more successful in pursuing a strategy with intermediate targets, although they may not always have done so without difficulties, think such a procedure is also sensible for the future. Germany, or more precisely the Bundesbank, is not the least among these. With such an approach the Bundesbank has not only been successful in keeping price rises in Germany over the longer term at a comparatively low level in international terms but, on the strength of this strategy, has in fact been able to provide Germany's European partners with an anchor, with whose help it has been possible to reduce the rates of inflation gradually to a level which, in some cases, is now even below Germany's[8].

Proponents of a one-step approach for monetary policy like to point out that it is ultimately the success in achieving its actual target, i.e. price stability, which counts when assessing the credibility of a central bank. It is precisely here, however, that a one-tier strategy may be fraught with difficulties. This is because experience has shown that in the short term, and even in the medium term, inflation is affected by a number of factors which are beyond the control of monetary policy makers. In Germany, which is generally considered to be a country with a reliable link between the trend in the money stock and the trend in prices, non-monetary factors have a considerable short-term influence on price movements while the growth in the money stock determines inflationary trends only in the long run[9].

Central banks such as those in the United Kingdom, Canada and New Zealand which try to achieve such a direct control of price movements are fully aware of these problems. Passages in their target statements make this clear. Yet there is a considerable risk that the central banks will be overstretched by such strategies due to the impatience of the public, they may tend to overreact as a result and this in the end may compromise the entire concept[10]. It is certainly true that those central banks which shifted to such a direct strategy in the past few years appear to be successful up to now. However, the trial period for monetary policy concepts is measured in decades rather than in years.

A number of options has been discussed to date in choosing an intermediate target, but only in a few cases have these actually been put to the test. It was a widely held belief in academic circles in the eighties that one should use nominal GNP as an intermediate monetary target[11] However, there have always been many objections, particularly from those implementing monetary policy, to a concept of this kind[12]. These objections are mainly to the effect that the movement in GNP is subject to a variety of influences and, at best, central banks can only try and control such a variable over a period far in excess of a year. Consequently, it is likewise impossible to set targets for a manageable period and to use these to illustrate one's commitment to price stability. It is therefore not surprising that ideas of this kind have still not been tried out in practice. However, academics have also expressed doubts, especially with respect to the symmetrical treatment of growth and inflation in this approach[13]

A traditional candidate for an intermediate monetary target has always been interest rates as a price variable in contrast to the money stock. Various aspects have recently been studied in this context. Nowadays it is less common to specify a certain nominal interest rate level; instead, the yield curve and the real interest rate are the variables proposed for use. It is intended in this way to take the standard objections to interest rates as an intermediate target in monetary policy into account[14]. Interest in the role of real interest rates was revived not least as a result of a statement by A. Greenspan to the US Congress[15].

There is no doubt that the difference between short and long-term interest rates can often indicate how restrictive monetary policy is although I admit that that is not always certain. In Germany we have been observing a flat yield curve; in the minds of the apologists of yield curves this is certainly being interpreted as a sign of a policy that is still restrictive. Yet the long-term interest rate in Germany is now (October 1993) below 6%, which is lower than it has been for most of the post-war years; at the same time the current inflation rate is at an above-average level. Interest rate patterns of a similarly flat nature were recorded at the end of 1980 and in early 1982. However, the overall interest rate level at that time was running at around 9 %. Indeed, a clear correlation between interest rate patterns and interest rate levels just does not exist. From the point of view of a policy geared to maintaining monetary stability it is of prime importance to avoid assuming that price stability is dependent on a specific interest rate pattern. Consequently, the yield curve cannot be used as a nominal anchor for monetary policy[16].

It is true that the use of a real interest rate as an intermediate monetary policy target can help, in principle, to avoid the risks which arise when nominal interest rates are targeted. For example, the central bank which uses nominal interest rates as its target runs the risk that, in failing to take inflationary expectations into account, it will try to stabilise a disequilibrium interest rate and will therefore trigger off a cumulative deflationary or inflationary process. On the other hand, it is not easy to fend off this risk by using real interest rates as one's goal either because, at best, fixing an equilibrium real interest rate can only be done with a large margin of uncertainty. Apart from that, there is a considerable danger that in the event of unsatisfactory cyclical trends the blame will be pinned on the central bank, which will then be suspected of having set an inappropriate intermediate target. Precisely because of the uncertainty involved in establishing the equilibrium rate of interest it will not be easy for an independent central bank either to resist the associated pressures. These problems would be exacerbated at the level of a European monetary policy, as interest rates play a very wide variety of roles in the individual member state economies. Consequently, it is difficult to imagine that on this basis the Governing Council of the ESCB could agree on the appropriate intermediate target.

Finally, the smaller countries in particular have frequently targeted exchange rates. Not a few central banks in Europe have opted for this strategy and have obtained good results. The Nederlandsche Bank is a case in point. On the other hand, resistance to setting such targets has always been considerable in relatively large countries such as the United Kingdom. At any rate, however, an anchor country is essential for a policy of this kind. A central bank which is responsible for monetary policy in Europe with the primary objective of price stability is unable to apply such a concept from the outset.

3. MONETARY TARGETING FOR THE EUROPEAN CENTRAL BANK

Having said all that, the question remains as to the suitability of the money stock as an intermediate monetary target in the European Monetary Union.

The use of a money stock as an intermediate target for European monetary policy is advisable for a number of reasons. Given an appropriate range of instruments and protection from external shocks by means of a flexible exchange rate, it can probably be assumed that the European Central Bank will be able to manage the growth of such a variable at its discretion; besides, it should be borne in mind that in the short term exact control is unnecessary. By setting and announcing a monetary target the central bank's responsibility is documented vis-à-vis the general public. Admittedly, this presupposes that the theoretical basis, in other words, the link between monetary expansion and price trends, is maintained.

Besides these advantages, which are generally applicable, a few other specific points argue in favour of a money stock target in the case of the European Central Bank, in particular. As a new institution, the European Central Bank will be especially subject to the scrutiny of those who wish to use the new currency as investors, borrowers or in connection with some other business transaction. This is particularly true in view of the fact that a supra-national central bank is something new. No doubt the European Central Bank Act, thanks to its statutory establishment of independence and its clear commitment to price stability, will provide an excellent institutional basis for monetary policy.

In the early days, however, the ESCB will not be able to point to its own success record on stability or to offer proof of its tenacity even in difficult situations. It will therefore be essential for it to be able to take over as much credibility from its predecessors as possible. To try and inherit the good record of the Bundesbank, which also owes its past stability successes to the medium-term orientation of its policy of monetary targeting, a procedure which it has now been pursuing for almost 20 years, would seem to be the obvious thing to do. Adopting its concept would no doubt increase these chances. Such an approach is also advantageous in view of the distribution of roles in the context of European economic policy. One of the basic ideas of medium-term monetary targeting is that the central bank thereby provides the other economic policy decision makers with a monetary framework which makes it easier for them to base their decisions on it and to coordinate these decisions with each other. In Europe that will be particularly important because, although there will be a joint monetary policy from the start of stage three, most decisions will continue to be made decentrally in other spheres such as finance and wage policy.

With good reason central banks tend to be among the more cautious institutions of this world. Experience has shown that they do not adopt a given concept until they have examined it from many points of view. On the other hand, in view of the credibility problems already mentioned and given the necessity of having to pursue an appropriate policy from the first day of stage three, it would be problematical if the ESCB were to start operating without having a clearly defined idea of its concept. What is more, such a basic decision will have to be taken at an early stage if only because it will have a far-reaching effect on other important decisions, such as the choice of instruments, on which there must be clarity at an early stage quite simply because of the preparation time necessary for them. In such a dilemma it is absolutely necessary to discuss possible objections and difficulties arising from such a strategy comprehensively and in good time.

One objection to a medium-term monetary targeting approach concerns the fact that such a concept is based on rules. The question arises as to whether such an approach based on rules is at all possible in view of the potential disruptions associated with the transition to stage three, in view of the general uncertainty regarding the structural parameters of the future European economy and also in view of the unpredictability of any future shocks to which the European Economic and Monetary Union will be exposed. What is certainly true is that in such an environment flexibility will be essential; however, it is also true to say that precisely in this situation rules are important.

In the uncertainty of the initial phase, which will bring a mixture of high expectations and intense fears, it will be virtually impossible for the European Central Bank to face the danger of transitory inconsistencies appropriately if it does not have a set of rules in the sense of a precommitment of its policy. A matter for consideration is to what extent this policy formula for the normal state of affairs has to be supplemented from the beginning by a clear definition of proviso clauses for exceptional cases. There will certainly be no shortage of pressure to deviate from the intermediate target. Deviation may well be justified in a given set of circumstances, but in that case there must be convincing reasons for it[17]. Incidentally, there are good reasons for the theory that a European economy as a total entity will be less exposed to external shocks than each of the individual national economies in the Community. (Of course, one counterargument is that the exchange rate as an adjustment instrument between the individual national currencies will disappear. However, such problems cannot be solved by a single monetary policy.)

One specific objection to monetary targeting for the ESCB concerns the stability of the demand for money in Europe during stage three. This is basically an empirical question and cannot therefore be answered with certainty before the beginning of the final stage and, indeed, even then it can only be answered after some experience in this stage has been gained. Nevertheless one can examine a few arguments which might suggest that the stability of the demand for money as required as a basis for monetary targeting is at risk. An immediate word of caution here concerns the danger of trying to set requirements which are too high. R. Gordon's argument that the concept of a short-term demand for money and its stability is not actually important may be a little exaggerated but it certainly does have an element of truth in it[18].

Actually, very short-term periods of instability are no hindrance, in principle, to setting medium-term monetary targets. On the other hand, central banks which have adopted monetary targets have always announced these annually. Conceptually, this appears to be set at the minimum of what one should be striving for. For example, J. Niehans was in favour of an approach in which the period of reference was a complete economic cycle. Ideas from A. Meltzer and B. McCallum can be similarly interpreted[19]. The Swiss National Bank has been following a strategy since 1991 in which a monetary target is set for five years. However, one should not be under any illusions here. In practice, extending the time horizon for monetary targeting almost inevitably results in a reduction of the disciplinary effects obtained from monetary targeting[20]. All in all, the arguments are probably in favour of continuing the practice of setting annual monetary targets.

Financial innovations are often cited as a significant source of future instability in the demand for money. This is an objection which one has to consider very carefully. Financial innovations can affect monetary relations not only marginally and in the short term. Those central banks which were compelled through such developments to abandon a strategy based on monetary targets have, as a rule, observed clear breaks in their monetary statistics even if, with a little hindsight, fears regarding long-term instability were sometimes possibly a little exaggerated[21].

Whether or not stage three of monetary union will be a period of increased financial innovation remains to be seen. There are those who fear that it will be[22]. However, there is considerable reason to be more optimistic. Firstly, there is the fact that financial innovations multiply best in periods of high inflation and in the wake of administrative regulations and subsequent de-regulations in the financial sector. If stage three begins with prices as stable as possible and the European Monetary Union becomes a zone of stability, the preconditions for keeping the dangers from this quarter in check will be good. The future appears to be bright as far as administrative regulations are concerned, too. Credit controls, interest rate ceilings and capital controls etc. no longer exist in many European countries while in others their significance is continually declining. The Treaty of Maastricht commits the central banks to observe in their actions the principles of an open market economy with free competition. As a result, administrative regulations disappear from monetary policy, as does the impetus which the corresponding restrictions give to attempts at evasion.

Incidentally, the significance of financial innovations is certainly a question which is also dependent on the choice of specific intermediate targets. History has shown us that in countries which have seen a particularly rapid growth of financial innovations not all monetary aggregates have been affected to the same extent. It will therefore be necessary to check which definitions offer protection against such risks or whether, for example, different weightings of the monetary components do so. In this connection there are good arguments in favour of a relatively broad monetary aggregate. However, one should not overlook the fact that such a tendency may reduce the potential of its manageability.

Another question to arise is whether a change in regime associated with stage three will lead to instability in the demand for money. One of the aspects which are being addressed here is the fact that in many European countries today it is not a monetary target which is being pursued but rather an exchange rate target. However, Goodhart's law warns us that the transition to controlling the money supply can destabilise a previously stable demand for money. Whether this argument still applies in a world where the financial markets have been liberalised for a fairly long time, where monetary policy does not aim to achieve monetary targets in the short term but where it seeks to manage the money stock indirectly by influencing interest rates seems questionable.

The question may be put the other way round, incidentally: what would be the consequences for a European monetary policy aimed at maintaining targets if the Bundesbank were to abandon its concept. At any rate, it would not be a foregone conclusion that the monetary transmission process in Germany and in Europe would remain unaffected and that, as a result, the effects of monetary policy measures could under these circumstances be assessed on the basis of past experience.

If, despite all these possible future problems, one follows the present results of estimates on the European demand for money, the outcome is surprisingly good[23]. Many studies show that the stability of the demand for money in Europe is better than that in most of the individual countries and is similar to that of the demand for money in Germany. This provides important arguments for monetary targeting in stage three.

It is not quite clear why a European aggregate performs so well despite the obvious problems which exist in, for example, aggregating various national money stock definitions. Some are of the opinion that it is the problems of currency substitution and the holding of money balances outside national boundaries that lead to problems at the national level but which disappear when aggregated[24]. It is doubtful, however, whether such problems of currency substitution in Europe have actually been a significant factor. In Germany, where cross-border holdings have become quite significant (they currently amount to over 10% of the traditional money stock M3), it is predominantly

Euro-D-Mark deposits, which are not held for reasons of currency substitution, that are involved in such financial investments. In other countries, too, other reasons for holding money abroad are in the forefront.

Analyses of European monetary aggregates with and without such cross-border holdings give reason to doubt that the secret of a stable European demand for money is to be found here[25]. Another possible explanation for the good properties of the European money stock is that the stability of German monetary demand is reflected here and that the problems of smaller countries become less significant in a larger aggregate and can be subsumed in a random disturbance. Whereas in the first case it is virtually a negative correlation between the quality of the statistical properties of a European demand for money and the demand for money in the individual countries which would be expected and we should see such a development in the course of stage two at the latest, in the second case European monetary targeting is essentially dependent on stable conditions in Germany.

Of course, the decision to use the money stock as an intermediate target in monetary policy would only be a first step. Decisions would also have to be made on at least two other points. This applies, firstly, to the rule according to which the money stock concerned should grow under normal circumstances. Secondly, it applies to the way in which the money stock is to be managed.

Although many central banks have set monetary targets, the rules which they have used for this have seldom been disclosed. One of the few exceptions was the Bundesbank. Not only has the Bundesbank announced monetary targets annually since the middle of the seventies – initially for the central bank money stock and later for the money stock M3 – it has also explained how it has arrived at these targets. The basic elements of its derivation have remained virtually unchanged from the outset: potential growth and a target for an acceptable inflation rate[26]. To what extent such a fundamentally simple and comprehensible procedure can provide the basis not only for the long-term realisation of the desired price developments but also, in the case of difficulties, the satisfactory return to equilibrium is dependent on many factors ranging from the interest rate elasticity of the demand for money and goods to the sensitivity of wages and prices to imbalances in the labour and goods markets. If the Bundesbank has been successful on the whole, this has certainly been due to the fact that, overall, these conditions have been favourable.

However, such conditions cannot be seen entirely exogenous to the central bank. It should not be forgotten here that the reputation which the central bank has built up over the years has itself played a role here when, for example, it had been necessary to keep inflationary expectations in check. Indeed, this seems to be the most promising way of reducing the costs of a disinflationary policy[27]. On the other hand, other attempts, for example, on the basis of indexing, have proved unsuccessful[28]. It is important for these reasons, too, that the introduction of a European stability policy is convincingly successful in order to bring about a virtuous circle and not a vicious circle. However, the conditions obtaining in the economic environment will be the decisive factor. Open borders to the rest of the world, competition on the goods markets and satisfactory public finances in the member countries, as is laid down as a precondition in the Treaty of Maastricht, are therefore essential if in the end a stability policy is to be generally acceptable and successful.

As far as the question of managing a European money stock is concerned, essentially two questions have to be answered. The first is which instruments the ESCB is to use in future. The second question, which has been frequently discussed, concerns the amount of scope that is to be allowed in European monetary policy for decentralised elements[29].

Regarding the range of instruments there has been a considerable convergence in the mechanism used by the individual central banks to manage the money stock over the past few years. Open market policy is at the centre of monetary policy everywhere. Yet there are also remarkable differences. One of these concerns the minimum reserves. In Germany this instrument has proved very useful not least in controlling liquidity on the money market[30]. Essentially, the arguments amount to the fact that minimum reserves act as a buffer against short-term fluctuations in the money market and that the minimum reserves avoid the necessity of the central bank intervening every day to maintain an equilibrium. On the other hand, it must not be forgotten that the tax character of such a minimum reserve requirement can also have undesirable effects, for example, by encouraging evasive innovations. The European Central Bank will have to take account of all of these arguments.

With respect to the question of centralisation-decentralisation there are various concepts which range from a centralised management of monetary policy to a decentralised form[31]. While a centrally organised monetary policy is the norm, significantly decentralised models would certainly have an experimental character. On the one hand, it is almost natural that national central banks will look for decentralised solutions in Europe. Some also argue that, in this case, far more account can be taken of the national peculiarities which will continue to exist. It should not be forgotten, however, that in stage three there must, by definition, be a single market for central bank money; to that extent independent action by national central banks would lead to arbitrage with its attendant costs at best. However, worse consequences may result. A development where different signals would reach market participants or where central banks would be encouraged to compete for customers through interest rates is to be avoided at all costs[32].

The argument that individual central banks are particularly familiar with the peculiarities of their domestic financial markets must be considered with care because it is doubtful whether past behaviour, which has frequently been determined by the differences in the various operating methods of central banks, is a suitable model for stage three. At any rate, what is essential is that the control procedure used by the ESCB also underpins the soundness and credibility of future monetary policy.

4. CONCLUSION

The transition to stage three of European Economic and Monetary Union will no doubt be a difficult period. Much will be new and unfamiliar, both for those inside the European Central Bank as well as for those outside. Success and failure will vitally depend on how confident the population is with regard to the European currency. It will be important in such a situation that wherever possible one can fall back on what has been tried and tested. This is the principle pursued in the Treaty of Maastricht. Committing the ESCB to pursue price stability and the granting of independence to this institution are not least a reflection of these efforts. Even when the guidelines for the monetary policy instruments were established, this principle was followed. It would also seem to be advisable now to decide on a strategy for stage three.

A monetary policy based on rules and incorporating monetary targets based on medium-term considerations has proved itself in the past whenever it has been necessary to achieve the goal of price stability. With this policy over the past few decades the Bundesbank has ensured a relatively high degree of stability for the value of the D-Mark. Even during the particular difficulties associated with German unification this policy has ultimately proved its worth. In any case, it is difficult to imagine that we could have met our statutory mandate better with another strategy.

Monetary policy and therefore monetary targeting, too, will certainly not succeed without an element of pragmatism. However, it is important that the rule always remains the point of reference. The answer to the question how much flexibility is possible and necessary will never be easy. It would also be helpful here if one could fall back on the experience of a strategy which has proved itself in practice.

NOTES

1. Jack Guttentag wrote in an article in 1966: The main weakness of the (money market) strategy is its incompleteness, i.e. the fact that the Federal Open Market Committee (FOMC) does not set specific quantitative target values for which it would hold itself accountable for the money supply, long-term interest rates, or any other strategic "variable" that could serve as a connecting link between open market operations and system objectives. J. Guttentag (1966), "The strategy of open market operations", *Quarterly Journal of Economics*, pp. 1–30.

2. See B. Friedman (1973), "Targets, instruments, and indicators of monetary policy", *Journal of Monetary Economics*, pp. 443–473.
3. See B. Friedman (1990), "Targets and instruments of monetary policy", *Handbook of Monetary Economics, Vol. II*, pp. 1185–1230.
4. See F. Kydland and E.C. Prescott (1977), "Rules rather than discretion – the inconsistency of optimal plans", *Journal of Political Economy*, pp. 473–491.
5. M.J.M. Neumann took this line during the European debate on the subject. See M.J.M. Neumann (1991), "Central bank independence as a prerequisite of price stability", EC Commission (1991), *The economics of EMU*, Background studies for European Economy No. 44 "One market, one money". For an account of the general discussion of these points see S. Lohmann (1992), "Optimal commitment in monetary policy: Credibility versus flexibility", *American Economic Review*, pp. 273–286.
6. See M. Friedman (1968), "The role of monetary policy", *American Economic Review*, pp. 1–17.
7. For an account of experience in Germany see O. Issing (1993), *Central Bank Independence and Monetary Stability*, Institute of Economic Affairs, Occasional Paper 89.
8. For a comparison of the situation of the Bundesbank with that of the Bank of England see, for example, M. King (1993), "The Bundesbank: A view from the Bank of England", Bank of England, *Quarterly Bulletin*, May, pp. 269–274.
9. See Deutsche Bundesbank (1992), "The correlation between monetary growth and price movements in the Federal Republic of Germany", *Monthly Report*, January, pp. 20–28.
10. See also in this connection W.F Duisenberg (1993), "Monetary policy in a changing economic environment", *SUERF Paper on Monetary Policy and Financial Systems*, No. 16.
11. See, for example, J. Tobin (1983), "Monetary policy: Rules, targets, and shocks", *Journal of Money, Credit, and Banking*, pp. 506–518.
12. See, for example, commentaries by S. Axilrod and H.J. Dudler on R. Gordon (1985), "The conduct of monetary policy", in Ando et al. (eds): *Monetary policy in our times*.
13. See J. Taylor (1985), "What would nominal GNP targeting do to the business cycle", in: *Carnegie-Rochester Conference Series on Public Policy*.
14. Interest rate targets are fraught with well-known problems, namely that they encourage a pro-cyclical impact of monetary policy, that they can lead to cumulative inflationary and deflationary processes, that the trend in market conditions cannot be clearly interpreted and that the relevant long-term interest rates, at least, are controlled by the central bank only to a very limited extent. Yet in American literature the idea of applying interest rates as an intermediate monetary target has recently regained an element of popularity. See R. Barro (1989), "Interest rate targeting", *Journal of Monetary Economics*, pp. 3–30. Unfavourable past experience, however, argues clearly against resuming such attempts. See B. Friedman (1988), "Monetary policy without quantity variables", *American Economic Review, Papers and Proceedings*, pp. 440–445, L. Mote (1988), "Looking back: The use of interest rates in monetary policy", *Economic Perspectives*, Federal Reserve Bank of Chicago, pp. 15–29.
15. For the recent discussion on the role of the yield curve in a monetary policy strategy see, for example, A. Estrella and G. Hardouvelis (1990), "Possible roles of the yield curve in monetary policy", in Federal Reserve Bank of New York: *Intermediate targets and indicators for monetary policy; a critical survey*, pp. 339–362. For real interest rates see A. Greenspan (1993), Testimony to the Committee on Economic Growth and Credit Formation of the Committee on Banking, Finance and Urban Affairs of the US House of Representatives on July 20, 1993.
16. See also V. Reinhardt (1991), "Conducting monetary policy without a nominal anchor", *Journal of Macroeconomics*, pp. 575–596.
17. For a technical description of such a view see R. Flood and P. Isard (1989), "Monetary policy strategies", *IMF staff papers*, pp. 612–632.

148

18. R. Gordon (1984), The short-run demand for money: A reconsideration, *Journal of Money, Credit, and Banking*, pp. 403–434.
19. See J. Niehans (1978), *The theory of money*, Baltimore; B. McCallum (1987), "The case for rules in the conduct of monetary policy", *Weltwirtschaftliches Archiv*, pp. 415–429; A. Meltzer (1984), "Rules for price stability: An overview and comparison", in Federal Reserve Bank of Kansas City: *Price stability and public policy*.
20. For an approach to the determining of an optimal time horizon for monetary targeting which takes such arguments into account see M. Garfinkel and S. Oh (1993), "Strategic discipline in monetary policy with private information: Optimal targeting horizons", *American Economic Review*, pp. 99–117.
21. For an early overview of the consequences of financial innovations for monetary policy see M.A. Akthar (1983), "Financial innovations and their implications for monetary policy: An international perspective", *BIS Economic Paper* No. 9. For a discussion with respect to stage three in Europe see C. Sardelis (1993), Targeting a European monetary aggregate, *Economic Papers of the EC Commission* No. 102. For a reappraisal of the theory of instability in the demand for money as a consequence of financial innovations see, for example, J. Boughton (1992), International comparisons of money demand: A review essay, *IMF working paper*.
22. See C. de Boissieu (1992), Financial innovation and the implementation of a European monetary policy: A prospective view. Manuscript.
23. For an overview see A. van Riet (1992), "Studies of EC money demand: survey and assessment", De Nederlandsche Bank, *Quarterly Bulletin*, pp. 63–75.
24. See, for example, I. Angeloni, C. Cottarelli and A. Levy (1991), *Cross-border deposits and monetary aggregates in the transition to EMU*, IMF Working Paper No. 114.
25. See C. Monticelli (1993), All the money in Europe, mimeographed, Basle.
26. See O. Issing (1992), "Theoretical and Empirical Foundations of the Deutsche Bundesbank's Monetary Targeting", *Intereconomics*, November-December, pp. 289–300.
27. See B. Chadha, P. Masson and G. Meredith (1992), "Models of inflation and the costs of disinflation", *IMF staff papers*, pp. 395–431.
28. For a theoretical explanation see S. Fischer and L. Summers (1989), "Should governments learn to live with inflation", *American Economic Review, Papers and Proceedings*, pp. 382–387.
29. See C. Monticelli and G. Vinals (1992), The monetary future of Europe, mimeographed, Basle; P. Kenen (1992), *EMU after Maastricht*, Group of Thirty.
30. See W. Friedmann (1988), "Die Mindestreserve im deutschen Finanzsystem", *Kredit und Kapital*, pp. 79–91; for a comprehensive account of the role of the minimum reserves in monetary policy see Federal Reserve Bank of New York (1993): *Reduced reserve requirements: Alternatives for the conduct of monetary policy and reserve management*.
31. See L. Hoogduin and G. Korteweg (1993), "Monetary policy on the road to EMU", in S. Eijffinger and J. Gerards (eds): *European monetary integration and the financial sector*, pp. 61–83.
32. See also P. Kenen (1992), "The European Central Bank and monetary policy in stage three of EMU", *International Affairs*, pp. 457–474.

Comment on Benjamin Friedman:
Intermediate Targets versus Information Variables as Operating Guides for Monetary Policy

ALEXANDRE LAMFALUSSY

Bank for International Settlements

I have read with great interest Professor Friedman's paper on intermediate targets versus information variables. He has for sometime now been a major contributor to both the technical literature in this area and to the public policy debate. I was therefore interested to see how his position on this topic has evolved, particularly in light of the Federal Reserve's July 1993 report to the US Congress announcing that it was "downgrading" the role of its M2 aggregate in policy-making.

Over the years I have heard the debate regarding intermediate targets surface in numerous discussions at the Bank for International Settlements; at a technical level in our central bank economists' meetings, when I was the head of the Monetary and Economic Department, and of course at the policy level, at formal and informal gatherings of central bank governors.

The intermediate target debate relates directly to the central issue of Professor Friedman's paper, the quality of information available to the central bank which will allow it to appropriately adjust its policy instruments. This implies having current information which is of use in anticipating future economic events, in particular the future performance of the ultimate objectives of policy. Moreover, reliable nominal targets, if available, are desirable not only for the purpose of setting policy, but also as means to convey to the public the policy intentions and to measure the performance of the central bank.

I do not think it should be taken as a criticism of Professor Friedman's paper if I begin by saying that the essential elements of the debate remain the same. We are, broadly speaking, addressing the classic debate of policy rules versus discretion. As he says early on in his paper: "The key role of the intermediate target variable is to provide the central bank with a ready rule for processing and acting on (this) new information" (p. 111). A reliable intermediate target is thus desirable, firstly because we believe it is related to some ultimate policy objective and, secondly, as a protective device against policy responses to "false signals".

While I believe most central bankers of the major economies periodically would admit to having serious doubts about the reliability of their monetary

149

J.A.H. de Beaufort Wijnholds, S.C.W. Eijffinger and L.H. Hoogduin (eds.), A Framework for Monetary Stability, pp. 149–152.
© 1994 *Kluwer Academic Publishers. Printed in the Netherlands.*

aggregates as intermediate target variables, I don't believe their continued attachment to them, as actual targets or useful information variables, reflects a nostalgic longing for earlier days. Their attention to them reflects what I would call a monetary policy "mini-max strategy" – that of minimising the policy-maker's maximum regret. And that maximum regret continues to be an unexpected and undesirable resurgence of inflation, requiring, as it has in the past, strong policies to counter its reappearance. This concern hangs over the shoulders of central bankers even today, where we observe low to moderate inflation in most of the major industrial economies.

I ask your indulgence in permitting me to refer to an article I wrote a dozen years ago on the question of policy rules, discretion and information[1]. The arguments I gave in favour of the use of monetary rules now look to be quite "old hat", but I believe they are the same as those used today: they provide a good basis for establishing central bank credibility and are helpful in defending against political pressures to run overly stimulative policies. But most important, I argued, full discretion requires the authorities to have near perfect information on how the economy actually functions. Complete policy discretion requires greater knowledge than policy-makers actually possess. This is one of the major reasons Milton Friedman, the major architect of monetarism, favoured monetary rules over central bank discretion.

In this same essay of mine I also attempted to find counter-arguments for the use of policy rules. Professor Benjamin Friedman's current paper I think provides some support for my earlier view. In my 1981 paper I specifically argued that "the definition of policy rules and their practical implementation will always require judgement". Indeed, abiding by a monetarist rule associated with an intermediate monetary target would require very considerable judgement, because it demands that we accept a specific notion of how the economy works.

An alternative to the strict adherence to a monetarist rule is the so-called "Poole rule". This paradigm recognises that the economy can be subject to purely random shock, in which case sticking to a particular intermediate target may actually be destabilising. William Poole raised the important question of whether, in the face of random shocks to the economy, an interest rate inter-mediate target or a monetary target would better stabilise real income. This policy choice, however, also requires considerable judgement. It demands that we know whether the shocks originated from the financial or the real side of the economy.

Benjamin Friedman has demonstrated that since the early 1980s in the United States neither M1, M2 nor a credit aggregate have been stably related to output growth or inflation. This has meant that short-run policy has increas-ingly relied on interest rate target setting and less and less on intermediate monetary targets. This in turn has required US policy-makers to cast their information net wider and sample the potential informational and predictive content of a number of variables, such as the term structure of interest rates and the spread between yields on private-issued and government paper. This could lead to the criticism that the Federal Reserve is following a "look at everything" approach to policy setting, and indeed this may be a valid criticism. Yet the validity of the criticism can be judged only in relation to the quality of the observed performance. On the basis of inflation behaviour in the United States since the mid-1980s, I do not believe the information variable approach, which I think the Federal Reserve has followed, has done a bad job.

My general opinion regarding the appropriate role of monetary aggregates is in most respects quite in accord with Benjamin Friedman's major conclusion – that the conditions do not exist for closely relating short-run movements in policy instruments to the behaviour of the intermediate monetary target. I am somewhat surprised, however, to read that Professor Friedman believes this to be a conclusion one can only recently have drawn for the United States.

Here I think I need to be a bit more specific to make my point clear. In my reading of events, only during the period 1979–82 can the Federal Reserve be interpreted as having followed anything like a formal monetary rule, in which the short-term instrument, the Federal funds rate, was systematically adjusted in response to deviations of money growth from its targeted range. After 1982 I interpret the Federal Reserve as having followed an increasingly judgmental, non-rule oriented, monetary policy, despite it having formally announced monetary targets. Monetary aggregates were over time increasingly used as information variables and not as strict targets in any technical control manner. The monetary aggregates may have had greater "weight" in policy than the broad private credit aggregate, but this was because the credit aggregate could not be easily controlled with the available instruments. The same problem now plagues the M2 aggregate.

What also changed was the manner in which the Federal Reserve adjusted its short-term instrument, the Federal funds rate, in response to bank reserve growth. But here I am not enough, or at all, an "insider" to know what practical relevance the shift from non-borrowed reserve targeting, to borrowed reserve targeting, to no reserve targeting had with regard to the setting of the Federal funds rate instrument. What I feel more confident about is that after 1982 monetary aggregates in the United States moved increasingly away from their use as intermediate target and were used more and more as "information variables". Policy by necessity became more judgmental. In Professor Friedman's words, the movement in information variables "merely create the presumption that a development has occurred that merits attention and that may warrant action depending upon circumstances" (p. 110). I think it had been clear to many observers long before July 1993 that the monetary aggregates were used in this manner.

While my original sympathies with dogmatic monetary rules could never be interpreted as having been particularly strong, I nonetheless appreciated, and still do, the risk central banks run without reliable intermediate nominal targets. The long-standing criticism that interest rate targeting by the central bank could lead to pro-cyclical money and credit growth is still applicable. The absence of a reliable intermediate target is one reason, among others, that some European countries decided to peg to the currency of a country with a stable monetary aggregate. This permitted them to borrow credibility and stabilise price expectations. This contributed to a sizable decline in inflation in several countries. Without nominal intermediate target variables a central bank is confronted with the problem of not knowing with any precision what weight to attach to particular information variables, running the risk that it may wait too long to respond before a serious problem emerges. Nor will the general public be informed of the central bank's intentions.

Unfortunately, reliable intermediate monetary targets are in diminishing supply. Furthermore, events of the past few years have complicated matters even further. For even with a dependable intermediate target, which is stably related to nominal income and standard measures of inflation, its behaviour may be quite at variance with that of asset prices. This, I think, is the new dimension of monetary policy in an increasingly deregulated and integrated global financial environment. Whether and how the authorities should respond to asset price bubbles, such as those we have seen in recent years, is not at all clear and is subject enough for another conference. Yet it is a subject I think we will be returning to in the future. It is made difficult by the simple fact that we have a poor fundamental knowledge of asset price determination. This resulted in some financial authorities reacting too slowly, in retrospect, to the asset price cycle which developed during the second half of the 1980s. We are now living with some of the financial and conjunctural consequences of this important policy dilemma.

In conclusion, I am in general agreement with Professor Friedman's argument regarding the information variable approach to monetary policy, but hardly reassured by it. A number of central banks have perforce moved from a world of policy rules with modest discretion to one of considerable discretion without rules. The policy-maker's problem is to know how to utilise this discretion in an increasingly uncertain economic environment.

NOTES

1. See Alexandre Lamfalussy (1981), "Rules versus discretion: an essay on monetary policy in an inflationary environment", *BIS Economic Papers*, No. 3, April, Bank for International Settlements, Basle.

Comment on Otmar Issing:
Monetary Policy Strategy in the EMU

PAUL DE GRAUWE

Catholic University Leuven

This is an interesting paper focusing on the advantages of monetary targeting. The main point of the paper is that the future European Central Bank (ECB) would do well to follow similar procedures of monetary targeting as those that exist in the Bundesbank.

I will not go into the issue of the use of intermediate targets in monetary policy, and the relative merits of different money stock targets. What I want to concentrate on are the international implications of money stock targeting, an issue which is not discussed by Otmar Issing. More particularly I want to discuss, first, the problem of monetary targeting by Germany in the context of the EMS, and second monetary targeting in the future before the introduction of a common European currency.

1. MONETARY TARGETING IN THE EMS

The working of the EMS has been based on a division of responsibilities in which Germany targets its money stock and the other countries target their exchange rates with the DM. This division of labour has generally been interpreted as providing discipline in the system, thereby increasing the credibility of the EMS.

It can be shown, however, that this division of labour leads to unattractive outcomes when asymmetric shocks occur. In order to show this, I use a two-country model of the money markets. I call the two countries Germany and France respectively.

The model is presented graphically in Figure 1. The downward sloping lines are the money demand functions. The vertical lines are the money supplies. We assume that interest parity holds, i.e. that the fixity of the exchange rate commitment is fully credible. As a result, interest rates must be identical in the two countries. Germany (the country which targets its money stock) fixes its money stock at the level M_G^1. France pegs its exchange rate with the mark, which is identical in its effects as pegging the French interest rate to the German one. Note that in this EMS setup only one country can target its money stock.

153

J.A.H. de Beaufort Wijnholds, S.C.W. Eijffinger and L.H. Hoogduin (eds.), A Framework for Monetary Stability, pp. 153–156.
© 1994 *Kluwer Academic Publishers. Printed in the Netherlands.*

154

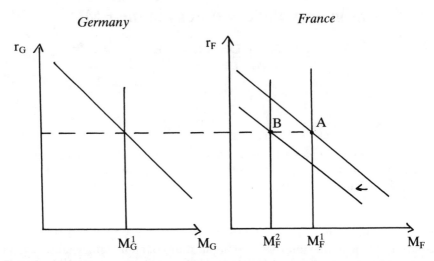

Figure 1.

The other country is forced to follow interest pegging policies. Suppose an asymmetric shock occurs in the goods market reducing output in France, while it remains constant in Germany. (Alternatively one could have an increase in income in Germany, and no change in France. All that matters is the asymmetry in the shock). We show the effects in Figure 1 by letting the money demand curve decline in France. Nothing happens in Germany. As a result, money market equilibrium in France moves from A to B. France is forced to let its money stock decline despite the fact that it experiences a recession. Note also that although Germany pegs its money stock, the total money stock in the system declines. Thus, the monetary arrangements in the EMS lead to volatility in the total money stock when the system is subject to asymmetric shocks. Monetary targeting in Germany does not translate into monetary targeting in the system as a whole. Under certain asymmetric shocks, the money stock may behave in a procyclical manner in the system as a whole, thereby intensifying the business cycle in the peripheral countries.

The paradox is that the monetarist inspired policy of targeting the money stock in Germany forces the other countries (as long as they peg to the German mark) to follow procyclical interest pegging policies.

What can be concluded from all this? A system in which one country targets its money stock and the others the exchange rate will lead to great tensions when asymmetric shocks occur. Large asymmetric shocks occurred during the nineties (in particular the German unification), and imposed undue monetary deflation on the peripheral countries. The tensions that

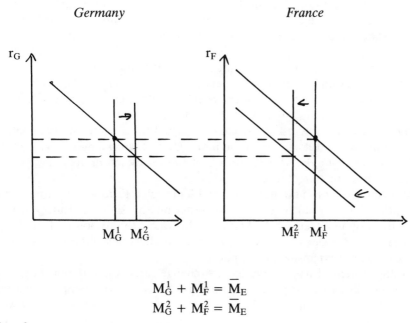

$$M_G^1 + M_F^1 = \overline{M}_E$$
$$M_G^2 + M_F^2 = \overline{M}_E$$

Figure 2.

arose from this were too large to maintain the credibility of the fixed exchange rates.

2. THE THIRD STAGE

The discussion by Issing of monetary targeting by the future ECB is based on the assumption that in the final stage of EMU, one currency will have displaced the national currencies, and that the ECB manages this currency. This allows Issing to transpose all the issues relating to monetary targeting that have been identified in individual countries like Germany or the US to the European level. In the final stage, Europe will be a blown-up version of Germany today, and we can discuss all the arguments as applying to the future ECB.

It is more likely, however, that the third stage will be an incomplete monetary union, i.e. one characterized by the continued existence of national currencies, albeit at "irrevocably" fixed exchange rates. This arrangement poses very different issues of monetary management than a system where only one common currency will be in existence.

Let me illustrate one of the problems of such an incomplete monetary union. Suppose the ECB sets a target for the European money stock. This will have to be translated into national targets since national currencies continue to exist. This will quickly lead to problems of under- and overshooting of the targets at the national level, if asymmetric shocks occur. We show this in Figure 2. The ECB sets a European money stock target at the level $\overline{M_E}$. The asymmetric shock, represented by the downward movement of the money demand curve in France, leads to a redistribution of the money stock from France to Germany. (Note also that the interest rate declines). Thus, European monetary targeting will require a lot of flexibility at the national level. Germany will have to be willing to accommodate for the shock in France by letting its money stock increase above the target level.

It is interesting to note that if we had had such a European Central Bank today the monetary policy response to the asymmetric shocks in Europe would have been quite different. As Figure 2 illustrates, the response of the ECB which targets its money stock, would have led to a lowering of the interest rates, and a monetary expansion in Germany.

In the system of irrevocably fixed exchange rates, the different targeting strategies will also affect the exchange markets, with possible implications for the credibility of the fixed exchange rates. These are issues that are not well understood today, but that merit attention because the "irrevocably" fixed exchange rate system is more likely to be the prevailing system, at least initially, during the final stage.

Dinner Speech:
To Cut or Not to Cut Interest Rates:
Some Remarks on the ERM

WIM F. DUISENBERG
President of De Nederlandsche Bank

1. INTRODUCTION

Ladies and gentlemen,

As announced in the conference programme, I am expected to deliver a separate course of tonight's menu. I intend to serve some food for thought. Indeed, I would like to draw your attention to the European exchange rate mechanism, or ERM for short, once more. This is an appropriate subject given the title of our conference, but also, after reading some of your articles in the journals, newspapers and magazines, I have the distinct feeling that the various people present here hold different opinions on current developments and on the future of the ERM. And since I obviously do not subscribe to all of your views, I take this opportunity to present my opinion on some of these matters.

I will start by examining the developments within the ERM since the summer of last year. I will then discuss the important subject of the significance of the level of short-term interest rates and stable exchange rates in Europe. Finally, I conclude with some remarks on the near future of the exchange rate mechanism and economic and monetary union.

2. THE DEVELOPMENTS SO FAR

As we all know, the ERM has been experiencing difficult times since the last five quarters or so. Practically all participating currencies came under pressure at one time or another. Eventually, we ended up with a situation that can probably be best described as a potential float. In reviewing the events, and with the benefit of hindsight, it is necessary to draw a clear distinction between the recent July-August tensions on the one hand and the other crises since the summer of 1992 on the other.

One may safely say that in the summer of 1992 the level of some exchange rates was out of line with economic fundamentals. Since the last general realignment in 1987, government deficits had deteriorated sharply and differences in inflation performance had caused shifts in countries' competitive

157

J.A.H. de Beaufort Wijnholds, S.C.W. Eijffinger and L.H. Hoogduin (eds.), A Framework for Monetary Stability, pp. 157–161.
© 1994 Kluwer Academic Publishers. Printed in the Netherlands.

positions. Markets and authorities, blinded as they were by the '1992-europhoria', did not pay sufficient attention to the accumulation of divergences. The eye-opening results of the Danish and French referenda on the Maastricht Treaty, however, caused some major changes in this respect. They tempered euro-optimism promptly and encouraged markets to examine economic fundamentals again. Soon, doubts were raised as to the feasibility of a European economic and monetary union, thereby undermining the credibility of the ERM and existing parities.

In the end, the pound sterling and the Italian lira left the mechanism on 'Black Wednesday' in September 1992. Devaluations of the Spanish, Portuguese and Irish currencies followed in the ensuing months. Even though these adjustments did not take place in an orderly manner, the resulting exchange rate levels could generally be justified, for they were more in line with underlying competitive positions again. This is in accordance with the rules of the game.

The story is clearly different for the recent July-August crisis, which did not involve overvalued exchange rates. This time the ERM was severely put to test by a combination of three factors.

Firstly, the credibility of the ERM had already been seriously undermined by previous currency devaluations and withdrawals, making the markets very nervous and sensitive to current economic and political developments and to any comment made by any official.

Secondly, cyclical conditions had deteriorated further, accompanied by rapidly rising budget deficits. The effect of the German unification is a major factor here. Initially it boosted ERM economies. Later it intensified the cyclical downturn, because of the tight monetary policy necessary to keep inflation under control.

Thirdly and in close connection with the other factors, markets doubted authorities' determination to keep interest rates high enough to defend existing parities. Political statements contributed to the perception that there was a difference of opinion among the main ERM participants on the appropriate stance of monetary policy.

It is interesting, but, as you may understand, not very helpful from my point of view, that a number of academic economists, mainly from across the Atlantic but some of them tonight at this side of the ocean, called on countries with weak economic activity and high unemployment to abandon their currencies' close link to the Dmark and to cut interest rates significantly in order to promote economic recovery.

Eventually, pressure became too strong at the end of last July when the Bundesbank, in contrast to market expectations, decided not to cut its discount rate, while other countries were not prepared to raise their interest rates in order to resist speculative pressure. After two turbulent days of heavy interventions on the exchange markets, it was decided to leave existing parities unchanged. However, the ERM was given more breathing space by widening the fluctuation margins to 15% for all countries with the exception of Germany, which came to an agreement with the Netherlands to maintain the original 2.25% margin.

In my view these decisions were rightly based on the observation that, given underlying economic fundamentals, there was no need to adjust ERM parities. The 15% fluctuation margins are therefore mainly to be thought of as a means to restore a two-way risk in the markets. They should certainly not be seen as providing extended room for manoeuvre for monetary policy, nor as a move towards a floating exchange rate regime. It is for this very reason that I described the current situation as a potential float.

3. THE IMPORTANCE OF SHORT-TERM INTEREST RATES AND STABLE EXCHANGE RATES IN AN INTERDEPENDENT EUROPE

Let me now proceed to the crucial question: what next? Some of you might respond: 'Give the weak European economies a boost, fight unemployment by prompt and aggressive interest rate cuts and tolerate concomitant and inevitable depreciations'. Others might even exclaim: 'The ERM is dead, long live the free float'. My opinion is a different one. Let me dwell on this subject somewhat more.

Right from its start, monetary stability was the ultimate goal of the exchange rate mechanism, and it still is of course. In Europe, monetary stability should not merely imply price stability, but certainly also exchange rate stability. This is a fact I cannot overemphasize, particularly not in tonight's audience. Sometimes, the crucial notion of exchange rate stability as an essential foundation of the functioning of the single internal European market is strongly underestimated. In the very open and highly interdependent continental European economies exchange rate volatility is much more damaging to trade and general economic developments than in, for instance, the United States, which, as a matter of fact, has a very diversified economy and yet one single currency.

Therefore, it is of the utmost importance to avoid strategies of competitive devaluation or depreciation, also under the current unfavourable economic circumstances. By definition, such policies, when pursued by many countries, cannot be successful in generating positive effects on the business cycle. They only result in increased uncertainty and inflationary pressures. For this reason, it is indispensable that European exchange rates be managed in one way or another.

The importance of interest rates, too, in continental Europe is considerably different from that in Anglo-Saxon countries. Here, long-term interest rates are far more important for investment and growth than short-term rates. In explaining this, for some perhaps surprising, phenomenon several reasons can be mentioned. The most import ones are: relatively low and stable rates of inflation and regulations promoting a long time-horizon.

In the short run, changes in short-term interest rates in continental Europe do not have a large impact on the disposable income of consumers and enterprises. Moreover, these effects, even limited as they are, show themselves only with a considerable time lag, and hence possibly far too late. The limited importance of short-term interest rates in the short term is remarkably often ignored by Anglo-Saxon commentators when they ask for continental European central banks to cut short-term interest rates aggressively in order to boost the economy. Hence, I attach great importance in stressing the fact that continental central bankers do not have the means to substantially influence the course of the business cycle. It is also not their primary task to do so. I add that European unemployment is mainly of a structural character. It is not a problem that can be solved by monetary policy. It is primarily the result of labour market rigidities. The solution is to attack these rigidities instead of forcefully pushing the wrong (monetary) policy button.

After the July–August crisis, all ERM countries continued to pursue cautious monetary policies. Since it is in difficult times that central banks show their true colours, one may safely say that recent experience has shown central banks' colours to be much more alike than many people expected. None of the ERM countries has tried to boost its economy by using its so-called increased room for manoeuvre to cut short-term interest rates aggressively. Interest rates were cut only gradually.

Central banks have several good reasons for a cautious approach. Firstly, relatively high interest rates are called for to induce reflows of capital in order to replenish stocks of international reserves. Secondly and more importantly, countries do not want to squander the substantial gains in terms of decreasing long-term interest rates which have been achieved over the last few months. In France, for instance, long-term interest rates have come down by half a percentage point since the July-August crisis. At approximately 6% they are now near Dutch and German long rates, below UK rates and at their lowest level since the middle of the 1960s. This level is a clear reflection of relatively favourable inflation prospects and should not hinder economic recovery.

Under such circumstances, attempts to force down short-term rates aggressively might very well stir up inflationary expectations again, thereby causing the opposite of what was intended: higher instead of lower long-term interest rates. It is precisely for this reason that European monetary policy must continue to be geared clearly and convincingly towards price stability. Official interest rate cuts must be made cautiously and gradually in line with this ultimate objective. This is particulary vital for the anchor country Germany, which is still suffering from a rate of inflation beyond the 0–2% target.

4. ERM's FUTURE

It is clear that stable exchange rates remain of great importance to European countries. It is, however, neither wise nor possible to return to narrow(er) margins in the ERM at short notice. It is beyond any doubt that such a return ought to be a well-considered and credible one. For it is very likely that each and every single move will be closely watched by the markets. Because of this, it is inadvisable, and probably even counterproductive, to establish an explicit timetable for the move towards narrow margins.

Furthermore, as far as the rules of the ERM are concerned, no major technical adaptations are necessary. The point is widely recognised and indeed convincingly made by two studies by the EC's Monetary Committee and Committee of Governors of the Central Banks. It was not so much flawed rules, but rather a non-adherence to the rules that contributed to the ERM problems.

Experience in the ERM has clearly shown that fixed and even semi-fixed exchange rates cannot be realised without a considerable degree of convergence, not only of economic fundamentals but also of policy views. In order to restore the credibility of the mechanism important efforts in both respects have to be made. Further progress in realising central bank autonomy will be helpful in rebuilding credibility. In addition, fiscal consolidation must be given absolute priority. At the moment no less than eleven EC countries run the risk of facing an excessive deficit in Maastricht Treaty terms. This will probably draw heavily on the excessive deficit procedure which will become applicable as from 1st January 1994.

A return to the 'old-style ERM' will presumably be easier in a period with better economic prospects, for in a more favourable cyclical environment monetary policy dilemmas are perceived less frequently than during the recent crisis. The political acceptance of a stability-oriented policy would benefit greatly from such a climate as well, just like the international willingness to cooperate and to have attention for each other's problems.

Finally, looking further ahead no doubt the establishment of an economic and monetary union in Europe remains worthwhile. The road to get there may be longer and more winding than expected. The EMU has to be a solid union. Therefore, it is of paramount importance that in the years ahead policies be directed towards achieving the convergence criteria and closing gaps in policy views. That is the best way to create an enduring framework for monetary stability in Europe.

Having said that, I again arrive at the theme of our conference. I hope and expect that like the first day, the second day will provide insightful and stimulating discussions. I wish you a pleasant night, an interesting second day of the conference and a good stay in Amsterdam, the monetary capital of Europe, . . . at least for these two days.

PART B

Friday October 22, 1993

SESSION IV: THE APPLICATION OF MONETARY POLICY
Rules versus Discretion in Monetary Policy

ANDREW D. CROCKETT

Bank of England

1. INTRODUCTION AND OVERVIEW

The debate about whether monetary policy decisions should be governed by rules or discretion has a long history, extending back at least as far as Henry Simons (1936). This debate has continued in the post-war period and still continues today. I will argue in this paper that the elements of a consensus are now beginning to emerge. Neither pure discretion, nor fixed adherence to an intermediate monetary target have proved satisfactory. In their place, several countries are moving toward a regime in which there is a clear target for the ultimate objective of monetary policy, together with a statement of the authorities' decision making practices that is as open and transparent as possible.

Looking at how thinking on this subject has evolved, it is possible to discern three broad phases in the approach to policy making in the postwar period. Up until about the late 1960s, it was taken for granted that formulating monetary policy required a substantial amount of judgmental discretion (although outside the United States, the exchange rate obligations of the Bretton Woods system acted as a constraint on policy). From the early 1970s until the 1980s, there was a growing emphasis on rules. This reflected both the persuasive theoretical and empirical work initiated by Friedman and Schwartz (1963), and dissatisfaction with the acceleration of inflation that had taken place under a more discretionary approach. Nearly all major industrial countries adopted targets for the growth of monetary aggregates, and most central banks intensified their attempts to find stable demand for money functions.

By the late 1980s, however, the pendulum began to swing away from rule-based policy regimes. The relationship between intermediate targets and ultimate objectives became more variable under the influence of financial liberalisation and innovation. It became clear that monetary authorities would have to approach the application of monetary targets with greater flexibility. One by one, countries that had adopted monetary targets as the basis for policy began to downgrade their importance, in the face of growing evidence of a loosening of the relationship between money and income. Even the Deutsche Bundesbank, which retains a monetary growth target as the centrepiece of

165

J.A.H. de Beaufort Wijnholds, S.C.W. Eijffinger and L.H. Hoogduin (eds.), A Framework for Monetary Stability, pp. 165–184.
© 1994 *Kluwer Academic Publishers. Printed in the Netherlands.*

its policy, has countenanced substantial departures from its announced objectives.

In recent years, therefore, most central banks have recognised the need for a return to greater discretion in the use of monetary instruments. But this has not been simply a reversion to the practice of the earlier post-war period. The lessons that have been painfully learned about the importance of credibility and time consistency of policies have taught us to avoid this. Rather the aim has been to use policy commitments and institutional arrangements to strengthen the credibility of the ultimate objective of policy (price stability), and at the same time to improve the information available to market participants about the systematic factors guiding the use of policy instruments.

The present paper begins with a definition of terms. This is particularly necessary in a subject where the same expression can be used to mean different things by different authors. Central banks use policy *instruments* to pursue ultimate policy *objectives*. Along the way, they are concerned with *intermediate variables, which are part of the policy transmission process, as well as with indicator variables* which may provide information about the impact of policy, without themselves being part of the transmission mechanism. It is important to be clear, as I shall try to demonstrate, which variables are to be subject to rules, and which to discretion, as well as what precisely is meant by the terms "rules" and "discretion".

After dealing with terminological issues, the paper considers the theoretical case for the use of rules as against the continuous exercise of judgment. It then goes on to consider how this case has worked in practice, and how experience has caused central banks to change the focus of the policy rules they use.

I end up with a discussion of the inflation targeting framework now used in the United Kingdom. I see this as just one among several examples of where the debate on rules versus discretion stands at the present time. At the risk of giving away the conclusion, I see the current state of debate as follows: there are no intermediate variables (in the sense I will define) whose relationship to ultimate objectives is reliable enough to permit them to be used as rules for monetary policy. But markets do require clear guidelines on the *objectives* of the policy authorities, as well as on the likely response of the authorities in the face of disturbances affecting the system. Hence, it is appropriate for the authorities to announce their medium-term policy objectives, and to be as transparent as possible about how they will approach them.

2. Objectives, Targets, Instruments and Indicators

The *objectives* of economic policy can be defined as those which have relevance for welfare in their own right. These include full employment, economic growth, price stability and the equitable distribution of income. For monetary policy, the central objective must be the achievement and maintenance of price stability. This is not because price stability is more important than other objectives of economic policy. But it is the one objective that is within the power of monetary policy to achieve. And it is generally accepted that price stability not only contributes to social equity, but is central to the goal of improving resource allocation and strengthening the basis of economic growth.

It used to be believed that there was a trade-off between price stability and economic growth, at least over a certain range (Phillips, 1958). If this were true, there would obviously be an important element of political choice (or discretion) in the setting of monetary policy. Policy makers would have to decide how much price stability they were prepared to forgo to increase economic growth or how much growth they were prepared to forgo to achieve price stability.

There is now general agreement that the "Phillips curve" is vertical in the long-run (Brunner and Meltzer, 1976). There is therefore nothing to be gained in having a higher long-run rate of inflation. Indeed, there is probably quite a bit to be lost, since a higher *level* of inflation is likely to be associated with greater variability and uncertainty in the inflation rate. Greater uncertainty about future price levels will reduce the level and diminish the efficiency of investment, thus impairing growth.

The same does not apply in quite the same way to the short-run, however. There probably is a short-run trade off between inflation and output. When an economy is hit by an inflationary or deflationary disturbance, the decision of *how quickly* to return to the trend rate of price increase does have implications for the level of output in the transition period. It is therefore appropriate to define the objectives of monetary policy to include not just the achievement of price stability in the medium term, but the smooth adjustment to price disturbances in the short term.

The *instruments* of monetary policy are those variables that are *directly* under the control of the monetary authorities. They can be divided into those that affect *quantities* of financial assets and those that affect *prices*. More precisely, the authorities can control the *supply* of base money in the system (through open market operations); banks' *demand* for base money (through changes in reserve requirements) or the *price* of base money (through setting the interest rate at which they are prepared to provide reserve assets). None of these policy instruments is directly related to economic welfare. The purpose of controlling them is simply to influence other variables which are more directly related to welfare.

In a non-stochastic system, setting interest rates would be the dual of fixing quantities. In practice, however, there are differences. Fixing the quantity of base money is likely to lead to fluctuations in price (interest rates) in response to swings in demand. Fixing interest rates means that the quantity of base money becomes endogenous.

In practice, all central banks use control of short-term interest rates as their day-to-day operating instrument. This is because interest rates are part of the channel of transmission of monetary policy and no useful purpose is served by wide fluctuations in interest rates. The only exception is when the central bank is attempting for demonstration purposes to bring home the need to tackle the root cause of inflation. This motivation probably lay behind the Federal Reserve's willingness to use a more quantitative monetary policy instrument in the 1979–82 period.

The fact that interest rates are the proximate instrument of monetary policy for most central banks does not mean that quantities do not play a role. Movements in quantities can provide the trigger for discretionary changes in interest rates. But it is the interest rate that is nearly always the proximate instrument on which central banks act.

Intermediate variables are those which the monetary authorities may attempt to target because of their presumed relationship with the ultimate objectives of monetary policy. Like the immediate instruments of policy, they do not have direct significance for economic welfare. Because, however, they are further along the channel of transmission, it may be convenient to direct policy to controlling them.

The most common example of an intermediate variable is some definition of the money or credit stock. To the extent that growth in a monetary aggregate is stably related to the ultimate objective of monetary policy (the steady growth of the nominal value of output) and to the extent that it is more feasible to control the money stock than nominal output, it makes sense to direct policy instruments towards the achievement of an intermediate variable.

Most monetary aggregates cannot, of course, be directly or precisely controlled. But if the monetary authorities are prepared to vary their policy instruments in order to achieve a given value of the monetary aggregate, there is no doubt that they can achieve such control over a period beyond the very short term.

It is such an objective that is usually meant by a rules-based policy approach. In other words "rules" are generally taken to require the authorities to use the instruments of monetary policy to achieve a given predetermined path for an intermediate variable (usually a monetary aggregate). I will return to this issue in more detail later.

Indicator variables can be defined as those that have information value about the impact of instruments on policy outcomes, but are not themselves an object of control. In fact, the whole range of economic quantities have a bearing on monetary policy decisions. They can include variables that, in another context, may be viewed as an intermediate target. For example, the growth rate of the money stock can be regarded as an object to be controlled. It can also be regarded as one indicator (among others) of the potential strength of demand in the economy. This underlines an important point: just because a monetary variable is not used as an object of control does not mean that it does not play an important role in evaluating the stance of monetary policy.

Other indicator variables are those that convey information about the future evolution of the economy, and the balance between recessionary and inflationary forces. They include all variables relating to the current and prospective level of real economic activity (GDP growth, industrial production, retail sales, consumer and business spending surveys, etc). They also include cost and price indicators (wages, import costs, consumer and producer price indices), and expectational indices, including expectations derived from financial variables such as the shape of the yield curve.

The distinction between whether variables are to be treated as indicators or intermediate targets is crucial to the distinction between rules and discretion. However, the distinction between rules and discretion is not straightforward, and deserves to be discussed further.

The use of discretion in monetary policy is clearly not intended to imply randomness in decision-making. A discretionary policy action usually reflects a systematic response by policy authorities, taken in the light of their objectives, and their perceptions as to how the economy will respond to particular economic stimuli. To quote from Bryant et al. (1993): "Any systematic procedure for making decisions can in principle be described by its originators in a manner that permits its replication and implementation by others. With an elastic stretching of conventional language, any systematic procedure, no matter how complex, could thus in some broad sense be construed as a set of decision rules".

By the same token, even a straightforward rule, such as a monetary target, involves discretion. The authorities have to decide which variable to target, the quantitative value for the target, when to change it, and ultimately whether or not to abandon the rule.

But if there is no absolute distinction between rules and discretion, there are certainly important differences between points on the continuum. Most observers can distinguish instinctively between a policy regime that can be classified as "rule-based" and one that relies on judgmental discretion. A rule-based system is normally one in which:

a. There is a target for a single intermediate variable (in the sense defined above).

b. The numerical value of this target is revised at infrequent intervals (say annually).

c. The setting of monetary policy instruments is adjusted primarily in order to achieve the target value of the intermediate variable.

When I come to discuss the operating history of different policy regimes later in this paper, I will use the foregoing criteria as the basis for distinguishing rule-based and discretionary regimes. It has to be recognised, of course, that other criteria are possible. For example, a "rule" could be expressed in terms of the exchange rate, as was done under the Bretton Woods system or in the European Exchange Rate Mechanism. Although an exchange rate commitment is undoubtedly a "rule", in the conventional use of the word, it raises a rather different set of issues than those usually covered in the "rules-versus-discretion" literature, and will not be pursued further here.

It is also possible to devise "rules" with more or less complex feedback mechanisms (Taylor, 1993; Meltzer, 1990). To the extent that such rules embody conditional responses, which presumably could be altered periodically (just as the numerical values of more simple rules can be changed), it becomes hard to distinguish them from discretion.

3. Arguments for Discretion and Rules

It was argued above that one traditional argument for discretion cannot be accepted. There is no medium-term trade-off between price stability and economic growth. Consequently, there is no reason for the authorities to make a deliberate choice between two objectives. Price stability is the best environment for the achievement of other economic goals.

But there are at least three other arguments for allowing the monetary authorities discretion in the formulation and implementation of economic policy.

First, economies are subject to both supply shocks and demand shocks. The appropriate monetary policy response will be quite different in the two cases. Consider, for example, an incipient increase in demand that, with unchanged interest rates, would lead to an increase in the money stock and prices. In such circumstances, it would be appropriate to limit the increase in the money stock by allowing interest rates to rise and choke off the excess demand. Imagine, however, that a rise in the price of imports causes an increase in the demand for credit. In such circumstances, allowing interest rates to rise would cause a reduction in domestic economic activity. As Poole (1970) has shown, the different disturbances affecting the economy can be thought of as movements in the IS and LM curves respectively. Provided the authorities can identify the nature of different shocks, they will be able to improve welfare by exercising discretion in how they respond to them.

A *second* argument for discretion lies in the fact that the speed with which an economy returns to price stability following an inflationary or deflationary shock has implications for output and employment. The recent inflationary impetus in Germany following unification is a case in point. It would have been possible, in principle, for the Bundesbank to have restored price stability very quickly. The cost would have been even higher interest rates than actually resulted, followed by a sharper downturn in activity. The use of discretion enabled the Bundesbank to tolerate some overshooting of the monetary targets, to allow the return to price stability to take place in a more orderly manner.

A *third* argument for discretion is that the structure of the economy is changing through time in ways that cannot easily be predicted in advance. The relationship between intermediate variables and the ultimate objectives of policy can be affected by technical developments. For example, the desire of the private sector to hold money balances is influenced by regulatory changes and the development of new financial instruments. These can either make money balances more attractive (say by providing for the payment of interest on previously non-interest bearing assets), thus reducing velocity; or they may make money relatively less attractive (say by investing non-money assets with payment attributes), thus lowering the velocity of circulation.

If velocity trends are subject to relatively unpredictable shifts, it will be desirable for the monetary authorities to take a variety of indicators into account in deciding the setting of monetary policy.

The case for rules was set out by Friedman (1953) in terms of the costs of avoiding gross errors of policy. Those who, like Friedman, favour rules, do not dispute that the application of discretion can, in principle, improve on the outcome produced by an inflexible rule. However, they argue that with rules (strictly, with the *right* rules), errors are self limiting, whereas with discretion policy mistakes may grow to major proportions. This concern probably springs from the monetarists' interpretation of the causes of the Great Depression (Friedman, 1963).

There are several strands of thought behind the advocacy of rules. One is the avowedly libertarian principle, that in a democracy, as much decision-making discretion as possible should be removed from individuals and vested in laws or rules. Leaving this on one side, perhaps the most important economic argument for rules is that there is a fundamentally stable relationship between an intermediate variable (a monetary aggregate) and the ultimate objective of monetary policy (the growth of nominal income). The benefits of discretion are therefore small, since it is not possible to improve much on the outcome generated by adopting a stable money growth target. On the other hand, so the argument goes, the costs of discretion are potentially large. The implicit argument is that the "wrong" policy instrument is selected and adhered to for too long. Typically, what monetarists fear is that a nominal interest rate objective may be selected and retained even when it is resulting in a cumulative contraction or expansion in the quantity of credit.

A subsidiary argument for rules is that financial markets operate most efficiently in the presence of certainty. If, in addition to the inherent uncertainties generated by outside economic shocks, there is uncertainty about the authorities' policy response, the difficulties faced by markets will be compounded. This argument has been formalised in the literature on the time-consistency problem and the value of rules that "pre-commit" the authorities to a particular course of action (Kydland and Prescott, 1977).

It will be seen that the arguments in favour of rules are based more on the *quality* of discretionary action, than on discretion per se. If the authorities are capable of distinguishing between "good" and "bad" policy responses, then in principle discretion ought to improve welfare by broadening the available choice set. It remains possible to select the policy response indicated by a "rule"; but it is also possible to depart from it if the rule is destabilising. Similarly, even if markets do not know exactly how the authorities will respond to outside shocks, the knowledge that they would act so as to dampen them should serve to reduce aggregate uncertainty.

To some extent, therefore, the argument for rules versus discretion is an empirical one. In the absence of binding rules, are central banks prone to make errors that could be avoided by prescribing rules?

It can be argued that discretionary monetary policy is subject to two systematic sources of adverse bias: "too little, too late", and a greater willingness to lower interest rates than to raise them (Kohn, 1993). It is not hard to see why such biases might exist. If there are costs to making discretionary changes in monetary policy, then policy-makers will be tempted to wait for conclusive evidence of the need to change policy before undertaking an action. These costs need not necessarily be real economic costs; they could be the psychological costs of abandoning a previous conviction about how the economy was developing; or the "image" costs of being seen to chop and change decisions.

Similarly, it is easy to see why policy makers may be more willing to make easy and popular decisions (lowering interest rates) than to make ones which are more likely to lead to public opprobrium (raising rates). This is, of course, especially the case when central banks are not independent, and when governments are aware that interest rate decisions will affect their electoral fortunes. But even independent central banks cannot be oblivious to public opinion. Apart from the natural human temptation to prefer bringing good news to bad, independence can be endangered if central banks ignore deeply held public preferences.

Rule-based policy regimes can help overcome these temptations. The rules themselves provide a vehicle for educating public opinion to the longer-run relationship between money and prices. And the need to adhere to a rule provides valuable "cover" for unpopular decisions.

4. RULES AND DISCRETION IN PRACTICE

The introduction to this paper identified three phases of the post-war approach to monetary policy making. Discretion predominated until the late sixties. The 1970s and early 1980s saw an attempt to identify and follow rules. And the most recent period has seen a disillusionment with rules and a return to discretion. In this section, I will try to show that this latest development represents a development crystallisation of the lessons of earlier experience, not simply a return to former practice.

Since much of the *early postwar period* (say until the late 1960s) was under the gold exchange standard, the scope for discretionary monetary policy was limited. But it was by no means absent. For the anchor country (the United States), the exchange rate was not much of a constraint on monetary policy, and the obligation to maintain convertibility of the dollar into gold was of notional significance only for much of the period. Even for the other countries in the system, there was considerable freedom for an independent monetary policy, given the existence of exchange controls and limited capital mobility.

For various reasons, most central banks considered it appropriate to operate monetary policy through the discretionary adjustment of interest rates in response to perceived changes in aggregate demand conditions. In the *first* place, monetary policy was seen as the junior partner in aggregate demand policy, and the objective of macroeconomic policy was seen as maintaining full employment. *Second*, there was no body of empirical evidence suggesting a stable relationship between money and income. Even if one had been found, it would probably have been thought due to the accommodation of the money stock to demand, rather than indicating an independent causal role for monetary control. A *third* reason was the importance accorded to funding the government's borrowing requirement as cheaply as possible. This was a particularly important motivation in the United Kingdom, as reflected in, for example, the Radcliffe report (1959).

The shift towards rule-based approaches that took place in the 1970s can likewise be attributed to several factors. Perhaps the most persuasive intellectually was the work of Friedman and Schwartz and their followers. This work seemed to show that there was a stable, lagged relationship in the United States between changes in the rate of growth of broad money (M2), and changes in nominal income. A key conclusion was that monetary policy mistakes had been largely responsible for the length and severity of the Great Depression. Subsequent studies showed that it was possible to detect a statistically significant relationship between money and income over a wide range of countries and time periods.

These findings did not, of themselves, produce a rapid shift in the basis for formulating and implementing monetary policy. But interest in monetary rules grew as inflation surged in the wake of the first oil shock. Indeed, the oil shock itself could plausibly be attributed to the failure to control creeping inflation over the previous two decades (Fried and Schultze, 1975).

At the same time, the discrediting of the long-run Phillips curve analysis persuaded most policy makers that there were no benefits to allowing the inflation rate to ratchet upwards. One after another, the major industrial countries adopted monetary targets as a guide to policy making, if not as its central feature.

Germany began using targets for Central Bank Money in 1975, the United States followed suit in 1976, and Japan adopted targets (strictly "forecasts") for M2 in 1978 (with CDs being added in 1979). Table 1 shows the dates at which various countries adopted targets, and the aggregates to which they applied. In general, central banks used targets for the money stock rather than the stock of liabilities under the direct control of the central bank (central bank money). This is presumably because it is the broader definition of money that is theoretically related to income, and most central banks felt that they could use the instruments at their command to achieve the desired result for monetary growth. An exception was Germany, which targeted central bank money (reserves plus currency in circulation) from 1975 to 1989, only moving to an M3 target at the latter date. The US was also an exception for three years from 1979, using a bank reserves target to reinforce the public perception of the shift to a determined anti-inflationary policy.

Table 1. Monetary targeting by the G7.

Country	Target	Date
Germany	Central Bank Money	1975
Canada	M1	1975
USA	M1	1976
France	M2	1977
Japan	M2 + CDs	1978*
UK	M3	1979
Italy	M2	1984

*CDs were added in 1979.

Judged by the anti-inflationary results, the period of monetary targeting was very successful. All countries with intermediate monetary targets experienced a sustained disinflation following the peak of price increases in the early 1980s. (See Figure 1).

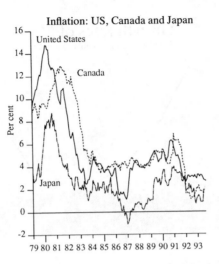

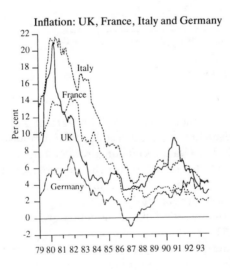

Figure 1.

However, it is not clear that the pursuit of intermediate policy targets was behind this success, as opposed to a more general willingness to pay the price of bringing down inflation. Indeed most countries missed their monetary targets by a considerable margin, and did not always move quickly to come back within them. The United Kingdom is a case in point. Figure 2 shows that monetary growth in the United Kingdom was frequently outside its target range, and that such over-shooting was generally absorbed into subsequent targets (base drift):

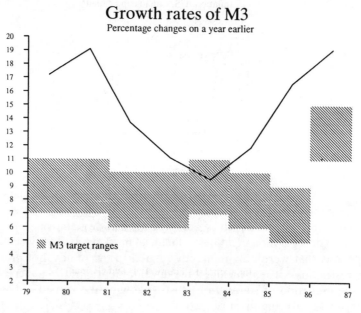

Growth rates of M3
Percentage changes on a year earlier

Fiscal years except 1979.

Figure 2.

Since the *late 1980s* there has been a downgrading of monetary rules as a guide to policy. Canada has already reduced the emphasis given to monetary aggregates in 1982. The United Kingdom dropped broad money targets in 1986 and continued to monitor only M0 (which is approximately equal to currency in circulation and therefore not an intermediate variable in the sense employed above). Japan reduced the emphasis given to monetary aggregates in 1992. The United States informally redesignated monetary growth targets as "monitoring ranges" during 1993.

The United States has a complex history of monetary targeting. Since the experiment with base money control was ended in 1982, the authorities have been gradually de-emphasizing monetary aggregates (Friedman, 1993). Only in 1993, however, did Chairman Greenspan state that M2 had been "downgraded as a reliable indicator of financial conditions in the economy, and no single variable has been identified to take its place".

To some extent, the downgrading of monetary targets, and the avowed shift towards greater discretion in monetary policy making, may reflect earlier successes in controlling inflation. With prices increasing at 5 percent or less in most countries (despite the upward blip in 1988–89) inflation had receded as a central element of concern. Of more significance, however, was the further weakening in relationships between intermediate variables and ultimate objectives.

In many countries, the trend of velocity changed abruptly and unpredictably (Figure 3). In the United Kingdom, for example, the growth of broad money had been slower than that of GDP for most of the 1960s and 1970s. Velocity had therefore declined gently. A continuation of the decline in velocity was incorporated in the monetary targets adopted by the Conservative government elected in 1979. In the event, however, broad money growth turned out to be much more rapid than intended, without adversely affecting the disinflationary process. Indeed, inflation receded more rapidly than had been envisaged or planned. (See Figure 3.)

The reasons for this experience in the United Kingdom are almost certainly to be found in the far-reaching economic liberalisation and deregulation that took place in the 1980s, and was particularly marked in the financial sector. To some extent, this was the result of policy decisions: the removal of exchange controls, and deregulation in domestic financial markets. It also owed much to developments that were only indirectly related to the removal of previously existing restrictions. These included the development of new financial instruments, the reduction of transactions costs following the spread of computer technology, the growing institutionalisation of savings channels, and the securitisation of investment media.

Similar developments have affected most countries in greater or lesser degree. They have had the effect of causing changes in patterns of intermediation, and therefore shifts in the relationship between particular financial aggregates and real variables. Those countries where financial liberalisation has proceeded furthest (the United States and United Kingdom) have experienced the largest disturbance to demand for money relationships. Those that have had less far-reaching change (eg Germany) have continued to place reliance on money demand relationships. Even in Germany, however, judgmental departures from monetary target have proved increasingly necessary. If more far-reaching changes in financial structure are allowed to take place, there is every reason to suspect that further unpredictable shifts in monetary velocity may come about.

Is this phenomenon (that of unpredictably shifting velocity) simply a characteristic of transition? In other words, when the process of financial deregulation and innovation has settled down, will stability in underlying money demand relationship reassert itself? This is certainly possible, though one

178

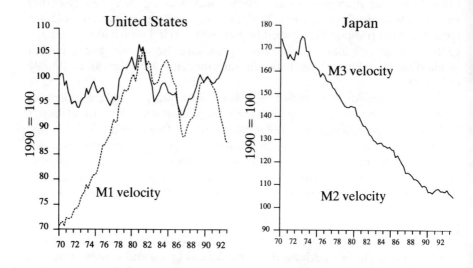

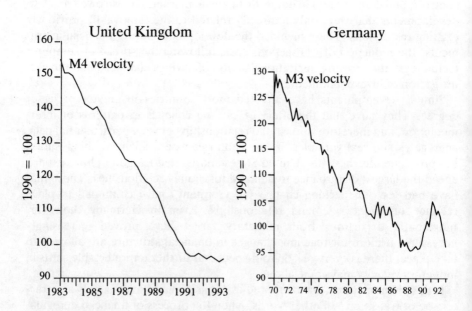

Figure 3. Money velocity.

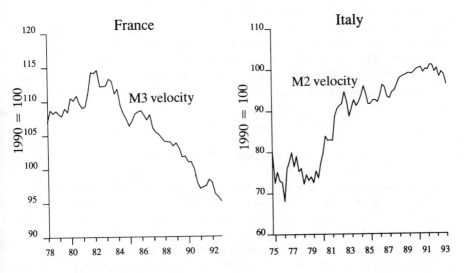

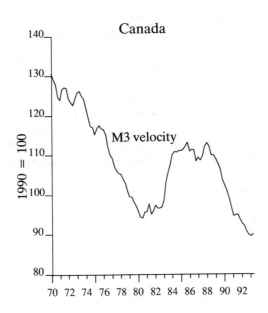

Figure 3. (cont.)

should not underestimate the capacity for further dynamic change, in capital markets and payments practices. Some observers (eg Sanford, 1993) foresee an accelerating process of change within the financial system, leading to further concentration in the banking system as we know it (and even to the eventual phasing out of money as an asset). Sanford's view of the world is seen by some to be inspired by "Star Trek". But even before our time comes to say "Beam me up, Scotty", the changes still in store for the financial system make it unwise to rely on rules that depend on stable relationships between money and income.

5. Towards a synthesis

The lessons of past experience of monetary policy are, broadly speaking, two.
- Without clearly expressed objectives for the conduct of monetary policy, markets are left uncertain about how the authorities will react, and the authorities themselves are exposed to the temptation to act in ways which cause inflation to be higher and more variable than necessary.
- There is no single intermediate variable which provides a satisfactory anchor for stability oriented policy.

These two "stylised facts" have prompted the search for a different framework for monetary policy, one that can combine the disciplinary benefits of rules, with the ability to take into account a suitably wide variety of economic indicators.

One alternative is of course to target monetary policy on the exchange rate. This can have important advantages, not least in the clarity of the objective. There are two reasons, however, why it cannot be a complete statement of monetary policy. *First*, it simply transfers the task of formulating monetary policy to another authority. The pegging country can define its policy in terms of exchange rate peg; but the anchor country still has to choose a regime of rules or discretion, and to set policies within it. *Second*, unless the pegging country is small and closely integrated with the anchor country, its domestic monetary policy requirements will inevitably clash occasionally with those of its partner. It was such a clash that eventually provoked the capital flows that made it impossible to retain ERM margins.

With the currencies of most major industrial countries floating freely, or within very wide bands, how should monetary policy be conducted?

Several countries have chosen to redefine the targets of monetary policy in terms of the ultimate objective of inflation, instead of some intermediate value, such as the monetary growth rate. This is intended to provide an element of guidance to markets, as well as added self-discipline on the monetary authorities.

Among countries that have adopted inflation targets as a centrepiece of their monetary policy are Canada, New Zealand, Sweden, Finland and the United Kingdom. In the remainder of this paper, I will attempt to describe the key features of the approach used in the United Kingdom, and how it relates to the ongoing debate about rules versus discretion.

Our starting point is the uncontroversial proposition that economies will function best, and employment and growth will be maximised when prices are reasonably stable, and can be relied on to remain so. A second proposition is that sustained inflation is an essentially monetary phenomenon, in the sense that inflationary pressures will only show up in a sustained rise in the price level if they are validated by monetary policy.

From these propositions comes the conclusion that the authorities should set a clear objective for price stability, together with a firm commitment to use the instruments of monetary policy to achieve it. There are two key elements to the choice of an inflation target: which *measure* of inflation should be used?; and what should the *target level* (or range) be?

The choice of a publicly announced target for inflation involves a trade-off between conceptual purity, and presentational familiarity. The ideal index would be one which captured only domestically generated increases in costs. This would measure best the magnitude that was under the influence of domestic monetary policy. For this purpose, the GDP deflator (at factor cost) might be the most suitable index. It excludes terms of trade effects and the contribution of indirect taxes. But the factor cost deflator suffers from practical drawbacks. It is available only with a significant lag. It is subject to subsequent revision. It is not free of "noise" which generates reversible fluctuation in measured inflation (Bank of England , Inflation Report, May 1993). Perhaps most significant, it does not have the degree of public familiarity to make it a useful tool in influencing labour market contracts.

The retail price index (RPI) is a much more familiar measure, but contains elements which are not directly related to underlying inflation. These include import prices and indirect taxes. Most importantly, however, the RPI in the United Kingdom includes the interest costs of owner-occupied housing. This severely distorts the underlying inflation picture at times of changing interest rates. Measures introduced to control inflation (a tightening of monetary policy) have the initial effect of causing a sharp increase in measured inflation.

The British Government has chosen to set its inflation objective in terms of the measurement increase in the Retail Price Index, *excluding* Mortgage Interest Payments (RPIX) (Lamont, 1992). Over time, it may be desirable to focus on a more sophisticated measure of internally generated price pressures; or at least to take explicit account of the extent to which external factors are pushing RPIX up or down when judging how to respond as measured inflation departs from the target.

The British government has also decided to express its inflation target in the form of a *range* rather than a fixed point. Although this has been criticised by some, in my view a range is more credible than a fixed point. Since a fixed target will never be hit (except briefly and accidentally) it provides little information about what kind of response the authorities will make when departures from the target occur. A range, on the other hand, reflects an intention to take action to prevent RPIX from moving outside the designated range.

The range has been set at 1–4 percent for the remainder of the present Parliament (ie probably until about 1996 or 1997). It is the intention to bring inflation into the lower half of the range by the latter part of this period. These targets are slightly higher than the rate of 0–2 percent inflation that, after allowing for quality improvements, is usually considered consistent with longer-term price stability. This reflects the fact that there is already a certain amount of inflation in the pipeline following the depreciation of sterling and increases in indirect taxation. The rapid elimination of inflation involves costs that could be avoided by the gradual convergence to price stability that is planned.

The setting of an inflation target cannot be a complete definition of monetary policy in itself. It needs to be complemented by a strategy of how monetary policy instruments will be set in order to achieve the stated objective of policy. Such a strategy is needed, both to guide the formulation of policy, and to provide appropriate guidance to market participants on how the authorities are likely to react. The strategy also needs to be stated publicly and embedded in an appropriate institutional framework. This is necessary to persuade private market participants that the authorities will not be tempted into time-inconsistent behaviour (ie, stating intentions now that they will have an incentive to abandon later).

The instrument of monetary policy in the United Kingdom is the level of short-term interest rates. It is convenient to view the indicator to which this instrument responds as the projected level of inflation 1–2 years ahead. Future rather than current inflation is used because the lag between changes in monetary policy and their impact on inflation is almost certainly quite substantial.

This framework calls for two types of judgment. *First*, how current trends in the determinants of inflation are likely to affect the actual rate of price increase. *Second*, how interest rate changes are likely to modify the projected outcome. Neither of these responses are capable of quantification with a great deal of confidence. Nevertheless, it is possible to use empirical evidence to make an estimate of the relevant effects.

Taking the inflation projection first, a starting point is the *current* underlying rate of inflation. This will be subject to upward or downward pressure as a result of both the *level* and *rate of change* of the output gap.

These may be thought of as demand-side influences on inflation. Supply-side influences will be reflected in variables such as the rate of increase of input prices (which is heavily dependent on commodity price trends and the exchange rate) and the growth of unit labour costs. The authorities' perceptions about inflation prospects derived from these measures can be cross-checked against private expectations. These are expressed in survey evidence, and can also be inferred from yields on financial assets.

When it appears that there is a danger of inflation accelerating to the top of the target range, it will be appropriate to tighten monetary conditions through raising interest rates. The impact of changes in monetary conditions on future inflation is not easy to estimate. Some indication of the potential impact on future price changes can be derived from looking at the effect of interest rate movements on the exchange rate and asset prices. But it will always be difficult to judge when a given degree of tightening of policy is sufficient, given the lags at work.

A final element in the UK approach to inflation targeting is the openness with which the authorities reaction function is expressed. The Treasury has undertaken to publish monthly an interpretative assessment of the various information variables that are taken into account in monthly policy reviews. And the Bank of England publishes a quarterly *Inflation Report* (Bank of England 1993), providing analysis of how the various determinants of inflation interact to produce a given expected path for the price level.

The purpose of the Inflation Report can be seen as threefold:
1. To convey to markets a clearer understanding of the authorities' reaction function (the goal of improving the *transparency of policy*).
2. To permit informed outsiders (especially in the press and academia) to make a contribution to improving the basis of policy making (the goal of improving the *efficiency of policy*).
3. To provide an external discipline, by making it more difficult for the authorities to ignore indicators calling for policy changes (the goal of improving the *consistency of policy*).

I have described the British approach to inflation targeting at some length, because I believe it is one expression of a new consensus on the appropriate balance between rules and discretion in the formulation of monetary policy. Rules are appropriate for the *ultimate objectives* of policy, because there is nothing to be gained by varying these objectives, or by concealing them from the public. And the more publicly the rules are stated, the more difficult it will be for the monetary authorities to go back on them. This should help credibility. Discretion is appropriate in the *setting of policy instruments*, because the economic circumstances to which the authorities must respond are too varied to be captured in simple rules. Lastly, clarity of institutional responsibility is of central importance in defining, and preserving, the appropriate frontier between rules and discretion.

184

REFERENCES

Bank of England, "Inflation Report", various issues.

Brunner, Karl and Allan Meltzer (1976), *"The Phillips Curve & Labor Markets"* North Holland Publishing Company.

Bryant, Ralph C, Peter Hooper and Catherine L Mann (1993), *"Evaluating Policy Regimes and Analytical Models"*, The Brookings Institution.

Fried, Edward R and Charles L Schultze (eds.) (1975), *"Higher Oil Prices and the World Economy: The Adjustment Problem"* (The Brookings Institution, Washington DC).

Friedman, Benjamin M (1993), "Ongoing Change in the US Financial Markets: Implications for the Conduct of Monetary Policy". Paper presented to a symposium on *"Changing Capital Markets: Implications for Monetary Policy"* sponsored by the Federal Reserve Bank of Kansas City, Jackson Hole, Wyoming, August 19–21.

Friedman, Milton (1953), "The Effects of Full-Employment Policy on Economic Stability: A Formal Analysis" in M. Friedman (ed.) *Essays in Positive Economics*, University of Chicago Press, 117–132.

Friedman, Milton and Anna J Schwartz (1963), *A Monetary History of the United States, 1867–1960*, Princeton University Press.

Kohn, Donald, Comments on paper presented by Benjamin M Friedman (see above).

Kydland, Finn E. and Edward C. Prescott (1977) "Rules Rather than Discretion: The Inconsistency of Optimal Plans", *Journal of Political Economy* June.

Lamont, Norman (1992), Letter of 8 October 1992 from the Chancellor of the Exchequer to John Watts, MP, Chairman of the Treasury and Civil Service Committee.

Meltzer, Allan H (1990), "The Federal Reserve at Seventy-Five" in Zvi Eckstein (ed), *Aspects of Central Bank Policy Making* Springer Verlag, Berlin.

Phillips, A W (1958), "The Relation between Unemployment and the Rate of Change of Money Wage Rates in the UK, 1861–1957", *Economica* Nov.

Poole, William (1970), "Optimal Choice of Monetary Policy Instruments in a Simple Stochastic Macro Model", *Quarterly Journal of Economics* (Volume LXXXIV).

Radcliffe Report (1959), Committee on the Working of the Monetary System, (CMND 827).

Sanford, Charles (1993), "Financial Markets in 2020" Luncheon address to Symposium in *"Changing Capital Markets, Implications for Monetary Policy"*, sponsored by the Federal Reserve Bank of Kansas City, Jackson Hole, Wyoming, 20 August 1993.

Simons, Henry C (1936), "Rules versus Authorities in Monetary Policy", *Journal of Political Economy* (Volume 44, 1–30).

Taylor, John B (1993), "Discretion versus Policy Rules in Practice", *Carnegie Rochester Conference Series on Public Policy*, 39.

The Role of Monetary Policy in IMF Programs

MANUEL GUITIÁN*

International Monetary Fund

> ". . . development of a new . . . approach to the
> theory of the international monetary system . . . I
> believe . . . that its intellectual lineage can be traced
> back, via Mundell's period of service in the . . . Inter-
> national Monetary Fund under J. J. Polak, to the . . .
> work on monetary equilibrium of the Dutch economist
> J. G. Koopmans and the subsequent development by
> M. W. Holtrop and the Netherlands Bank . . . ."
>
> Harry G. Johnson
>
> *(Inflation and the Monetarist Controversy, 1972)*

1. INTRODUCTION

The main purpose of the International Monetary Fund has been the promotion of economic and financial cooperation among its member countries. In order to fulfill this purpose, the Fund has come to play a central role in the international monetary scene, a role that includes the provision of financial assistance to members facing actual or potential balance of payments difficulties in support of their efforts to overcome them. The responsibilities of the Fund as a source of financial assistance are laid out in the Articles of Agreement of the institution. This basic document prescribes *inter alia* that the Fund will help in shortening the duration and lessening the degree of imbalance in members' balance of payments in the context of a liberal multilateral payments system characterized by the absence of exchange restrictions and the prevalence of exchange stability. To this end, the Fund has stood ready to make its financial resources available to member countries to help them correct balance of payments imbalances without resorting to measures that run counter to national or international prosperity. In the discharge of this responsibility, an important requirement of the Articles of Agreement is that the Fund adopts policies that will provide reasonable assurances that members' use of the institution's resources will be temporary[1]. Consequently, the Fund makes resources available to members in support of policies of economic and financial adjustment undertaken either to solve their actual, or to avert their potential, balance of payments problems. The design and content of these policies have evolved in line with changes in the world economic environment and they have always reflected the particular characteristics of individual countries. But they have also sought policy adjustment paths that in the light of available financing

---

* The views expressed in the paper are mine and they should not be attributed to the International Monetary Fund.

J.A.H. de Beaufort Wijnholds, S.C.W. Eijffinger and L.H. Hoogduin (eds.), A Framework for Monetary Stability, pp. 185–209.

possibilities would ensure both a measure of uniformity of treatment and temporariness in the use of Fund resources.

A central aspect of the economic adjustment programs typically agreed between a member country and the Fund focuses on monetary policy in its broadest interpretation, that is, an interpretation that encompasses exchange rate management and exchange arrangements in general. Monetary and exchange developments are closely linked with balance of payments performance and the role of monetary policy in IMF programs, the subject matter of this paper, is based on their interactions.

The plan of the paper is as follows. First, the rationale for the role of monetary policy in the process of stabilization and adjustment will be provided (section 2). Second, the implementation of monetary policy in Fund programs will be examined from an analytical standpoint (section 3). Then, the paper will conclude by drawing a few final observations (section 4). An Annex appended to the paper contains a summary of monetary policy features in a selected sample of Fund member countries.

2. THE RATIONALE

An economy typically needs to adjust and stabilize whenever a sustained demand for resources arises that exceeds their actual or prospective availability, either domestically or from abroad or both. Clearly the causes of an imbalance are important factors influencing the strategy for its correction, but the magnitude of the imbalance and the resources available to deal with it are factors that will play a critical role in the choice of strategy[2]. Imbalances can be financed or adjusted or typically, both. The linkage between *adjustment* – the correction of an imbalance – and *financing* – the use of resources to pay for it – is generally perceived as competitive in nature, that is, as involving a trade-off between them. While true at first sight, this perception conceals a more fundamental relationship between adjustment and financing. In reality, imbalances can hardly ever be adjusted immediately and, unless transitory and reversible, they can rarely be totally financed. A mixture of adjustment (policy action) with financing (use of reserves or recourse to borrowing) will be required under virtually all circumstances.

2.1. General framework

The process of stabilization and its particular aspect of correction of macroeconomic imbalances entail policy measures that can be classified in two main categories: those that affect the level and composition of aggregate demand; and those that influence the rate and structure of production in the economy.

A frequent source of demand expansion is fiscal or public sector expenditure proceeding on a scale above available tax and other fiscal revenues and therefore, requiring resort to domestic or foreign financing, or both. In general, fiscal policy, a subject that is beyond the scope of this paper, will be the instrument appropriate to keep the flow of public outlays on a sustainable relationship with fiscal revenue. This is the *fiscal dimension of macroeconomic management*. Reliance on sources of finance outside the public sector, e.g., the rest of the economy or the rest of the world, entails the use of other policy instruments. In general, monetary and domestic debt management is involved when the financing is internal. Action on the domestic financing side will influence mainly the level of demand, a variable on which monetary and credit as well as domestic debt management policies have a most important bearing. This represents the *monetary and domestic debt dimensions of macroeconomic management*. The level of demand will be also affected directly by the accumulation of external debt and by the use of international reserves, as will, of course, the availability of goods and services in the economy. Therefore, foreign borrowing flows have a direct bearing on the expenditure-income balance as well as an indirect one resulting from its potential to replace domestic credit expansion. There are, thus, also *external debt and international reserve dimensions to macroeconomic management*[3].

2.2. Monetary policy and exchange rate regime

The broad framework for stabilization and adjustment just outlined focuses on the relationship of the flows and patterns of global expenditure with those of income and on the effects of diverse economic policies on those critical variables. Among the latter, there are policies that have a time dimension, such as monetary and credit expansion as well as foreign borrowing flows, and there are policy actions that are of a one-and-for-all nature, such as price adjustments or interest rate or exchange rate changes which affect the economy in a correspondingly diverse fashion.

The close relationship between monetary policy and exchange rate management from the standpoint of stabilization and adjustment will now be examined. For this purpose, a first point that must be stressed is that the traditional propositions of monetary theory and their implications for monetary policy are very much influenced by the openness of economies. And openness is a feature common to all economies to a larger or lesser degree; therefore, the recognition of its existence is essential from the standpoint of economic policy in general, and of monetary policy, in particular.

a. Absence of external constraint
Seen from the perspective of the money market, there are two main sources of liquidity in any (open) economy: the credit extended by the central bank and

more broadly, the banking system, to the rest of the economy by purchases of domestic assets; and the supply of money that is provided by net purchases in the economy of international reserves and foreign assets. For purposes of stabilization, balance in the money market calls for actual monetary expansions to be commensurate with the growth in the demand for money. This is the *flow equilibrium dimension* of the money market, which has as a broad counterpart the prevalence of balance between expenditure and income in the economy, that is, balance in the market for goods and services. But stabilization will require, in addition to flow equilibrium, *balance in the stocks* in the system, that is, that the actual and the desired stocks of money and international reserves be equal. In the absence of such stock-flow balance, adjustments will take place that may call for policy action.

In a *hypothetical closed economy*, there would only be one source of liquidity, that is, the purchase of domestic assets by the central bank or the banking system at large. In this setting, an excess expansion of credit – that is, credit flows that surpass the rate at which the economy is willing to increase its money holdings – will tend to raise expenditure over income. Prices, and temporarily output, will increase as a result. With them, the demand for cash balances will rise, thereby contributing to balancing the money market and with it, re-establishing a measure of stability in the economy at large. This, of course, is the sequence of events that would occur only if the state of excess supply in the money market does not persist. Otherwise, what would happen is that prices would continue rising – that is, inflation would take off – and output would stop growing – when resources became fully employed. As a consequence, the persistent money market imbalance would keep inflation going; if the degree of imbalance remains unchanged, so will inflation because the value of the excess nominal money holdings will be precisely eroded by given, constant, price increases and actual and desired real cash balances will once again coincide.

The hypothetical closed economy can be replicated by an open economy operating under a *freely fluctuating exchange rate*. In such a setting, there would be two potential sources of liquidity: domestic *and* foreign asset purchases by the central bank or the banking system. But the free fluctuation of the exchange rate on the basis of market forces will preclude net intervention in the foreign exchange market by the central bank, thus severing the link between foreign exchange flows and the money supply. A money market imbalance in this environment, besides pushing domestic prices (and perhaps output) upward, will create an incipient excess demand for foreign exchange and with it, pressure for an exchange rate depreciation. The price increase, the output rise (if any), and the devaluation will tend to correct the imbalance, provided its causes do not persist. If on the contrary, they do persist, the economy will enter a continuing process of inflation and depreciation. The respective rates and variability in prices and the exchange rate will be determined by the degree and variation of the imbalance in the money market.

b. Presence of external constraint

In open economies with a *fixed rate of exchange* or with limited exchange rate flexibility, there will be a link between the money supply and the balance of payments which must be taken into account in the formulation of monetary policy. Balance in open economies of these characteristics require coincidence between domestic credit expansion and money demand growth *together with* equilibrium in the balance of payments. This dual requirement is needed because a given rate of growth in the demand for money is compatible with different balance of payments results and therefore, money market equilibrium need not coincide with external balance.

The analysis so far has proceeded without considering *capital flows*. Their introduction adds a market for domestic and foreign securities. The presence of capital flows, however, does not alter the basic relationships already discussed. If anything, it strengthens the link between domestic credit, the balance of payments and the international reserve position of the economy. With capital mobility, excessive (insufficient) domestic credit expansion relative to the growth in the demand for money will induce a current account deficit (surplus), a net capital outflow (inflow) and hence, a decrease (increase) in net international reserves. The balance of payments thus continues to be one of the channels through which the supply of money is adjusted to its demand. An important consequence of capital movements that warrants early mention is the intimate linkage that they impose between monetary, interest rate and exchange rate policies. Any inconsistency between these policies will be rapidly eliminated by the free flow of capital.

3. THE IMPLEMENTATION

The analysis provided so far is generally accepted as the standard framework for monetary policy evaluation. But there is an issue in the area of monetary management on which consensus remains elusive. The issue concerns the choice of an instrument for the implementation of monetary policy and for the measurement of its stance. The lack of consensus often reflects lack of clarity in the distinction between policy instruments and policy targets. In the specific context of Fund programs, the issue has a bearing on the assessment of the appropriateness of monetary management and on the choice of appropriate domestic monetary policy variables for the objectives of the financial arrangements of the institution with member countries. This is a question with a relatively long history as made evident by its extensive treatment in the economic literature both outside and inside the Fund. Many of the analyses conducted on the subject were undertaken during the 1970s and little attention has been paid to it since then[4].

At present, the analysis and assessment of monetary policy are generally carried out in terms of either credit or money flows as if these were interchangeable. The time seems right for a re-examination of the issues involved in the choice of a monetary policy instrument, if only because the international economy has undergone significant changes over the last two decades, some of them of a fundamental nature, such as those in the area of exchange rate arrangements and in the domain of capital movements. The arguments will be presented from the standpoint of Fund programs. But the basic conceptual and operational considerations to guide the choice of the appropriate monetary policy variable apply in the general context of domestic monetary management.

3.1. Policy understandings in Fund programs

Fund programs contain policy understandings the institution reaches with its members to guide their access to Fund resources. Prominent among these understandings are quantitative estimates of policies under the programs to measure the effectiveness of their implementation. In the institutional vocabulary, these quantitative understandings are called *performance criteria*. A basic principle behind the use of performance criteria in Fund arrangements has been the need to reach an acceptable balance between two major institutional aims: first, the provision of a firm assurance to Fund members regarding the circumstances under which they can have unquestioned access to the institution's resources; and, second, the establishment of an equally firm assurance to the Fund that its resources will be used by members in manners consistent with the prescriptions of the Articles of Agreement.

With regard to the first aim, this basic principle led to the formulation of performance criteria in terms of policy variables that were under the authorities' control and also amenable to objective description in quantitative terms. The second aim is a direct reflection of an essential objective pursued by the Fund in its relations with members, that is, the attainment and maintenance of a balance of payments position that allows freedom from restrictions on international transactions to be achieved and sustained in a setting of sound economic growth and price stability. From an operational point of view, a clear manifestation of the progress made by a member toward the attainment of this key objective is that its policies improve its balance of payments position and therefore, its use of Fund resources will be temporary, as prescribed by the Articles of Agreement, to ensure that access to the Fund will revolve among Fund members.

These two fundamental institutional aims point to the desirability of mutually agreed quantitative performance criteria to guide a member's access to Fund resources. This said, however, in an uncertain environment and in particular, in a setting of rapid financial innovation and closely integrated capital markets, it is of course advisable to supplement quantified policy action with an opportunity to exercise judgment, that is, an opportunity to assess the continued validity of the agreed quantitative policy commitments. This supplement is always included in IMF programs in the form of so called *review clauses*. These clauses call for consultations between the member and the institution to evaluate, inter alia, the appropiateness of the quantified criteria and reach understandings on the circumstances under which modifications or adaptions are warranted. In this manner, a measure of balance is sought between the *predictability* of performance criteria and the *flexibility* required in an uncertain and constantly changing environment.

3.2. The choice of a policy instrument

The conceptual framework described in the previous section for the formulation of monetary policy is based on the existence of a demand for money that is a stable function of a relatively limited number of variables[5]. Consequently, a critical ingredient for the process of policy implementation is the accuracy of the estimate of the demand for money and of the corresponding forecast of its developments; such an ingredient is of relevance regardless of whether the money supply or domestic credit is postulated as the policy instrument.

Situations where specific control over the money supply is advocated can be generally characterized by the persistence of inflation, interpreted as reflecting essentially money market conditions. Behind the argument in favor of the use of the money stock as a policy variable has been a concern to avert rates of monetary expansion that could threaten the attainment of inflation targets. It has been reasoned that the degree of control over the inflationary process that needs to be exercised in such circumstances can only be assured by strict monitoring of developments in the money supply. Therefore, according to this argument, situations where a decisive and visible reduction in the rate of inflation is deemed critical for the effectiveness of an adjustment effort call for policy action to ensure direct control over the rate of monetary expansion.

Attention toward monetary aggregates has been particularly drawn in situations of significant uncertainty concerning the magnitude of the net capital inflows that could be expected following the adoption of an adjustment policy program. The concern typically expressed in this context has been over the likelihood of unduly large capital inflows rather than over capital flows of a volatile nature in both directions[6]. The consequences of such uncertain capital inflows will depend on the characteristics of the economy including, in particular, the degree of its openness and the specific exchange rate regime under which it operates.

In an open economy with a fixed exchange rate system, a larger than anticipated capital inflow would increase the stock of money in the economy, thereby adding to undesirable inflationary pressures, unless the inflows were to be sterilized in some fashion (admittedly, at the risk of perpetuating the incentives for their continuation). A similar set of circumstances in the context of *an open economy with a flexible exchange rate system* would lead instead to an unexpected appreciation of the domestic currency, an outcome that, in contrast, would exert a moderating influence on inflation (at the possible expense, though, of competitiveness). In the more common setting of *an open economy with an exchange regime but where the exchange rate is not totally flexible*, larger than anticipated capital inflows would lead toward a combination of increases in the money stock (thus, contributing to inflation) and exchange rate appreciation (thereby, tending to contain inflationary pressures).

Depending on the type of exchange rate regime in operation, the logic behind the choice of the money supply as a policy variable is thus based on the following reasoning. Where a totally flexible exchange rate prevails, the emergence of unanticipated capital inflows would not influence the money supply as the external accounts would always balance. In these circumstances, what happens is that money and domestic credit expansion will in fact coincide, and it can be argued that such coincidence renders money equivalent to domestic credit as a policy instrument. In the case of open economies with fixed or only partly flexible exchange rate arrangements, large capital inflows could threaten the attainment of the objective to control inflation by unduly raising domestic monetary expansion. Therefore, it becomes necessary to seek means to ensure that the monetary consequences of unexpected balance of payments developments do not place an economy's efforts to control inflation in jeopardy.

Among the possible means to this end, there is direct control of the money supply. If the prospects for net foreign exchange inflows are uncertain or if there is a risk that they may be a priori incompatible with the inflation objective, strict adherence to a monetary expansion path will make it necessary to sterilize the undesired foreign exchange inflow. Such a sterilization can be effected either through a compensating open market sale of domestic securities (an operation logically equivalent to an offsetting reduction in the rate of domestic credit expansion) or by direct sales (or absence of purchases) by the authorities of the excess foreign exchange itself or by a combination of both methods. For a given inflation rate, the choice of one or the other method of sterilization will result in a different combination of paths for domestic interest rates (which will be higher than otherwise in the case of offsetting open market sales of domestic securities) and for the exchange rate (which will be higher – i.e., a more appreciated domestic currency – than otherwise in the case of offsetting sales or absence of purchases of foreign exchange).

In summary, the considerations for the adoption of the money supply as the direct policy variable are based on the combination of two propositions: first, that the control of inflation has clear priority among the policy objectives sought by the adjustment program; and second, that prospective balance of payments developments conflict with the attainment of the inflation objective.

From a conceptual standpoint, the alternative formulation of policy in terms of domestic credit expansion is also partly based on the interpretation of the imbalance prevailing in the economy as perceived from the conditions that prevail in the money market. Domestic credit policy is typically formulated in relation to an estimate or a forecast of developments in a money demand function as a means to attain the authorities' objectives in the areas of balance of payments and the exchange rate as well as on the domestic price and economic activity fronts. Again abstracting from considerations of economic activity or growth, the rationale behind the approach is that when domestic credit is allowed to expand by less (more) than the expected growth in the demand for money, this will tend to be accompanied by an incipient balance of payments surplus (deficit) or an incipient appreciation (depreciation) of the exchange rate and a consequent decline (rise) in either inflation or in domestic prices; in effect, the most likely outcome will be some combination of all of these events.

The logical sequence behind the credit approach is that the rate of *domestic credit expansion* is particularly closely related to developments in *aggregate expenditure and demand* in the economy. On the other hand, an important and well-known determinant of the *demand for money balances* is the economy's *global income*. Thus, a discrepancy between expenditure and income can be translated into an imbalance between the rates of expansion of credit and money.

The actual operation of domestic credit policy in a situation where large unanticipated capital inflows are actually registered, will depend on whether or not these unexpected developments are determined by the demand for money. When the unexpected foreign exchange surpluses reflect developments in the demand for cash balances, the sequence of events in *an open economy with a fixed exchange rate* is as follows: net international reserves and the money supply will expand at a higher than programmed rate; but no unexpected inflationary pressures will emerge as a result, because the additional money balances will be held voluntarily. In the case of *an economy with a flexible exchange rate*, the balance of payments surplus and resulting monetary expansion will not materialize. Instead, the exchange rate will appreciate and downward pressures on inflation or on the domestic price level will tend to emerge. In this particular case, while ex post credit and monetary developments will coincide in fact, this coincidence is not sufficient to infer from it that it renders money and credit equivalent as policy instruments because the logic that policy action should be formulated in terms of its impact on domestic credit expansion remains. This is because the ex post coincidence between credit and money in these circumstances does not eliminate the need to keep aggregate expenditure under control, and the rate of domestic credit expansion rather than the money supply is the most effective instrument to control this particular variable[7]. With *a partially flexible exchange rate*, a combination of monetary expansion and upward domestic price pressures will occur on account of the accumulation of foreign exchange that takes place; and downward pressure on the rate of increase or the level of domestic prices will also materialize because not all the foreign exchange surplus will be absorbed. Ceteris paribus, once the impact of the unexpected foreign exchange flows works itself through the economy, the level of real (though not the nominal) money balances should be the same (for a given domestic credit policy stance) in the three categories of instances.

An unexpected foreign exchange surplus that does not reflect developments in the demand for money will result in a different set of events, however. *In the fixed exchange rate case*, the additional domestic cash balances thus generated would not be willingly held. As a consequence, domestic expenditure would rise, thereby either reducing the rate of foreign exchange accumulation or placing upward pressure on domestic prices and most likely operating through both channels. With *a fully flexible exchange rate*, the impact of the inflow will be totally deflected toward the exchange rate, which will appreciate, thereby, exercising a moderating influence on inflation. In the case of *incomplete exchange rate flexibility*, a combination of these two sets of outcomes will materialize: a more limited exchange rate appreciation would be associated with some monetary expansion and upward domestic price pressure.

The process in these three sets of circumstances is not open-ended. In the first (fixed exchange rate) case, the pressure on aggregate demand and on domestic prices will deflect more and more spending toward the balance of payments, thereby eliminating the impact of the foreign exchange inflow on the domestic money market. A similar diversion of expenditure abroad will be brought about by the exchange rate appreciation in the second (flexible exchange rate) case until the pressure toward appreciation is offset. A combination of higher domestic prices (as in the first case) and lower foreign prices (in domestic currency, as in the second case) will divert expenditure in a similar direction in the intermediate case[8].

In sum, the considerations for policy formulation in terms of domestic credit expansion are based on the proposition that, under most circumstances, the money supply in an open economy is an endogenous variable, and although influenced by the authorities, it cannot be solely determined by policy action on a sustained basis. In addition, the credit approach also contends that, again in most instances, there can be no durable conflict in the attainment of inflation and balance of payments objectives.

3.3. Operational implications of the choice

The alternative approaches discussed in the previous section have implications for the formulation of specific policy criteria. They are based on the need to distinguish clearly in the process of policy making between policy objectives and policy instruments. Typical examples of policy instruments in Fund programs are fiscal and credit measures as well as certain prices of both commodities and factors of production which are important from an economy-wide perspective. Through the use of these instruments, influence can be exercised in a particularly direct fashion on aggregate expenditure and demand and indirectly also on the level and pattern of domestic supply. From this standpoint, global demand and supply are intermediate target variables which through their interplay contribute to the attainment of ultimate objectives of economic management such as prices, output, and the balance of payments.

Conceptually, the stock and the rate of expansion of monetary aggregates belong in the category of intermediate policy targets, rather than in the group of policy instruments. A direct way to illustrate this point is to note that for any given demand for money, different balance of payments, price, and output outcomes may be consistent with a given stock of money[9]. In the context of the domestic money market, the rate of increase of the domestic liabilities of the central bank (reserve money) or of the banking system as a whole (broader monetary aggregates) are, therefore, the joint outcome of the financial policy stance of the authorities and of the behavior of the rest of the economy regarding its willingness to add to its cash balances. Depending on the latter, it is possible for a given rate of monetary expansion to materialize in effect even in the absence of implementation of agreed policies on the part of the authorities. More generally (except in the case of a freely fluctuating exchange rate), the authorities have no ex ante assurance that the implementation of the agreed policy measures will in effect result in a rate of monetary expansion that has been determined a priori. Hence, in the context of Fund programs, the authorities would have no firm assurance that once they take the agreed policy actions, Fund resources will be made available. In addition, the possible lack of relationship between a given stock of money or rate of monetary expansion and a given set of policy actions severs the link with the attainment of program objectives, in particular, those on the balance of payments front. Consequently, there would be no assurance that the use of Fund resources would be temporary.

These shortcomings of monetary variables are particularly important because of the indeterminacy they allow with regard to the outcome for net international reserves, since the maintenance of monetary expansion within an agreed path is not sufficient to ensure a given balance of payments outcome. Elimination of this indeterminacy requires that money supply targets be accompanied by a specific, quantified balance of payments objective, regardless of the exchange rate regime in effect. Through this technique of combining a money supply target with a balance of payments objective, less favorable net international reserve outcomes than the one programmed in the latter test are in effect ruled out. However, this combination of performance criteria may also serve to eliminate the possibility of better than programmed balance of payments outcomes since the established objective can easily become equivalent to a maximum path for net international reserves. This is because whenever the balance of payments performance outlook is better than envisaged in the program, *ceteris paribus*, the rate of monetary expansion will tend to exceed the level permissible under the target. A relatively straightforward method of adherence to the monetary target in those circumstances would be for the authorities to avert buying or to sell the foreign exchange that would tend to flow into the economy in excess of the amount programmed in the balance of payments. This external objective thus risks becoming a ceiling on net international reserves, not only a floor below which they cannot fall, as is the case when domestic credit expansion is the policy variable.

If the better than expected balance of payments performance reflects fundamental factors in the economy and therefore is not transient, the approach of a monetary target-cum-balance of payments aim would impair adjustment and tend to perpetuate an imbalance between the demand for and supply of cash balances, thereby forcing the full adjustment to be effected through price and exchange rate movements. If, on the contrary, the balance of payments improvement is transitory, the money approach would provide a direct incentive to keep monetary expansion on the programmed path, but at the expense of forfeiting a higher than otherwise net international reserve accumulation.

From a conceptual standpoint, the stock and rate expansion of domestic credit are closer than their money counterparts to the category of policy instruments[10]. A clear way to illustrate this point would be to indicate that, ceteris paribus, for a given path for the demand for money, the rate of domestic credit expansion will determine the outcomes for the balance of payments, prices, and output. In effect, the attainment of these external and internal objectives will be contingent on the relationship between the demand for additional cash balances and the rate of domestic credit expansion. Balance of payments outcomes are determinate when ceilings are specified in terms of domestic credit expansion. With a fixed exchange rate, there is no need to add a specific balance of payments criterion: the attainment of the net international reserve target implicit in the credit ceiling will depend on whether the demand for cash balances has been underestimated (leading to balance of payments overperformance, that is, a larger-than-expected surplus), or overestimated (leading to balance of payments underperformance). In either set of circumstances, the attainment of balance in the money market will not be impeded by attempting to adhere to the ceilings. With a totally or partially flexible exchange rate, domestic credit ceilings need to be supplemented by a balance of payments test.

This approach will allow a stronger than expected balance of payments performance to be totally reflected in domestic monetary expansion. If the stronger external performance is permanent, such an outcome would be compatible with money market balance. If it is transient, it could put upward pressure on domestic prices pari passu with the larger than programmed net international reserve accumulation. Therefore it ensures that additional resources are available to cope with the consequences of a higher-than-programmed rate of price increase.

Areas of potential difficulty can be created by excessive capital inflows. Of particular concern are those inflows that lead to rising domestic expenditure and which therefore conflict directly with the objectives sought by domestic credit ceilings. These inflows, then are equivalent to foreign borrowing and have led to the inclusion in Fund arrangements of limits on such borrowing to ensure effective aggregate domestic expenditure control. These limits have basically encompassed foreign borrowing by those sectors where imbalances are most likely to be generated: in particular, the limitations have affected the public sector to keep its spending under control and the commercial banks to control the rate of their domestic lending. Concerning the private sector, its foreign borrowing has not been normally constrained, except indirectly, through the establishment of limits on the extension of official guarantees to private foreign borrowing operations. To the extent, however, the governments tend to assume the foreign liability when the private sector is unable or unwilling to repay, a strong argument can be made in defense of constraints on total foreign borrowing[11].

3.4. The proper scope for the policy variable

Whether policy is to be formulated in terms of money growth or of domestic credit expansion, a choice must be made concerning the definition of money that will be used. This choice, of course, concerns the spectrum of nominal assets that are to be considered as money, that is, whether it will be limited to the central bank (which places the focus on reserve or base money), or whether it will encompass the whole banking system (thus stressing a variety of broader money definitions depending on the range of bank liabilities they include), or whether it should cover in addition other financial intermediaries. Depending on the money concept that is adopted, there will be a counterpart domestic credit variable that is compatible with it[12].

The issue addressed here, though, will be confined to considerations on whether the scope of the monetary policy variable should be coincident with the banking system at large or whether it should remain confined to the central bank or the monetary authority. Although a reasonable argument can be made that the evolution of nominal variables in the economy are related to banking system variables more closely than they are to central bank variables, there are relevant considerations to counter the argument. A choice of the narrower definition implies of course that the formulation of policy will be based on the stability of the relationship between broad and narrow monetary aggregates, that is, the multipliers. In normal circumstances, the presumption can be made, however, that should a stable demand for money exist, there would also be a measure of stability in the composition of its various components, which are the determinants of the multipliers[13].

The reasons in favor of anchoring policy formulation on monetary authority or central bank variables can be summarized as follows. First, an essential feature of policy variables in general is that they should be under the *control of the policy maker*. From this standpoint, there is no doubt that the relevant definitions of monetary variables are those that pertain to the central bank. It is on the central bank balance sheet that the monetary authorities exercise a measure of control[14]. Second, focus on the banking system rather than on the central bank *blurs the distinction* between public sector and private sector activities or more narrowly, *between the monetary authority and the banking sector*. An important by-product of such blurring is the risk of disintermediation that can be incurred potentially when policy aims at controlling broad monetary and bank credit flows[15].

4. FINAL OBSERVATIONS

The trend toward liberalization of national and international transactions together with the process of deregulation of domestic financial markets that have characterized the evolution of the world economy during the last decade has posed a number of challenges for the conduct of monetary policy. The challenges focus on the appropriateness of monetary targets as guides for domestic monetary policy as well as on their relevance in a setting where national monetary borders have become increasingly permeable.

With financial deregulation, *the boundary between banking and other financial activities has blurred*. This blurring has compounded the difficulty of identifying a monetary variable with a stable behavior capable of anticipating the evolution of other nominal variables in the economy. There are two aspects to this difficulty. One is that deregulation has affected stability of the demand for money in its various traditional definitions and therefore, it has impaired the usefulness of money demand forecasts as a basis for monetary policy implementation. Some of the arguments made in this context focus on the impact of the lifting of financial sector restrictions on the demand for money.

In itself, this factor should be of a once-and-for-all nature and disappear once deregulation has been completed. Another aspect of the issue is the increasing degree of substitutability between banking liabilities and those of other financial intermediaries. Rather than affecting the demand for money (however defined), this argument centers on the growing complexity of the definition of money, which no longer can be confined to central bank or banking system liabilities.

These considerations pertain to the national policy domain. But with the internationalization and globalization of financial markets, another challenge has arisen for national monetary policy implementation. While the first challenge underscores the blurring of the boundary between banks and other financial intermediaries, the second stresses the *growing disappearance of national economic frontiers*. The issue at stake here is the relevance and appropriateness of national monetary variables in an environment of increasing substitutability of currencies. This phenomenon, which acquires particular strength in the context of regimes like that in the European Monetary System, has validity on general grounds, as the experience with dollarization in a number of economies amply illustrates.

Rather than posing a conceptual question, these issues are empirical in nature. They relate to the *identification of the national monetary variable* with the relatively most stable behavior. And they concern the question of the relative stability and predictability of national or international monetary aggregates. In themselves, the challenges now confronting monetary policy makers do not affect the logical framework discussed in the paper. They only add to the complexities of actual policy implementation. The blurring between banks and other financial intermediaries calls for definitions of monetary variables that correspond to the financial sector at large. Domestic credit counterparts can be derived from whichever broad financial aggregate is determined. Still, the issue of the proper scope for the policy variable remains as outlined in the paper. Focus on the central bank highlights the importance of control as well as the separation between public and private sectors. Broader coverage, whatever merits it may have from other standpoints, will extract a price in terms of a more complex, and possibly a looser, relationship with broadening monetary variables as well as in terms of moral hazard risks. As for the *obsolescence of national monetary aggregates*, the important implication to draw is the *constraint it imposes on domestic monetary policy*. It essentially allows for little, if any, margin of error in the conduct of policy as such error would soon be corrected by international financial flows. Specifically, the pursuit of unduly restrictive or expansionary monetary policies no longer will yield the consequences expected in a more segmented international economic setting. Rather, they will only stimulate net financial inflows or outflows, thus confirming market forces as the main determinants of the stance of monetary conditions.

NOTES

1. These policies have become known by the term *conditionality*. See Joseph Gold (1979), Manuel Guitián (1981, 1987 and 1992a), John Williamson (1983), Peter B. Kenen (1986), Azizali Mohamed (1991), Jacques J. Polak (1992), and Alexis de Tocqueville Institution (1992) for discussions of this subject.

2. The causes of an imbalance may be either *exogenous* or *endogenous* to policy actions or *external* or *internal* in origin. Important though these distinctions are, the essential aspect is whether the imbalance is *transitory* or *permanent* because this is what will determine the need for policy adaptations. See Manuel Guitián (1981) for further elaboration.

3. While the direct effects of domestic and foreign financing fall on the *level* of domestic demand, their influence does not end there. Through their impact on interest rates they can also affect its *composition* between consumption and investment; in the particular case of foreign borrowing (or use of international reserves) the supply of goods and services in the economy – as noted in the text – will also be affected through increased imports. For a detailed discussion of fiscal adjustment and debt management issues, see Manuel Guitián (1989). And on external debt, see for example Jacob A. Frenkel, Michael P. Dooley and Peter Wickham (1989).

4. See Jacques Polak (1957), Jacques Polak and Victor Argy (1971) and Manuel Guitián (1973a) for illustrations of the analysis conducted within the Fund; see also William Day (1979). A similar approach has been followed for long in the Netherlands and this has been stressed by Harry G. Johnson (1972); see also Jacob A. Frenkel and Harry G. Johnson (1976). A comprehensive survey of the approach to monetary policy in the Netherlands will be found in Frits de Jong (1973); see also M.W. Holtrop (1957 and 1972); for an illustration of different views on the issue, see Richard T. Selden (1975) and Manuel Guitián (1977). A simple empirical test of the approach will be found in Manuel Guitián (1976).

5. This presumption has been under increasing challenge as the process of deregulation in many countries and the global liberalization of financial markets have unsettled the regularity of financial relationships in country economies and possibly the relevance of domestic monetary variables in at least some settings, such as those in the European Monetary System (EMS). For discussion of this subject see International Monetary Fund (October 1992).

6. It may be pointed out that the particular problems posed by volatile capital movements are not likely to be solved solely by the establishment of a money supply ceiling; capital flow variability will impair the effectiveness of domestic monetary policy, regardless of the particular fashion in which it is implemented.

7. In essence, this argument can also be put in the context of the market for goods and services: in a closed economy, aggregate demand and supply, ex post, always coincide. While policy measures can be designed to influence both, the policy challenge most frequently consists of keeping demand in line with supply. From the perspective of domestic financing, this challenge calls for policy action to be geared to the control of demand.

8. A consequence of this whole process may be that in reacting to the disturbance, the exchange rate may have become unrealistic and thus require adjustment. In this regard, there is a possible issue of conflict between the exchange rate impact of unexpected foreign exchange inflows and the maintenance of competitiveness in the economy. In the absence of distortions, it would seem that the change in the real exchange rate that may take place temporarily is not likely to be sustained, so that a conflict need not arise in this context.

9. Of course, the future evolution of the demand for money will depend on the particular constellation of results that obtains on the balance of payments, inflation, and output fronts, but this will be contingent on the behavior of the economy with regard to cash balances and not on direct policy action by the authorities.

10. This said, however, it should be added that the implementation of a given credit policy will be

effected typically through specific technical means, e.g., open market operations, reserve requirements, rediscount facilities, etc. Actually, it can be argued that both credit and money are intermediate target variables to be attained by the use of instruments such as those just listed. But given the control of the monetary authorities over domestic credit, which exceeds the one they exert over money, the former exhibits more the characteristics of a policy instrument than the latter. For an extensive discussion of specific monetary instruments, see Paul Hilbers (1993).

11. There are important issues of governance and moral hazard risks surrounding this whole question. I have addressed some of them in Manuel Guitián (1992b).

12. In this connection, the statement by Milton Friedman and Anna Schwartz (1970) that "After centuries of consideration, the best way to define money remains a live issue today" is as valid now as it was when they wrote it. For a discussion of the relationship between the definition of money and domestic credit, see Manuel Guitián (1973b).

13. The presumption here is that stability in the demand for money characterizes both the level *and* the composition of cash balance holdings; the latter depends on the behavior of variables like the currency-deposit and the reserve-deposit ratios which reflect, *inter alia,* the public's and the banks' preferences; see Milton Friedman (1960). But stability in the composition of cash balances need not obtain, particularly in circumstances of financial uncertainty, a possibility that of course would complicate monetary management.

14. It should be pointed out that in my 1973 article on the subject (Manuel Guitián, 1973a) I cast the argument in terms of money, not base money; however, the assumption behind such argument was that the monetary authorities had the "institutional arrangements to control the total domestic assets of the banking system." This said, I have acknowledged that the assumption was then and is now heroic.

15. Another practical consideration is that from an operational standpoint, the conduct of monetary policy calls for timely data. And such data are typically available more promptly for central bank transactions than for those of the banking system at large.

REFERENCES

Alexis de Tocqueville Institution (1992), *IMF Conditionality, 1980 – 1991* (Washington).

Day, William H.L. (1979), "Domestic Credit and Money Ceilings Under Alternative Exchange Rate Regimes", *IMF Staff Papers*, Vol. 26 (September).

de Jong, Frits J. (1973), *Developments of Monetary Theory in the Netherlands* (Rotterdam University Press).

Frenkel, Jacob A. and Harry G. Johnson (eds.) (1976), *The Monetary Approach to the Balance of Payments* (London).

Frenkel, Jacob A., Michael P. Dooley and Peter Wickham (eds.) (1989), *Analytical Issues in Debt* (Washington, International Monetary Fund).

Friedman, Milton (1960), *A Program for Monetary Stability* (New York, Fordham University Press).

Friedman, Milton and Anna J. Schwartz (1970), *Monetary Statistics of the United States* (New York, National Bureau of Economic Research).

Gold, Joseph (1979), *Conditionality*, IMF Pamphlet Series No. 31 (Washington, International Monetary Fund).

Guitián, Manuel (1973a) "Credit Versus Money as an Instrument of Control", *IMF Staff Papers*, Vol. 20 (November). The article has been reproduced in International Monetary Fund (1977).

Guitián, Manuel, (1973b), "Devaluation, Monetary Policy and the Balance of Payments", unpublished Ph.D. dissertation (Chicago, The University of Chicago).

202

Guitián, Manuel (1976), "The Balance of Payments as a Monetary Phenomenon: Empirical Evidence, Spain 1955–71", in Jacob A. Frenkel and Harry G. Johnson (1976), *op. cit.*.

Guitián, Manuel (1977), "Dutch Monetarism: A Comment", *Journal of Monetary Economics*, Vol. 3 (July).

Guitián, Manuel (1981), *Fund Conditionality: Evolution of Principles and Practices*, IMF Pamphlet Series No. 38 (Washington, International Monetary Fund).

Guitián, Manuel (1987), "Adjustment and Economic Growth: Their Fundamental Complementarity", in Vittorio Corbo and others (eds.), *Growth-Oriented Adjustment Programs* (Washington, International Monetary Fund and World Bank).

Guitián, Manuel (1989), "Fiscal Adjustment, Debt Management and Conditionality", in Mario Monti (ed.), *Fiscal Policy, Economic Adjustment and Financial Markets* (Washington, International Monetary Fund).

Guitián, Manuel (1992a), *The Unique Nature of the Responsibilities of the International Monetary Fund*, IMF Pamphlet Series No. 46 (Washington, International Monetary Fund).

Guitián, Manuel, (1992b), "Remarks on the Debt Crisis," in Paul Volker and Toyoo Gyohten, *Changing Fortunes: The World's Money and the Threat to American Leadership* (New York, Times Books).

Hilbers, Paul (1993), "The Use of Monetary Instruments During the Transition from a Centrally Planned to a Market Economy", unpublished (Washington, International Monetary Fund, July).

Holtrop, M.W. (1957), "Method of Monetary Analysis Used by De Nederlandsche Bank", *IMF Staff Papers*, Vol. 20 (February).

Holtrop, M.W. (1972), *Money in an Open Economy: Selected Papers on Monetary Policy, Monetary Analysis, and Central Banking* (Leyden).

International Monetary Fund (1977), *The Monetary Approach to the Balance of Payments* (Washington, International Monetary Fund).

International Monetary Fund (1992), *World Economic Outlook*, World Economic and Financial Surveys (Washington, October).

Johnson, H.G. (1972), *Inflation and the Monetarist Controversy* (Amsterdam, North-Holland Publishing Company).

Kenen, Peter, B. (1986), *Financing, Adjustment and the International Monetary Fund*, Studies in International Economics (Washington, The Brookings Institution).

Mohammed, Azizali (1991), "Recent Evolution of Fund Conditionality", in Jacob A. Frenkel and Morris Goldstein (eds.) (1991), *International Financial Policy: Essays in Honor of Jacques J. Polak* (Washington, International Monetary Fund and De Nederlandsche Bank).

Polak, Jacques J. (1957), "Monetary Analysis of Income Formation and Payments Problems", *IMF Staff Papers,* Vol. 6 (November). The article has been reproduced in International Monetary Fund (1977).

Polak, Jacques J (1991), *The Changing Nature of IMF Conditionality*, Essays in International Finance No. 185 (Princeton University, December 1991).

Polak, Jacques J. and Victor Argy (1971), "Credit Policy and the Balance of Payments", *IMF Staff Papers*, Vol. 18, March. The article has been reproduced in International Monetary Fund (1977).

Selden, Richard T. (1975), "A Critique of Dutch Monetarism", *Journal of Monetary Economics*, Vol. 1 (April).

Williamson, John (ed.) (1983), *IMF Conditionality* (Washington, Institute for International Economics).

Annex: Monetary policy features in selected IMF member countries

1. INTRODUCTION

The situations in countries that have adopted financial programs supported by arrangements with the Fund have exhibited wide differences in initial conditions (including, *inter alia*, their level of economic development, the degree of their "openness", and the type of their exchange regime) as well as diversity in the sources and extent of economic disequilibria. At the end of 1992, 50 member countries – including four states of the former Soviet Union (FSU) – had formal stand-by (SBA), extended facility (EFF), or (enhanced) structural adjustment facility (SAF/ESAF) arrangements with the Fund (Table 1). Over the last few years, high inflation, as well as external debt and balance of payments problems, have been largely contained in Latin America and Asian program countries, and a measure of progress has been made in stabilizing a number of economies of Eastern Europe. Macroeconomic management has increasingly focused on removing impediments to economic efficiency and on the appropriate mix of monetary, fiscal and incomes policies. Almost all African country programs, as well as those in a few low-income Latin American and Asian countries have undertaken comprehensive structural reforms conducive to economic growth. These programs have been elaborated under multiyear arrangements and supported by the Fund with concessional assistance. Important progress has been made in a number of these cases in removing rigidities and expanding the role of market forces in resource allocation. FSU states have been an important area of IMF work in the last two years, particularly in developing the legal, regulatory, and staff capabilities as well as the instruments of economic management; but progress toward reform as well as toward the adoption of financial arrangements with the Fund has varied across states.

2. EXCHANGE AND MONETARY POLICIES IN SELECTED IMF PROGRAMS

a) Sources of disequilibria

Countries with Fund programs in recent years generally have experienced both exogenous shocks – the effects of which have been in some instances aggravated by an inadequate domestic policy response – and domestic policy slippages. Some exogenous factors have been both temporary and reversible (such as adverse weather), but others (such as the collapse of previous economic systems and relationships, deterioration in terms of trade) have required significant changes in domestic policy. In many program countries, and in particular in (former) CMEA members, inappropriate fiscal (defined to include state enterprises) and incomes policies have been identified as key sources of imbalance, while monetary policy was seen to be accommodative, to varying degrees, of the resulting credit needs. In these cases, programs have focused on correcting the underlying fiscal problem (through discrete changes in tax rates, tax reform to improve the income elasticity of taxes and widen the tax base, removal of subsidies, budget expenditure cuts and restructuring, and enterprise reform and privatization) so as to contain aggregate expenditure, and thus avoid crowding out potentially more efficient users of domestic credit. In a number of (former) CMEA program countries, emphasis has also been given to restraining wage increases and removing labor market rigidities and other impediments to competition. In countries with high inflation, however, absorbing any existing liquidity overhang and tightening overall credit were seen as crucial to restoration of macroeconomic stability. Programs elaborated with SAF/ESAF eligible member countries have also contained policy benchmarks which gave substance to and set priorities on key structural reforms.

b) Exchange arrangements

Of the 50 countries with programs at end-1992, almost half maintained flexible exchange regimes. Most have adopted a floating or managed floating rate system with a unified rate determined by competitive forces in the interbank market or by linking an official rate to developments in a legal secondary market where the rate is market determined. In the latter case, the official rate may fluctuate within a pre-determined band or be adjusted at discrete intervals to maintain a desired spread relative to the secondary market rate. In some cases (e.g., Mexico and Uruguay), a crawling peg system has been adopted with a view to ensuring international competitiveness or to provide a nominal anchor in a high inflation setting.

A number of countries have opted instead for a fixed exchange rate regime,

Table 1. Summary of recent experience of monetary policy in selected Fund programs (as of December 31, 1992)

| | Number of arrangements | Intermediate monetary target | | | Exchange regime | | |
| | | Credit | | Money | Pegged | Flexible | |
		Central bank*	Banking system			Independently floating	Other
Africa	17	2	15	–	13	2	2
Asia	5	2	2	1	2	1	2
Europe	6	–	6	–	2	3	1
FSU	4	3	–	1	1	3	–
Middle East	3	–	3	–	2	–	1
Western Hemisphere	15	15	–	–	4	9	2
Total	50	22	26	2	24	18	8

Source: IMF
* Defined as the central bank or monetary authorities and, in the case of Panama, the National Bank.

setting the exchange rate as a nominal anchor. This group includes mainly (but not only) countries which are members of common currency areas (such as the CFA franc and the South African rand areas), or use another country's currency for domestic intermediation (typically, the U.S. dollar) and those with a historical relationship to an intervention currency (such as Barbados, Nicaragua, Nepal). The success of this strategy in containing inflation while maintaining balance of payments viability has depended on the flexibility of domestic wages and costs as well as the stability of inflation in the currency against which the rate was fixed.

c) Choice of intermediate target of monetary policy and policy instruments

Financial programs almost uniformly have adopted a credit variable as the intermediate target of monetary policy. The programs that targeted a more aggregated concept of credit (net domestic assets of the banking system or total credit) were generally those associated with countries (mainly in Africa but also some of the former CMEA members) with relatively un- or underdeveloped financial systems and whose central banks have a limited range of policy instruments, relying mainly on direct controls and/or relatively unsophisticated instruments such as reserve requirements or not fully market determined interest rates. Net domestic assets of the central bank has been adopted as the intermediate monetary target in 22 programs, including all Western Hemisphere countries. The policy instruments in these countries usually, but not always, have included open market operations.

d) Impediments to the transmission of monetary impulses

The conduct of monetary policy and the specification of performance criteria in recent years has been complicated by the liberalization of global capital markets as well as of the domestic financial sector. Financial sector reform also has exposed underlying weaknesses in the banking system of many countries. Financial programming and, specifically, the implementation of monetary policy have had to take account of unexpected foreign capital inflows and the effects of weak or insolvent domestic banks (including, in some cases, the central bank itself) on the transmission of monetary impulses. As a result of these factors, the stability and predictability of monetary aggregates have been reduced and the link of money and credit growth with inflation and balance of payments outturns has been weakened.

A significant number of countries with IMF programs (most of the Latin American countries as well as a few Asian and Middle East countries) have experienced *unexpected foreign capital inflows*. The underlying cause of the inflows, however, has not been easy to identify and, hence, it has been difficult to determine the extent to which they represented a sustainable increase in the demand for domestic currency. The recipient countries tended to be characterized by a measure of success in implementing adjustment programs, albeit with domestic inflation and interest rates that, nevertheless, have remained above those in their main trading partners.

Many of the countries delayed taking action to sterilize the inflows, not only because weak economic data impeded early identification of the source of liquidity, but also because the impact of inflows on inflation and the external current account deficit was apparent only with a lag. The resulting appreciation of the currency was perceived to be eroding past, hard won, gains in international competitiveness. The initial response of most countries was to tighten monetary policy by increasing statutory reserve requirements and/or through open market operations combined with intervention in the foreign exchange market. However, foreign exchange intervention in some cases added to the losses of the central bank while open market operations resulted in higher domestic interest rates (with consequent costs in fiscal terms) which in addition provided further incentives for the continuation of such inflows. Increasingly, the focus has shifted to the role of fiscal policy, with tightened budgets seen as consistent with achieving a targeted level of aggregate expenditure, while leaving greater room for private consumption and investment. A few countries did not adjust policy significantly, perceiving the inflows as a way of mobilizing private foreign savings (which had largely dissipated following the debt crisis of the early 1980s) thereby easing the burden of domestic adjustment, or as the repatriation of domestic flight capital and, hence, reflecting an increase in money demand. A number of programs have included trade liberalization and removal of labor market rigidities as important structural reforms aimed at enhancing wage and cost flexibility to offset the pressure on domestic competitiveness stemming from currency appreciation.

Central bank losses generally have reflected quasi-fiscal operations but also, in some cases, foreign exchange intervention. Such losses are a source of liquidity creation and they constrain monetary policy options. In program countries where the central bank losses are large, the burden of domestic liquidity control has had to be shifted to fiscal policy.

While *financial sector structural reforms* have emphasized enhancing the efficiency of intermediation as a basis for expanding supply potential, reforms have also exposed or exacerbated an underlying weakness in the banking system. Maintenance of positive real interest rates has been considered essential for the mobilization of savings and the efficient use of scarce financial resources and has generally been adopted as an early policy objective. Sharply higher interest rates (often compounded by reforms in other areas such as removal of subsidies and transfers to enterprises) have contributed to an increase in nonperforming loans of banks. Financial sector liberalization, often combined with weak prudential oversight by central banks, also contributed in some cases to increased risk-taking by banks, including through greater concentration of sector or customer group lending and/or undertaking operations in foreign exchange that were not adequately hedged.

3. EXPERIENCE WITH FSU STATES

The pace of, and commitment to, reform has varied across FSU states. Consistent with the differential pace of reform, the states were also at diverse stages in the adoption of stabilization programs that could be supported by Fund arrangements, and at the end of 1992 programs were in place with the three Baltic republics and Russia. When advising on macroeconomic policy, within or outside the framework of a formal program, the Fund has emphasized consistently the need to establish the prior conditions necessary for economic stabilization.

In order to determine the appropriate mix of fiscal, monetary and incomes policies, the main sources of *economic disequilibria* had to be identified. Generally, these could be divided into five broad categories: 1) systemic collapse of economic interrelations within the country, between republics and with other former CMEA trading partners; 2) terms of trade shock; 3) fiscal imbalances and, in particular, soft budget constraints of state enterprises accommodated by monetary policies; 4) consequent expansionary monetary policies made evident by the persistence of negative real rates of interest; and 5) incomes policies geared, to varying degrees among republics, to maintaining consumption.

With respect to *exchange regimes*, 9 of the 14 non-Russian FSU states remained in the ruble zone at the end of 1992. Of those with national currencies (including Russia), 4 republics have adopted a floating rate system with only Estonia pegging its currency. However, a number of states have indicated their intention to introduce their own currency during 1993. Moreover, interference with inter-state payment and settlements has accelerated the move to national currencies and 2 states (Belarus and Moldova) introduced "coupons" in parallel with the use of rubles.

With respect to *monetary policy*, a significant tightening of credit was considered an essential precondition to harden state enterprise budget constraints and to contain inflation. Restraining liquidity was a cornerstone of the first Russian program while the initial agreement that most states would remain within the ruble zone constrained the independence of their monetary policy. However, difficulties with payments and clearing systems, the creation of ruble deposits by the various central banks, the introduction of parallel near money instruments in some states, and the accommodative policy followed by the Russian central bank during 1992 undermined the potential stabilizing effect of a common currency area. Some states opted relatively early for the introduction of a national currency but progress in reducing inflation has been closely linked to the extent to this was supported by tight domestic policy. (Ukraine being the extreme case of an accommodative credit policy while the other end of the spectrum was represented by Estonia, which opted for a currency board and a corresponding fixed exchange rate regime).

The *main intermediate monetary policy variable* has generally been credit of the central bank since this was the variable that the authorities were best able to influence. However, not all states can be characterized as having an active monetary policy in 1992, since, especially for those where reforms are at an early stage, credit needs were largely accommodated. The conduct of monetary policy in some Baltic republics was complicated in 1992 by unanticipated capital inflows. Generally, this inflow was considered to represent "a flight from rubles," rather than an increased preference for holding local currency and, hence, it could turn out to be potentially destabilizing should conditions abroad change. Monetary policy has been implemented mainly through direct *instruments* (mainly bank-by-bank credit limits and/or directed credits from the central bank) with those states that have moved more rapidly to formulating a stabilization program also undertaking the shift to allocation of central bank credit on a market-determined basis. However, with the exception of Estonia and Latvia, market determination of interest rates has had little operative significance in an environment of easy access to central bank funding and where key borrowers – mainly state enterprises with monopoly positions – have not been price sensitive. In the event, real interest rates remained negative and the central banks have found it difficult to withdraw from indirect commercial lending activities.

The Fund has actively been engaged in – together with cooperating industrial countries and other multilateral agencies – *technical assistance programs* to develop the institutions, data bases and human resources necessary for market-based economic policy management. In the banking area, priority has been given to establishing the legal and regulatory framework; introduction of new central bank accounts to aid economic analysis and prudential oversight; introduction of a modern clearing and payments system; public debt and monetary management; foreign exchange operations; and central bank organization and staff training. The pace of absorption and implementation of the technical assistance provided thus far has varied widely across republics, depending on the commitment to economic transformation and, to a lesser extent, on the capabilities and continuity of local counterparts.

Comment on Andrew D. Crockett: Rules versus Discretion in Monetary Policy

JACQUES J. SIJBEN

Tilburg University

Mr. Chairman, I was very pleased to accept the kind invitation of the organising committee of this international conference, to put some remarks to Andrew Crockett's stimulating and interesting paper "Rules versus discretion in monetary policy". I find myself in broad agreement with most of what Mr. Crockett puts forward about the lessons we have learned from the past, but I have some questions with his main conclusions and the proposal of an eclectic approach in the rules versus discretion trade-off.

At present monetary policy operates in a quite different financial and economic environment than it did in the sixties and seventies. In the last decade the financial world changed drastically. Driven by financial deregulation, internationalisation and information technology, financial market innovations have eroded the distinction among monetary assets, weakened the stability of the money demand function and changed the monetary transmission mechanism. Moreover the globalisation of markets has increased the international effects of domestic policy through trade accounts and the exchange rates.

In this new international financial setting the question comes about how to conduct monetary policy, revitalizing the classical debate between a preannouncement of rules versus discretion in monetary policy. Like Mr. Crockett describes in the first part of his paper, I think it is a good idea first of all to discuss the lessons that can be drawn from the experiences of preceding decades, that have led central bankers to believe that monetary policy should take a longer-term perspective and that their primary goal should be price stability. However, this central policy objective implies that we have to guard against overburdening monetary policy.

During the sixties the policy view that dominated was aiming both at the achievement of a reasonable outcome for the level of output, employment and the rate of inflation and at the stabilization of real economic activity. At that time macroeconomic stabilization policy was based on discretionary demand-management by fiscal and monetary policies, making use of the Phillipscurve trade-off mechanism. However, those who believed in a long-run trade-off between unemployment and the rate of inflation were disappointed because it appeared that there were no benefits to allowing the inflation rate to ratchet

J.A.H. de Beaufort Wijnholds, S.C.W. Eijffinger and L.H. Hoogduin (eds.), *A Framework for Monetary Stability*, pp. 211–215.

upwards. Moreover, inflationary expectations and the disappearance of fiscal and money illusion had frustrated any attempt to use fiscal and monetary policy instruments to "fine tune" the real economy in a traditional anti-cyclical way. Since the first oil crisis in the early seventies, unemployment had increased substantially, without slowing down the inflationary process. Then inflation became the predominant problem and a growing number of western countries have adopted the practice of setting growth targets for the monetary aggregates. In this way policymakers made clear in advance the stance of monetary policy, giving a signal to the firms and trade-unions that inflationary expectations should be based on predetermined and credible future rates of monetary growth. As I already mentioned Mr. Crockett also puts forward that in the postwar period there was a shift from discretionary policies in the sixties to rule-based policy regimes in the seventies. However, on pages 165 and 166 he remarks that owing to the changed financial environment by the late eighties the pendulum began to swing away from rule-based policy regimes to the introduction of discretionary elements into the policy making process.

In the first part of the paper Mr. Crockett is dealing with some important terminological issues like objectives, targets, instruments and indicators, which provide information both about the impact of policy and the course of the transmission process. I agree with him that there is nothing to be gained in having a higher long-run rate of inflation because a greater variability and uncertainty in the inflation will reduce the level and diminish the efficiency of investment, thus impairing growth and employment in the long run.

In this context I will stress that not only financial innovation processes have affected the conduct of monetary policy, but that there is also a causality in the opposite direction. This means that monetary policy actions in the recent past have been an inducement to the kinds of innovation processes we have observed. Highly inflationary monetary policies in the past with the concomitant high nominal interest rates have given incentives to certain types of innovations, weakening the effectiveness of monetary policy. Therefore, the central goal of monetary policy must involve an elimination or reduction of the uncertainty of the public with regard to the future price level, resulting in sound and more stable monetary relations in the long run.

His remark with regard to the meaning of the smooth adjustment to price disturbances in the short run for real effects is in my view crucially dependent on the degree of policy credibility. The higher the credibility and reputation of the central bank with regard to maintaining monetary stability, the lower the sacrifice ratio and the more rapid the return to the trend rate of price increase with smaller output effects, and vice versa.

I can agree with his argument that wide fluctuations in interest rates are a demonstration of the central bank to bring home the need to tackle the root cause of inflation (p. 168). The sharp increase of short term interest rates organised by the Bundesbank in the last few years, with a downward-sloping yield curve, was a clear signal of the authorities to financial markets to give no room for a rekindling of inflationary expectations, so maintaining their credibility and reputation with regard to an anti-inflation policy.

On the pages 170–171 Mr. Crockett presents two arguments for allowing the monetary authorities judgmental discretion in the formulation and implementation of economic policy in an uncertain world. When there is a rise in the price of imports, like the oil crisis in the early seventies, or an inflationary shock like that following the unification in Germany at the end of the eighties, sticking to the monetary target, so to a rule-based policy regime, undoubtedly will result in a downturn in economic activity. But in my opinion the social costs of this disinflationary policy in terms of a loss in production and employment will be lower the higher the credibility of policy-makers, which will be reflected in a moderation of wage demands. The Bundesbank had built up so much reputation that there was no need "to bite the bullet", by creating a negative inflation shock.

I can agree with his third argument in favouring some discretionary elements, where he points out that because of regulatory changes and the development of new financial instruments the velocity of circulation of money can shift in a relatively unpredictable way, giving rise to a weakening of the stability of the money demand function. However, as I said before, unpredictable shifts in the velocity of circulation can be originated from allowing erratical fluctuations in inflation and interest rates and can be prevented or diminished by monetary stability and stable rules of the game, so by reducing monetary uncertainties.

I fully agree with his arguments in favour of rules in monetary policy, based on Friedman's view on the costs of avoiding great errors of policy and on the game-theoretic approach in monetary policy according to the Kydland-Prescott and Barro-Gordon analysis. These authors put forward that monetary policy characterized by cheating the public is not time-consistent, results in an "inflationary bias" and will deteriorate policy-makers' credibility and increase the uncertainty in the economy.

I don't understand on page 172 why the arguments in favour of rules are based more on the quality of discretionary actions than on discretion itself. I hold the view that in the asymmetric informational environment between policy-makers and economic agents it is very important for economic agents in forming their inflationary expectations to be able to distinguish as soon as possible between "hard" and "weak" policy-makers, according to the Backus-Driffill analysis about the macroeconomic outcomes of repeated games. I think that this identification process by the public is more relevant for policy-making than, as proposed by Mr. Crockett, the distinction made by the authorities between "good" and "bad" policy responses.

This means that the asymmetric information has to be eliminated, so giving the public sufficient information to get to know the true identity of the policy-maker's preferences. When the policy-maker had built up the reputation to be a strong-one, giving no room for discretionary actions, reputational forces of enforcement and temptation will be working and the public can form its inflationary expectations in a more easy way.

Summarizing, I am not in favour of Mr. Crockett's proposal for a new framework for monetary policy characterized by a balance between rules and discretion, so downgrading the use of monetary targets. He demonstrates his proposal by the current UK approach of a publicly announced target for inflation. Although it implies a rule-based regime for the attainment of price stability as the ultimate objective of policy and stresses the meaning of time consistency, there are too much discretionary elements in the implementation of policy, giving rise to unpredictability of policy behaviour to participants on financial markets. In my view, allowing too much room in setting monetary instruments, given the complex and shifting nature of the transmission mechanism, may easily impair the transparency and credibility of policy and may result in uncertainty among economic agents as to the course of future policy behaviour. In this context I will refer to Dr. Duisenberg's view, put forward recently at the Bocconi University in Milan, that in these circumstances, especially when the central bank is not independent, policy may easily tend to assume an ad hoc nature and may increase the risk that other considerations than the achievement of price stability may come to dominate. In this way time-inconsistent behaviour may be creep in gradually again, deteriorating the credibility and reputation of the central bank.

I hold the view that next to the option of an exchange rate target, with its disciplinary benefits and credibility effects, within the context of an exchange rate arrangement, an other potential monetary policy strategy exists by using a medium-term oriented target zone for a broadly defined monetary aggregate as the intermediate policy target variable. The basic monetary philosophy of a central bank should be that an excessive money supply will sooner or later lead to inflation, to the debasement of money.

A stable and preannounced target zone for such a monetary aggregate would help to prevent inflation and prevent inflationary expectations from being mistaken, restoring the information content of money and prices, and would make the monetary authorities more predictable. Moreover, such a guideline can have benefits precisely because it restricts future policy choices and will give the market participants a monetary framework in advance, setting some psychological data for the wage and price policy of the trade unions and the firms. However, to be successful and to avoid an overburdening of monetary policy, such a policy must be adequately supported by two other areas, namely wage and price policy and fiscal policy. In my view this policy can be achieved at best by a central bank as an independent body, with a statute which clearly states its task of maintaining the value of money, strengthening policy credibility.

Finally, such a framework can contribute also to a more stable financial and economic environment with less volatility in inflation and interest rates, resulting in a reduction of financial innovation processes and the associated unpredictable shifts in the velocity of circulation of money.

Comment on Manuel Guitián: The Role of Monetary Policy in IMF Programs

HENK JAGER

University of Amsterdam

Guitián's paper is an instructive analysis on the well-known theme of the implementation of monetary policy in IMF programs. It summarizes a decade-long tradition of theorizing concerning the choice of an instrument for both the implementation of monetary policy and the measurement of the monetary policy stance in a program country. With this goal in mind, the author extensively compares the nature of domestic credit expansion and money supply as performance criteria. His standpoint is that, in general, the former is preferable. In section 3 Guitián promises a re-examination of the issues involved in the light of significant changes in the framework within which monetary policy must be conducted. New challenges have arisen from domestic financial deregulation and the internationalization of financial markets, which have been fostered by international financial liberalization. Domestic deregulation has increased the degree of substitutability between banking liabilities and those of other financial intermediaries. Due to the internationalization of financial markets there is an increased substitutability of currencies. Nevertheless, the author concludes that these new challenges which now confront monetary policy-makers do not really affect the conventional arguments; they only add to the complexities of actual policy implementation. This position seems to have been built on an early statement (in section 2) that, if anything, the presence of capital flows strengthens the link between domestic credit, the balance of payments, and the international reserve position of the economy.

Guitián provides a comprehensive overview of arguments in favour of domestic credit and the broader money aggregate as performance criteria. In this respect I have nothing to add. In my opinion, however, the author's view that the new challenges of the financial liberalization do not really matter can be criticized. I will explain why this inference is far too sweeping.

Economic policy instruments or intermediate variables are appropriate as performance criteria, only when they satisfy two requirements. First, it must be possible to hold the policy-makers accountable for the value of the variable. Therefore, the variable must be controllable to a large extent. Domestic credit creation rather than money supply fulfills this condition. Second, when the policy-makers let the instrument or intermediate variable change, it must be

217

J.A.H. de Beaufort Wijnholds, S.C.W. Eijffinger and L.H. Hoogduin (eds.), A Framework for Monetary Stability, pp. 217–220.

possible at least to partly predict what the effect is on the ultimate economic goals[1]. Shortening the causal chain between the variable in question and the ultimate economic goals will, of course, contribute to this predictability: a possible instability of the relationship between domestic credit creation and the monetary aggregates, i.e. an instability in the multipliers, is circumvented. In this respect allocating a target value to the money supply is a more certain way to realize money market equilibrium and, in line with that, the desired rate of inflation and balance of payments than by fixing the value of the domestic credit variable. Guitián believes that this drawback of the domestic credit variable is insignificant, by arguing that the balance of payments imbalance – through changes in the monetary reserve component of the money supply – will close the gap between domestic credit and the money demand. In his reasoning, he in fact uses – implicitly – an exogenous price level. This assumption is standard in the monetary approach of the balance of payments and, later on, of the exchange rate. However, this unrealistic assumption can considerably distort the model outcome relative to practice, for example in the event of high capital mobility. Guitián is aware of this eventuality, but does not connect it with the process of financial liberalization – which he aimed to investigate. When substantial capital inflow occurs, however, the weakness of domestic credit creation as a performance indicator becomes apparent. This will be illustrated as follows.

It is to be expected that the start of an IMF program raises the credibility of the country's adjustment policy. This in turn stimulates capital inflow: particularly the flight capital flows will be encouraged to return. As Guitián shows in the Annex, this is not only an assumption as a significant number of countries with IMF programs have actually experienced unexpected large capital inflows. Under fixed exchange rates this will substantially increase money supply, amplified still more by the working of the multiplier. This will lower the nominal interest rate, particularly if the capital inflow does not reflect a growth in the demand for money. When the inflation expectations show a downward rigidity – as seems to be usual in the labour and goods markets – the real interest rate will decline. As a consequence, expenditures will increase and inflation will go up. Through the lower interest rate and higher price level, money demand is thus adapted to the higher money supply. The country will then fail to realize its inflation target, although domestic credit remains constant. The use of the money supply as a performance indicator would have signalled this undesired development.

This is a realistic example, which demonstrates the substantial impact of capital liberalization on the outcome of the choice between domestic credit and money supply as performance indicators and criteria. Up to this point there is no difference of opinion with Guitián. In section 3.2 he also postulates that situations where a reduction in the rate of inflation is critical and there is significant uncertainty concerning the magnitude of the net capital inflows are circumstances which call for direct control over the rate of money expansion, rather that domestic credit creation. However, it is quite surprising that Guitián does not continue this line of reasoning in the direction of the new challenges of financial liberalization. The process of internationalization of financial markets will boost both the average size of and the uncertainty about international capital flows and thus positively affect the relevance of money supply, relative to domestic credit creation, as a performance criterion. This result contrasts essentially with Guitián's viewpoint that the new challenges of financial liberalization and internationalization do not really affect the conventional arguments in this respect and that they, apparently, do not induce a shift in the choice of a monetary performance criterion.

As Guitián argues, within the framework of economic adjustment programs the Fund focuses on monetary policy in its broadest interpretation, encompassing exchange rate management. If in the adjustment process in the case discussed above, the exchange rate is allowed to float freely, the return of flight capital will induce a currency appreciation. Due to lower import prices, the country's inflation will not increase, but decrease. This is certainly an attractive outcome[2]. Hence, a mixture of the two policies discussed is well worth considering: a somewhat higher money supply and a moderate currency appreciation. It would restrict the worsening of competitiveness that results from the appreciation. So it would appear that the internationalization of financial markets not only affects the choice between domestic credit creation and money supply as performance criteria, but also the kind of exchange rate management. Again, Guitián seems to support the policy mix described but does not make the final logical step by taking account of the effects of the financial liberalization on the choice of performance criteria. The same holds for several instabilities which have come in the wake of financial deregulation and the globalization of financial markets, as well as the concomitant additional financial uncertainty, *viz.* in the demand for money, the composition of cash balances, and the money multipliers. Guitián does mention them, but neglects to spell out the clear consequences for the position of performance indicators.

This leads to my concluding suggestion. The challenges of financial deregulation and international financial integration are attended by a large increase of uncertainty. The example suggests that additional flexibility in the IMF policy stance could be constructive[3]. The time is now ripe to consider applying IMF rules in a somewhat looser way and adapting them more rapidly in the light of all the available information[4]. Then, Guitián's problem of whether to use either domestic credit creation or money supply is no longer topical. Instead, it is more sensible to regard the use of credit creation and money supply as mutually interdependent performance indicators. In short, this represents a shift from rules to a situation of rules with some scope for discretion with respect to the purely monetary variables. For the countries which apply IMF programs this does create the drawback of additional uncertainty about the IMF payments of future credit instalments: the relevance of fulfilling the money supply criteria declines. However, this additional uncertainty can be (partly) offset if the IMF intensifies the monitoring of these countries. This would greatly facilitate its ability to spot undesired policy developments in good time.

NOTES

1. In section 3.3 Guitián presents a somewhat extreme description of a policy instrument. A given money demand may be consistent with different balances of payments, prices and output incomes if the money supply is given. According to Guitián, this disqualifies money supply as an instrument. In fact, Guitián is in pursuit of the ideal, but non-existent, world for economists, where a single instrument is able to achieve the complete realization of many economic goals.
2. Here one escapes from the so-called Walters critique with regard to a country that joins the EMS while having a relatively high rate of inflation. In that case also the gain of credibility, generated by the start of the EMS membership, attracts foreign capital and thus boosts money growth. In the EMS, however, exchange rate changes are almost precluded.
3. That the IMF has indeed shown flexibility in the past in carrying out the policy of conditionality is made clear in, particularly, the lucid survey by J. J. Polak (1991). The changing nature of IMF conditionality, *Essays in International Finance*, no. 184, Princeton.
4. Polak, *op.cit.* (p. 35) shows that in an IMF program which started in 1989 a similar additional flexibility was already incorporated.

SESSION V: MONETARY POLICY AND EXCHANGE RATES

Italy's Experience within and without the European Monetary System: A Preliminary Appraisal*

MARCELLO DE CECCO[1] AND FRANCESCO GIAVAZZI[2]

[1]*University of Rome "La Sapienza"*
[2]*Bocconi University and Ministry of the Treasury, Italy*

Like most citizens of large countries, Italians tend to seek at home the explanation for things that go wrong with their economy. This may be slightly presumptuous on their part. Italy has experienced, since its inception as a united country, in 1860, several serious balance of payments crises. Each of them coincided with serious instability in the international financial system. This was true in 1866, 1893, 1907, 1926, and after the second world war, in 1947, 1964, 1976, 1992.

It is thus fair to say that an international financial crisis seems to be a necessary, if not a sufficient, condition for an Italian balance of payments crisis. What is more worrysome is that in spite of its tremendous growth record since unification, Italy seems to have remained at the mercy of what happens on the international financial markets, incapable to fend off the pushes towards disequilibrium it receives from them.

This conclusion, far from being negated, is reinforced by a study of the Italian experience as a member of the EMS. Almost fifteen years of partnership in an exchange rate mechanism which seemed to be based on monetary stability do not appear to have had as their result Italy's siding with the "strong currency" countries when crisis broke out in the international financial markets. On the contrary, the international financial turmoil of 1992 seems to have once again unchained a balance of payments crisis so serious to induce a heavy Lira devaluation which had all the features of an involuntary event, one which the Italian authorities had to bear with, in spite of all their intentions to the contrary.

A cursory look at the most serious Italian balance of payments crises will reveal that only in two instances did the Italian authorities manage to come out of crisis without massive devaluation or, in earlier times, without suspending Lira convertibility. In 1926, Mussolini adopted a policy of revaluation based on a strict authoritarian incomes and price policy and forced public debt conversion, which allowed him to restore full convertibility for a few years. This episode bears a peculiar resemblance to the similar policies adopted by the military Junta in Argentina in 1976. The other case in which a serious balance of payments crisis was brought to an end without recourse to devaluation is 1963–64. The crisis

---

* Opinions expressed in this paper must be considered to be the authors' personal ones, and can in no way be attributed to the institutions to which they belong.

J.A.H. de Beaufort Wijnholds, S.C.W. Eijffinger and L.H. Hoogduin (eds.), A Framework for Monetary Stability, pp. 221–238.

came as a crowning of five years of very fast growth which resulted from Italy's founding membership of the EEC. The Italian economy was abruptly exposed to the advantages of a large market for its industrial products, which were manufactured at labour costs much lower than those current in Germany or France. Italian industry, in order to exploit the newly found demand opportunities bid up the price of labour so energetically that the relative position of workers on the Italian social and political scene became suddenly much more powerful. At the same time, higher wages prompted a shift from the countryside and an increase in demand for food and other products which induced a trade imbalance, rendered more serious by a swift increase in investment goods imports. To make things worse, the political crisis engendered by the workers' parties' request of a place in the government induced a capital fight which was reinforced by the overvaluation of the Lira, and by the expectation that it would be redressed by a devaluation.

Italy being a member of the Bretton Woods system, devaluation was not out of the question. But, in view of serious dollar weakness and a very perturbed Eurodollar market, the U.S. government would not hear of it either for the Lira or Sterling, which had come under pressure soon after the Lira, as a result of the Labour Party's return to power after almost fifteen years. The Italian authorities were thus forced to adopt a very strict credit squeeze, accompanied by a savage cut in government expenditure. Domestic demand fell abruptly as a result, and Italian producers were pushed on the international market, in order to maintain cash flow on their greatly enlarged plant capacity. The fall in domestic demand thus heavily deflated total imports, while an export boom was swiftly engineered on a buoyant foreign market. The credit squeeze also compelled entrepreneurs to repatriate the funds they had invested on international financial markets.

It would be fascinating to write a comparative analysis of Italian balance of payments crises, of the factors responsible for their outbreak and of the policies adopted to bring Italian international accounts back to balance. This is however an exceedingly heavy agenda, which we have to postpone. In the pages that follow, we intend to confine our attention to the last two decades only, the 1970s and 1980s. They both recorded, if we extend the 1980s to 1992, a first class Italian balance of payments crisis, which culminated in a massive Lira devaluation.

The 1970s, however, saw economic authorities the world over having to adjust to two massive external shocks: the floating of the US Dollar and later the giant rise in oil prices. The 1980s started with another oil shock, witnessed the steep rise in interest rates, the wild gyrations of the US Dollar, and ended with German re-unification and the dissolution of the USSR. The purpose of this paper is to analyse how the Italian authorities reacted to these shocks, which severely affected the Italian economy.

At first glance, Italian economic policies in the two decades would appear very different. This difference we will try to spell out in some detail. But we must still consider that at the end of two very different economic policy episodes there were massive Lira devaluations, in 1976 and in 1992, both forced on the Italian authorities by exhaustion of international reserves.

One last preliminary remark: before the 1980s, all Italian domestic and external crises show a common pattern. A growth cycle is started by some external event, which for the Italian economy translates into a rise in the demand for Italian products. Exports, imports and fixed investment all tend to rise coincidentally. Enlargement of industrial capacity thus seems to be undertaken by Italian entrepreneurs always responding to a marked increase in foreign demand. It shows great elasticity of response, but very little ability to plan ahead of events. It indicates a permanent attitude to sail close to the wind. It also indicates a structure of production which can be added or removed at short notice, implying a minimum of sunk costs.

Faced with this behaviour on the part of Italian entrepreneurs, the Italian authorities, who can be said to consider an increase of Italy's share of world industrial production as a favourable event to be fostered at all costs, have waited before imposing demand-deflating measures until they have been sure the investment cycle had run its whole course. They have accommodated the rise in fixed investment as long as it was manageable to do so, consciously running the risk of fostering inflation. They have curbed demand only when the external accounts became too seriously imbalanced, because Italian exports became uncompetitive and when the composition of imports showed too marked a rise in the share of raw materials (indicating speculative build-ups) or consumer goods (indicating serious loss of competitiveness on the part of Italy's key industries).

With the exception of 1964, Italian authorities tended, as we have already said, to accompany the curb in domestic demand with a large devaluation of the Lira. This would maintain total demand for Italian products, reducing the impact on domestic employment, and on domestic producers' profits.

A swift redress of the Italian trade balance would follow.

The Italian authorities could rely on a sequence of policy measures like the one just mentioned because of the composition of Italian foreign trade. Italian exports are traditionally highly price elastic, consisting mainly of manufactured goods which are produced by many other countries. Italian imports consist of investment goods, and raw materials, which are directly affected by credit restrictions, and of consumer goods, which are affected by credit restrictions and by devaluation making national substitutes preferable. Domestic credit conditions also affect capital flight making Italian interest rates more alluring to domestic capital and at the same time compelling entrepreneurs to call back excess funds they placed abroad, which they now need to replace domestic bank loans curtailed by the restrictive credit policy enforced by the authorities.

1. DEVALUATION AND ADJUSTMENT IN THE 1970S

For the Italian economy, as well as for most other developed countries' economies, the 1970s were a decade of inflation. Taking 1985 as 100, the GNP price deflator rose from 12,8 in 1971 to 51,3 in 1980. Inflation did not really abate until 1985, but, compared to both the 1960s and the 1980s, the 1970s do stand out as the age of inflation. Compared to other European countries, Italy was affected by inflation with a certain delay. It was not really until well into 1972 that prices begun their race upward.

As befits a decade when price expectations were constantly high, fixed investment and inventories also showed high values. Total gross investment never fell much below 20% of GDP (its average value for the whole decade), while in the 1980s, and especially in the latter part of that decade, it fell as low as 16% of GDP, and averaged about 18%. Inventories also remained high for the whole 1970s, while they slumped to very low values in the 1980s.

Were it not for a dip to −2.5% in 1975, GDP growth was consistently high in the 1970s. Looking at real GDP growth rates, the first oil crisis cannot be detected. Nominal growth rates, on the other hand, tell a completely different story, which gives away the Italian authorities' policy choice in the 1970s. Faced with turmoil in the world economy of a level and kind unprecedented since the interwar years, the Italian authorities, who had to confront a very difficult sociopolitical context in their own country, decided that full employment had to be maintained at all costs to minimize social strife. Accordingly, they fostered growth and took the consequences on the balance of payments in their stride, benefitting from the newly inaugurated era of floating exchange rates. They used the exchange rate to maximize employment, as competitiveness gains could not be expected from rationalization of labour inputs, which the social context rendered unfeasible.

This policy stance, which the authorities maintained until the end of the decade, was based on what in the 1930s used to be called "elasticity optimism". Italian exporters showed for the whole period that the authorities' confidence in their abilities was well placed. From 13% of GDP in 1970, exports rose constantly in the decade, ending it at 18% (in nominal terms). Direction of Italian trade was able to move towards the markets which expressed the highest demand levels, and those which paid in high-valued currencies.

Such swiftness of foot, however, required a profound transformation of Italian industrial organization. The seventies were in fact the decade in the course of which Italian industry was completely transformed, small scale firms became much more dominant than they used to be, extensive sub-contracting became the order of the day for most large scale producers, and Italian foreign trade started being dominated by exports of light industrial products, while mass produced goods retreated, never to regain their prominence again.

Italian industry had always lived somewhat hand to mouth, never really engaging in large research and development (R&D) efforts, never organising foreign distribution of its products on a permanent basis, which would require large sunk costs, inconsistent with rapidly changing markets. In the 1970s, these features were enhanced to an almost caricatural degree, as small and medium sized firms entered the export market en masse. While other European countries enhanced their relative specialization in mass production goods, like motor cars, and in R&D intensive goods, Italy concentrated its forces on exports which were price elastic and organised production so as to be able to adjust to oscillating demand by readjusting output and by spreading profit losses on as many people as possible. This was accomplished while the better organised part of Italian industry was subjected to an increasing dose of labour rigidity, rapidly rising labour costs, and historically high labour unrest.

In view of the micro-economic situation, which was rapidly deteriorating for Italian large scale industry, with the continuous help of government measures which sought to purchase social peace at no matter what price, and even with the employers' federation agreeing to grant total indexation of wages, macro-economic policy measures tried to change distribution in the opposite direction to that indicated by micro-economic policies and events. This explains the inflation-accommodating policies which were adopted.

It is clear that, in spite of the favourable output growth rates we have mentioned at the start, the 1970s was a decade of survival in extremely troubled socio-political, as well as economic conditions. The Italian authorities as well as large scale industry obviously postponed long term readjustment, using inflation and devaluation as dilatory measures.

These were rough methods, and negative results could not be avoided. Huge external deficits, for instance, were recorded. Maintaining output and employment implied recourse to international organisations such as the IMF and the EEC, and to bilateral help like the swap arrangement with the Federal Reserve and a swap of gold against currency with the Bundesbank. There were also currency crises. At the beginning of 1976 the foreign exchange market had to be closed for over a month, on the occasion of a world-wide financial crisis which ended up with the Lira being masssively devalued.

It would be unfair to forget that in the years immediately following devaluation, and probably because of the shock which the sudden and large loss of international value of the Italian currency caused to the whole Italian population (which had hitherto been accustomed to the idea that a dollar was worth 625 lira, as indeed had been the case since 1947), social peace was obtained by a temporary grand alliance between government and opposition. The opposition restrained the unions and the latter agreed to de-index at least severance pay, and, which was much more important, to allow the government to maintain nominal income tax brackets and highly progressive tax rates in a context of rapid inflation. Thus tax revenues jumped, and this allowed the authorities to grant employers subsidies consisting in a sizable cut in employers' social security contributions.

As a result, in spite of indexation, private consumption fell from an average of 52% of GDP in the years 1970–75, to one of 50% in the following five years. At the same time profits recovered, in the second half of the 1970s, to the level they had been at before the oil crisis. In those same years, the opposite occurred in the other large European countries. After a short recovery, the share of profits in value added declined again.

The positive results we have mentioned on production, employment and the balance of payments were obtained in Italy not only by a social truce but also by declaring a state of economic emergency, which lasted well until the second half of the 1980s and whose more remarkable measure was the passing of a law which made capital exports a criminal offense. Strict capital controls stemmed the flight from the Lira and allowed the authorities to keep domestic interest rates a good 350 basis points lower than those on the Eurolira. Capital controls, however, stifled for more than a decade most international activities of the Italian financial sector. They contributed to insulate Italian banks from foreign competition, making them much less efficient than they could have been if they had continued to be able to participate freely in international transactions. While thousands of Italian firms appeared as exporters and importers of commodities, and Italy kept and even increased its large share of world visible trade, Italian financial firms were shut off from invisible trade. This very awkward imbalance was to be kept even when the state of emergency ceased.

2. ADJUSTMENT AND DEVALUATION 1980–1992

With the kidnapping and subsequent killing of Aldo Moro by the Red Brigades, in the spring of 1978, the grand alliance between government and opposition, which Moro had fostered, against domestic and external dissent, came gradually unstuck in the course of the same year. With it went the social peace the opposition had extracted from the reluctant unions. In the new atmosphere of open social confrontation, with mounting political strife, the Italian economic authorities could not possibly have imposed a new policy course on the economy, in spite of the fact that the rest of the developed countries had showed every intention to face the new hike in oil prices imposed by OPEC in 1979 with a policy of deflation, as opposed to the accommodation most of the same countries had chosen in the years immediately following the first oil crisis. The Italian authorities thus found themselves in the early 1980s persevering almost alone in the policy of accommodation of supply shocks. Their stance contrasted even more starkly with that of the countries with whom Italy had decided to form a joint floating system, the EMS which, as is known, started operating in March, 1979. The inflation differential between Italy and Germany went from 12% in 1979 to 16% in 1980. Admittedly, the Italian central bank had insisted on choosing a very low point of departure for the Italian exchange rate when the EMS was formed, and a wider band of fluctuation for the Lira. All the same, Italian macroeconomic variables could not have kept following the course of the previous ten years without a serious crisis developing in a very short time in the EMS, low exchange rate of the Lira and wider band notwithstanding.

A policy reversal was thus forcibly imposed by circumstances on the Italian authorities. The exchange rate was to be used in the following years rather than to maintain full employment, maximize export shares and profit levels, to enforce rapid deflation, or at least retreat from high inflation to more acceptable levels of price rises, more consistent with Italy's permanence in the EMS. It is not possible to understand the new course of Italian policy if we do not recall the remarkable change in central bank behaviour which occurred in the same years. The Italian central bank had no statutory autonomy from government. Having gained great authority and prestige over the decades of its existence, it was thoroughly immersed in economic policy making, sharing with the Government the design and implementation of most economic policy measures. After the inception of the EMS, which the central bank had been extremely reluctant for Italy to participate in, and after a despicable attack had been launched against it by politicians, now thoroughly discredited, who were in those years in the fullness of their power, the central bank decided that its survival as an institution depended on its ability to stand aside from cooperative policy making, and to define its role more strictly and narrowly as that of warden of monetary stability. This new stance coincided with similar ideas getting favourable reception in foreign political and economic circles. If the 1980s were to see a reentry from world inflation, central banks ought to be given strict terms of reference with respect to monetary stability, and be allowed to pursue them in isolation from political interference. The Bundesbank's alleged independence was associated with Germany's favourable record of low inflation and held as an example for all central banks to follow.

For the Italian central bank, the new course began to take shape with the so-called "divorce" from the Treasury with respect to the prices of Government bonds. As in the case of the Federal Reserve in the early 1950s, the policy of pegging interest rates on Public Debt was discontinued. It could have hardly been otherwise, given the escalation of world interest rates which resulted from the appointment of Paul Volcker to the Federal Reserve with a mandate to rapidly bring back the US from the brink of runaway inflation.

We have noted before that in the 1970s the Italian authorities made abundant use of exchange rates and foreign exchange controls to maintain growth, accumulation, employment, and increase exports to cover the much enlarged oil and raw materials import bill. A peculiar sort of incomes policy was in force in the years of the grand alliance between government and opposition, which consisted in allowing progressive taxation to hit rapidly increasing nominal wages with full force. In addition, large budget deficits were monetized.

The new autonomous monetary stance inaugurated in the early 1980s came to view Italy's membership of the EMS as a major tool for disinflation only gradually. The Bank of Italy had insisted, as we have already seen, on making absolutely sure that EMS membership would not require subjecting the Italian economy to an unrealistically severe deflation. A very low starting exchange rate and a wide fluctuation band had been secured for the Lira, which would allow Italy to stay within the ERM without too much trauma.

The EMS was at its inception not seen yet as a way for inflationary countries to borrow credibility from less inflationary ones, in order for the former to deflate with less sacrifice than they otherwise would without a "nominal anchor". Nor had the "advantage of tying one's hands" been yet appreciated by the authorities of profligate countries, or by analytical economists. The EMS, as everyone will recall, was an invention of French and German politicians, and its main aim was to prevent the EEC from being hit by all US exchange rate oscillations, which played havoc with, for instance, the Common Agricultural Policy arrangements. It was also a way of proclaiming a truce among European industrial producers, who had, in the 1970s, increasingly begun to fall prey to the allure of beggar thy neigbour policies, as an easy solution to the current account problems they had to face after the first oil crisis. The second oil shock and the deep fluctuations of the US dollar threatened to renew such problems. In addition, the US indictment of German monetary policy at the end of the seventies made it convenient for Germany to link up its currency to weaker ones, in order to partly stem the revaluation against the dollar the Deutschemark had experienced in the same years. It is useful to recall that at the end of the 1970s German exports had encountered difficulties on world markets due to the appreciation of the Deutschemark. Italian trade with Germany, for instance, had for the first time in memory swung into a surplus.

The EMS thus behaved, until well into the 1980s, as a crawling peg more than as a fixed exchange rate system. Realignments took place on average once a year until 1987. From the beginning of the decade, however, the Italian monetary authorities showed their intention to put their own house in order without waiting for the Italian government to do the same with theirs. Public deficits continued to grow in relative size, but the Bank of Italy made it very clear that it would no more let them mess up its monetary statistics. It expressed its new order of policy priorities as, first, to look after its own balance sheet. Only gradually did the monetary authorities begin to show interest in using the exchange rate to reduce the rate of inflation. When they did so they let the real exchange rate appreciate, by not fully accommodating domestic price changes by a corresponding devaluation of the nominal exchange rate. This new stance was accompanied by a return to positive real interest rates, and by a rapid climb in their levels, after almost a decade of negative real rates.

The return to positive real interest rates, plus the less than complete accommodation of nominal exchange rate devaluation was a clear signal to the private sector that the policy stance had changed. It was an effective signal because it caught private enterprises at a very high leverage level, which they had reached when real rates were negative and credit easily forthcoming. The incentive to draw down bank debt was therefore powerful, and it coincided with a rationalization drive by large industrial firms, which allowed them to return to satisfactory profit levels. When the European slump subsided, later in the decade, industrial firms were again to ask for bank loans. These were the years when the bonds were absorbed by individual savers and Italian public debt became, a unique example among developed countries, 70% owned by individuals. In order to make it palatable to the latter, the authorities devised, during the phase of high inflation, interest-indexed bonds, which became so popular that they still represent almost two thirds of total government debt. As long as individual savers will be asked to directly purchase government bonds, it is very unlikely that the share of fixed interest securities will grow by very much.

This change in the composition of public debt ownership was just one of the great structural changes which occurred in the 1980s. The other most important structural transformation involved the composition of employment. While in the 1970s the share of value added produced by industry had remained constant and industrial employment had slightly increased, in the first half of the 1980s both declined substantially. A million jobs were lost in industry. The index of industrial employment declined from 113 in 1980 to 100 in 1985. A similar decline had taken place in the great industrial rationalization which had occurred between 1963 and 1966. In 1967, however, industrial employment had started rising again, and had continued to rise until 1974. A plateau had then been reached, where the index had remained in spite of two oil shocks. The rationalization which took place in the 1980s lasted till the end of the period. In spite of a slight increase in the boom years 1988–90 the index never regained the 100 level.

Employment in the service sector, on the contrary, showed in the same decade a very strong positive dynamics. As a result, total employment did not suffer. At the same time value added in the service sector was gaining ground relative to value added in industry and agriculture. If one adds the fact that relative prices shifted in favour of services and against agriculture and especially industry, one begins to understand the limits of the monetary authorities' policy stance. Putting their own house in order, in addition to anchoring the Lira to the EMS, the monetary authorities managed to clean up their own balance sheet. The industrial sector, by rapidly drawing down bank debt and replacing it with new capital, achieved a profound rationalization which involved the destruction of some capacity and the creation of a large mass of industrial unemployment. Productivity increases thus obtained went some way towards replacing the easy productivity gains that had been achieved through devaluation and high levels of capacity utilization in the 1970s. And the new mass of unemployed industrial workers finally managed to break the back of union power. In 1984 the government tested union power by setting a ceiling to wage indexation for one year. This measure was challenged by a referendum called by the opposition, which the government turned into a resounding success. An important political strike called by the unions at the Fiat works in Torino was broken by a very successful march of white collar employees and plant supervisors.

It took these strong measures to convince Italian price setters to revise their inflationary expectations downwards. Linking the Lira to the EMS was certainly not enough, by itself, to produce an improvement in the output-inflation trade-off. Moreover, disinflation had to be real, involving the destruction of industrial capacity and employment and this, much more than a pegged exchange rate, induced the break in union power which in turn broke the back of high inflation.

Reentry from high inflation, however, has never, to this date, reached the levels achieved in most other countries of the EMS. In spite of the precipitous fall in oil prices and the coincidental fall in the external value of the dollar, Italian prices reached a lower plateau between four and six per cent annual rates of increase, and remained there until 1992.

The limitations of adversarial monetary policy, as we might call the type of policy characterized by monetary authorities looking after the soundness of the central bank's balance sheet and not worrying about its consequences on the economy, can be appreciated to the full if we review the five years that are comprised between the EMS last realignment in 1987 and the Lira devaluation of September 1992. This interesting period included the joining of the narrow band by the Lira in January 1990 and the complete liberalization of exchange transactions, for the first time since 1934. All these measures ought to have increased the pace of convergence towards the inflation rates extant in the rest of EMS countries. In fact, if we look at industrial prices, they did almost completely converge to the rates experienced in Germany and France. The prices of services, on the contrary, remained all the time well above the Franco-German levels. And public employees' wages recorded very high rises in the same period, just when the Italian economy was achieving the highest degree of openness and integration in the world economy it had ever experienced.

The rapid march towards the single European market, then, does not seem to have encouraged Italian convergence. The monetary authorities' internal and international credibility was certainly greatly enhanced by the stern policy stance they adopted and maintained in the 1980s. Together, the European fast movement to complete integration and the Italian monetary authorities' acquired credibility resulted in a massive flow of foreign capital into Italy in the last five years of our story, and in particular since the signing of the Maastricht Treaty and the fixing of clear dates for the further phases of European monetary unification.

Paradoxically, however, the ease with which the Italian monetary authorities were able to keep the Lira at a level well above PPP reduced the urgency with which the Italian political leaders had to address the structural problems of the Italian economy. Like in the 1920s, a *fool's paradise* was created in Europe with foreign short term capital inflows validating the virtuousness of monetary authorities and the profligacy of political authorities, putting fiscal and monetary policies on collision courses which foreign capital inflows temporarily managed to hide from view.

The policy stance inaugurated by the Italian monetary authorities early in the 1980s and kept by them for the whole decade, until the Lira was forced to devalue in September 1992, must be thus considered a counsel of despair, taken because cooperative economic policy making with a profligate government was no more advisable for a self respecting central bank.

We must now turn to consider the large analytical problem of whether the monetary authorities' new stance in the 1980s had anything to do with public debt becoming unsustainable, a phenomenon which occurred in the same period. Italy entered the 1980s with a public debt/ GDP ratio of 60%, high for a developed country of its size, but not excessively high by its own historical standards. Since 1861, we notice that, historically the debt/ GDP ratio never fell lower than 60% except in the decades following the second world war. The post-war anomaly occurred because, in 1947, existing debt was drastically reduced in real terms by a bout of inflation which some analysts (Friederich and Vera Lutz prominent among them) believed to have been a conscious debt reducing policy on the part of a government which did not want Italy to start its democratic life burdened with a debt largely created by the Fascist Regime to wage its wars.

The ratio remained very low until the second half of the sixties, when it started to escalate rapidly. The escalation became really serious in the 1970s, when the 60% ratio was reached again, a doubling in ten years.

The monetary policy adopted in the 1960s and 1970s allowed the government to go on increasing the wedge between public revenue and expenditure without having to pay the price for its profligacy. The capital value of the debt doubled, but debt service was, because of real interest rates staying negative as a result of inflation, heavily negative too.

Had the 1980s come to coincide with a radical change of government, as had been the case in 1947, the newcomers might have burned up the existing debt with a bout of runaway inflation. This was, however, a course of policy hardly open to Italian politicians. The same coalition that had ruled the country since 1947 had returned to power after a brief experiment with an alliance with the opposition. They could not have disclaimed a debt they had consciously incurred to curry electoral favour for almost two decades. Had the rest of the world, and in particular the United States, stayed on the course of high inflation they had themselves chosen in the 1970s, the Italian government could have been excused if it had followed suit. But in the US Paul Volcker had been called in to take the country back from double digit inflation, and had elected to do it by controlling the money supply, disregarding what happened to interest rates.

The jump world interest rates experienced as a result of the new US policy stance made itself immediately felt on Italian public accounts. While the government itself started a policy of gradual retrenchment, more consonant with the country's membership of the EMS, the debt service part of the deficit started growing uncontrollably. The question to ask is whether, in view of the monetary strictness the US had adopted, imitating more virtuous countries like Germany and the UK, the Italian monetary authorities could have carried on with their previous policy of deficit monetization and negative real rates. If we recall that deficit monetization had, since 1976, required capital exports to be made a serious criminal offence to keep inflation from completely getting out of control as a result of devaluation, we can easily understand that the freedom of action of the Italian authorities was limited. Not only was it bounded by Italy's membership of the EMS. More important still, it was bounded by Italy's large participation to world trade, and by geographical composition of its foreign trade. More than half of total Italian trade is conducted with its EEC partners. Taken together, these features of Italian trade seriously limit what the authorities can possibly impose in the way of restriction of capital movements. Italian traders have been since time immemorial masters of the art of leading and lagging, of overinvoicing and underinvoicing, as befits people who have taught these techniques to the rest of the world since at least the middle ages. If the Italian authorities, even without the EMS, had persevered in a monetary policy of negative interest rates, inflation, and deficit monetization, Italy would have rapidly ended up like Argentina, with a total delegitimation of the Lira as a saving currency, and the complete disintermediation of the Italian banking system. Italy's foreign traders, that is to say a large part of its entrepreneurial class, would have just kept the proceeds of their exports abroad.

Since the inception of the center left coalitions, in 1963, successive Italian governments had banked on favourable initial conditions to accumulate primary deficits, which grew increasingly heavy as time went by and sociopolitical problems mounted. They had also sailed close to the wind blowing internationally as long as the United States had kept a largely inflationary stance, as they did until 1979.

When the US monetary policy finally changed course, the spectre of their former decades of high spending and lax taxing came to haunt the Italian government. Barring the destruction of existing debt, the course of their policy was largely traced for them. A policy of increasing the burden of taxation and of cutting expenditure was required, and it was adopted, but even if the pace at which government accounts had swung from primary deficit to primary surplus had accelerated, as it did since 1987, the sustainability of public debt would have been, given the dreadful initial conditions, very difficult to regain for more than fleeting periods.

Short term interest rates and GDP rates, and the primary balance itself, depend, in the case of Italy, which is highly integrated in the European and the world economy, on what happens in Europe and in the rest of the world.

Here we come back to what we said at the beginning. As long as the European economy continued on a pace of rapid growth, and the credibility of exchange rates was not put in doubt, the difference between real interest rates and real growth rates would not be too high. Suppose for instance the Danes had not voted against the Maastricht Treaty in the June 1992 referendum and the Bundesbank not raised its discount rate the following July. The chain of events which followed would have probably not come by, and the huge capital flows from US pension and investments funds would have carried on playing the "*convergence game*", to be invested, that is to say, in the bonds of countries intent in bringing down interest rates from the very high levels they had reached. The Italian authorities would have probably been able to buy more time to put their house in order, as the difference between real interest rates and real GDP growth would not have been so punitive for their debt service requirements.

This is, however, counterfactual history, based on our disregard of the important external shock which occurred in 1990 with German political reunification involving a monetary union based on one to one exchange rate between the East and West Marks. This event sparked the series of consequences which have in reality followed. The German economy experienced a prolongation of high demand levels for two more years, rapid fiscal deterioration, and a collision course between a fiscal policy feeling the need to spend on re-equipping the Eastern *Länder* with modern infrastructure and to maintain the incomes of Eastern workers hit by industrial reorganisation, and a monetary policy which reflected the deeply ingrained belief of the Bundesbank in an inflation model where the main transmission is from M3 to prices and from the exchange rate to prices.

It is not unfair to ascribe at least partly to an unease with a neighbour too suddenly grown in size the negative outcome of the Danish referendum. The *primum mobile* of recent European events is thus German reunification. The train of consequences which followed sparked the international financial crisis which hit Italy while it was intent on walking the tightrope of debt sustainability, in the much more difficult context created by its recent repeal of exchange controls.

Summing up on this issue we may conclude that, by the end of the 1970s, the Italian national debt had reached a size which made its sustainability wholly dependent on the continuation of the international context which had prevailed in that decade: floating exchange rates and high inflation in the United States. A country as highly integrated in the European and world economy through trade as Italy could have not charted for itself a monetary policy course independent from that chosen by the leading countries. We thus view the decision to join the EMS as not being crucial in this context.

Much more crucial was the Italian monetary authorities' decision to end their tradition of cooperative involvement with the government in economic policy making. At the beginning of the eighties cooperative solutions to Italian economic policy problems would have probably yielded slower disinflation and lower real interest rates for Italy, resulting in higher GDP growth rates and slower debt accumulation. Even cooperation between policy makers, however, would have been only a palliative for the Italian public debt problem. By 1980, almost twenty years of mounting primary deficits had given rise to a stock of debt which made Italian economic policy too easily destabilized by sudden changes in world growth rates and international interest rates. It had become a veritable hostage to fortune.

Had the international financial crisis of 1992–93 not broken out, what would have happened to Italian economic policy?

Traditionally, Italian domestic reforms, though needed for many years, only get actually carried out under the pressure of some external trauma, which allows the country's political leaders to overrule adversarial politics and demagogic consensus seeking. Had the international financial crisis not broken out in the late summer of 1992, the Italian government would have probably been able to continue to finance the strong currency option it had inaugurated in 1981 and enhanced, since 1987, by a continuation of the inflow of foreign short term capital, without having to worry, at least for some time, about the sustainability of its public debt. The tightrope walk, however, would have become increasingly difficult for the Italian authorities. A look at a chart showing Italian export performance, for instance, immediately reveals that, in the years following 1989, the strong currency option had become rather heavy for Italian industry to bear. Imports had started pouring in and exports had markedly slowed down. Italians fell increasingly prey to the allure of cheap foreign travel, and began even to buy up property abroad at a remarkable rate, while service sector prices kept growing apace.

All these elements rendered the continuation of the strong currency option problematic. Incidentally, it has been reasonably observed that the Maastricht Treaty, by mandating that two whole years without any realignment had to elapse before Stage Two of the EMU could be entered, made the timing of the last realignment wholly predictable to market operators, and unchained the financial crisis of September 1992, as the deviation of actual exchange rates from PPP became really too large and obvious for some of the EMS currencies.

If what we just said is correct, that Italian reforms, even if badly needed for years, can be convincingly adopted only in the face of an international crisis which allows the country's politicians to break momentarily loose of the demagogic stalemate in which they are normally frozen, we can call the international financial crisis of 1992–93 the *deus ex machina* which made the adoption of stern economic reform possible and indeed precipitated it.

What the Italian government has been able to do, once the international financial market dictated a massive Lira devaluation, is indeed remarkable. We must however remember that the abolition of wage indexation was agreed upon by government and trade unions in the Summer of 1992 actually to attempt to stave off devaluation, and to stem the outflow of capital which had begun in earnest.

The aftermath of devaluation resembles many another such phase in Italian recent economic history. Imports are slumping, exports are booming, the current account is further improved by the end of capital flight and by the return of tourists to our cities. Not much can be done about the increase in foreign debt service charges which has occurred in the 1980s. Altogether, however, the price elasticity of demand for Italian goods and services seems to have remained quite high, and the same can be said about the price elasticity of Italian demand for imports and foreign real estate.

Economists are currently marveling about one allegedly strange feature of this post-devaluation phase. Domestic prices have not responded to devaluation, and have kept slowing down their rate of advance. Some analysts have been ready to advance a novel theory of virtuous devaluation. Not only is a massive fall in the exchange rate good for production and the trade balance, it is also good as an inflation fighter. A little pause should be needed before venturing into statements as bold as that. Analysts ought to have memories longer than the five to ten years they seem to be able to span currently. If we go back to the aftermath of the 1963–64 crisis, we see that it was the only other time in recent years when domestic demand was thoroughly deflated, both in its private and public components. The same has happened in the last year. The anti-corruption drive by Italian magistrates has paralyzed disbursements on already appropriated public works projects. In addition, the government has postponed all but the most necessary new public works projects, and has launched on an anti-waste campaign which is yielding an across the board cut in expenditure on all government purchases.

Private consumption also has fallen because pensions have been drastically cut, and private employment has been curtailed both by industry and, for the first time in many years, by the service sector. Private investment is also down, since firms have had to rely solely on foreign demand to keep plants operating, and thus have needed no additional capacity.

In the previous episode we have just recalled prices remained stable for several years. There was no devaluation, but we can surely compare the 4.5% prices' increase of the last year to the virtual price stability of the mid-sixties. Essential to the behaviour of the price level in the last year has been the dramatic slump in the prices of food products, which have still pride of place in the Italian consumer price index. A fierce war between retail food chain stores has been responsible for this rare phenomenon.

We are therefore of the opinion that before declaring Italian structural inflation a thing of the past, we would be wise to wait for a pick up in aggregate demand which may encourage price setters to try their luck again.

What we can say, however, is that the restructuring of the Italian economy which two decades of hand to mouth adjustment to world and domestic economic, social and political turmoil had rendered necessary did not seem to be made any easier by the adoption of the enhanced strong currency option of the five years prior to devaluation.

The question remains, however, whether even the extremely strict package of measures adopted by the Italian government in the last eighteen months will be sufficient to put the country on a safe path to a less than ephemeral readjustment. We have seen that the policy stance of the 1970s amounted to a second-best solution. It allowed the country to forgo painful adjustment measures and still generate a growth level consistent with the maintenance of social peace. The package of measures adopted in the last eighteen months can undoubtedly be described as first best. Massive devaluation redresses the current account, and moderates the slump in domestic demand induced by the straightforward axing of public expenditure, freezing public sector salaries, and by the reform of social security. The public debt stock situation, however, is such as to require a continuation of service payments which will remain as a very high share of GDP even under the most favourable, yet realistic, forecasts on future interest rates. Service charges have thus a momentum which will allow to stabilize debt in 1998 at the earliest.

Stabilizing a debt stock as high as the Italian is, moreover, a rather tricky affair, especially in the world of no exchange controls which has recently come about in Europe. Any time a commotion occurs on the international exchanges those who hold Italian bonds have to take a view about their future value. As we said above, Italian public debt has the unique feature of being two thirds of total in the hands of individuals, who shun the non-indexed bonds and favour the indexed ones, as they consider their holdings as the equivalent of trust or pension funds. The advantage individual ownership yields to the public debt managers is that the stock is eminently stable, as bond holders cannot find substitutes with the same features and a better yield. On the other hand, a drastic reduction in world interest rates, such as the one which has occurred in the last year, cannot be fully exploited by the Italian authorities because demand for public bonds remains stable as long as their yield remains attractive to people who are eminently income-minded, as the holders of interest-indexed bonds must be.

Would the authorities be well advised if they offered bond holders to swap their interest-indexed bonds with a newly issued fixed real interest bond, a fixed real interest consol, yielding, let us say, two per cent over the consumer price annual inflation rate?

Would this debt conversion exercise, in addition to reducing debt service charges, make the demand for the existing stock of government bonds more stable? Italian economists are currently debating this issue, but no consensus opinion has so far emerged.

As a result of continuous turmoil on the exchange market, the EMS authorities decided last August to widen the fluctuation bands to 15% each way, leaving the ERM in a state of suspended animation. Other EMS countries have thus joined Britain and Italy in their lifting of the nominal anchor and sailing into the choppy seas of floating rates. Lifting the nominal anchor was obviously caused by the well known contradiction which exists between freedom of capital movements and fixed exchange rates. This contradiction, however, spent almost five years in quasi-abeyance. Complex analytical efforts involving rational expectations and credibility were launched to explain the non-appearance of the monster. It finally manifested itself, and with a vengeance, in the Summer of 1992, and thus, belatedly but powerfully, confirmed traditional analysis.

Why such a delay for the well known contradiction to make itself felt? Had the EMS authorities not fixed a deadline for the last realignment before the final exchange rate lock-in, some economists have remarked, the Bundesbank's raise of its discount rate and the outcome of the Danish referendum might have not by themselves been able to bring down the whole house of cards. This is not a convincing argument, however. International speculation returned on the scene as late as 1992 because in the few previous years American, Japanese, and British banks had very little time or money to spare, as they had been intent in cutting the huge losses induced by their domestic lending excesses. In addition, as American interest rates decreased rapidly because of the recession and the need to fight it by monetary means, British and American pension funds and investment trusts felt the pinch from lower income and were compelled to look for higher yielding assets. They found them partly in the stock markets of the Pacific and Latin America, and partly in the convergence game which the IMF Capital Markets Report for 1992 has so well described.

As no member of the EC seems in the least inclined to restore exchange and capital movements control, it is unlikely that peace will return to the foreign exchanges as long as low interest rates will prevail in the US, the UK, and Japan, or as long as high interest rates will remain in Germany.

In spite of the Lira's massive devaluation, Italian policy makers will be as affected to the gyrations of the international financial markets as others. Without exchange controls, the asset part of the balance of payments will be as relevant to the adjustment of the Italian economy as the trade part. There is in fact no assurance that demand for the stock of Italian public debt will remain as stable as it has been thus far. Moreover, the peculiar structure of Italian public debt ownership cannot be relied upon to last forever. If the authorities want to keep it as it is, they must court the bond holders with higher rates, thus imperilling the public debt stabilization effort and the rebound of aggregate demand. If they allow it to change, they must lay the ground for an orderly transition to a more orthodox structure of public debt ownership, by designing alternative assets that may appeal to institutional investors, and by, first and foremost, encouraging the development of institutional investors much more openly than they have done hitherto.

A last word on the Italian privatization policy. From what can be gleaned so far, a solution which relies on widespread stock-ownership seems to be preferred. If this will be the case, the stability of the Italian financial market would be best assured if the public were allowed to pay for the shares of the privatized companies they purchased with their government bonds. Retirement of public debt would thus coincide with privatization, and would probably boost the government's credibility.

Monetary Policy and Exchange Rates:
The French Experience

ANDRÉ ICARD

Banque de France

For nearly 15 years now, France has distinguished itself amongst the Group of Seven countries by maintaining the same course of monetary policy based on two objectives. One of the objectives is external, and it stems from strict compliance with the rules of the European Exchange Rate Mechanism. The other objective is domestic and is aimed at controlling money supply growth. Indeed France has used money supply targeting since 1977 and has taken part in all of the EMS mechanisms since the system was set up in 1979.

Overall, this monetary policy has produced the desired results. At the end of the 1970s, the annual inflation rate was in the region of 12%. It now stands at less than 2.5%. In the same vein, the differential between French and German ten-year bond yields stood at 5.8 percentage points in 1981. It then fell to 3.1 points in 1987 and has now disappeared.

These developments were parallel to sweeping deregulation, epitomized by the lifting of what had often been very restrictive controls on bank credit and international capital flows at the end of the 1980s.

Nonetheless, it must be recognized that the two intermediate targets of France's monetary policy act in different ways. The external exchange rate target has been a powerful tool for eliminating inflation expectations and it has guided day-to-day choices concerning interest rates.

The annual money supply growth target is a long-term nominal benchmark that markets can use to gauge policy intentions. It helps to shape expectations by stressing the authorities' abiding commitment to price stability.

This paper will highlight three main points.

First of all, stable exchange rates are imperative for Europe and for France. This explains the prominent role played by exchange rate policy in French monetary policy.

Next, as exchange rates are the most important transmission mechanism for monetary policy, pegging the exchange rate of the franc within the ERM has been a key factor in reducing French inflation over the last ten years.

And to conclude, the consequences for French monetary policy of the widening of the ERM fluctuation bands to 15% on 1 August 1993 will be discussed.

J.A.H. de Beaufort Wijnholds, S.C.W. Eijffinger and L.H. Hoogduin (eds.), A Framework for Monetary Stability, pp. 239–255.
© 1994 *Kluwer Academic Publishers. Printed in the Netherlands.*

1. STABLE EXCHANGE RATES ARE IMPERATIVE FOR EUROPE AND FOR FRANCE

Stable exchange rates and monetary cooperation have been constants in the history of the European Economic Community, which stretches back over nearly four decades. The Treaty of Rome, which itself was drafted within the international context created by the Bretton Woods Agreement, rests on the principle of realistic exchange rates between the Member States and sets fixed parities as one of its objectives. The Treaty also instituted the Monetary Council to meet the need for monetary cooperation.

At the end of the 1960s, the "Barre Plan", followed by the "Werner Report", set the goal of achieving Economic and Monetary Union within the Community rapidly. The initial completion date was to be 1980. The creation of the monetary "snake" was part of this approach aimed at limiting the damage done by floating exchange rates.

When the EMS was set up in 1979, it incorporated the lessons that had been learned from the snake. The EMS avoided the weak points of the snake by reinforcing the institutional framework and by using more than one fluctuation band. There was no doubt about the determination of the countries in the Exchange Rate Mechanism to make the fight against inflation their top priority and to accept genuine discipline in exchange rate matters. The results were plain to see: price increases slowed in all of the ERM countries and closer convergence emerged within the system, which, as it was meant to, managed to ensure increasing exchange rate stability up until the crises in 1992 and 1993. Lately, the ERM was weakened because the parities remained fixed despite discrepancies between price trends from one member country to the next, and because of instability on financial markets. But this does not detract in any way from its contribution to reducing inflation and improving the way both the common market and the single market work.

1.1. Stable exchange rates and community mechanisms

Stable exchange rates are needed if the single market is to work, and they are required if the European Community itself is to function.

All barriers to cross-border movements have been lifted in the single market. This has entailed sweeping harmonization of laws, regulations and taxes to remove or reduce the hidden barriers that existed in such areas. The exchange rate is a key factor in price formation and it had been kept stable within the ERM throughout the run-up to the single market. It is unthinkable that this market should now be left without any arrangement for maintaining stable exchange rates and that monetary barriers should once again be allowed to emerge, after having been largely abolished through the efforts undertaken over the last decade or so.

Even though businesses can hedge against exchange rate risk, it would be settling for far less than the original plan to accept more variable rates. It would give rise to discrepancies in a market that was supposed to be as harmonious as possible. The single market could not withstand excessive and unpredictable swings in exchange rates.

The fiscal operations of the European Community itself would be seriously hampered if exchange rate instability between the member states were to become a common occurrence. We have already seen how the rapid adjustment of the "green" exchange rates to much more volatile exchange rates has hobbled the Common Agricultural Policy. Similarly, the relationship between national budgets in national currencies and the Community budget denominated in Ecus is bound to be disrupted in the event of greater variability of exchange rates between the member states.

In many ways, the defence mounted by the Banque de France to protect the franc during the successive crises in recent months shows that France's aims are twofold. First, it intends to preserve the policy of competitive disinflation that it has conducted with persistence and success since 1985. Secondly, it aims to prevent any disruption in the functioning of the European Community. The French authorities' concern for persisting with a strategy aimed at the medium and long-term stability of the franc within the wider band proves France's determination to stick to its twofold strategy.

1.2. International integration of the French economy

France has a highly internationalized economy that is fully integrated into the EC. This gives the French all the more reason to be concerned about the stability of their currency vis-à-vis those of their European partners.

The ratio of the external openness of France's economy, expressed as half the sum of imports and exports to GDP, stands at 22.5%. This is less than the Netherlands' ratio of 41%, but it is greater than the German ratio of 21.8%, the British ratio of 19%, the Italian ratio of 15%, and it is much higher than the 8% ratios posted by the United States and Japan alike.

The internationalization of France's foreign trade is strongly oriented towards the rest of the EC. France's trade with its eleven Community partners accounted for 51% of its total foreign trade in 1980 and 61% in 1992.

With respect to international portfolio investment, it is noteworthy that non-residents' holdings of French securities have been increasing steadily. The negotiable government debt held by foreigners reached 620 billion French francs at the end of 1992, which works out to nearly 10% of France's GNP and 30% of the outstanding government securities. This is an important factor in the external constraint on the French economy and it has a major influence in the shaping of monetary policy.

Finally, the European Community accounts for a growing share of the direct investment flows between France and the rest of the world. Outflows and inflows to and from EC countries accounted for nearly three-quarters of these transactions in 1992, up sharply from previous years when the Community's share stood at half.

This high degree of integration into the world economy, and the European economy in particular, shows how important the exchange rate is as a transmission mechanism for France's monetary policy.

1.3. The role of the exchange rate in French monetary policy

There was a long period where France frequently resorted to devaluation. The authorities thought that it was a means of boosting growth and businesses found it a convenient way to offset their lack of competitiveness.

In fact, the extra growth obtained through devaluation was rapidly eroded by the stop-and-go policies that had to be implemented to prevent overheating. In any case, most of the extra growth was merely an illusion, because it was cancelled out by the depreciation of the franc. France's real GDP has grown at the same rate as Germany's since 1980, but changes in exchange rate parities up until 1987 have caused per capita GDP growth expressed in dollars to be 16% lower in France than in Germany.

Businesses had little incentive to call on their own strengths in order to increase their market share. They just increased their margins, rapidly eating up the artificial gains in competitiveness and gradually sapping industry of its flexibility.

The most obvious result was that France's inflation rate was higher than that of its partners. All of the economic agents, including employers and employees, got used to devaluation and factored further depreciations of the currency and renewed inflation into their expectations. The self-perpetuating cycle of depreciation, inflation and then more depreciation had set in and its operation was very clearly visible in the early 1980s.

In France, the unhealthy spiral was broken in the mid-1980s. This was achieved chiefly through four important steps that reshaped the behaviour of economic agents:
– a commitment to a firm policy to uphold the external value of the franc, which some observers have called the *"franc fort"* policy, and which the monetary authorities call the *"franc stable"* policy,
– a prudent stance for domestic monetary policy,
– the end of the index–linking of wages to prices,
– a better grip on public finances.

This drive for a stable exchange rate has had an undeniable impact on inflation by modifying expectations and by its automatic implications for interest rate policy.

Therefore, it is worthwhile to analyze how changes in interest rates affect the French economy.

A range of macroeconomic research[1] has shown that the main effects of France's interest rate policy are exerted through variations in the real exchange rate. These variations have an impact on growth in the short term, but their influence on prices is even greater. In the medium term, however, the extra growth caused by a depreciation of the exchange rate is transitory and mainly illusory, because of renewed inflation. The other effects of interest rate changes are less pronounced. They can be seen in the credit aggregates and, to a lesser degree, in monetary aggregates, as well as in incomes. Moreover, the impact of interest rate changes on domestic spending, via the financial sphere or income effects, is much less predictable. This is proof, if proof is required, that monetary policy without a strong exchange rate component would not be very effective in France. It also shows that the best means of enhancing the external component of economic growth is not currency depreciation, but greater competitiveness through stable exchange rates and better control of costs.

2. 1979–1993: FRANCE REDUCES INFLATION WITHIN THE EMS FRAMEWORK

The figure and table in Annex 1 show how far France has come in the fight against inflation since 1981. It is hardly surprising to see that, starting in 1984, this process was parallel to a shift in French macroeconomic policy to two main objectives: the strengthening of monetary policy, both in terms of domestic objectives and the franc's peg in the ERM, and a rebalancing of France's policy mix, as evidenced by the smaller government deficits and moderate pay rises.

The effort to stabilize the franc within the narrow band of the ERM was indisputably a powerful factor in curbing inflation. However, such clear-cut results could not have been achieved without incorporating the exchange rate constraint into rigorous economic and monetary policies.

2.1. Convergence in disinflation in France and in Europe

One of the greatest achievements of the ERM has been to promote convergence on lower inflation rates. The best results in this field were turned in by the founding members of the ERM in the narrow band.

The inflationary pressures in 1979 to 1981, following the second oil crisis, gave way to falling inflation rates as oil and commodity prices declined. During the period from 1986 to 1988, inflation rates were at their lowest levels since 1974. This convergence was achieved by alignment on the lowest inflation rates. The average annual inflation rate for the twelve EC Member States (as measured by the private consumption deflator) fell from 12.1% in 1981 to 3.8%

Table 1. Private consumption deflator: annual variation (%).

	1976–1978	1979–1980	1981	1982–1985	1986	1987	1988	1989	1990	1991	1992
France	9.5	12.2	13.4	8.8	2.9	3.3	3.0	3.3	3.4	3.1	2.8
EC12	11.0	12.2	12.1	8.1	3.8	3.5	3.7	4.9	5.7	5.1	4.3
Dispersion	4.8	5.4	4.7	4.4	4.2	2.9	2.7	2.6	3.4	2.6	2.0
EC7[a]	6.6	8.0	9.3	5.7	1.2	1.8	2.0	3.2	3.0	3.3	3.3
Dispersion	2.9	3.7	3.6	2.3	1.4	1.2	1.0	0.7	0.4	0.3	0.6

[a] Belgium, Denmark, Germany, France, Ireland, Luxembourg, Netherlands.

in 1986. With the fall in oil prices, the decline in inflation accelerated in 1987, when the average annual inflation rate for the EC fell to 3.5%. Since 1989, however, the trend has been less uniform.

Furthermore, throughout the period from 1979 to 1992, the dispersion of inflation rates narrowed, and at the end of the period the dispersion reached values even lower than those recorded during the 1960s.

The reduction of inflation rates and their dispersion was most pronounced in the countries that belonged to the narrow band of the ERM since the beginning. The average rate of inflation for these countries fell from 9.3% in 1981 to less than 2% between 1986 and 1988. More importantly, the dispersion of the inflation rates in this group of countries was sharply reduced, until it became negligible in 1990 and 1991.

But, there was a break in the convergence process in 1992, when the effects of German unification on that country's price performance showed up in the Community-wide inflation rate and in a slight increase in the dispersion between national rates in the narrow band.

Of course, the ERM countries were not the only ones to reduce inflation during the 1980s, the improvement involved all of the industrialized countries. However, while there was overall progress in the fight against inflation in the OECD area during that time, the average rate of inflation for the non-ERM countries and the divergences from one country to the next narrowed less than in the countries belonging to the European Exchange Rate Mechanism.

2.2. France has benefited from the fall in European inflation because of its membership of the ERM and the increased credibility that it has entailed

France had a long tradition of higher inflation than some of its neighbours, as was long the case vis-à-vis Germany and the Netherlands. The decision to belong to a stable exchange rate system with other countries, which were less inflation-prone at the time, was a strong incentive to disinflation. It made constant efforts to improve competitiveness necessary and gradually curbed import price increases.

Little by little, the fixed nature of the exchange rates within the system was reinforced as parity realignments became smaller and less frequent and then stopped altogether after 1987. In France's case, this was fully justified by the fundamental economic indicators, and especially the inflation figures.

The stability of the franc in the ERM and the curbing of inflation after 1986 helped reduce the real exchange rate of the franc vis-à-vis most of the other currencies in the system. This gave rise to a lasting competitive advantage that helped change expectations concerning the franc. This was especially true for resident firms, whose positions in export markets were strengthened through a virtuous cycle.

Gradually, an interactive process between the exchange rate constraint and stable domestic prices was created. And, gradually, France's performance on inflation came into line with those of the least inflationary countries in the ERM.

The firm commitment to keeping the franc in the ERM has given it a degree of credibility that would have been impossible to achieve so quickly outside of the Exchange Rate Mechanism. This is consistent with the basic credibility model[2]. Pegging the franc to a strong currency helped reduce the cost of disinflation by curbing inflation expectations. The fact that this was done when France had a high inflation rate, and that it was accompanied by credible economic policy commitments, was undoubtedly another factor that increased the influence of the intermediate exchange rate target[3].

Even though there is no credibility effect on the labour market, because German wages and prices have little influence on French wages, an effect of this type can be seen in the foreign exchange markets and in the way producer prices are determined. Price adjustments have reflected expected changes in the exchange rate and competitiveness less and less, thus proving that economic agents no longer count on a depreciation to offset excessive rises in their production costs[4].

This means that one of the main sources of French inflation has been eliminated.

2.3. The foreign exchange rate constraint as a determinant of French interest rates and the yield curve

In theory, one of the expected effects of the ERM was to be greater convergence in the member countries' interest rates, as their currencies gradually became more interchangeable. Interest rate convergence is also one of the criteria set out in the Maastricht Treaty for entry into Economic and Monetary Union.

The figures and the tables in Annex 2 show the fall in interest rates in France that accompanied the franc's stability within the narrow band of the

Exchange Rate Mechanism. The one-month rate now stands at 7.25%, as opposed to more than 12% in 1983. Over the same period, long-term rates fell by 7.5 percentage points and are now at their lowest levels since the 1960s. These changes show how much has been gained through disinflation in terms of lower interest rates, and especially in the case of long-term rates.

There has also been a substantial reduction in the differential between French and German interest rates. The gap between one-month rates stood at 6.8 percentage points in 1983, while the differential between long-term rates was 5.6 percentage points. In 1992, the differentials averaged 0.9 points for short-term rates and 0.6 points for long-term rates. As these words are being written, the differential has been narrowed to 40 basis points on the one-month rates and on long-term rates, the differential has disappeared and ten-year government bonds yield 6.15% in both France and Germany.

Membership of the ERM and the enhanced credibility it has conferred on French monetary policy have made a substantial decline in French interest rates and convergence with German rates possible.

A look at real French and German interest rates, using the figures in Annex 3, shows that the trend from 1983 to 1991 was similar for both short and long-term rates. Then, a differential emerged in 1992, as Germany's real interest rates declined due to a higher inflation rate.

Nevertheless, the real French one-month rates are at their lowest level since the end of 1989 and they are close to matching the levels seen between 1986 and 1989. Real long-term rates are at their lowest level since 1982. In Germany, the last time real interest rates were so low was in the mid-1970s, at the time of the first oil crisis.

It would be a mistake to attribute the sluggishness of the French economy and investment to the current real interest rate levels. Indeed, real one-month interest rates are only slightly higher in France than in Britain and France's real long-term rates are much lower than Britain's, where an economic recovery seems to be under way all the same. It should be remembered that real interest rates of around 5%, like those in France today, were consistent with lasting economic growth in the industrialized countries throughout the 1980s and, in particular, with the recovery following the second oil crisis[5].

2.4. The exchange rate peg was only able to play its role in the disinflation process because it was supported by economic and monetary policy

In 1983, as the French Government formally reasserted its commitment to pegging the exchange rate of the franc, it also shifted back onto the path of sound macroeconomic conditions and a balanced policy mix.

2.4.1. Policy mix

As can be seen in the table in Annex 1, France's government deficit was gradually trimmed and then kept at a low level in comparison to the deficits in most of the other leading industrial countries. It did not grow again to any substantial degree until 1992, when the slowdown of the economy and the effect of automatic stabilizers caused it to rise.

Along with this effort to reduce the deficit, decisive moves were made to break out of the index-linking procedures for wage settlements. This led to more restraint in wage increases, which still continues. The result was an easing of former recurring inflationary pressures and increased competitiveness for French industry.

The determined effort made on these two important macroeconomic fronts (fiscal policy and incomes policy) helped strengthen the franc's peg in the ERM and played an important role in bringing down inflation.

Furthermore, it is very likely that it would have been much more difficult for the government to make these economic policy choices, and much more difficult for the public to accept them if it had not been for the strong signals sent by the repeated crises of the franc within the European Exchange Rate Mechanism between 1981 and 1983.

Therefore, it can be argued that pegging the exchange rate had a major influence on the reshaping of French macroeconomic policy after 1983.

2.4.2. The role of domestic monetary targets

Domestic monetary policy also helped reduce inflation by setting intermediate money supply targets.

The purpose of the annual announcement of money supply targets is to set a nominal anchor that links, however imperfectly, the monitoring of monetary trends to the ultimate medium-term goal of fighting inflation. The targets give the markets a reference point and influence expectations by stressing the authorities' abiding commitment to price stability[6].

When the formulation of the targets is part of the annual exercises in economic forecasting, as it is in France, it becomes more than merely a monetary matter and fits into an overall policy mix, thus enhancing the influence it has on shaping expectations.

However, the announced policy must be credible if expectations are to take the right direction. This means the targets must be credible, as well as the means implemented to attain them. The domestic money supply targeting must be sustainable in the long term and the targeted aggregates must show a stable relationship to the ultimate goal of price stability. The latter requirement explains why M2 was dropped as the targeted aggregate in 1991 and replaced by a broader M3 aggregate that includes short-term mutual fund shares.

In the end, a monetary targeting policy is only really credible if the central bank enjoys a sufficient degree of independence from government authorities. France has made a clear commitment to granting its central bank this independence.

It has often been argued that it is pointless to announce money supply growth targets within the framework of an exchange rate system like the ERM. But, in addition to the long-term stabilization effect mentioned earlier, there are several arguments that can be put forward to justify this policy:

– Monetary policy based solely on an exchange rate target would be unbalanced in a large economy like that of France, where, in spite of the massive scale of its foreign trade, domestic demand is still the main component of the Gross National Product.
– The harmonisation of national monetary objectives within the framework of the "ex ante" exercises conducted by the Committee of Governors of the Central Banks of the European Economic Community has made these targets considerably more meaningful.
– The domestic money supply growth target has been a stable component of French monetary policy since 1977. The widening of the ERM fluctuation bands to 15% on 1 August does not call the exchange rate stability objective into question, but it confirms the importance of France's domestic monetary targeting.

2.4.3. Potential conflicts between domestic and external objectives

Svensson[7] showed that, in theory, when a exchange rate target is credible, keeping it within the bounds of a fluctuation band is compatible with relative monetary independence. This would seem to show that maintaining a domestic target is justified. The relative independence is based on the so-called "honeymoon" effect, whereby the existence of a fluctuation band and a firm commitment to defend it help to stabilize the exchange rate within the fluctuation band. However Svensson shows that this independence is restricted by:

– the fact that it only applies to short-term interest rates,
– the narrowness of the band, which may be reduced even further if national monetary authorities voluntarily abstain from using their independence over a long period,
– the gradual fading of the "honeymoon" effect over time and its final disappearance when systematic deviations from the central rate occur, especially where past experience shows that a move towards the limits of the fluctuation bands is a prelude to realignment.

In France's case, recent work[8] has shown that the stability of the exchange rate gradually reinforced the credibility of the exchange rate peg from 1987 to 1992.

From an empirical point of view, we merely have to see if the use of interest rates to meet the exchange rate constraint has led to a loss of control over the domestic target.

In general, any conflict that comes up cannot last. When the basic balance is fragile and there is a pronounced inflationary tendency, as was the case in France up until the beginning of the 1980s, conflicts between the objectives are rare[9]. In this situation, relatively high interest rates are a means of fighting inflation and they also ensure a sound basic balance by attracting external capital and thus help stabilize the exchange rate. In countries with a surplus in their basic balance and low inflation conflicts between the objectives are neither frequent nor long-lasting.

France did not experience any conflicts of this type between its objectives between 1984 and 1989. The conduct of monetary policy was aimed at meeting the exchange rate requirements within the framework of the ERM and overall money aggregate growth was in line with the targets set.

After that, however, the situation within the ERM became paradoxical. The currencies of some countries suffering from domestic economic imbalances were kept at the upper limit of the Exchange Rate Mechanism by high nominal interest rates. This led to a conflict between the need to keep the franc stable within the ERM through high interest rates, and France's sluggish economy and high unemployment, which, on the contrary, called for a cut in interest rates. Money supply growth fell short of the targets in 1991, which would seem to prove that monetary policy was tight.

In 1992, rising inflation in Germany and the Bundesbank's tight policy forced the Banque de France to keep interest rates high in spite of a flagging economy, but this did not prevent money supply growth targets from being met. On the other hand, the persistence of the problem in 1993 is very likely to mean that M3 growth will fall short of the target.

3. CONCLUSION: MONETARY POLICY ISSUES IN THE CONTEXT OF THE 15% FLUCTUATION BANDS

The widening of the ERM fluctuation bands to 15% on 1 August 1993 is only meant to make the potential use of intra-margin exchange rate movements more effective, but it does not imply that the objective of stability has been dropped.

With the narrow 2.25% ERM fluctuation band, the exchange rate target was set automatically by the commitment to keep the franc in line with the other currencies in the narrow band. The temporary widening of the band carries a message and a danger. Firstly, there is an all-important confirmation that the bilateral central rates are consistent with the economic fundamentals of the member countries. Secondly, erratic and uncontrolled short-term swings in exchange rates are not compatible with the medium and long-term success of the common market and the single market.

The message is that the short and medium-term mutual stability of the various ERM currencies around their central rates confirms the very foundations on which the Treaty of Rome is based and sustains progress towards Economic and Monetary Union as it is defined in the Maastricht Treaty, which remains totally valid.

The danger gives the message more impact. The existence of the common market itself could come under threat more rapidly than many people think if erratic exchange rate variations were to create invisible borders like those that spring up and fade away between the yen, the dollar and the bloc of Community currencies. This poses a threat, to more than just the ERM, the implementation of the Maastricht Treaty and the Single European Act. It poses a threat to the Treaty of Rome itself.

Of course, French monetary policy must take proper account of these institutional elements, even though the wider fluctuation bands may change the way in which practical action is taken.

There are other good reasons why France should remain vigilant in its exchange rate policy:
– The French economy is highly internationalized and the fact that a sizeable portion of French public debt is held by non-residents makes the external constraint very powerful.
– A substantial depreciation of the franc could spark off the cycle of depreciation and inflation that was a feature of the French economy up until the mid-1980s. This makes it vitally important to prevent French economic agents from forming fresh expectations about a depreciation of the franc.
– The sluggishness of the economy and the effect of automatic stabilizers have increased the fiscal deficit and done some harm to the sound policy mix that had been a feature of French economic policy for several years. In this context, it would be dangerous to weaken one of the essential mechanisms of monetary policy.
– French long-term rates are at an historic low. This is a key to renewed investment and, thus, renewed growth. But these low rates could not be maintained if the outlook for monetary stability were to deteriorate.

All in all, if the franc is to be a stable and credible currency vis-à-vis the world's major currencies, it must first and foremost be stable and credible in its own natural sphere, which is Europe.

However, the way the ERM is working now means that the M3 growth target and the price stability objective are more prominent than before. Price stability, by definition, encompasses both intermediate objectives, because it cannot be achieved without a stable franc, and the growth of monetary aggregates must be monitored to prevent inflationary pressures from building up. Furthermore, the targets for inflation and the money supply are even more harmonious since a criterion for the potential for non-inflationary growth has been factored into the M3 growth target range as of this year.

It is particularly important to note that the credibility of France's anti-inflationary policy survived the changes introduced by the 2 August agreement intact, as can be seen in the recent trend in its long-term interest rates. Before 2 August, the focus of the French monetary authorities' action had already been to defend this credibility. Since that date, the focus has probably become even more forceful.

This policy will probably have to rely on a wide range of indicators, with prices and monetary aggregates occupying key positions. But other indicators also have their place, including long-term interest rates, which are a valuable indicator of how credible the exchange rate stability objective is. Other indicators to watch are total domestic debt, financial aggregates and the balance of payments.

4. FINAL REMARKS

The temporary widening of the fluctuation bands to 15% marks a change in the operation of the European Exchange Rate Mechanism. It does not alter the objective of France's monetary policy, even though this policy is adapting to the new framework. Indeed, the attainment of this objective will now depend more on the credibility stemming from the consistency and quality of monetary policy itself. This means that there is reason to be optimistic about the outlook for the future. First of all, the markets have ratified France's firm long-term commitment to price stability. Secondly, the granting of independence to the Banque de France has reinforced this commitment. Finally, and this is perhaps the most important point, French public support for the ten-year-old policy of keeping the franc stable domestically and externally is growing, in spite of the intense debate about the future direction of the country's macroeconomic policies. This trend is very encouraging for the monetary authorities, because no lasting defence of a currency's purchasing power can be mounted without widespread public support.

NOTES

1. Cordier, Jean (1993), "Effets économiques de la baisse des taux", *Bulletin Mensuel de la Banque de France* no. 44, August.
2. Barro, Robert and David Gordon (1983), "Rules, Discretion and Reputation in a Model of Monetary Policy", *Journal of Monetary Economics* vol. 12, number 1, July.

3. Egebo, P. and S. Englander (1992), "Engagements institutionnels et crédibilité de la politique économique", *Revue économique de l'OCDE* no. 18, – Printemps 1992.
4. Artus, Patrick and Raoul Salomon (1992), *The EMS Credibility and Disinflation: The French Case*, Caisse des Dépôts et Consignations, Document de travail no. 1992. 17/E, Décembre.
5. Chomette, J.-P. et al. (1993), "Taux d'intérêt réels et activité économique", *Bulletin Mensuel de la Banque de France*, no. 43, Août.
6. Icard, André (1992), "Les effets de la politique monétaire dans un environnement financier en mutation", Colloque Banque de France – Université, Novembre 1991. *Cahiers Économiques et Monétaires* no. 40 – 4e trimestre.
7. Svensson, Lars (1992), *Why exchange rate bands? Monetary independence in spite of fixed exchange rates*, NBER Working Paper no. 4207.
8. Magnier, M. (1992), "Théorie des zones-cibles et fonctionnement du SME", *Economie et Prèvision* no. 104.
9. Icard, André (1992), *The Transmission of Monetary Policy in France*, Colloquium National Bank of Switzerland, March, forthcoming in: *Journal of Monetary Economics*.

REFERENCES

Krugman, Paul (1988), *Target zones and Exchange rate dynamics*, NBER Working paper no. 2481.
IMF (1992) *French–German Interest rate differentials and time varying devaluation risk*.
Monetary Policy Coordination in the ERM, Economic Unit. Committee of Governors of EEC (1992), Central Banks, June.
Pfister, M. (1993), *The Coordination of Monetary Politics in Europe. A French View*, Colloquium National Bank of Austria.
Jaillet, P. and M. Pfister (1993), "Du SME à la monnaie unique", *Economie et Statistique* no. 262.
Cordier, Jean et al. (1993), "La conduite des politiques économiques et le policy mix dans l'UEM". *Economie et Statistique* no. 263.

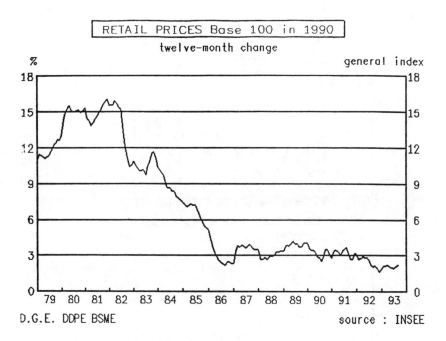

	1982	1983	1984	1985	1986	1987	1988	1989	1990	1991	1992
Twelve month change in retail price (%)	10,9	10,4	7,5	5,2	2,3	3,5	3,4	4,0	2,8	3,1	1,9
Wages increases (annual rate in %)	12,6	9,8	6,4	5,2	3,2	3,6	3,4	4,4	5,2	4,1	3,5
Actual Government deficit as % of GDP	2,5	3,5	3,2	3,1	2,6	1,7	2,0	1,9	1,6	1,8	3,0

Annex 1. Retail prices, wage increases and government deficit

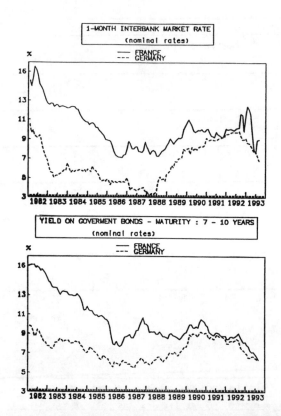

1-MONTH INTERBANK MARKET RATE (nominal rates) FRANCE GERMANY

1-MONTH INTERBANK MARKET RATE (on annual average)											
	1982	1983	1984	1985	1986	1987	1988	1989	1990	1991	1992
FRANCE	14,7	12,4	11,6	9,9	7,7	8,1	7,7	9,2	10,1	9,5	10,4
GERMANY	8,8	5,6	5,8	5,3	4,6	3,9	4,2	6,8	8,2	9,1	9,5
SPREAD	5,8	6,8	5,9	4,6	3,1	4,2	3,5	2,4	1,9	0,5	0,9

YIELD ON GOVERMENT BONDS - MATURITY : 7 - 10 YEARS (on annual average)											
	1982	1983	1984	1985	1986	1987	1988	1989	1990	1991	1992
FRANCE	15,7	13,6	12,5	10,9	8,4	9,4	9,1	8,8	9,9	9,0	8,6
GERMANY	8,9	8,0	7,8	6,9	6,0	6,0	6,2	7,1	8,9	8,7	8,0
SPREAD	6,8	5,6	4,7	4,0	2,5	3,5	2,8	1,7	1,0	0,4	0,6

Annex 2. Nominal short-term and long-term interest rates

REAL SHORT-TERM INTEREST RATES
Monthly average, per cent

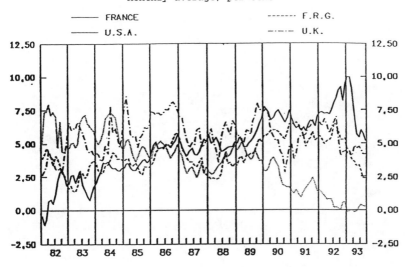

REAL LONG-TERM INTEREST RATES
Monthly average, per cent

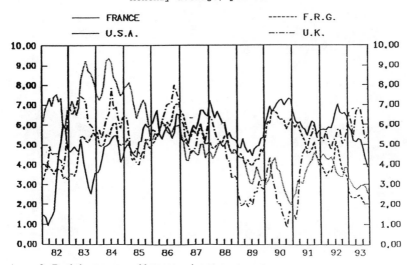

Annex 3. Real short-term and long-term interest rates

Comment on Marcello De Cecco and Francesco Giavazzi: Italy's Experience within and without the European Monetary System: A Preliminary Appraisal

GUNTER D. BAER*

Committee of Governors of the EC Central Banks

The controversial debate on EMU among academics and policy-makers might not have come to final conclusions but has certainly helped to improve our understanding of the costs and benefits associated with an irrevocable locking of exchange rates or, what amounts to the same, the adoption of a common single currency. The pros and cons of such a regime are probably best summarised in the terms familiar from the early discussions on optimal currency areas. The main advantage of a single currency lies in the reduction, if not complete elimination, of various transaction costs which, furthermore, can enlarge the dimension of markets by facilitating a better use of economies of scale, thus adding to economic growth. The main disadvantage is the loss of an instrument to ease the adjustment to economic shocks: the possibility of changing nominal exchange rates and of offering national monetary policies a greater degree of freedom in being geared toward domestic objectives.

Analogous arguments can be applied to the costs and benefits of an exchange rate regime with fixed but adjustable rates. If successful, the regime can reduce exchange rate variability and thus generate some of the same direct and indirect economic benefits as a Monetary Union, although on a smaller scale. Smaller benefits are fortunately associated with smaller costs, since the policy instrument will remain available: when it is *really* needed, parities can be changed. From this angle, exchange rate regimes do not seem too bad a deal: for a, perhaps small, reduction in benefits the loss of a valuable policy instrument can be avoided. The trouble is that in the real world the deal is rarely so unequivocal. Exchange rate arrangements have shown a tendency to break down suggesting that under certain circumstances the costs of maintaining the exchange rate system were felt to be excessive. Why is that so?

In order to understand the reasons behind the difficulties experienced with systems of fixed, but adjustable parities, it may be useful to start from the circumstances in which the exchange rate should be adjusted.

The need for a parity change can arise, as is well known, from two different developments:

* The author expresses his own views.

257

J.A.H. de Beaufort Wijnholds, S.C.W. Eijffinger and L.H. Hoogduin (eds.), A Framework for Monetary Stability, pp. 257–262.
© 1994 *Kluwer Academic Publishers. Printed in the Netherlands.*

a) The occurrence of asymmetric shocks which affect permanently or temporarily the equilibrium real exchange rate. As an example, let us think of a scenario in which the reform process in Eastern Europe succeeds and owing to markedly lower wage costs these countries will be highly competitive in low-technology manufactures and agricultural products. Given their different economic structures not all countries in Western Europe would be affected in the same way by the growing competition, and thus a change in the exchange rates between their currencies could be helpful to cushion, at least partially, the effects of the fall in demand.

b) Divergent economic performances – reflecting either structural differences in growth potential or the protracted divergence of some policies, such as persistent fiscal expansion – which also alter the equilibrium real exchange rate and, in a world where prices and wages are sticky, are thus best accommodated by a change in the nominal exchange rate.

Shocks are sudden and unexpected, lead to "jumps" in equilibrium exchange rates, and hence there is a sufficiently precise indication for the appropriate timing of a change in parities. In contrast, the effects of structural and/or policy divergences are typically felt only gradually. Changes in the equilibrium exchange rates are creeping and imbalances build up slowly over time, and this poses difficulties to decide when the change in parities should be made. Indeed, like visits to the dentist, devaluations are typically delayed until the pain becomes unbearable.

But apart from the difficulties linked to the decision of the timing, a bigger problem has to be faced when changing parities: the choice regarding the size of the realignment. The issue is not new, but it is as thorny as ever both for policy-makers (meetings where realignments are decided normally end in the middle of the night, no matter when they start) and the economists, as shown by the formidable technical difficulties, as well as by the need to rely on questionable assumptions, which are associated with the estimation of FEERs (Fundamental Equilibrium Exchange Rates).

However, it should be borne in mind that these questions relating to the appropriateness of parities hinge more or less implicitly on the view that the determinants of the exchange rate movements ultimately reside in developments in the real economy. The often referred to criteria of Purchasing Power Parity and Current Account Sustainability just reflect this view, i.e. exchange rates are looked at primarily against the background of movements in the relative price of domestic and foreign goods.

But even casual observation is sufficient to realise that exchange rate fluctuations have a very weak link with these factors, especially in the shorter run. Since the emergence of euromarkets, and in particular after the widespread abolition of capital controls, exchange rate fluctuations have originated primarily in capital markets. Exchange rates, like any other asset price, are then determined by stock equilibrium and portfolio considerations. Nominal exchange rates come to depend mainly on the risk/return characteristics which markets participants attribute to each currency on the basis of present and expected interest rates. Interest rates, in turn, are influenced by the authorities' actions and so markets focus on present and expected policies, or, more generally, on the wide range of factors which can affect policy choices.

In so far as this characterisation captures the essential features of exchange rate determination, it follows that the maintenance of nominal parities is not so much challenged directly by the shocks affecting the real side of the economy or by the anticipation of the longer-term impact of current policies. Rather, the main challenge comes from any market perception, accurate or whimsical as the case may be, that policies or policy intentions will change. This reasoning implies that the stability of nominal exchange rate parities is attainable if, and only if, markets perceive present and future policies to be compatible with a given constellation of exchange rates. The criteria employed by market participants to assess such a compatibility are, as a matter of fact, shrouded with mystery. It may perhaps be reasonable to surmise that the factors considered by markets in their assessment are not very different from the fundamentals resting in the real side of the economy and therefore market views will eventually converge to the opinions of authorities and economists. Yet, the important point here is to note that, for maintenance of exchange rate stability, it is not so much the present policy stance which matters, and possibly even less the policy intentions announced by the authorities. What matters most are the market expectations of future policy actions.

As a result, the scope for autonomous policy actions on the part of participating countries is considerably narrowed by the objective of ensuring that the parities are sustainable, that is, are not challenged by violent speculative attacks. For this policy stances of the various countries must not only be credible and time-consistent at the national level but must also be perceived as mutually consistent in the eyes of the market.

Is this an advantage or a disadvantage?

As usual in economics, it depends. It depends on the degree of economic and financial integration between the countries involved, on the type of shocks prevailing at a particular point in time, on the credibility of the different national authorities; not to mention broader political objectives, which are often forgotten in economic analysis. It is apparent that plenty of factors may affect this assessment, but it may be useful to focus on the distinction between small and large countries.

Small countries (which import sizable spillover effects from the policies and shocks affecting large countries but do not exert a significant influence on foreign economic conditions) may, for two kinds of reasons, find exchange rate targeting a useful strategy for the orientation of domestic policies. With regard to the conduct of monetary policy, the analysis by Turnovsky[1] has shown that the choice of the exchange rate as an intermediate target may present "technical" advantages on the basis of the classic arguments à la Poole which link the choice of the optimal monetary instrument to the type of shocks hitting the economy. In addition, exchange rate targeting may present other advantages, as it can enhance the credibility of the authorities through exerting a disciplinary effect and through the "borrowing" of foreign authorities' anti-inflationary stance so much emphasised in the discussions about the ERM.

These benefits, however, can basically be reaped by small countries through a unilateral exchange rate pegging with no particular need, on economic grounds, for an exchange rate regime which implies some form of mutual involvement in the setting and maintenance of parities. Both authorities and market participants in fact know that the large country will have a limited economic interest in the success of the pegging, since the economic influence exerted by the small country is in any case not very significant. Recent European events tend to confirm that the reference to a multilateral framework is not crucially important for the success of the pegging strategy pursued by small countries: the link to the Deutschemark has been successful for countries both within (Netherlands) and outside the ERM (Austria), while at the same time it proved difficult for countries both within (Denmark and Ireland) and outside the ERM (Sweden's and Finland's link to the ECU).

The situation is very different for big countries characterised by a high degree of interdependence stemming from the importance of the reciprocal spillover effects associated with economic shocks and policies. When economic interlinkages are important, the management of an exchange rate regime requires a close co-ordination of policies. Even the benign neglect of one large country could be sufficient to undermine, either de facto or in the eyes of the markets, the consistency between prevailing parities and actual as well as expected policies, since this attitude would imply that the consequences of economic interdependence are not fully considered in the setting of policies. Indeed, the strong pressures towards policy co-ordination which are inherent in an exchange rate arrangement may be regarded as the main advantage of the pursuit of exchange rate stability, in that countries are "forced" to internalise spillover effects and to avoid beggar-thy-neighbour policies, such as competitive devaluations. Moreover, there is the possibility that peer pressure among large partners results in a discipline effect and triggers a virtuous circle of stability-oriented policies.

Still, in practice exchange rate systems rarely deliver these results for extended periods. There are several reasons for that:

Firstly, the understanding of the mechanisms and transmission processes through which policy instruments are linked to policy objectives is limited, as shown by the continuing controversy regarding the properties of competing econometric models, both for single countries and at the multi-country level.

More importantly, national policies are ultimately decided in a decentralised way by several authorities, which may often be, if not in conflict, in less-than-full agreement even at the country level. The attainment of consensus on such wide a basis as the one required to ensure the effective and cohesive co-ordination of economic policies which should underpin a robust exchange rate regime is a formidable task, if only because of the sheer number of decision-makers potentially involved.

Even more importantly, international policy co-ordination can only be a voluntary undertaking. There are often incentives for the single country to deviate from the co-operative behaviour and chances are that the inefficient non-co-operative solution may prevail, as illustrated by the example of the prisoner dilemma. General declarations of goodwill and precise policy intentions may not convince markets: even in the absence of shocks, parities will be vulnerable if authorities, for some reason or another, are expected to deviate from the path of policies which is perceived to be consistent with the maintenance of exchange rate stability. Needless to say, difficulties are compounded in the case of asymmetric shocks which give rise to obvious policy dilemmas.

All these arguments point to the importance of combining an exchange rate system with a mechanism to mitigate policy conflicts when they arise. Of course, a precise definition of the rules of the game in case of disagreement could go a long way in guaranteeing that the policy actions necessary to the maintenance of the system are undertaken. And market participants would then have less reasons to doubt that mutually consistent policies would be actually implemented.

Is the establishment of such an effective mechanism possible or will we – even with all best intentions – be left with the notorious "let us agree to agree", which implies that when conflicts occur negotiations start afresh with no presumption that the consensus on a consistent set of policies will eventually be reached?

Once again there is no panacea. Whether it is realistic to believe that the smooth solution of conflicts is possible and that solid, welfare-improving exchange rate regimes can be established depends on a host of factors. But two of them seem the most important. In the first place, the effort of close policy co-ordination must be worth the national authorities' while. The gains which are expected from co-operation must be substantial. Unfortunately, the evidence on this issue obtained from economic and econometric analysis is far from conclusive, as recently reasserted by the studies collected in the volume *Evaluating policy regimes* edited by Bryant, Hooper and Mann, from The Brookings Institution. Secondly, the time horizon which underlies the choices of the policy-makers must be sufficiently long, if the exchange rate agreement is not to hold only during good times. When a policy conflict arises, say because economic cycles are not perfectly synchronised, even an agreement on how to respond jointly will imply that there are losers and gainers, at least in terms of the policy objectives which national authorities initially set. Such an outcome will be acceptable only if each party is expecting future benefits and is willing to wait long enough for the gains to take place.

Even tentative conclusions are difficult to draw on such a complex and controversial matter as the costs and benefits of exchange rate regimes. However, the arguments I have presented suggest that if a country is willing to pursue an unequivocal commitment to the exchange rate, this strategy can be successful if two conditions are satisfied: if the implied loss of autonomy is accepted without raising serious internal controversy and if consistent macroeconomic policies are actually implemented, leading foreign exchange markets to believe that appropriate policies will also be carried out in the future. When exchange rate regimes are instead based on an agreement which is multilateral in its essence, they require a close policy co-operation and the establishment of a mutually-agreed mechanism to solve conflicts when they arise; only then could they be expected to be successful and to hold also during difficult times. But the common framework necessary to satisfy these conditions implies that countries are willing to relinquish to a significant extent domestic autonomy in exchange for a jointly exercised autonomy. In the final analysis this may indeed imply creating a strong institutional framework which would mean in practice a move in the direction of Monetary Union. If exchange rate systems are not reinforced by such co-ordination mechanisms, either because they are not politically acceptable or because the economic benefits are seen to be insufficient, exchange rate regimes are likely to function satisfactorily only for a limited period of (good) time(s) and in the absence of asymmetric shocks and policy conflicts.

NOTES

1. Turnovsky, S. J. (1984) "Exchange market intervention under alternative forms of exogenous disturbances", *Journal of International Economics*, pp. 279–297.

Comment on André Icard: Monetary Policy and Exchange Rates: The French Experience

RALPH C. BRYANT

The Brookings Institution

1. INTRODUCTION

My comment on Mr. Icard's paper will address broad issues about the conduct of French monetary policy and about exchange rate stability. I will sharply question several of the main themes emphasized in the paper.

My comments may have rather too much the flavor of a North American perspective, for which I ask forgiveness in advance. North Americans are frequently not well enough informed about European problems, or do not grasp some important nuances of the issues. Yet to some extent a transatlantic gap in understanding is probably inevitable. My hope is that mutual learning can take place if we North Americans constructively voice a different perspective, even if we do get some of the nuances wrong.

2. DOMESTIC MONETARY CONTROL COMBINED WITH AN EXCHANGE RATE PEG?

My first major puzzlement is about the contention that it is possible for France both to maintain an exchange rate peg and to successfully pursue a domestic monetary aggregate target. Mr. Icard acknowledges on page 248 that many analysts regard these two objectives as – at least sometimes, and possibly most of the time – incompatible. But he is less than fully persuasive in rebutting this concern.

One conceivable way of removing my puzzlement would be to argue that the French variety of intermediate monetary targeting is the "compromise" soft version, of the sort alluded to yesterday afternoon by Andrew Crockett. Under this hypothesis, the French monetary aggregate target (formerly M2 and now M3) is a device for signalling aspirations about long-run inflation control, which has communicative value in influencing expectations. But in this interpretation, the monetary targeting is very loose (in any operational sense) and unambiguously plays second fiddle to the exchange rate peg.

One must read carefully between the lines in the Icard paper if the preceding

J.A.H. de Beaufort Wijnholds, S.C.W. Eijffinger and L.H. Hoogduin (eds.), A Framework for Monetary Stability, pp. 263–268.

interpretation is correct. If, instead , one argues that the French monetary aggregate target is of the serious, strict variety, I cannot make my puzzlement go away.

Of course I can imagine that the exchange rate peg and a domestic aggregate target can be compatible during some periods of favorable conditions. For much of the 1980s, for example, probably everyone believes that the exchange rate peg served French interests well. French commitment to reducing inflation was anchored to the already credible reputation of the Bundesbank as an inflation fighter, which over time permitted the gradual build-up in reputation of the French government itself. During this period, moreover, the domestic monetary target and the exchange rate peg would probably not have been incompatible in any serious way, and the two may to some extent have reinforced each other.

But in recent years, since the onset of German reunification, the compatibility of the two appears to me to be very much in doubt. The barest outline of the familiar story reveals the conflict. German reunification placed immense strains on the German government budget. Unfortunately, decisions were made in Germany to deal with these strains by permitting the budget deficit to bloat rather than by raising tax revenues. The Bundesbank was forced to tighten German monetary conditions sharply, producing the undesirable mix of lax fiscal policy and stringent monetary policy. The strong upward pressure on the Deutschemark to appreciate was resisted, which necessarily transmitted high German interest rates to the other ERM countries. High French interest rates in turn caused weaker than hoped-for growth in domestic monetary aggregates, especially in 1991 (which caused in part the shift from an M2 to an M3 target) and apparently also this year in 1993.

The recent past thus seems to me a classic example of a situation in which a domestic monetary aggregate target was incompatible with maintenance of the exchange rate peg, and de facto (though not in the rhetoric) the domestic target had to be abandoned to keep up the defense of the exchange rate peg. A few sentences in Mr. Icard's paper acknowledge the conflict. But his language is very guarded. And, for my taste, he downplays the difficulty of the tradeoff between the external and domestic objective and the hard choices confronting the French government.

I can't take more time to venture into other aspects of monetary targeting in France. And in any case, the really overriding issues turn on the exchange rate peg itself.

3. FOREGOING THE OPTION OF EXCHANGE RATE ADJUSTMENT?

Mr. Icard emphasizes that "stable exchange rates are imperative for Europe and for France." President Duisenberg in his speech at the dinner last night emphasized the overriding importance, in his view, of intra-European exchange rate stability.

In North America, as you know, a majority of economists and policy-makers tend to be skeptical about foreswearing the possibility of changes in exchange rates as an economic adjustment mechanism.

It is not so clear why there should be as large a difference in presumptions as typically is observed. As economists, we all have equal access to the extensive literature on exchange rate arrangements and so-called optimal currency areas. The general theoretical considerations are not so controversial:
- National economies between which labour is highly immobile are poor candidates for exchange rate pegging or monetary union. When labour can move smoothly across the borders of national economies, on the other hand, macroeconomic adjustment need not rely as much on flexibility in the real exchange rate.
- If economic disturbances tend to be predominantly nation-specific, the case is strongest for maintaining separate national currencies and for individual nations pursuing autonomous macroeconomic policies. Conversely, if shocks are shared or relatively symmetric across countries, a common monetary policy may promote economic adjustment fairly smoothly.
- When a national economy is very open to the rest of the world, the means-of-payment and unit-of-account services provided by a separate domestic currency may be less beneficial than the corresponding services provided by an external, widely used currency.
- Fixed exchange rates and currency unification are relatively more attractive to smaller than to large economies.
- Inflation-prone countries may be able to profitably peg their currencies to a foreign trading partner whose central bank credibly maintains a nominal domestic anchor. Conversely, if one's own country is less prone to inflation than others, flexibility of the exchange rate can help to insulate the domestic economy from foreign monetary mistakes.
- Nations or regions within which institutions exist that facilitate fiscal federalism are more propitious candidates for exchange rate pegging or monetary union than those in which such institutions are absent or weak.

Political considerations are no less important. For example:
- Nations and governments wanting to maintain open goods markets may wish to try to suppress exchange rate flexibility and/or opt for currency unification as a way of warding off pressures for protectionist restrictions on cross-border trade.

- Cross-border cooperative arrangements for sectoral policies – the Common Agricultural Policy being the archetypal example – are more difficult to maintain in the face of frequent adjustments in exchange rates.
- Separate currencies are viewed politically as a key symbolic attribute of national sovereignty. Monetary union cannot occur without a marked diminution in this political preoccupation.
- A nation might want to surrender monetary sovereignty in exchange for political gains in some other issue area (e.g., the contention that Germany has been a supporter of EMU because it would gain in exchange an expanded role in the formulation of an EC-wide foreign policy).

Analytical agreement on propositions such as these is fairly high. Nevertheless, North Americans and Europeans seem to give different weights to the general considerations and to come out very often at different points on the questions of if, when, and how a European nation may be better off by foreswearing the possibility of exchange rate adjustment.

Europeans, for example, seem to believe that the single market would be jeopardized seriously, in part because of protectionist backsliding, if exchange rates are adjustable. They emphasize the difficulties of adjusting the "green" exchange rates in the Common Agricultural Policy. They conjecture that a common currency would substantially reduce transactions costs. They understandably stress the high degree of trade and financial interdependence among EC economies. And so on.

What puzzles many North Americans, on the other hand, is the tendency to give relatively small weight to the analytical points about asymmetric shocks and limited factor mobility.

Let me come back again to the salient example of the German reunification shock. By disallowing an appreciation of the Deutschemark after it became clear that the policy mix in Germany was going to be skewed toward lax fiscal policy and very tight monetary policy, the ERM countries ensured that all ERM countries would have to experience together this skewed policy mix. A real supply-side shock of the magnitude occurring in Germany is a paradigmatic example of an asymmetric real shock that ought – other things being equal – to be considered as a candidate for producing adjustment of the real exchange rate (in this case between Germany and its major trading partners). With relatively low labour mobility among Germany, France, and other EC countries, the unwillingness to facilitate adjustment partly through changes in real exchange rates has markedly adverse consequences for French employment and output.

To many of us in North America, the costs of this foreswearing of exchange-rate adjustment seem high indeed. And the politics are also hard for us to understand.

If I had been a French citizen in the last several years, I would have been quite restive with political and economic developments within Germany and how France was forced to dance to the tune of those developments. I can imagine arguing "we French attached our anti-inflationary policies to Germany – thinking of Germany as a credible, stable monetary center. And then, alas, we find that major shocks originated in the center itself. Did Germany give significant weight to community-wide welfare in making its macroeconomic policy decisions? Apparently not. Is it then appropriate for us in France to make large sacrifices for community welfare and for building European institutions? Is the benefit-cost ratio for France really high enough to continue foreswearing adjustment via change in the real exchange rate?"

4. WHAT HAPPENS NEXT ABOUT EXCHANGE RATE ARRANGEMENTS?

Unhappily or fortuitously, whichever is the appropriate perspective for France and the rest of Europe, the last 15 months in the ERM/EMS have forced a retreat from the dominant role of an exchange rate peg. A significant amount of exchange rate adjustment has occurred, albeit of course with some disagreement about whether the changes have been in accordance with economic "fundamentals."

Even if one accepts the premise that monetary union is eventually the appropriate institutional framework for Europe, or at least a core of Europe, the road to that objective seems even longer and bumpier than many thought it was in the first half of 1992. Realistically, the wide bands in the ERM prevailing today seem unlikely to be narrowed again in the short run, quite possibly not even in the next several years. I am unable to tell from the balanced, cautious language in Mr. Icard's paper – or from President Duisenberg's crafted remarks last night – just what the committed but realistic long-run supporter of EMU ought to hope for about a re-narrowing of the bands and further concrete steps toward monetary union.

I confess to some cowardly agnosticism myself about the appropriate long-run attitude.

Economists, especially North American economists, make several analytically sound arguments about why European monetary union may not be feasible, or why it would be costly even if it were feasible. But perhaps those economists need to be reminded of the attitude embodied in a famous remark of Benjamin Jowett, the classical scholar who many years ago was head of Bailliol College Oxford. When a young woman came to Jowett with many difficult theological questions, he is supposed to have said to her: "My dear, you must believe in God no matter what the theologians say!" Perhaps, just perhaps, we need to believe in European monetary union despite what the economists say.

But as a North American skeptic, someone who finds it difficult to keep suppressing how expensive it might be for European economies to foreswear exchange rate adjustment until many other structural changes will have been made, a cross-cutting theological aphorism also pops into my head. EMU may symbolize stability and virtue, analogous to the cross on the cathedral's altar table. But, says the cautious whisper of the skeptic: "*Le diable se couche derrière la croix*" (the devil hides himself behind the cross). And while EMU might eventually bring European monetary salvation, there may be numerous dances with the devil before the goal really comes within reach.

SESSION VI: MONETARY POLICY IN EASTERN EUROPE AND LATIN AMERICA
Can Russia Control Inflation?

RICHARD LAYARD[1]

London School of Economics

1. THE RECORD

In the most essential ways, the generation and control of inflation in Russia happens in the same way as in any other country:

(i)   Money affects real interest rates and thus real aggregate demand (with a lag).

(ii) Real aggregate demand affects inflation (with a lag).

In addition, since Russia is a rather open economy (with exports equal to nearly a half of GNP[2]), there is an important transmission mechanism through the exchange rate:

(iii) The real interest rate affects the real value of the rouble, with low real interest rates lowering the value of the rouble and thus directly fuelling inflation.

Let us review the history, beginning with monetary growth and its effect on inflation. This is shown in Figure 1.

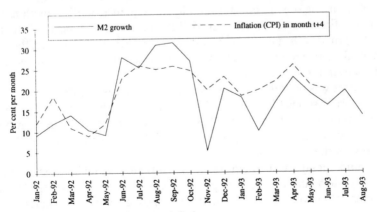

Figure 1. Monetary growth and subsequent inflation.

269

J.A.H. de Beaufort Wijnholds, S.C.W. Eijffinger and L.H. Hoogduin (eds.), A Framework for Monetary Stability, pp. 269–281.

Monetary policy has gone through three main phases. The first phase from January to June 1992 was one of relative tightness. On January 2nd most prices were liberalised and jumped on average by a multiple of 3.5. But the central bank did little to accommodate this increase, since the aim of the liberalisation was to eliminate the pre-existing monetary overhang. Instead the bank pursued a quite cautious policy, which led to a money growth M_2 of around 10% per month up to May 1992.

But by that time strong pressure had developed in favour of greater credit expansion. At the meeting of the Congress of Peoples' Deputies in April, one enterprise director after another spoke of the shortage of working capital, and from June onwards the authorities responded. In the orgy of credit creation in "phase 2" the central bank, which comes under the Supreme Soviet, happily took the lead.[3] But the reform members of the government were also forced unwillingly to agree to large "directed" credits through the Ministry of Finance. As a result monetary growth leaped up to over 25% per month for the next five months.

This had a disastrous (lagged) effect upon inflation (see Figure 1). In response to the relatively responsible policy at the beginning of the year, inflation had fallen steadily to around 10% per month in August. But it then leaped to a plateau of around 25% per month for the rest of the year. By the end of the year there was a general fear of hyper-inflation.

This led to a third phase of monetary policy (more restrained), which began with Yegor Gaidar's establishment of the Credit Commission in October 1992 and was intensified with the appointment in January of Boris Federov as Deputy Prime Minister for macroeconomics. He at once announced targets for the growth of central bank credit up to the end of the year. These were to follow a declining growth path, reaching roughly 20% per quarter in the third quarter and 15% in the fourth. In April the central bank agreed to the target for central bank credit in the second quarter, and in consequence credit growth fell from 57% in the first quarter of the year to 38% in the second quarter. (The target was 32%.) In May the government and bank agreed with the IMF on the targets for central bank credit mentioned earlier, which do not include the credits provided to the government by the IMF. But unfortunately performance in the third quarter was nearer to 40% rather than the target of 20%.

The more responsible "phase 3" monetary policy has already led to some improvement in inflation, which has fluctuated around 20% a month since March. However sustained improvement will depend heavily on what happens in the rest of the year.

The fundamental problem in controlling inflation is that in the short-run this involves a fall in output. The Phillips curve is alive and well in Russia.[4] Inflation only falls when output falls. Tight money does not immediately reduce

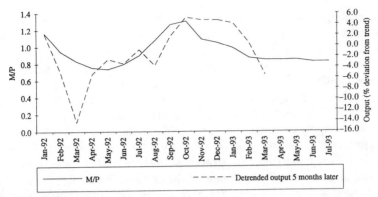

Figure 2. Effect of real balances on output (5 months later).

inflation. It reduces real balances which in turn reduces output, and thus ultimately inflation.

Figure 2 shows the history of real balances and of output (net of trend). As can be seen, the tight money policy of the first half of 1992 led to a steady fall in real balances, which in turn accelerated the fall in output. But from June to October real balances rose, leading to a stable level of output from September until early 1993. Since then output has again been falling, due to the tighter stance of monetary policy.

Real balances affect real output partly through their effect on real interest rates. Market real interest rates have risen from around minus 14% in November 1992 to around minus 4% in mid-1993 (see Figure 3). And the central bank refinance rate has now moved up to close to the market rate.

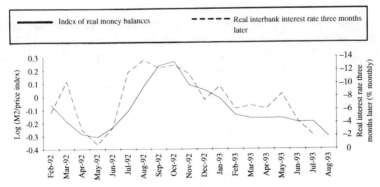

Figure 3. Real money balances and the real interest rate.

The real interest rate affects not only output but also the real value of the rouble, as is predicted by the standard interest parity condition and the notion that in the long-run the real exchange rate is determined by real rather than monetary forces. Real interest rates have risen sharply from around minus 14% November 1992 to around minus 5% in mid-year 1993. This is the main explanation for the sharp real appreciation of the rouble since mid-June. From mid-June to late September (when the Parliament was dissolved) the nominal value of the rouble was roughly constant at around R1000 to the dollar. This is perhaps the most tangible success of the new monetary policy. A rise in the dollar wage (from 25 in November 1992 to 60 in August 1993) can only be good for inflation. Following the suspension of Parliament the exchange rate fell to nearer R1300, due to increased uncertainty. Since then new policy measures have been announced and their effects on the exchange rate remain to be seen.

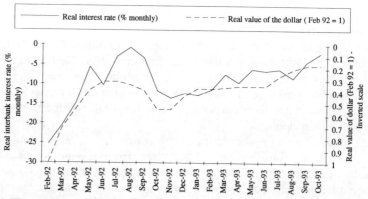

Figure 4. The real interest rate and the real exchange rate.

Can the policy last and can Russia really control inflation? There are a number of major problems which we have to consider:
(i)   Can central bank credit to the budget and to enterprises be controlled?
(ii) What about credits to the rouble area?
(iii) Will control of central bank credit lead to control of commercial bank lending?
(iv) May not velocity explode? and
(v)   What about inter-enterprise credit?
In the rest of the paper we address these issues in turn.

2. CENTRAL BANK CREDIT, UNEMPLOYMENT AND GRADUALISM

The biggest single problem is controlling central bank credit. In 1992 the growth in central bank credit equalled 40% of GNP.[5] This level of seigniorage is almost without parallel and was only possible because Russia's primitive payments system prevented an increase in the velocity of circulation of money (see below).

If inflation is to be controlled, new central bank credit will have to be severely curtailed. According to the agreement reached in May with the IMF, central bank credit (excluding that financed by sale of IMF dollars) would grow by the following percentages of GDP:[6]

1992	40
1993 Q2	14
1993 Q3	7
1993 Q4	5

This would be difficult to achieve because of pressures coming from all three recipients of central bank credit – budget, enterprises and other CIS states. In many ways the distinction between finance for the budget and for enterprises is somewhat artificial, since the budget props up enterprises through explicit subsidies, while credits at negative real rates do the same through an implicit subsidy from the banking system.

The budget

Even so, it is worth recording that the budget (and extra-budgetary funds) have not been the main sources of credit creation. In 1992 total taxes (including revenue of extra-budgetary funds, like the Pension Fund) amounted to around 60% of GNP – almost exactly the same as total expenditure.[7] The record of tax collection has been one of the unsung triumphs of the economic reform.

In 1993 the balance of the rouble budget was positive up to the middle of the year – due as before to the principle of sequestering applied by the Ministry of Finance. In July however the Supreme Soviet made a bigger challenge on the budgetary front than ever before and this (together with its attack on privatisation) was a major factor leading to the dismissal of the Parliament.

Given the huge pressure for credit to enterprises, the optimal target for credit to the government (excluding credit to enterprises) is negative. To achieve such a balance will require further efforts to increase government revenue especially from the energy sector. After the July price rise the price of gas was still only about 10% of the West European level (at the prevailing exchange rate), and taxes on gas are minimal (a 15% excise). Russia should be using its huge energy sector as a milch cow for the budget.

An important step towards non-inflationary budgetary finance would also be the sale of government bonds. The government is currently taking a small step in this direction, but the scope for this is limited due to the current popular distrust of government.

Credit for enterprises

In any event the main problem has been and remains the problem of finance for enterprises (whether "directed credits" issued through the Ministry of Finance or commercial credits through the commercial banks). This is the area where the main macroeconomic battle has been fought and will continue to be fought. Enterprises want credits above all to pay wages,[8] and to avoid the pain of restructuring. In 1992 inflationary finance provided them with a major transfer of resources from households, as the following figures show:

	% of GDP in 1992
Credit to enterprises	31
– Inflation tax on enterprises	–21
Net transfer to enterprises	10
Inflation tax on households	14

The real money balances of households are now so low that the scope for any future transfer to enterprises is limited. Enterprises now pay nearly all the inflation tax – a fact which should make them less enthusiastic about inflationary finance. But there will still be enormous pressure for finance to avoid layoffs, i.e. inflationary finance which transfers resources from sound enterprises with good bank balances to weak ones that may never repay their debts.

Will such pressures prevail? Two main arguments are used in favour of credits – that they will prevent unemployment and that they will enable enterprises to continue to finance housing and health care.

Unemployment

At present Russia has an official unemployment rate of 1.4%[9]. This is clearly well below any conceivable long-run equilibrium rate of unemployment, which is roughly 9% in Western Europe and perhaps the same in Poland and Hungary. Unless Russia moves at a reasonable pace towards its equilibrium unemployment rate, inflation is bound to increase. Will Russia choose unemployment or hyper-inflation?

There are some grounds for optimism:

(i) Public opinion polls reveal strong aversion to inflation. Inflation affects everybody. Unemployment will affect a minority, though the fear of unemployment is of course widespread.

(ii) Resignation in the face of misfortune has been a long-standing feature of Russian life. This is reflected in the absence of organised social protest against the economic reform, and in the weakness hitherto of the trade union movement (though this could change in the absence of easy wage increases).

(iii) Even in the West unemployment has on most occasions, but not all, led to apathy rather than unrest.

However there are two special features in Russia which give ground for concern:

(i) Enterprises are major providers of social services, especially housing, health, kindergartens and holiday facilities. Unless housing and health can be off-loaded onto local government, enterprises will be able to mount a convincing argument that they should be supported. And if these responsibilities are transferred to local authorities, this will put more strain on the budget.

(ii) For the next nine months Russia will be in an election campaign (for the Duma in December and for the President in June). This will make tough policies difficult, so that it remains quite likely that stabilisation in Russia will happen by stealth.

Gradualism

Such a gradualist stabilisation would be very unusual by world historical standards. Is it conceivable?

There are standard arguments to the contrary, which go roughly as follows. A policy can only work if it shows results. So long as inflation is high, everybody waits till they know what relative prices will prevail. Sales of goods whose prices are held down (like energy) remain low, waiting for future price rises – and this adds to the shortages. Investment is suspended and barter is everywhere. Enterprises with bad debts gain at the expense of those with solid bank balances. On this view the situation deteriorates steadily till a clean break is made.

That view may well be correct for standard capitalist economies. It is not so clear for a transforming economy, where the scope for improvement is so great that it may occur even in an environment of macroeconomic disorder. Indeed some Russians concerned with privatisation believe privatisation will work better in an environment of abundant inflationary finance rather than one of monetary tightness.

I doubt the last of these arguments. My own preference would be for a clean and quick stabilisation. But as a forecaster I would not rule out the possibility of a gradual stabilisation by stealth.

The government's current plan falls in between the extremes of stealth and shock therapy. It involves a clear timetable for disinflation, but no specific moment of stabilisation.

The timetable is a timetable for central bank credit. This involves not only tight credit for the Russian economy but also tight credit for the other former republics of the Soviet Union.

3. THE ROUBLE AREA

In 1992 about a quarter of new central bank credit went to the rouble area outside Russia. This financed the trade deficits of the other states with Russia. But the roubles thus created were of course paid to Russian enterprises and thus increased the base money supply in Russia.

Up to July 1992 the provision of credit to other states was almost automatic. Each state's central bank created its own non-cash roubles, and these could then be used to pay Russian suppliers. But from July 1992 onwards Russia refused in principle to accept net payments from other republics beyond agreed limits. All payments from (say) Kazakh enterprises to Russian enterprises had to be made through the Kazakh central bank and the Russian central bank and there were agreed limits to the extent of deficit permitted to the correspondent account of the Kazakh central bank with the Russian central bank. Thus in effect the (non-cash) Kazakh rouble became a different currency from the Russian rouble.

But there was no organised foreign exchange market in Russia for exchanging these currencies. Bit by bit such a market is developing. Kazakh commercial banks can now hold correspondent accounts with Russian commercial banks in Moscow, so that some trade can be financed through direct bank-to-bank payments rather than through the Kazakh and Russian central banks. This will help the development of this foreign exchange market.

But so far the existence of separate, non-convertible currencies has had a serious impact on inter-state trade. Inflation in each state has also wreaked havoc with trade, both between states and within. Barter is still a major method of inter-state trade.

There are now essentially two possible types of monetary arrangement to restore trade. One, favoured until recently by the IMF and the EC, is to maintain the single currency area with credit rationing by Russia, or at least to operate a fixed exchange rate system with current account convertibility and some kind of payments union or inter-state bank providing limited credit to deficit countries. The problem of any such system is that the pressure for excess credit creation would be intense.

The alternative is separate currencies, floating against each other. This too would be subject to strong inflationary pressures. For Russia runs a massive current account surplus with most other states. If this is cut speedily, it will cause major hardship and President Yeltsin does not want to sour relations with his neighbours. Thus it is not going to be possible to operate without some on-going rouble credits or subsidies to the successor states.

But these need to be explicit acts of political will, and not a haphazard outcome of monetary operations. Any subsidies or credits to other republics should be included in government budgetary outlays and covered, if necessary, by credit issued to the government.

The second approach seems less likely to lead to excessive credit creation. If eventually the other CIS states want to peg their currency to the Russian rouble, that would be fine. But first they must learn to manage their currencies on their own.

The actual trend of affairs here remains somewhat unclear. In September, six countries signed up to a rouble zone controlled in principle by Russia, but involving dangers of massive credit creation.

Foreign aid

The final element affecting the generation of central bank credit is foreign aid. If this aid goes to the government (or central bank) the dollars can then be sold for roubles, thus reducing base money.

The Russian GNP is so small (under $100 billion) that foreign aid can make an enormous difference. The IMF Systemic Transformation Facility is $3 billion – of which the second half ought to be released and disbursed this year. The proposed Stand-By is $4 billion and if the government now produces a good programme that should begin flowing early in 1994. In addition trade credits should be provided as far as possible to the government – to be sold in exchange for roubles. Subsidised sales of such credits should cease, which will limit demand. But such finance can at least double the flow of dollar sales beyond that provided through the IMF and World Bank,[10] all of which will help to restrain the growth of central bank credit.

4. THE PYRAMID OF CREDIT

If central bank credit can be controlled, two further links must hold if inflation is to be controlled:
(i) The money multiplier (M_2/M_0) must not explode, and
(ii) Velocity (PY/M_2) must not explode.
Let us consider first the money multiplier.

Russia has a two-tier banking system with some 2,000 commercial banks, about 10 of which account for the vast majority of banking business. Some of these ten are elements of the old structures (the savings bank, the agricultural bank, the industry and construction bank, the Moscow Business Bank and so on) and some are new.

Commercial banks are subject to a required reserve/deposit ratio of 20% (since April 1992).[11] However they also hold excess reserves which have increased from almost nothing in April 1992 to over 15% of deposits (on average) in the early months of this year. The reasons for this increase are unclear. It is unlikely that the payments system deteriorated since April 1992, so we cannot assume that these excess reserves correspond to a necessary float. It is more likely that they are the accumulated effect of continued emission of central bank credit plus increasing uncertainty about the solvency of potential borrowers. The obvious danger is that, if credit emission becomes more restrained, this will lead banks to lend a higher fraction of their assets, thus offsetting in part at least the intended effect of the credit squeeze.

As Rostowski shows,[12] this is a standard pattern in situations where credit growth first expands and then contracts: at first the money multiplier decreases and then (during the stabilisation) it expands. This has been found not only in Latin America but also in Poland and Yugoslavia.

To guard against this danger, a number of policies are available. Raising the reserve ratio is a crude way, which could unfairly penalise banks with low existing ratios. A fairer method along these lines would be a new and higher marginal reserve ratio, so that extra deposits would require a higher addition to reserves. Alternatively reserves above some limit could be converted into bonds. But some kind of action does seem advisable.

The second element in the money multiplier is the currency/deposit ratio. This too has risen from 20% when the reform began to over 30%. Nothing can be done about this but there is again the obvious risk that, if inflation comes down and payments systems improve, the currency/deposit ratio could fall, increasing the money multiplier. Thus the authorities need to keep a tight watch on M_2 as well as simply central bank credit.

5. VELOCITY AND THE PAYMENTS SYSTEM

But suppose bank credit and M_2 remain under control. Is this enough to control inflation? It depends of course on what happens to velocity.

In most countries velocity rises when credit is easy, and it falls when credit is tight. This has not been the Russian experience. Figure 5 gives the history of velocity. It is not well correlated with inflation.[13] The remarkable thing is how low velocity has remained, despite a year of 20–25% inflation per month.

The explanation seems to lie in the crudity of the payments system. Firms can only draw currency to pay wages, which is done every two weeks as it has

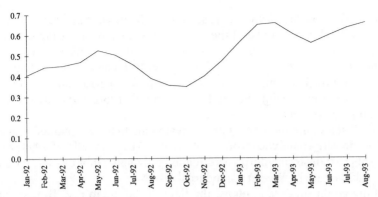

Figure 5. Monthly velocity of M$_2$.

been for very many years. And payment of non-cash money by money order is subject to unpredictable delays and obstruction, making it necessary for enterprises to hold abnormally large bank balances. Dollars are used as a means of payment in quite limited sectors of the economy.

But the situation is extremely fragile. The payments system is bound to improve now that correspondent accounts between banks are legal and all clearing does not have to go through the central bank. Similarly, dollarisation of transactions can easily spread, if inflation continues. The Tanzi-Oliveira effect is a less likely source of hyper-inflation, as most tax payments are made in advance on the basis of forecast liabilities. But a rise in velocity could quite easily come from nowhere. Enterprises already have dollar deposits of around $11 billion in Russian banks – roughly the same value as their rouble deposits. If the dollar became a regular means of payment, velocity could easily take off. It is this which makes progress in disinflation so vital.

6. INTER-ENTERPRISE CREDIT

There is a widespread belief that monetary policy cannot control inflation in Russia due to the absence of effective bankruptcy laws. According to this argument, if bank credit is squeezed, purchases and sales of goods will continue to occur at ever-rising prices, and firms will become more and more indebted to each other.

This belief was reinforced by the "arrears crisis" of mid-1992. Under the old communist system, firms took limited responsibility for paying their bills (which corresponded essentially to the costs of physically allocated supplies). Instead bills were sent to the debtor's bank, which paid them according to pre-assigned priorities as and when money came into the debtor's bank account.

During 1992 overdue payments rose sharply from virtually zero to about 3 months' GDP by the middle of the year. Unfortunately, a netting-out process was instituted for all debts up to 1st July – so that all net debtors ended up clear, and net creditors were credited by the central bank[14]. Since then many statements have been made ruling out any repeat performance, and urging sellers to check on the liquidity of their customers. More and more sellers now insist on prepayment.

Since last autumn the arrears problem appears to have remained well under control, despite some vociferous complaints. At the middle of 1993 overdue payments to industrial enterprises equalled only half a month's GDP – a quite respectable figure by Western standards[15].

As the credit squeeze tightens, the figure is bound to rise. But, so long as creditors do not expect to be paid if they sell to bankrupt enterprises, the arrears problem will remain under control. Even in 1992 it was completely wrong to assert that Western style monetary policy could not control inflation in the absence of effective bankruptcy laws. The whole of East European experience demonstrates this fallacy and it is equally fallacious in Russia.

NOTES

1. I am extremely grateful for the help over the last two years in Russia of M. Ellam and P. Orszag, and for everything that I have learned from other colleagues, especially A. Aslund, P. Boone, B. Granville, A. Illarionov, S. Ignatiev, J. Rostowski, J. Sachs and S. Vasiliev. The paper draws heavily on *Russian Economic Trends*, the monthly journal produced by the Working Centre for Economic Reform, Government of Russia in collaboration with the Centre for Economic Performance, London School of Economics, and published by Whurr Publishers (Fax: 071.226.5290). For an interesting discussion of most topics covered in this paper see J. Sachs, "Prospects of Monetary Stabilisation in Russia" in A. Aslund, (ed.), *Economic Transformation in Russia,* Pinter Publishers, London, 1994. See also his earlier paper 'Remaining Steps to a Market-Based Monetary System', in A. Aslund and R. Layard, (eds.), *Changing the Economic System in Russia*, Pinter Publishers, London, 1993.

2. This is at mid-1993 exchange rates which clearly undervalue domestic sales. Using this exchange rate imports were about 20% of GNP in mid-1993.

3. Mr. Geraschenko became Chairman in mid-July.

4. There are not enough time series observations to estimate the curve. But on a cross-section of 38 manufacturing industries there is a clear relationship between the change in wages and the change in employment (comparing December 1992 with January/February 1991) – see *Russian Economic Trends*, Vol.2, No.2, p.65.

5. Due to high central bank profits from interest charges and some accumulation of government deposits in the central bank, M_0 grew by only about 25% of GNP.

6. The government's fourth quarter target is now unclear on the assumption that the second tranche of the IMF's Special Transformation Facility is not now provided in the fourth quarter, as originally planned.

7. *Russian Economic Trends*, Vol.2, No.2, pp. 8–13. Other estimates are in the range 52–54%.

8. An incomes policy could be very dangerous in the difficult political situation in Russia.

9. A World Bank/Goskomstat household survey reports a figure of 3%.
10. The Bank is now negotiating a second Rehabilitation Loan of around $0.6 billion.
11. The ratio was 5% in January 1992 and rose in monthly steps up to April.
12. J.Rostowski, "Dilemmas of monetary and financial policy in post-stabilisation Russia", in A.Aslund, (ed.), *Economic Transformation in Russia*, Pinter Publications, London, 1994.
13. The best explanation of velocity comes from the simple equation illustrated in Figure 1. According to that

$$\dot{p} = \dot{m}_{-4}$$

where $\dot{p}$ is inflation and $\dot{m}$ is monetary growth. This implies that the change in velocity is $\dot{y} + \dot{p} - \dot{m} = \dot{y} - (\dot{m} - \dot{m}_{-4})$ which is dominated by the term $(\dot{m} - \dot{m}_{-4})$. Thus velocity *rises* in a disinflation, due to the lagged response of price inflation to reduced monetary growth. As we point out later, this relationship could easily change.
14. It appears that total net debt equalled only about 14% of total gross debt (R450 billion, compared with R3200 billion). Most of the R450 billion was used to pay taxes. However one cannot be sure that, without the netting out process, most of the taxes would not have been paid in some other way.
15. Total outstanding payments (overdue and other) to industrial enterprises amounted to just over one month's GNP.

Stabilization and Monetary Reform in Latin America

RUDIGER DORNBUSCH

Massachusetts Institute of Technology

Latin America does everything in extremes. In the past decade, many countries in Latin America have gone from the most dismal financial performance including hyperinflation and default to macroeconomic stabilization and institution building, financial opening and record returns to investors[1]. In some countries, notably Chile, the agenda has been completed: institutions, consensus, and a remarkable growth performance create a background that is likely to stand up. Other countries have gone some of the way – Mexico and Argentina, for example, but have left serious problems to be dealt with later. These include, specifically, very low rates of investment and crass overvaluation of their currencies. Finally, in Brazil reform has not even started.

The paper reviews the inflation experience, issues of inflation stabilization and the special role of financial opening and international capital flows in this context.

Latin America has struggled with inflation for 100 years[2]. In the late 19th century monetary instability and high inflation was a problem just as it was in the recent past. Uncontrolled issue of money, speculative frenzy, and collapse were the rule then as they have been in the 1980s. While there were instances of "chronic inflation" since the 1950s, the acute flaring up does not start until the 1970s and comes to full flower in the 1990s. Not all countries had a history of "chronic inflation" to use Pazos (1972) term. Notably Colombia, Mexico and Venezuela had very moderate experiences prior to the late 1970s. Moreover, in some economies inflation never went beyond the moderate range of say 15–30 percent[3].

The origin of the 1980s inflation can be found in a conjunction of four developments:[4]

– The tradition of *some* inflation, an acceptance of inflation or even a belief that inflation was an essential or at least inevitable part of the social and economic development process, and a monetary accommodation of inflation.
– A return to the capital market in the 1970s with borrowing that had little regard, in most cases, for sound public finance or profitability criteria.
– External shocks from oil and interest rates, including credit rationing. These

283

J.A.H. de Beaufort Wijnholds, S.C.W. Eijffinger and L.H. Hoogduin (eds.), A Framework for Monetary Stability, pp. 283–298.
© 1994 *Kluwer Academic Publishers. Printed in the Netherlands.*

284

Figure 1. Latin American inflation pre-crisis.

Table 1. Inflation performance (percent per year).

	50–60	60–70	70–80	80–91	1992	1993[a]
Argentina	28	14	134	417	25	12
Brazil	22	44	39	328	1,009	1,507
Chile	38	33	188	21	15	13
Colombia	7	11	22	25	27	25
Mexico	7	3	18	67	16	10
Peru	8	9	30	287	74	50
Venezuela	2	1	14	21	31	36

[a] Most recent 12 months
Source: IMF and World Bank

shocks brought with them the need to depreciate the real exchange rate which, in the context of indexation, meant a sharp inflation boost.
– Political opening, with the resulting challenge to deliver prosperity or at least minimize the impact of shocks and deny reality.

It is useful at the outset to separate two kinds of inflation. There is extreme inflation and there is moderate inflation. The former means inflation rates of 20 or 30 or more percent per month, the latter 15 to 30 percent per year. Each kind involves very different considerations when it comes to stabilization.

1. THE EXTREME INFLATION CASE

Inflation at extreme rates is almost always driven by money financed budget deficits. In such a situation lags between the exchange rate, prices, and wages vanish and the central fact becomes the creation of money which nobody wants to hold and which therefore is being destroyed, in real terms, by hyperinflation.

The way to such a situation involves typically three channels of instability. The first is financial adaptation to high inflation. This implies a reduction in the scope for (non)inflationary financing of budget deficits. The second channel is the widening of deficits as the real yield of taxation falls victim to accelerating inflation. Lastly, existing indexation arrangements shorten as wage earners try and catch up with prices and the exchange rate. The adjustment process is intrinsically unstable and leads to ever higher rates of inflation.

Stabilization of extreme inflation starts from the recognition that without bringing money creation under control, inflation will not end. Accordingly, budget balancing or a shift to external financing of the budget is the central step which *ultimately* assures that inflation will come down and stay down. But the mechanical process of stopping inflation typically involves, just as in the 1920s, steps to stabilize the exchange rate. Since all pricing will have come to focus on the exchange rate, stopping currency depreciation is an immediate forceful way to establish de facto stability. The next issue then becomes how to sustain that stability. Argentina serves as a case study.

Argentina

The 1960s were the last cycle of expansion and since then there has only been bad news: dictatorships and a "dirty war" on domestic dissent and guerilla, a mad war on Britain over the Malvinas, massive capital flight and a few hyperinflations. Raped over and over again, Argentina ultimately fell into full and complete disillusionment. By 1991 the economy was almost completely dollarized and a massive part of wealth had moved abroad. Inflation became endemic, deficits became structural and the country fell into cycles of populism and stabilization.

Table 2. Argentina: Long-term performance.

	1960–80	1980–90
Growth per capita	1.8	−2.3
Inflation	71.7	440.0

In the 1980s the debt crisis was particularly severe. Having financed massive capital flight in 1978–82 by borrowing abroad, the country had no way of facing the large debt service burdens that emerged with the end of voluntary lending, world recession and record high dollar interest rates in the early 1980s. Net investment had been negative for almost a decade. A once great country has been run down to the point where millions of people in Buenos Aires were fed at soup kitchens. Real GDP per capita was back to the levels of the early 1960s.

In March 1991, following yet another burst of extreme inflation, Argentina

Table 3. Argentina: The stabilization process.

	1990	1991	1992	1993
Budget deficit	2.7	1.3	–0.7	–1.4
Revenues	14.4	15.9	17.2	17.7
Privatization	0.5	1.2	0.8	0.8
Inflation	1,344.0	84.0	18.0	6.8
Growth	0.1	8.9	8.7	6.5

Source: Argentina: Ministerio de Economia

moved finally to a radical stabilization. The program was centered on the "convertibility plan". Under this plan the government guaranteed the convertibility of pesos at a fixed exchange rate into U.S. dollars *and* undertook not to print any money except in the course of buying dollars in the foreign exchange market. Since foreign exchange reserves in the central bank exceeded the dollar value of the domestic money supply the program was "credible" provided the government stuck to the constitutional commitment not to print money to finance the budget.

So far the promises have been kept. The currency has become strong in the sense that there has been a major rebuilding of monetary assets in the form of peso currency holdings and deposits. Moreover, the government has started executing sweeping reforms in the economy and success is showing.

Privatization is proceeding if not at breakneck speed, at least in a determined fashion; Deregulation is pervasive; Trade liberalization has been pushed aggressively and is seen as a key building block in a more rational and productive use of the nation's resources; Fiscal reform is equally ambitious, although the progress is inevitably only gradual.

All of this is splendid. If kept up and pushed further, year after year, the reform program cannot fail to give Argentina the same stability that Chile has secured from a decade of adjustment. For the time being, the willingness to do more is strong and the program and the government command wide support. Of course, there are areas of vulnerability. The picture would not be complete without talking of two acute problems. First, fiscal correction notwithstanding, the budget continues to be precarious. Second, competitiveness is a serious issue. Over the past year, on a fixed exchange rate but with inflation of 20 percent, competitiveness has been eroded.

Argentina's case demonstrates that endemic instability takes long to reverse even when great determination and skill are applied. A century ago, in 1899, Argentina was described in *Banker's Magazine* in the following terms:

They are always in trouble about their currency. Either it is too good for home use, or as frequently happens, it is too bad for foreign exchange. Generally, they have too much of it, but their own idea is that they never

Figure 2. Argentina: Real broad money.

have enough . . . The Argentines alter their currency almost as frequently as they change presidents . . . . No people in the world take a keener interest in currency experiments than the Argentines.

So far the experience has been mostly positive because in the past two years there was a boom driven by consumption. The hard work of rebuilding the productive economy still lies mostly ahead and may come to cast a shadow over the accomplishments of the past two years and the surprising degree of stability.

Post-stabilization issues

The very moment that the currency is stabilized, the central bank will obviously experience reserve *in*flows. As is typical, monetization of these reserve inflows will allow a rapid remonetization of the economy. But that process cannot go on for long without a question about the sustainability of the fixed rate. At this stage a plausible story about budget deficit reduction or financing will have to come. If there is no plausible ("credible" in the jargon) story, just as in Germany in the winter of 1923, inflation will return and blow up again.

Even if the budget deficit is corrected or its external financing is provided for, there is a problem area on the side of the exchange rate. A fixed rate means that any lingering inflation will translate into real appreciation. If inflation is not quite dead – say 1 percent per month – real appreciation will soon become a serious problem. At that stage the question emerges whether the rate should be allowed to depreciate at a pace offsetting the inflation differential or whether an extra stand should be made to kill inflation once and for all.

A third issue in the aftermath of extreme inflation is dollarization. It appears that even after stabilization has succeeded and price stability has been sustained for many years, monetary habits simply do not revert to their pre-inflationary situation. Specifically, the ratio of dollar deposits relative to local currency in the domestic banking system will remain very large and possibly rising. The same is true for dollars as hand to hand currency. This persistent dollarization, apparent in Bolivia, Peru or Argentina, involves both a loss of seigniorage but also problems of intermediation. This point can be observed most strikingly in Bolivia. In 1987, 2 years after hyperinflation was stopped, foreign currency deposits amounted to 67.7 percent of all deposits. By 1992, with continued very moderate inflation, the ratio had risen to 81.2 percent. The point here is that credibility does not do wonders if, almost 10 years after stabilization the trend is still toward increasing dollarization.

The fact of high and rising dollarization long after stabilization raises an important question: why have a national money. If the economy is highly dollarized to start with, much of the loss of seigniorage has already been incurred. In the course of stabilization, the existence of a domestic money and the associated credibility problems create formidable obstacles.

Would the costs of stabilization not be far lower if domestic money were totally discarded or, at the most limited to small change? As long as there is a domestic money, however formidable the arrangements for making the currency credible, the suspicion lingers that it will ultimately go. Nobody thinks of a peso as appreciating, most think that the exchange rate at best is constant or else the currency will go down. That imparts an inflationary bias which ultimately will be self fulfilling or else forces a very costly roll back of accumulated inflation and real appreciation. Bolivia, Peru and Argentina would all have done well getting rid of their national monies. Governments are reluctant to go that far, burning their bridges. But the very fact that they are reluctant, reserving money creation as the means of last resort, creates the very bias toward inflation which creates post-stabilization problems.

The bias and the resulting cumulative real appreciation leads, inevitably, to distortions in financial intermediation. The term structure of interest rates on the active and passive side will be upward sloping. Currency optimists gamble on stability and borrow short to lend long while sceptics go the other way. This betting, one way or another, creates financial problems. If the currency does go, so will the optimists; if it does not go, the pessimists will go down. The financial system inevitably is weakened by this betting which is unrelated to productive activity.

Table 4. Argentina: Term structure (June 1993).

	Deposits		Loans	
	Pesos	Dollars	Pesos	Dollars
Liquid	4.5	2.8	6.0[a]	–
30–89 Days	9.9	6.3	10.5[b]	7.8[b]
>90 Days	12.8	7.2	–	9.1[c]

[a] Interbank
[b] 30 Days
[c] 90 Days
Source: Banco Central

2. MODERATE INFLATION

When inflation proceeds at moderate rates, say in the 10 to 30 percent range, budget deficits typically are not in the foreground. Implicit or explicit indexation of wages, the exchange rate and prices are the central fact that keeps inflation going.

The inflation process can be expressed in terms of an accelerations Phillips curve where p, e, and y represent the inflation rate, the rate of depreciation and the GDP gap:

$$\dot{p} = \alpha(e - p) + \beta y \tag{1}$$

Because of inertia generated by implicit or explicit indexation, inflation today is basically that of yesterday. The only deviation comes from exchange rate shocks (or terms of trade and public sector price shocks) or from the impact of economic activity measured by the gap.

In this model inflation can only be brought down by one of three strategies, or by a combination of these elements:
- The rate of currency depreciation is slowed down relative to the prevailing rate of inflation. As a result, inflation decelerates but the real exchange rate appreciates.
- A big recession is created in order to force down wage inflation relative to price inflation and the rate of depreciation.
- Incomes policy can accomplish a simultaneous reduction of wage and price inflation and an accompanying reduction in depreciation. If inertia is an issue then incomes policy is the answer. This typically requires some *pacto* to coordinate the disinflation in a situation of overlapping pricing and wage setting. Mexico and Chile offer interesting examples.

Chile

Chile in the 1970s followed the first model. The exchange rate was fixed and a boom drove the economy over the cliff. Real appreciation accumulated and ultimately translated into a deep collapse of activity and a resurgence of inflation. The real depreciation would have forced up inflation, had it not been for extremely high levels of unemployment.

Table 5. Chile: The 1980s orthodox stabilization.

	Growth	Unemployment	Inflation	Real exchange rate[a]
1981	5.5	11.1	9.5	100
1982	14.1	22.1	20.7	90
1983	–0.7	22.2	23.1	93
1984	6.3	19.3	23.0	74
1985	2.4	16.3	26.4	64
1986	5.7	13.5	17.4	61

[a] Real effective exchange rate index.
Source: Dornbusch and Edwards (1993)

Figure 3. Chile: Inflation.

Sustained depression levels of unemployment – the rate including relief workers reached 35 percent in 1983 – kept a sharp hold on wages and as a result real depreciation and disinflation could go hand in hand. Chile then is the case of orthodoxy; interestingly, it is also the case of unquestioned success. It is open to question whether this strategy could have been pursued by a democratic government. But it did succeed and was the foundation for the extraordinary expansion and consolidation that has taken hold since 1986.

Mexico

Until the 1970s, Mexico had a tradition of very low inflation and substantial growth. The important reforms of the past few years, following on inflation peaking near 300 percent, are designed to bring back that environment.

On the macroeconomic front, essential reforms included trade liberalization, deregulation, a debt deal, a massive fiscal restructuring and a coordinated disinflation program. The central device for disinflation was an incomes policy agreement, evaluated and repeated at agreed intervals, that brought together the public sector, labor and enterprises. These pactos set

Table 6. Mexico: Long run performance.

	Per capita growth	Inflation	Operational budget (% of GDP)
1955–72	3.3	5	n.a.
1973–81	2.6	22	–4.4
1982–88	–2.2	83	–1.5
1989–92	1.6	20	1.9
1993*	–1.0	9	2.0

* Forecast
Source: Banco de Mexico

ceilings for a key basket of goods, guidance for private price setting and limits to wage increases. The government's contribution came from public sector prices – despite a major removal of subsidies – and from setting the pace of the exchange rate to support disinflation.

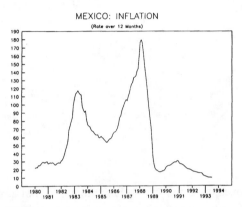

Figure 4. Mexico: Inflation.

The disinflation program is immensely successful if judged just on its own. Inflation is coming down toward U.S. levels and may get there in a year or so. But that is too narrow a focus in evaluating the success. Because the exchange rate was made to carry a major burden in the disinflation, the real exchange rate has appreciated for more than 3 years. A good portion of the real appreciation is appropriate simply because Mexico has moved with big strides toward modernity: reforms, return to the world capital market with applause, the forthcoming NAFTA. All these factors support real appreciation. But the sharp trade liberalization points in the other direction. Trade liberalization typically requires real depreciation to avoid large imbalances and loss of growth.

The high level of the Mexican real exchange rate is showing in three ways. First, the external deficit of almost 5% of GDP. This is not a world record, but it is extremely high and questions about sustainability or vulnerability are appropriate. Second, interest rates in real terms have been high. Third, the combination of a high real exchange rate, a high real interest rate and fiscal restraint have caused the loss of growth. Real GDP is now barely growing and in per capita terms it is falling. Moreover, no growth and high real interest rates combine into serious problems for the banking system. A few years into stabilization, this is not a good sign.

In Chile the effort to maintain a super competitive exchange rate is now the basis for a broad-based growth; in Mexico the softer stabilization has carried forward a major handicap. Mexico's stabilization then is not complete until growth returns on a sustained and sustainable basis.

292

MEXICO–U.S.: RELATIVE WHOLESALE PRICES
(Index 1985=100, in Common Currency)

Figure 5. Mexico – U.S.: Relative wholesale prices.

3. BRAZIL: UNFINISHED BUSINESS

Brazil is uniquely exasperating. With a favorable external environment – low interest rates and low oil prices – why can't the country turn the corner, get stabilization done and move ahead? Moreover, with poor income distribution and strained democracy, even political considerations now point to the urgent need to do something. Old approaches are debunked as useless and not credible, new alternatives are either declared nonexistent or else politically impossible.

In the past, Brazil had an extraordinary record of growth. Of course, there were momentary setbacks such as the instability of the early 1960s, but even so the long run growth record was nothing but spectacular. As to inflation, Brazil has always been special – living with inflation has been the rule; amazingly both inflation and the country are still alive. A very elaborate indexation, perfected in the course of the 1960s reform and stabilization, was designed to assure that domestic capital markets could function even in the presence of inflation, that the exchange rate would not become endemically overvalued and that wage adjustment to offset inflationary erosion would occur automatically rather than result in strikes and instability.

Table 7. Brazilian performance.

	1960–73	1975–82	1982–92
Growth	7.2	4.5	1.9
Inflation	36.0	61.0	470.0

By 1980, inflation had increased to 83% even though a full pass-through of oil price increases had not been accomplished. Large external and budget deficits were being financed by borrowing. Demand restraint to contain inflation and the deficit resulted in the first and largest recession so far. But there were no lasting benefits. By 1986 Brazil was ready for the first "heterodox" stabilization program – the Cruzado Plan. The advent of democracy and the lack of appeal of traditional IMF programs with their focus on breaking inflation by deep recession made the market for an alternative approach, namely the emphasis on incomes policy. The interest in such an approach was all the larger in that inertia of inflation (in the downward direction, primarily) was understood as a central feature of the Brazilian inflation process.

The Cruzado Plan of 1986 was built around fighting inflation inertia. Workers who had just gotten a wage increase were rolled back, those who had not had any for some time were compensated for part of the accumulated loss in real wages, and firms were subjected to a firm and unyielding price freeze. From one day to the next inflation was gone and that picture continued for quite a while. Along with incomes policy came adjustment rules for wage and debt contracts all of which had built in the assumption of high inflation and needed to be adjusted to the new world of price stability.

Figure 6. Brazil: Inflation.

For a few months the Cruzado Plan was a striking success. Price stability was the rule and, as a result, the political popularity of President Sarney skyrocketed as did the stock market, demand and output. Brazil seemed to have discovered a free ride to stability and prosperity. Of course, that could not last. The controls became increasingly difficult to enforce, the runaway growth strained capacity, the freeze at arbitrary relative prices became binding in the areas of parts and components, and soon housewives had to be mobilized to "police the freeze". As virtually all price control schemes – kept on too long, abused for record growth rather than prudent transition, the Cruzado Plan became as disaster. Higher inflation than even before the scheme was the penalty for trying to override the laws of economics. The same story applies to every plan since.

Brazil is tired of inflation and even more tired of shocks. The cooling off required to deal with the Collor program turned down growth and inflation. But in Brazil that can never last; once again, after a brief respite, inflation is back on the rise. The latest reading on inflation is 34% per month or 3,255% per year. The official definition of hyperinflation is 50% per month; the distance is not far.

Table 8. Brazil's recent performance.

	1990	1991	1992	1993[a]
Growth	−4.4	0.9	−0.9	5.0
Inflation	2,599	399	991	2,500

[a] Estimate, last 12 months

There are broadly three options to stabilize. The first is to try and contain the damage with an emphasis on further fiscal consolidation. Two problems arise with this strategy. First, the results are very slow and as a consequence deteriorating inflation may preempt whatever positive effects are accomplished on the fiscal front. In fact, even with bold steps on the budget, fiscal performance may still fall behind.

The second option takes a lesson from Argentina: try and dollarize the economy and then use a fixed exchange rate strategy together with an institutional reinforcement of the central bank as the new anchor. The trouble with this approach is that Brazil is a large inward looking economy which today is *not* at all dollarized. Because of pervasive indexation, flight into the dollar never happened on the scale in which it occurred in Bolivia, Peru, Argentina or Russia. As an implication of a lack of dollarization, politicians surely are not going to opt for a strategy that first puts the house on fire with dollarization only then to call in the fire brigade. However successful a currency board strategy elsewhere, it can only function in dollarized economies and Brazil is not (yet) one. Hence stabilization must look elsewhere.

The third strategy is to use the positive experience with the Cruzado Plan, supplement it with serious moves on privatization and the budget and get it right. Since there is no alternative, it helps to spell out that stabilization is possible, can be popular and, above all, can work.

Brazil is no different from any other mismanaged economy. To fix the mess, a consistent four part program is the answer: Rapid, pervasive privatization must signal major change. Put the best companies on the table, startle the world by doing something unconventional, but in the right direction. Privatization is the best strategy toward sound public finance. Next, a freeze on wages, prices, and the exchange rate for a two months period must be used to break inflation. Wage-price fixing always and rightly has a bad name, but with 30% inflation per month and pervasive indexation unusual steps are indispensable. (Yes, the Cruzado Plan of 1986 which employed these measures was a great success until it overstayed its welcome.) An important stabilizing factor is a lengthening of wage indexation periods to 6 months. The acceleration of inflation is due in large measure to a shortening of indexation intervals; lengthening them back to a 6 months period assures that the new and low inflation rate has inertia. That inertia in turn will influence price setting patterns: firms who do not see a wage adjustment for 6 months (and no major exchange rate realignment) do not have to fear a renewed outburst of high inflation and hence can afford to go with very moderate price increases. That fact in turn makes the lengthened wage indexation plausible and thus closes the circle.

Moderate inflation cannot be attained without the third piece: budget balancing, including tax reform and effective control of the public sector. Finally, a targeted anti-poverty program such as the Mexico solidarity scheme can act as a shock absorber and a key function of the new State.

An essential point for a winning package is this: the freeze can only be very short and then indexation, fiscal restraint, privatization, serious monetary policy must carry the full weight in holding back inflation. The objective ought to be bringing down inflation to less than 20% per year – not the magic zero which nobody accomplishes and which ultimately tempts policy makers in staying too long with a fixed rate.

Stabilization will benefit greatly from the exceptionally strong external position. Reserves are plentiful and the trade surplus and current account are strong. Thus there is plenty of room to use a fixed currency – temporarily fixed and then soon crawling – as one of the anchors of the program.

4. Lessons

In 1964, in a conference to assess the Latin American inflation problem, two positions were sharply delineated. Graene Dorrance, speaking for the IMF and monetarism, held firmly and unambiguously[5]:

"An attempt to slow down an inflation will take a long time to be effective and its final result will be uncertain . . . Unless the authorities are firm in their attack, the atmosphere of financial stability necessary to induce a revival of output..will not emerge. . . . However, if the economic system has been allowed to get out of hand, the authorities must decide to stabilize or not to stabilize. There is no doubt that the process of stabilization is difficult, but, difficult or not, it is a prerequisite for rapid economic growth."

Dudley Seers. speaking for Latin American structuralism, took the other side[6]:

> "The charge that can be made against the monetarist school is that it directs attention away from the fundamental problems of economic growth, and so discourages the search for political strategies and economic plans to solve these problems. It puts forward a panacea, irrespective of social reality. Consequently, overemphasis on monetary measures involves serious risks. The paradox is that though the monetarist is normally far from a revolutionary, and his preference is for peace and quiet, his policies may lead to social disorder and eventually regimentation of one form or another.
>
> . . . . Perhaps we are best advised to proceed empirically rather than dogmatically, testing the local political framework before we throw on it the full weight of policies derived from a doctrine which was developed for the needs of another century and another part of the world."

What would we conclude after the experience of the 1980s? Most observers would recognize in Seers' advice the seeds for the monumental mess of the 1980s and they would, reluctantly but firmly, side with Dorrance.

But four questions must be added today:

– Can institutions such as fiscal rules and an independent central bank or a dollarization make a stabilization more effective in the sense of softening the output loss and assuring lower realized real interest rates? Independent central banks now exist in Argentina, Chile, Mexico and Venezuela; discussion to have an independent central bank (along with a Brady deal, cellular phones and an emerging market hoopla) are on the agenda everywhere.

   The answer is yes; institutions that assure confidence and stability do help. But, of course, only to the extent that they in fact can deliver this assurance. Do not expect too much.

– Is there a room for incomes policy as part of a serious program? That it is not a substitute is by now clear; whether it is a very positive complement is still debated after the fiascos of the 1980s.

   The answer is yes; incomes policy that does not translate into bottlenecks or overvaluation can take some of the sting out of stabilization. Again, do not expect too much.

– How does one move from stabilization to growth? The answer here is the most disappointing. Much of the impetus for growth must come from an improved supply side *and* increase in real aggregate demand. Economies that emerge from stabilization with optimism and competitiveness will do well; others will limp along.

– How helpful is access to external capital? The answer is, of course, that access to the world capital market is immensely helpful in supporting stabilization. But it is also very perilous. The world capital market is not an effective monitor; it falls far too easily in love with high yields and it cannot be relied upon when the going gets tough.

Notes

1. See World Bank (1993).
2. See Subercaseaux (1920) for monetary problems and the quest for institutions in the late 19th century in Latin America. Professor Edwin Kemmerer and Sir Otto Niemeyer were the money doctors of the 1920s.
3. See Dornbusch and Fischer (1993) on moderate inflation.
4. See Pazos (1972) and the conference volume edited by Baer and Kerstenetzky (1964) for important studies of inflation in Latin America. The latter portrays the debate between monetarists and structuralists. The recent experience is reviewed in Dornbusch, Sturzenegger and Wolf (1990) and Vegh (1992).
5. See Baer and Kerstenetzky (1964, p. 68).
6. See Baer and Kerstenetzky (1964, p. 103).

References

Agenor, P. (1993), "Credible Disinflation Programs", Mimeo, Washington DC, International Monetary Fund.

Baer, W. and I. Kerstenetzky (1964) (eds.), *Inflation and Growth in Latin America*, New Haven, Yale University Press.

Bruno, M. (1991) et al. (eds.), *Lessons of Economic Stabilization and Its Aftermath*, MIT Press.

Calvo, G. et al. (1993), "Capital Inflows and the Real Exchange Rate", *IMF Staff Papers*, Vol. 40, No.1, March.

Calvo, G. and C. Vegh (1992), "Inflation Stabilization and Nominal Anchors", Mimeo, International Monetary Fund, December.

Chadha, B., P. Masson, and G. Meredith (1992), "Models of Inflation and the Costs of Disinflation", *IMF Staff Papers*, June.

Dornbusch, R., F. Sturzenegger and H. Wolf (1990), "Extreme Inflation: Dynamics and Stabilization." *Brookings Papers on Economic Activity*, No. 2, 2–84.

Dornbusch, R. and S. Edwards (1993), "Chile: Exchange Rate Policy and Trade Strategy", Mimeo, Massachusetts Institute of Technology.

Dornbusch, R. and S. Fischer (1993), "Stopping Moderate Inflation", *World Bank Review*, Vol. 7, No. 1, January.

Englander, S. (1992), "Institutional Commitments and Policy Credibility. A Critical Survey and Empirical Evidence from the EMS", *OECD Economic Studies*, Spring.

Galbis, V. (1993), "High Real Interest Rates Under Financial Liberalization", Mimeo, International Monetary Fund, Washington DC.

Hanson, J. (1992), "An Open Capital Account: A Brief Survey of Issues and the Results", World Bank, Working Paper WPS 901.

Khan, M. ,P. Montiel, and N. Haque (1991) (eds.), *Macroeconomic Models for Adjustment in Developing Countries*, Washington DC, International Monetary Fund.

Khor, H. and L. Rojas-Suarez (1991), "Interest Rates in Mexico", *IMF Staff Papers*, December.

Krugman, P. (1992), *Currencies and Crises*, MIT Press.

Mathieson, D. and L. Rojas-Suarez (1993), *Liberalization of the Capital Account*, Occasional Paper No. 103, International Monetary Fund, Washington DC.

Pazos, F. (1972), *Chronic Inflation in Latin America*, Praeger, New York.

Persson, T. and G. Tabellini (1992), *Macroeconomic Policy, Credibility, and Politics*, New York, Harwood.

Polak, J. (1989), *Financial Policies and Development*, OECD, Paris.

Rodriguez, C. (1978), "A Stylized Model of the Devaluation-Inflation Spiral", *IMF Staff Papers*, March.

Rodriguez, C. (1993), "Money and Credit Under Currency Substitution", *IMF Staff Papers*, Vol. 40, No. 2 June.

Subercaseaux, G. (1920), *Le Papier Monnaie*, Paris, M. Girard & E. Briere.

Vegh, C. (1992), "Stopping High Inflation: An Analytical Overview", *IMF Staff Papers*, Vol. 39, September, 626–695.

World Bank (1992), *Latin America and the Caribbean. A Decade After the Debt Crisis*, Washington DC.

Comment on Richard Layard: Can Russia Control Inflation

OLEH HAVRYLYSHYN

International Monetary Fund

For this session on "Monetary and financial reform in Central and Eastern Europe", we have before us a paper entitled "Can Russia control inflation?". I am not quite sure what, if any, meaning to give to this. Is this an application of the new *Monroevsky Doctrine*[1] to economic policy questions in effect saying that we need only worry about monetary stability in Russia and it will then ensure the same follows in the region? Or does it mean that Russia typifies the situation for all former socialist economies, and understanding one means understanding all? In that case the choice might better have been Ukraine which I regret to admit has the highest inflation in the region. Such a choice would also have avoided adding another grain of sand to the growing mound of perception of the primacy of Russia, a perception which does little to offset the growing internal sentiments in Russia favoring a Monroevsky role for the country.

As to whether Russia typifies post-socialist economies on the matter of monetary and financial reform, it should be easy to agree the answer is "yes" and "no". We see this succinctly in the phrase from Layard's paper (p. 274) "the main problem has been and remains the problem of finance for enterprises. . . . . . Enterprises want credits above all to pay wages". *Yes*, it has been the same for all transition economies, but *no* it no longer is the primary problem in several countries where stabilization has been so far successful – Poland, Czech Republic, Hungary, the Baltic States, Slovenia, Albania – while it remains a problem for many like Ukraine, Russia, etc. In countries with successful stabilization, restructuring has also advanced in varying degrees, and the main problem in the financial sector is deepening and maturation of the banking process, starting in particular with improvements in the intermediation function. There are even some countries where the most important problem lies in a still earlier phase of financial sector evolution: establishing an adequate central bank operation.

But I have come to comment on a paper, not to write one, so I will say no more on the situation in specific countries or groups of countries in Central and Eastern Europe[2], and focus on what Prof. Layard has written. Five sub-questions are put:

J.A.H. de Beaufort Wijnholds, S.C.W. Eijffinger and L.H. Hoogduin (eds.), A Framework for Monetary Stability, pp. 299–303.

- control of central banks credit
- control of rouble area credit
- control of the money multiplier
- control of velocity
- control of inter-enterprise arrears.

These are the right questions and I shall concentrate on the first two only, because I have little argument with the discussion on the others.

On control of central banks credit, first I might ask the author to update and clarify the record. On pages 270 and 273, several target numbers are cited for the government's and IMF program targets on monetary expansion, 20% in Q III and 15% in Q IV of 1993. The author is cited in a *Financial Times* article[3] referring to an expected 40% rise in Q III. What are the most recent actual and targeted rates?

More importantly on central banks credits, Layard makes a good but too brief effort (pp. 274–5) to go below the simple and widely understood surface notion that inflation can only be stopped if directed credits to enterprises are sharply reduced. He discusses two kinds of pressures and arguments made in favor of credits: averting unemployment, and continuing provision of housing and social services through enterprises (I presume *kolkhoz* and *radkhoz* are included here). But his discussion stops at the level of the interest of the populace and workers, when in fact it is probably a much smaller elite interest group that is effective in lobbying for continued credits: the directors of enterprises, of kolkhoz, of retail organisations, of "new" commercial structures. It is not unusual in economic history that populism is captured by the interests of a relatively small group of people who succeed in their political efforts by crying "unemployment – cuts in social services", and rallying around them the support of the populace.

Soviet directors were more than managers, they were "patriarchs" dispensing favors such as first rights on housing or better housing. They will not easily give this up – especially after two years of seeing that their power is nearly as strong as it ever was. Thus, in the simple minded diagram of Figure 1, demand for credits is more than simply normal working capital and investment requirements as in a "market" economy environment (MD^M), but includes the patriarch's needs (MD^P). So far this differs from Layard's description only in that his "P" appears to stand for "the Populace", my "P" stands for "the Patriarchs". But there are two added elements which will more strongly differentiate my view from Layard's analysis.

Besides the patriarchs, there is now a solidly entrenched rentier-capitalist interest which feeds itself on a combination of easy credits (and by the way, *cheap* credit, an important point not explicit in Layard's paper), continued price distortions leaving wedges between domestic and world prices (especially in natural resources); and a continued high degree of foreign trade licensing,

especially for exports. Easy low-interest credits finance not only dollar "speculation" (less true now in Russia than elsewhere) and capital flight, but also
access to below world-price natural resources which can either yield a higher
profit in domestic use, or if a license can be obtained, in exports. Capital flight
also follows this second route. Popular wisdom on the street labels these
rentier-capitalist interests variously as the mafia, the "old-new" nomenklatura,
etc. It also relates this kind of activity to widespread graft and corruption,
which, while prevalent, is of secondary importance to the underlying incentives
for such activities – many of which are entirely legal. The implication is well
known in the rent-seeking literature: the opportunity to make large and quick
profits. These rentiers will devote considerable energy and resources lobbying
to ensure such a situation continues, and to oppose the systemic changes which
would close the wedges and remove the profit opportunities.

The impact on Figure 1 analysis is twofold. First, it adds yet another big
source of demand for credit (MD^W) – referring to wedges in pricing). Second,
the inherited (and perhaps even strengthened) influence of these interests puts
them very close to the levels of policy-making, hence, money supply decisions
are not simply the standard central banker and policy-maker's macro judgment on
stimulation versus inflation-control (MS^M), but unfortunately demand becomes
endogenized in the supply decision to give us (MS^P) and the all-inclusive MS^M.

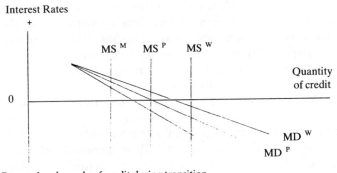

Figure 1. Demand and supply of credit during transition.

Such an endogenized accommodation of credit demands lies behind not only
the repeated history of failed efforts to control money supply in most transition
economies (especially in Eastern Europe, less so in Central Europe), but it also
explains the continuation of highly negative rates of interest – which incidentally are an important aspect of monetary policy not adequately discussed by
Layard[4].

What to do next? As a well known transformer of societies asked earlier this
century. By all means, consider whether one could simply ignore the pressures

of this powerful set of lobbyists, and if so, stick to MS^M, starve them of their future patriarchal or rentier profits[5] until their power is reduced.

But the pressures will be immense and will continue as long as state property arrangements prevail or soft-budget conditions continue, and as long as price-wedge opportunities for rent-seeking continue. Here I will perhaps rejoin Layard in his resigned assessment of gradualism (p. 275). It would have been far easier to be tough and stick with MS^M as part of a monetary and reform shock about two years ago, when the players in this rentier-capitalist game were off-guard and perhaps even unaware of their potential new power. It will be far harder today, without making even greater concessions to them, without reducing the pressure in some way. Such concessions may (and already do) include more "spontaneous" "insider" privatization to drain off these accumulated profits and to allow hard-budget imposition[6]. Most important, it will be essential to complete the process of price and trade liberalization, closing the wedges and eliminating licensing while certainly leaving a relatively high degree of tariff protection for some time. A credit shock without these supporting changes will be unsustainable.

Let me finish with a few comments on the rouble-area problem which was defined by many analysts as a moral-hazard problem three years ago; came close to extinction as a problem when by early 1993 Russian authorities were strongly urging any laggards to introduce a separate currency; and now lo and behold is once again a problem with a reconstructed rouble area agreement being put in place on September 6. Layard correctly worries about the implied "dangers of massive credit creation", as one suspects do many economic policy-makers in Russia[7]. Why then the willingness of Russia to accommodate? Layard's suggestion that President Yeltsin "does not want to sour relationships with his neighbors" does not quite capture it.

Perhaps this rouble area see-saw demonstrates a final reversal of Marx's economics: his dictum that "economic matters are at the root of politics" is overturned and we now can say political matters are at the root of economics. If one of the aspects of the question "Can Russia control inflation" is in the likelihood of limiting credits to rouble area countries (or its economic approximation, a Russian current account surplus with these countries), its answer might better be sought not in economic logic, but in the foreign policy trends of Russia in relation to its "new" regional role[8]. More important will then be foreign policy statements of President Yeltsin, Minister of Foreign Affairs Kozyrev, and the still important Chairman of the Parliament Committee of Foreign Affairs, Mr. Ambartsumov. As for the economics of issuing rouble-area credits, should they be allowed to prevail over political issues, the advice given by Prof. Layard is unquestionably right: don't do it, but if you must, do it transparently as budget items covering any Russian current account surplus.

NOTES

1. While written by Mr. Ambartsumov, what has come to be called the Russian Monroe Doctrine was most fully exposed recently by Minister Kozyrev at the U.N., *Washington Post*, September 29, "Russia Asserts Role in Ex-Soviet Republics."
2. I appreciate the Conference organizers' vision in the use of this term to encompass all relevant countries while avoiding the cumbersome and inadequate term, FSU.
3. *Financial Times,* Oct. 2, "Impact of Yeltsin's Moves on Economic Reforms."
4. This circle of policy-making influence and impact on economic reform prospects is discussed more fully in O. Havrylyshyn "Ukraine and Western Financial Assistance," a paper prepared for symposium at York University, October 8–9, 1993.
5. The two groups doubtless overlap, and indeed, conceptually the economic benefits of patriarchal status may also be considered a rent.
6. Though one should not assume that private ownership of enterprises will mean an automatic end to such pressures, especially of the "W" variety. The history of soft-budgets in countries such as Argentina and Brazil is testament to the problem.
7. Reuters Press Service "Rouble Zone Could Bring Problems for Russia," October 14, 1993.
8. Peter Reddaway, The *New York Times*, Sunday, October 10, 1993, describes the re-assertion of Russian influence in the areas of the two old empires.

Comment on Rudiger Dornbusch:
Stabilization and Monetary Reform in Latin America

GUILLERMO ORTIZ*

Ministry of Finance, Mexico

As usual with Dornbusch's papers, the paper "Stabilization and monetary reform in Latin America", is clear and touches on the crucial issues facing Latin America today. We agree with the important distinction made between moderate and extreme inflation, as well as with the fact that these two forms of price increases have different principal causes, as well as the solutions to the problems generated by them. We also agree that the current stabilization and development strategies are not over yet, with several measures pending in order to consolidate and allow a further positive evolution of the results obtained so far.

1. GENERAL COMMENTS

Nevertheless, we have several comments on various aspects of the presentation. Even though a distinction is made between several developments and countries in Latin America, we feel that the differences in circumstance between countries needs to be further stressed. That would allow a clearer perspective and analysis' benchmark, in a region where diverse inflation and growth results have emerged, both in the present and historically.

2. MEXICO

Even though the importance of the reform programs undertaken in Mexico is recognised, a skeptical view towards Mexico is expressed, regarding several issues. Specifically, three issues need further clarification: low rates of investment, overvaluation of the currency and low growth perspectives.

Low investment

Real growth rates of investment have averaged 9.46% for the period 1988–1992. It is clear, then, that rates of investment in Mexico have been growing

* *This comment was delivered by Martin Werner of the Ministry of Finance, Mexico.*

305

J.A.H. de Beaufort Wijnholds, S.C.W. Eijffinger and L.H. Hoogduin (eds.), A Framework for Monetary Stability, pp. 305–307.
© 1994 *Kluwer Academic Publishers. Printed in the Netherlands.*

in a consistent and significant way. The proportion investment/GDP has been growing from a 17.3% in 1989 to 21.7% in 1992, without yet reaching the level attained in 1981, which equalled 26.5%.

An interesting characteristic of the investment's composition and evolution is left aside, as private investment represented 54.7% of total investment, or 14.5% of GDP, in 1981, while the proportions for 1992 are 80.3% of total investment and 17.4% of GDP. These numbers are indicative of the fundamental transformation that has taken place in the Mexican economy, with the private sector as the principal promoter of growth, and a government which indulges, overall, in fundamental social investment activities. This change seeks to promote an allocation and utilization of resources by the entities that are more efficient in each of these two elementary activities.

Overvaluation of the currency

It is true that the Mexican currency has appreciated, but such a fact is far from implying a strong overvaluation of the currency. That depends on the equilibrium level of the real exchange rate, which is difficult to calculate, adding to the fact that the peso had undergone a strong devaluation before the current stabilization effort started, which probably made it to be undervalued. As you say, the appreciation process is a natural, and not necessarily negative, consequence of the reform process in Mexico.

An element that is not explicitly included is the high rate of growth in productivity that has prevailed the last few years. This rate of growth signifies that the appreciation that has taken place does not necessarily mean a loss in overall competitiveness.

Low growth perspectives

We agree with the fact that high interest rates can pose an obstacle to growth. We must add, however, that real interest rates in Mexico have been coming consistently down for the last months, reaching a level close to 5% in long term, five-year AJASTABONOS, securities. Rates have also come down on nominal interest rate instruments, such as CETES.

Last year's growth rate was low, as will be this years[1], but the basis for a strong and stable growth has been established. Several reasons explain why the growth has been lower than expected. First, the new investments that have taken place require a certain period of time to enter their productive stage. As we have seen, investment has grown considerably for the past five years; and it does not seem unreasonable to suppose that a very significant proportion of this investment is yet to start producing. Second, actual GDP measurements tend to misrepresent new industries as well as gains in competitiveness. These two elements are crucial in assessing the prospects of an economy that has gone under considerable reform, deregulation, and trade liberalization programs. Both of these elements have had a positive evolution during the last few years. Third, two considerable reform programs have taken place which will modify substantially the functioning of the Mexican Economy. These two programs, the reforms in Agriculture and in Education, imply long-term results, with scarce impact on immediate GDP numbers.

3. FINAL REMARKS

Finally, we feel that an important factor was left untended when surveying the different cases. This factor is time consistency, which leads to credibility gains and further consolidation of results. It is clear that political economy in Mexico has been time consistent since 1982.

Even though we agree with you in the sense that there remain significant actions to be undertaken, we are not invulnerable to different negative shocks, and that we have not finished with the necessary undertakings that will allow Mexico to reach much higher levels of development, we are confident that the environment prevailing in the Mexican economy is much better than it would seem at a first and quick glance. This environment is the basis for a consistently growing, developing, and internationally projected, Mexican economy.

NOTES

1. There will probably be no per capita growth this year, but a decrease of 1%, as foreeasted in the paper, seems very exaggerated.

A Framework for Monetary Stability – General Report

SYLVESTER C.W. EIJFFINGER*

CentER and Tilburg University

Opening and Keynote Speeches
(*Wim Duisenberg and David Mullins Jr.*)

Recently, in many countries both political and monetary authorities have shown an increasing interest in the objective of monetary stability and the position of the central bank. In Western Europe, there is a clear tendency to establish (more) independent central banks and to foster, thereby, monetary stability. According to the Maastricht Treaty, the independent European Central Bank is only committed to the goal of price stability in the final stage of Economic and Monetary Union (EMU) by 1997 or later.

Furthermore, in some Anglo-Saxon countries, e.g. Canada, New-Zealand and the United Kingdom, monetary authorities are trying to achieve monetary stability by an inflation-reduction target. Countries in Central and Eastern Europe, such as Hungary, Poland and the Czech republic, and in Latin America, like Argentina, Chile and Mexico, are looking for a way to strengthen the position of their central bank in order to realize some degree of price stability.

It is not by accident that a conference under the theme "A Framework for Monetary Stability" is held in the Netherlands. De Nederlandsche Bank (DNB) is one of the most independent central banks in the world and this country has a long-standing tradition of monetary stability. Moreover, this stability-oriented monetary policy was founded on the so-called "Dutch monetarism", tracing back to Professor *Koopmans*' famous essay "Zum Problem des 'Neutralen' Geldes" of 1933. In his opening speech President *Duisenberg* emphasized, once more, the importance of monetary stability as a precondition for economic growth in the long run. This view was also supported by Vice-Chairman *Mullins Jr.* (Federal Reserve Board), although he considers price stability not as an objective *per se*, but as a means to accomplish higher growth and welfare.

* The author wants to express his gratitude to Eric Schaling for his essential support in making this general report.

J.A.H. de Beaufort Wijnholds, S.C.W. Eijffinger and L.H. Hoogduin (eds.), A Framework for Monetary Stability, pp. 309–330.
© 1994 *Kluwer Academic Publishers. Printed in the Netherlands.*

In this General Report, I will give my personal view on the papers and comments presented during the last two days. It is however not my intention to give a complete overview of the conference. Finally, I will close my report with three personal conclusions which can be inferred from this conference.

Formal Targets for Inflation Reduction:
The Canadian Experience
(*Charles Freedman*)

Charles Freedman discusses the Canadian experience with formal target bands for reducing the rate of inflation (CPI) setting out an explicit time path towards price stability. These inflation-reduction targets were announced in early 1991 both by the Bank of Canada and the government to achieve not only the short-term objectives of preventing a further wage-price spiral and reducing the prevailing inflationary expectations, but also the longer-term goals of realizing price stability and gaining credibility in monetary policy. By the end of 1992 the floor of the first target band (2–4%) was achieved with a twelve-month inflation rate of 2.1% suggesting that such targets should not be introduced at a time of upward inflationary pressure, but rather of downward pressure by, among others, sluggishness of the economy.

According to Freedman, inflation-reduction targets have played a useful role in communicating and making more concrete the Bank's policy of moving to price stability. Furthermore, he argues that these targets can be thought of as allowing for a form of automatic stabilization in response to demand shocks and, thus, for partial stabilization of output fluctuations. Consequently, he ignores the problem of long and variable transmission lags from monetary instruments to the policy goal. Finally, Freedman concludes that, although inflation-reduction targets are neither necessary nor sufficient to achieve price stability, the Canadian experience thus far proves that they can be helpful in attaining price stability and in improving credibility. However, he admits that one should await the inflation performance over a whole business cycle before drawing firmer conclusions about the role of these targets.

John Driffill states that the introduction of inflation targets does commit the Canadian government to sticking to a low inflation policy in the future, when economic conditions would be less favourable (i.e. less recessionary). He argues that in the context of economic theory, especially game theory, the way the Canadian government announced the targets can be described as "cheap talk". According to Driffill, this is because the targets *per se* impose no restrictions on the future actions of the authorities, and there are no costs involved in the announcement *per se* of one target rather than another.

The Costs and Benefits of Disinflation
(*Stanley Fischer*)

Stanley Fischer analyses the costs and benefits of disinflation. The basic theory of disinflation states that there is a trade off between the short-term costs of lower output and recession, associated with the reduction of inflation, and the longer-term benefits of a lower inflation rate and better economic performance associated with it. He makes a distinction between a long-run inflation target and a long-run price stability target, meaning that the goal is to keep the price level constant and predictable. By taking inflationary uncertainty into account, short-term price variability will generally be larger with a price stability target than with an inflation target (and long-term variability will be smaller).

The argument for a low inflation target are the negative effects of inflation on output growth because real balances serve as a factor of production: i.e. higher inflation means less certain inflation and price level uncertainty decreases the efficiency of the price system. The evidence points, according to Fischer, to an optimal inflation range of 1–3%. However, it is questionable whether lower inflation within this range is associated with higher productivity growth (because of the limited gains of very long-term nominal contracting and the possibility of a Phillips-curve trade off at very low inflation rates).

Once inflation has been brought down, the challenge is to keep it within the optimal target range and to preserve the gains of low inflation. For industrialized countries, Fischer recommends an independent central bank as part of the solution, stressing that the fundamental support of the public is needed to make the central bank an effective inflation fighter. In this respect he refers to the example of the Deutsche Bundesbank. Moreover, he emphasizes the accountability of the central bank, i.e. that it has to explain its actions, to subject itself to cross-examination and to be held responsible for not achieving its goals. Fischer states that the Bundesbank is not accountable in these senses. However there is, in my opinion, a trade off between central bank independence and accountability.

At the end, he suggests that the cost of inflation and price level uncertainty could be reduced by providing hedges against unanticipated price level changes, for instance, through the introduction of indexed government bonds (as has been the case in the United Kingdom).

In his comment on Fischer's paper, *José Luis Malo de Molína* states that – due to the irrefutable existence of output costs of disinflation – the inflation target cannot be set independent of the initial inflation rate. However, the implied gradualism may give rise to time inconsistency and credibility loss. Finally, Malo de Molínas remarks that the proper functioning of the economic system implies constant changes in relative prices, and that the existence of information costs and uncertainty may favour a positive – albeit minor – rate of inflation. The latter argument reinforces Fischer's preferred 1–3% target range and may explain why no central bank has succeeded in sustaining absolute price stability.

Commitment through Delegation, Political Influence and Central Bank Independence
(*Alex Cukierman*)

Alex Cukierman takes the view that the delegation of authority over monetary policy to (partly) independent central banks is used as a (partial) commitment device by politicians in office. By specifying the objectives of a central bank more or less tightly and by giving it broader or narrower powers, politicians determine the extent of commitment to a policy rule. The stronger this commitment and the more independent a central bank is, the more politically costly it is for politicians to override the decisions of the central bank.

Therefore, Cukierman wants to identify the economic and political factors that induce politicians to delegate more or less authority to the central bank. Of course, attempts to use monetary policy for stimulating economic activity and financing public expenditure lead to a (suboptimally) high inflation rate. This inflationary bias may be reduced by giving the central bank independence, i.e. the mandate to focus on price stability as the single policy goal. See e.g. the Deutsche Bundesbank and De Nederlandsche Bank. According to Cukierman, a certain degree of independence is granted in order to reduce interest payments on government debt and, in many cases, the larger the debt the more politicians tend to delegate authority to the central bank. An example is the "divorzio" between the Banca d'Italia and Italian Treasury in 1981. When capital markets are deep (e.g. in Germany and the U.S.) it is likely that government will try to raise more funds through the capital market and, thus, will delegate more authority to the central bank. However, counter-examples are Japan and the U.K.. Referring to the U.K. and the anti-inflation stance of its civil service, Cukierman states that the tendency to delegate authority to the central bank is likely to be lower if there is a strong preference for price stability within the executive branch of government.

Finally, he concludes that the stronger the inflationary bias under discretion and the larger the political polarization and instability are, the greater the need to rely on central bank independence.

In his comment on Cukierman's paper *Eduard Bomhoff* points to the recent literature on political business cycles supporting a relation between the nature of the party system on the one hand and government debt and inflation on the other hand. However, the model of Cukierman only features a two-party system. Bomhoff thinks the analysis would benefit from more sophisticated modelling of the political process. Among other things, this means that parties should be able to influence their election probabilities (which are exogenous in

Cukierman's model). Moreover, the analytical framework lacks uncertainty about the way the economy works. Including the latter real world phenomenon would also improve Cukierman's otherwise very advanced analysis.

Central Bank Autonomy:
Policy Issues
(*Onno de Beaufort Wijnholds and Lex Hoogduin*)

Onno de Beaufort Wijnholds and *Lex Hoogduin* analyse a number of policy issues related to central bank autonomy on the presumption that central banks should be autonomous. First of all, they conclude that it appears possible to maintain central bank autonomy both in case of the separation and combination of monetary policy and (micro) prudential supervision. The choice between separation and combination depends on the structure of the banking system, as well as the conduct of monetary policy in a country.

Furthermore, central bank autonomy requires a codified legal basis but is not hampered by accountability in the general sense of explaining and making visible a central bank's policy. It may even strengthen its credibility and policy acceptance by the public.

However, De Beaufort Wijnholds and Hoogduin emphasize that price stability should be the final objective of monetary policy which should be conducted in a medium-term framework. Autonomy can be reinforced by using intermediate targets in monetary policy making: preferably a monetary target or, for an open economy, an exchange rate target against the currency of a large economy (e.g. Germany).

Moreover, they stress that central banks should be granted a considerable degree of freedom in designing and using their instruments. Central banks should not be "too visible" in the money markets leaving some scope for market participants' influence on short-term interest rates.

Finally, De Beaufort Wijnholds and Hoogduin admit that there are reasons to make the political authorities responsible for decisions on exchange rate regimes and parity changes within an adjustable peg system despite the possibility of conflicts with the objective of price stability. The central bank should protect its autonomy in this respect mainly by making public its advice on exchange rate matters and other practical actions.

In his comment on De Beaufort Wijnholds and Hoogduin, *Manfred Neumann* argues that the functions of monetary policy making and banking supervision should be kept institutionally separated, both in smaller and larger countries. Further, he stresses the securing of a Thomas-Becket effect, i.e. inducing central bankers upon appointment to safeguard the value of the currency as their personal *leitmotif* and to cut all former political ties. Finally, Neumann pleads for completing central bank independence by transferring the sovereignty over exchange rate matters (including parities) to central banks to provide them with the undivided power over monetary and exchange rate policies. In the discussion, the authors pointed out that, to their knowledge, there is no central bank with complete autonomy over exchange rate matters. If this were the case, it would have far-reaching constitutional implications.

Intermediate Targets versus Information Variables as Operating Guides for Monetary Policy
(*Benjamin Friedman*)

Benjamin Friedman focuses on the role of intermediate targets and information variables as operating guides for monetary policy, particularly in the United States. Since 1975 the Federal Reserve System has been required under law to set money growth targets and to report semi-annually to Congress on its success or failure in meeting them. He stresses that the basic challenge of most central banks is to maintain price stability and/or full employment and that stable money growth is not the most reliable way to achieve these objectives, because the empirical relationships between money and income, and between money and prices have largely broken down. The latter explains Chairman Greenspan's statement in July 1993 that M2 "has been downgraded as a reliable indicator of financial conditions in the economy, and no single variable has been identified to take its place".

After discussing the distinction between an intermediate target and an information variable and the collapse of intermediate targets (M1, M2 and broad credit) in the United States, Friedman makes the case for an alternative class of policy making procedures relying on money and other indicators as information variables. Instead of the automatic pilot of an intermediate target procedure, under which every deviation of the target requires corrective action, he prefers a judgemental information variable procedure implying that divergences merit attention and may warrant action depending upon circumstances. Clearly, Friedman chooses for an eclectic approach to monetary policy.

First of all, rather than aiming at only one intermediate target, the central bank should use as information variables a broader range of financial and non-financial measures with potential predictive content, varying from the term and risk structure of interest rates to goods orders, building permits, ground breakings etc.. This is already done by the Federal Reserve. Furthermore, information variables should be exploited intensively through frequent re-examinations of what they are signalling about the current and future development of the economy and about the effects of the central bank's own actions.

Friedman concludes that judgemental discretion will always be needed, because even the most reliable information variables can give false signals as a consequence of changing exchange rate regimes, financial market structures and business practices. However, simply proceeding on an intermediate target is, in his view, an invitation to error.

Regarding Friedman's argument in favour of the information variable approach to monetary policy, *Alexandre Lamfalussy* argues that even with a dependable intermediate target, its behaviour may be quite at variance with that of asset prices. According to Lamfalussy, this is the new dimension of monetary policy in an increasingly deregulated and integrated global financial environment. The question is then whether and how monetary authorities should respond to asset price bubbles. This question is difficult because of poor fundamental knowledge of asset price determination.

Monetary Policy Strategy in the EMU
(*Otmar Issing*)

Otmar Issing evaluates the design of a monetary policy strategy for the third stage of EMU. He stresses that the transition to stage three will be difficult, vitally depending on the confidence of the public in the European currency. Therefore, it will be important to fall back on the experience of a strategy which has proved itself in practice, e.g. that of the Deutsche Bundesbank. In stage three the European Central Bank is committed to the ultimate objective of price stability and granted independence from European and national authorities.

However, the monetary policy strategy of the European Central Bank is still to be decided upon. According to Issing, the wide range of proposals for this strategy can be roughly categorised in: a two-step approach of pursuing the ultimate objective indirectly by using an intermediate target and a one-step approach of achieving the final objective in one move, directly. The one-step approach is nowadays popular in some Anglo-Saxon countries, such as the United Kingdom, Canada and New-Zealand, not because they consider such a strategy superior, but because they cannot identify any suitable intermediate target. On the contrary, the two-step approach is used in many continental European countries, e.g. Germany, as a consequence of "the long and variable lags" in monetary policy making.

Issing prefers a two-step approach with a broad monetary aggregate as an intermediate target for a number of reasons. First of all, the link between money growth and inflation has a sound theoretical and empirical basis. Further, the control of the money supply reflects the central bank's responsibility and is easily to assess by the public. Finally, with a policy based on rules and incorporating monetary targets based on medium-term considerations the European Central Bank can ensure, similar to the Bundesbank over the past decades, a relatively high degree of price stability. He sees, just like *De Beaufort Wijnholds* and *Hoogduin*, no good alternative to a medium-term monetary targeting strategy. Although monetary policy and, thus, monetary targeting will not succeed without an element of pragmatism, it is important that the rule always remains the point of reference.

According to *Paul de Grauwe*, Issing's discussion of monetary targeting by the future ECB is based on the assumption that in the final stage of EMU, one currency will have displaced the national currencies, and that the ECB manages this currency. However, de Grauwe points out that it is more likely that initially the third stage will see an incomplete monetary union, i.e. one characterized by the continued existence of national currencies, albeit at 'irrevocably' fixed exchange rates. In the latter regime, in case of asymmetric shocks European monetary targeting leads to under- and overshooting of targets at the national level.

Rules versus Discretion in Monetary Policy
(*Andrew Crockett*)

Andrew Crockett analyses the debate on rules versus discretion in monetary policy both theoretically and empirically for the postwar period. Rules are advocated to commit central banks to a predetermined time path for an intermediate variable, mostly a monetary aggregate (M1, M2 or M3), while discretion is favoured because of unpredictable shifts in the demand for and supply of money by a variety of factors. He argues that neither pure discretion, nor fixed rules have proved to be satisfactory, but that the elements of a consensus are now beginning to emerge.

After discussing some terminological issues (objectives, targets, instruments and indicators) and the theoretical case for rules against judgemental discretion, Crockett examines how this case has worked in practice for the main industrial countries. He discerns three broad phases in monetary policy making during the postwar period: until the late 1960s, a substantial amount of discretion was taken for granted; from the early 1970s to the 1980s, increasing emphasis was put on rules by adopting targets for money growth ('monetary targeting') in order to reduce inflationary expectations; and by the late 1980s the pendulum began to swing away from rules to more discretion. By the loosening of the relationship between money and income, many central banks – even the Bundesbank – were forced to downgrade their monetary targets and to take a wider range of indicators into account. Crockett concludes, however, that this need for greater discretion does not imply a return to the earlier postwar practice. The lessons about the importance of credibility and time-consistency in monetary policy have been painfully learned. He refers to the inflation-targeting framework in the United Kingdom as one example of a possible synthesis of rules and discretion. Rules are appropriate for the ultimate objective of monetary policy, i.e. price stability, because there is nothing to be gained by varying or concealing this objective. Nevertheless, discretion is appropriate in the setting of monetary instruments but the decision making must be as open and transparent as possible to improve the information available to market participants.

Jacques Sijben agrees with Crockett that, because of regulatory changes and financial innovations, the velocity of circulation of money can shift in a relatively unpredictable way, thus favouring discretionary elements in monetary policy. However, Sijben points out that in turn the financial innovations and the associated shifts in velocity were induced by highly inflationary – i.e. discretionary – monetary policies in the first place. According to Sijben, these unpredictable shifts in velocity can be diminished by reducing monetary uncertainty, i.e., by stable rules of the game.

The Role of Monetary Policy in IMF Programs
(*Manuel Guitián*)

Manuel Guitián discusses the role of monetary policy in IMF programs within the context of the basic principles of, firstly, the interest of member countries in a firm assurance of the conditions for access to IMF resources and, secondly, the interest of the ,IMF in an equally firm assurance of the fostering of its purposes by member countries. Of course, both principles have consequences for the design and implementation of monetary policy. Although money growth influences the inflation rate and balance of payments position, Guitián argues that this relationship should not imply the control of monetary aggregates. Even if the control of money growth would be possible, its relationship to inflation and external developments reflects a link of domestic credit expansion (DCE) with aggregate demand in the economy. Clearly, his analysis is based on the familiar monetary approach to the balance of payments. Therefore, the monetary authorities have to formulate targets for domestic credit expansion in order to realize the goals of price stability and balance of payments or exchange rate stabilization.

Furthermore, Guitián stresses two important challenges facing the national monetary authorities in many countries: on the one hand the process of deregulation of domestic financial markets and of liberalization of international capital movements, on the other hand the corresponding trend towards internationalization and integration of financial markets during the last decade. Financial deregulation and liberalization has blurred the boundaries between banking and other financial services and, thereby, the differences between money and other financial assets (*All Finanz* or *bancassurance*). Thus, it has affected the stability of the demand for money and has impaired the usefulness of money demand forecasts as a basis for monetary policy making. Finally, financial internationalization and integration has weakened the national economic frontiers between countries and has increased the substitutability of national currencies. Ultimately, both challenges put heavy constraints on the effectiveness of domestic monetary policy by the mobility of international capital flows.

In his comment on Guitián's paper, *Henk Jager* criticizes Guitián's view that the new challenges of financial liberalization do not really matter for the choice of intermediate targets. With respect to Guitián's belief that the drawback of domestic credit as an intermediate target is insignificant, because of adjustments of the monetary reserve component of the money supply, Jager remarks that Guitián implicitly assumes an exogenous price level. This assumption distorts the outcome in the event of high capital mobility. According to Jager, under more realistic assumptions the money supply is better suited as an intermediate target, because it is a better indicator of inflation performance.

Italy's Experience within and without the European Monetary System: A Preliminary Appraisal

(*Marcello De Cecco and Francesco Giavazzi*)

De Cecco and *Giavazzi* evaluate Italy's experience within and out of the EMS exchange rate mechanism. Almost 15 years of partnership in the exchange rate mechanism did not result in the siding of Italy with the " strong currency" countries. The currency crisis of 1992 has triggered a balance of payments crisis inducing a heavy Lira devaluation. Until September 1992, the ease with which the Italian monetary authorities could keep the Lira well above its PPP level reduced the urgency for politicians to restructure the economy. Foreign short-term capital inflows validated the virtuousness of monetary authorities and the profligacy of politicians, creating a fool's paradise. The currency crisis did hit Italy, while it was walking on the tightrope of debt sustainability after the lifting of exchange controls. The accumulation of national debt during the 1970s and 1980s had made Italian monetary policy too easily destabilized by fluctuations of world growth rates and interest rates.

Nevertheless, De Cecco and Giavazzi consider the currency crisis as a *deus ex machina*, which made the adoption of stern economic reform possible by allowing the politicians to break loose of the demagogic stalemate in which they were frozen before. The question remains whether the extremely strict package of policy measures adopted by the Italian government in the last 18 months will be sufficient to induce a more structural adjustment process. However, the public debt stock will still require interest payments to be a very high share of GDP in the near future, despite the advantage that two thirds of total debt is in the hands of individuals who see their holdings as the equivalent of trust or pension funds. This does not imply that the demand for Italian public debt will remain as stable as it used to be. The monetary authorities should lay the ground for an orderly transition to a more orthodox structure of public debt ownership by designing alternative assets for institutional investors and by encouraging ownership by them much more openly.

In his comment on De Cecco and Giavazzi's paper *Gunter Baer* argues that the evaluation of exchange rate regimes depends on whether they are based on multilateral or individual country agreements. In the latter case unequivocal commitment to the exchange rate is successful only, if the implied loss of autonomy is accepted and if appropriate macroeconomic policies are adopted now and in the future. In the case of a multilateral agreement exchange rate regimes require close policy-cooperation and the establishment of a mutually-agreed mechanism to solve possible conflicts. According to Baer, in practice this may imply a strong institutional framework, like a move in the direction of EMU.

Monetary Policy and Exchange Rates:
The French Experience
(André Icard)

André Icard examines the French experience of monetary policy making within the EMS exchange rate mechanism since 1979. The conduct of monetary policy is based on two objectives: an external objective, stemming from compliance with the rules of the exchange rate mechanism, and an internal objective, aiming at the control of money growth within the framework of monetary targeting used by the Banque de France from 1977 on. The external exchange rate target has been an important tool for eliminating inflationary expectations and has guided policy in the (very) short run, while the internal money growth target (until 1991 M2 and presently M3) is a long-term benchmark for financial markets and reflects the central bank's commitment to price stability.

Icard emphasizes that stable exchange rates are imperative for Europe and for France, explaining the prominent role of exchange rate policy in French monetary policy. Furthermore, he stresses that exchange rates are the dominating transmission mechanism in France. The pegging of the (nominal) exchange rate of the franc to the Deutsche mark has been crucial for reducing French inflation over the last ten years. The temporary widening of the EMS fluctuation bands to ± 15% from August 1993 is only meant to make use of intra-marginal exchange rate movements (two-sided risk), but it does not imply that the goal of price stability has been abandoned. However, this widening of the bands carries a message and a danger. The message is that the bilateral parities are consistent with the economic fundamentals of the member countries. The danger is that erratic and uncontrolled short-term fluctuations of exchange rates are not compatible with the long-term functioning of the single market and even of the common market, if these swings create invisible borders like those that occur between the U.S., Japan and the European Community.

According to Icard, there are reasons to be optimistic about the outlook for future monetary policy in France. First of all, the French long-term commitment to price stability has been acknowledged by the financial markets. Moreover, the law to make the Banque de France (more) independent from government has reinforced this commitment. Finally, public support for the policy of stabilizing the franc is still growing both domestically and externally.

In his comment on Icard's paper *Ralph Bryant* is puzzled about the contention that it is possible for France *both* to maintain an exchange rate peg *and* to successfully pursue a domestic monetary aggregate target. According to Bryant, German reunification – being a huge asymmetric shock – is a classic example of a situation in which monetary and exchange rate targets are incompatible. As a North American economist, Bryant finds it hard to understand why this shock failed to produce a realignment, i.e. he thinks the policies of the ERM countries are hard to understand.

Can Russia Control Inflation?
(*Richard Layard*)

Richard Layard discusses the way in which Russia can control inflation and the difficulties associated with it. He starts by reviewing the recent history of Russian monetary policy. Since the reform, monetary policy has gone through three phases: from January to June 1992 a phase of relative tightness (i.e. low money growth), until October 1992 a phase of substantial loosening and, after that, a phase of gradual tightening. In April 1993 declining targets for central bank credit were agreed upon, reducing inflation progressively from a steady 20% per month. Next, Layard considers five major problems connected with this policy of bringing inflation down gradually.

Firstly, can central bank credit to the budget and to enterprises really be controlled? The control of central bank credit is under heavy pressure, e.g. by the role of enterprises as providers of housing and health care.

Secondly, the controllability of credit to the rouble area, i.e. other former republics of the Soviet Union. This would be easier if all countries in the area have an own currency and if their currency was fully convertible with the rouble.

Thirdly, will control of central bank credit lead to control of commercial bank lending? If the reduction of base money growth is offset by an explosion of the money multiplier, as frequently happens in a credit squeeze, inflation will not decrease.

Fourthly, the velocity of circulation of money (M2) may also explode. The velocity is quite low (about seven times per year) because of the primitive payments system, but could rise rapidly when this system improves.

Fifthly and finally, the velocity of money can increase as well by more inter-enterprise credit instead of bank credit. He states that the limited solvency of enterprises makes this danger unlikely. However, Layard concludes that, despite the above mentioned problems, Russia will not experience hyper-inflation so long as the present reform government remains in power, but the period of disinflation might be prolonged by these problems.

In his comment on Layard's paper, *Oleh Havrylyshyn* argues that Layard makes too brief an effort to go below the surface notion that inflation can only be stopped if direct credits to enterprises are sharply reduced. According to Havrylyshyn, Layard should have addressed the role of smaller elite interest groups effective in lobbying for continued credits such as the directors of enterprises, of kolkhoz, of retail organisations and of "new" commercial structures.

Stabilization and Monetary Reform in Latin America
(*Rudiger Dornbusch*)

Rudiger Dornbusch evaluates the process of stabilization and monetary reform in Latin America. In some countries, like Chile, this process has already been completed, in other countries – e.g. Argentina and Mexico – it is en route and in a country such as Brazil the reform has not even started.

He distinguishes two kinds of inflation: extreme inflation, meaning inflation rates of more than 20% per month, and moderate inflation, i.e. 15 to 30% per year. Extreme inflation is mostly driven by money financed budget deficits and, thus, a hugh creation of money. Hyperinflation may only be stabilized by controlling money creation through the balancing or external financing of the budget. In this respect, Dornbusch discusses the case of Argentina in the 1980s.

Moderate inflation is, however, not caused by high budget deficits, but is kept going by implicit or explicit indexation of wages. It can be brought down by a real appreciation of the currency, a big recession to force down wage inflation and/or incomes policy. Examples are Chile in the first half of the 1980s and Mexico during the 1980s and early 1990s. While stabilization in Chile has been orthodox and successful, the softer approach of Mexico resulted in no growth and high real interest rates.

Nevertheless, in Brazil there is no stabilization and reform at all. Brazil has three options to stabilize hyperinflation: further fiscal consolidation, dollarization of the economy and/or fighting inflation inertia. Dornbusch's conclusion from the experience of the 1980s is that the process of stabilization, difficult or not, is a prerequisite for rapid economic growth. Moreover, this process should be supplemented by four measures: the estabishment of an (more) independent central bank to assure confidence and stability , like in Argentina, Chile, Mexico and Venezuela; incomes policy to take the sting out of stabilization; improving the supply side and increasing real aggregate demand to stimulate economic growth; and access to the world capital market to draw upon external financing.

Guillermo Ortiz's comment – delivered by *Martin Werner* – addresses Dornbusch's view on the Mexican economy. Ortiz points out that the *composition* of investment is left aside. He argues that in the last decade the Mexican economy experienced a fundamental transformation due to a surge in private investment. With respect to the overvaluation of the currency, he stresses that – prior to the current stabilization – the peso had experienced a strong devaluation. Therefore, the following appreciation process is a natural – and not necessarily negative – consequence of the reform process.

Some Personal Conclusions
(*Sylvester Eijffinger*)

What may be concluded from the papers, comments and discussions presented at this conference? I think at least three general conclusions can be drawn on the conduct of monetary policy and the position of the central bank not only in Western Europe and North America, but also in Central and Eastern Europe, Latin America and other continents. Of course, these conclusions are not exhaustive.

The *first conclusion* is associated with what are, in my opinion, the two basic elements of monetary policy making in the main industrial countries. The conduct of monetary policy comprises a *structural* element, based on the degree of central bank independence, and a *cyclical* element, depending on the influence of the political cycles on policy decision making by the central bank. With the overall tendency to establish (more) independent central banks in many countries, the structural element increases and, thus, the cyclical element decreases but will never vanish completely. Even in countries with a very independent central bank (e.g. Germany, the Netherlands and Switzerland) monetary policy making is still influenced to a lesser extent by the political cycle.

Nevertheless, both theory and empirical evidence give further support to the well-known inverse relationship between the degree of central bank independence and the level of inflation. Moreover, neither theory nor empirical evidence find a clear-cut relationship between central bank independence and the level of real output growth in the long run. Hence, there is wide-spread support for the proposition that having an independent central bank is like having a *free lunch*: the benefits of lower inflation are high and the costs in terms of real output growth are not apparent.

The absence of a long-run trade off between inflation and economic growth has also important implications for the rules versus discretion debate in monetary policy. Independent central banks will put much emphasis on rules for monetary growth (if they have an internal target) or for their exchange rate vis-à-vis the anchor country (if they have an external target) to reach and maintain the goal of price stability. Dependent central banks will place more weight on discretion both in case of monetary targets and of exchange rate targets. Although there have been changes in the trade off between rules and discretion during the postwar period in the main industrial countries, these changes were relatively greater for dependent central banks (like the Federal Reserve and the Bank of England) than for independent central banks (such as the Deutsche Bundesbank and De Nederlandsche Bank).

The *second conclusion* is that the earning of reputation in the financial markets is best achieved in *"bad weather"* (low economic growth) rather than in *"good weather"* (high economic growth). Naturally, the independence of a central bank is the basis for its reputation and credibility. However, only in periods of low (or even negative) economic growth can an independent central bank prove its decisiveness to stick to the ultimate goal of price stability by not accommodating inflationary pressures from politicians, labour unions and other economic agents. Just then this stubbornness of the central bank not to inflate and to stimulate economic growth will pay in the long run because of the higher reputation of that central bank in the financial markets and, thereby, of a less than otherwise necessary restrictive monetary policy in future.

In this respect one may compare the *German–Dutch* model (the Bundesbank and De Nederlandsche Bank) with the *Anglo-Saxon* model (the Federal Reserve and the Bank of England). Both the Bundesbank and De Nederlandsche Bank cherish their image of a *"hard-nosed"* policy maker preserving and extending their reputation and, thus, reducing inflationary expectations. On the contrary, the Federal Reserve and the Bank of England behave more as a *"soft-nosed"* policy maker excavating their reputation ("too little, too late"). Therefore, these central banks conduct a stop-go policy raising inflationary expectations and uncertainty and, subsequently, risk premia demanded by investors.

The mobility of international capital flows and the integration of financial markets in most industrial countries have made the reputation and credibility of the central bank its only instrument of monetary policy. Therefore, politicians and other policy makers should restrict themselves as much as possible from policy advice to their central bank. Otherwise, they force the central bank to prove its reputation unwillingly by a more than necessary restrictive monetary policy.

The *third conclusion* is that every country gets the central bank it deserves. Although one could favour a (very) independent central bank for every country (based on the theoretical and empirical arguments given before), not every government or public will accept such a position of its central bank. In this respect, the difference between the German-Dutch model and the Anglo-Saxon model is also striking.

In Germany and the Netherlands public and, thereby, political support for an independent central bank and a policy directed to monetary stability is widespread and overwhelming. The Bundesbank and De Nederlandsche Bank know that their policies are backed by the vast majority of the people. This puts them in a relatively comfortable position.

However, in countries such as the United States and the United Kingdom central banks have a limited autonomy. Government and parliament may give directives to the central bank or even override its decisions. The Federal Reserve has some autonomy in monetary policy making but is "independent *within* government". If the Federal Reserve would conduct a really restrictive monetary policy (e.g. in the early 1980s under Chairman Volcker) for a long time, it is almost certain that Congress will ultimately restrict its legal autonomy further by amending the Federal Reserve Act. The Bank of England is clearly less independent than the Federal Reserve. British politicians and policy makers are always stressing the accountability of the central bank to parliament.

Finally, in many countries the position of the central bank is being discussed and sometimes new legislation is underway. Especially in Europe, the process of monetary integration has triggered a trend to make central banks more independent: the Banque de France, the Banca d'Italia, the Banco de Espâna and, perhaps in the future, the Bank of England. However, it should be emphasized that *legal* independence is a necessary but not a sufficient condition for the *actual* independence of a central bank. In my opinion, actual independence implies a tradition and culture of monetary stability not only within the central bank but also within the government and parliament of that country. Such a tradition will not be established overnight.

Authors, Discussants and Chairpersons at the Conference 'A Framework for Monetary Stability'

Mrs Bodil N. Andersen (Chairperson)
Governor
Denmarks National Bank
Havnegade 5
DK-1093 Copenhagen K
Denmark

Gunter D. Baer
Secretariat of the Committee of Governors
of the Central Banks of the
Member States of the EEC
Centralbahnplatz 2
CH-4002 Basel
Switzerland

J. Onno de Beaufort Wijnholds (Organiser)
Professor of Economics/ Deputy Executive Director
De Nederlandsche Bank
P.O. Box 98
1000 AB Amsterdam
Netherlands

Eduard Bomhoff
Professor of Economics
Erasmus University Rotterdam
Department of Economics
Burgemeester Oudlaan 50
3062 PA Rotterdam
Netherlands

Ralph C. Bryant
Senior Fellow
The Brookings Institution
1775 Massachusetts Avenue N.W.
Washington, D.C. 20036–2188
USA

J.A.H. de Beaufort Wijnholds, S.C.W. Eijffinger and L.H. Hoogduin (eds.), A Framework for Monetary Stability, pp. 331–338.

Marcello De Cecco
Professor of Economics
University of Rome
c/o Research Department
International Monetary Fund
Washington, D.C. 20431
USA

Andrew D. Crockett
Executive Director
Bank of England
Threadneedle Street,
London EC 2R 8AH
England

Alex Cukierman
Professor of Economics
Tel Aviv University and CentER
Faculty of Social Sciences
The Eitan Berglas School of Economics
Ramat Aviv
Tel Aviv 69978
Israel

Rudiger Dornbusch
Professor of Economics
Massachusetts Institute of Technology
Department of Economics
Cambridge, MA 02139-4307
USA

John Driffill
Professor of Economics
Department of Economics
University of Southampton
Highfield
Southampton SO9 5NH
England

Wim Duisenberg
President
De Nederlandsche Bank
P.O. Box 98
1000 AB Amsterdam
Netherlands

Sylvester C.W. Eijffinger (Organiser)
Associate Professor of Economics
CentER and Department of Economics
Tilburg University
P.O. Box 90153
5000 LE Tilburg
Netherlands

Stanley Fischer
Professor of Economics
Massachusetts Institute of Technology
Department of Economics
Cambridge, MA 02139
USA

Charles Freedman
Deputy Governor
Bank of Canada
234 Wellington Street
Ottawa, KIA 0G9
Canada

Benjamin M. Friedman
Professor of Economics
Harvard University
Littauer Center 127
Cambridge, MA 02138
USA

Paul de Grauwe
Professor of Economics
Centrum voor Economische Studiën
Catholic University Leuven
Van Evenstraat 2 b
B-3000 Leuven
Belgium

Manuel Guitián
Associate Director
Department of Monetary and Exchange Affairs
International Monetary Fund
Washington, D.C. 20431
USA

Oleh Havrylyshyn
Alternate Executive Director IMF
International Monetary Fund
Washington, D.C. 20431
USA

Lex H. Hoogduin (Organiser)
Manager Research Department
De Nederlandsche Bank
P.O. Box 98
1000 AB Amsterdam
Netherlands

André Icard
Director General of Research
Banque de France
P.O. Box 140–01 F 75049
Paris Cedex 01
France

Otmar Issing
Member of the Board
Deutsche Bundesbank
P.O. Box 100602
D-6000 Frankfurt/M 1
Germany

Henk Jager
Professor of Economics
University of Amsterdam
Department of Economics
Roeterstraat 11
1018 WB Amsterdam
Netherlands

Alexandre Lamfalussy
General Manager
Bank for International Settlements
P.O. Box 262
CH-4002 Basle
Switzerland

Richard Layard
Professor of Economics
Director Centre for Economic Performance
London School of Economics
Houghton Street
London WC2A 2AE
England

José Luis Malo de Molina
Director General of the Research Department
Banco de España
Apartado de Correos 15
28080 Madrid
Spain

David W. Mullins, Jr.
Vice Chairman
Board of Governors of the
Federal Reserve System
Washington, D.C. 20551
USA

Manfred J.M. Neumann
Professor of Economics
Institut für Internationale Wirtschaftspolitik
University of Bonn
Lennéstrasse 37
D-53113 Bonn 1
Germany

Kumiharu Shigehara (Chairperson)
Head of Economics Department
OECD
2 Rue André Pascal
F-75775 Paris Cedex 16
France

Jacques J. Sijben
Professor of Economics
CentER and Department of Economics
Tilburg University
P.O. Box 90153
5000 LE Tilburg
Netherlands

Arnout Wellink
Executive Director
De Nederlandsche Bank
P.O. Box 98
1000 AB Amsterdam
Netherlands

Martin Werner
Director Public Debt
Ministry of Finance
Palacio Nacional Primer Patio
Mariano Piso 3
Of. 3039 Col. Centro
06066 Mexico DF
Mexico

Other Participants at the Conference
'A Framework for Monetary Stability'

David Archer
Acting Chief Manager
Economics Department
Reserve Bank of New Zealand
2 The Terrace, P.O. Box 2498
Wellington 6000
New Zealand

A. Lans Bovenberg
Senior Research Fellow
CentER
Tilburg University
P.O. Box 90153
5000 LE Tilburg
Netherlands

Martin M.G. Fase
Professor of Economics/Deputy Executive Director
De Nederlandsche Bank
P.O. Box 98
1000 AB Amsterdam
Netherlands

Henk de Haan
Professor of Economics
University of Groningen
Department of Economics
P.O. Box 800
9700 AV Groningen
Netherlands

Jakob de Haan
Associate Professor of Economics
University of Groningen
Department of Economics
P.O. Box 800
9700 AV Groningen
Netherlands

Harry P. Huizinga
Professor of Economics
CentER and Department of Economics
Tilburg University
P.O. Box 90153
5000 LE Tilburg
Netherlands

Kagehide Kaku
Director Research and Statistics Department
Bank of Japan
C.P.O. Box 203
Tokyo 100–91
Japan

Theo van de Klundert
Professor of Economics
CentER and Department of Economics
Tilburg University
P.O. Box 90153
5000 LE Tilburg
Netherlands

Jeroen J.M. Kremers
Deputy Director
Directorate for General,Financial and Economic Policy
Ministry of Finance
P.O. Box 20201
2500 EE The Hague
Netherlands

Padraig McGowan
Deputy General Manager
Central Bank of Ireland
P.O. Box 559
Dame St., Dublin 2
Ireland

Aldo Pelosio
Head of Representative Office
Banca d'Italia
Hertogstraat 47
1001 Brussels
Belgium

Jean Jacques Rey
Director
National Bank of Belgium
Boulevard de Berlaimont 14
B-1000 Brussels
Belgium

Georg Rich
Director of Economic Division
Swiss National Bank
Bundesplatz 1
CH-3003 Bern
Switzerland

C.L. Stals
Governor
South African Reserve Bank
Pretoria 0001
P.O. Box 427
South Africa

Jerzy Stopyra
Director
Credit and Monetary Policy Department
National Bank of Poland
P.O. Box 1011
PL 00–950 Warsaw
Poland

E. D. Tromp
President
Bank of the Netherlands Antilles
Breedestraat 1 (P) Willemstad
Curacao
The Netherlands Antilles

Hans Visser
Professor of Economics
Free University Amsterdam
Department of Economics
De Boelelaan 1105
1081 HV Amsterdam
Netherlands

Franz Weninger
Deputy Head
Economic Research Division
Austrian National Bank
P.O. Box 61
A-1011 Wien
Austria

Sweder van Wijnbergen
Professor of Economics
Department of Economics
University of Amsterdam
Roeterstraat 11
1018 WB Amsterdam
Netherlands

FINANCIAL AND MONETARY POLICY STUDIES

* 1. J.S.G. Wilson and C.F. Scheffer (eds.): *Multinational Enterprises*. Financial and Monitary Aspects. 1974   ISBN 90-286-0124-4

* 2. H. Fournier and J.E. Wadsworth (eds.): *Floating Exchange Rates*. The Lessons of Recent Experience. 1976   ISBN 90-286-0565-7

* 3. J.E. Wadsworth, J.S.G. Wilson and H. Fournier (eds.): *The Development of Financial Institutions in Europe, 1956–1976*. 1977   ISBN 90-286-0337-9

* 4. J.E. Wadsworth and F.L. de Juvigny (eds.): *New Approaches in Monetary Policy*. 1979   ISBN 90-286-0848-6

* 5. J.R. Sargent (ed.), R. Bertrand, J.S.G. Wilson and T.M. Rybczynski (ass. eds.): *Europe and the Dollar in the World-Wide Disequilibrium*. 1981   ISBN 90-286-0700-5

* 6. D.E. Fair and F.L. de Juvigny (eds.): *Bank Management in a Changing Domestic and International Environment*. The Challenges of the Eighties. 1982
                    ISBN 90-247-2606-9

* 7. D.E. Fair (ed.) in cooperation with R. Bertrand: *International Lending in a Fragile World Economy*. 1983   ISBN 90-247-2809-6

  8. P. Salin (ed.): *Currency Competition and Monetary Union*. 1984
                    ISBN 90-247-2817-7

* 9. D.E. Fair (ed.) in cooperation with F.L. de Juvigny: *Government Policies and the Working of Financial Systems in Industrialized Countries*. 1984   ISBN 90-247-3076-7

 10. C. Goedhart, G.A. Kessler, J. Kymmell and F. de Roos (eds.): *Jelle Zijlstra, A Central Banker's View*. Selected Speeches and Articles. 1985   ISBN 90-247-3184-4

 11. C. van Ewijk and J.J. Klant (eds.): *Monetary Conditions for Economic Recovery*. 1985
                    ISBN 90-247-3219-0

* 12. D.E. Fair (ed.): *Shifting Frontiers in Financial Markets*. 1986   ISBN 90-247-3225-5

 13. E.F. Toma and M. Toma (eds.): *Central Bankers, Bureaucratic Incentives, and Monetary Policy*. 1986   ISBN 90-247-3366-9

* 14. D.E. Fair and C. de Boissieu (eds.): *International Monetary and Financial Integration*. The European Dimension. 1988   ISBN 90-247-3563-7

 15. J. Cohen: *The Flow of Funds in Theory and Practice*. A Flow-Constrained Approach to Monetary Theory and Policy. 1987   ISBN 90-247-3601-3

 16. W. Eizenga, E.F. Limburg and J.J. Polak (eds.): *The Quest for National and Global Economic Stability*. In Honor of Hendrikus Johannes Witteveen. 1988
                    ISBN 90-247-3653-6

* 17. D.E. Fair and C. de Boissieu (eds.): *The International Adjustment Process*. New Perspectives, Recent Experience and Future Challenges for the Financial System. 1989   ISBN 0-7923-0013-0

 18. J.J. Sijben (ed.): *Financing the World Economy in the Nineties*. 1989
                    ISBN 0-7923-0090-4

FINANCIAL AND MONETARY POLICY STUDIES

19. I. Rizzo: *The 'Hidden' Debt.* With a Foreword by A.T. Peacock. 1990
                                                    ISBN 0-7923-0610-4

*20. D.E. Fair and C. de Boissieu (eds.): *Financial Institutions in Europe under New Competitive Conditions.* 1990   ISBN 0-7923-0673-2

21. R. Yazdipour (ed.): *Advances in Small Business Finance.* 1991   ISBN 0-7923-1135-3

*22. D.E. Fair and C. de Boissieu (eds.): *Fiscal Policy, Taxation and the Financial System in an Increasingly Integrated Europe.* 1992   ISBN 0-7923-1451-4

23. W.C. Boeschoten: *Currency Use and Payment Patterns.* 1992   ISBN 0-7923-1710-6

24. H.A. Benink: *Financial Integration in Europe.* 1993   ISBN 0-7923-1849-8

25. G. Galeotti and M. Marrelli (eds.): *Design and Reform of Taxation Policy.* 1992
                                                    ISBN 0-7923-2016-6

*26. D.E. Fair and R. Raymond (eds.): *The New Europe: Evolving Economic and Financial Systems in East and West.* 1993   ISBN 0-7923-2159-6

27. J.O. de Beaufort Wijnholds, S.C.W. Eijffinger and L.H. Hoogduin (eds.): *A Framework for Monetary Stability.* Papers and Proceedings of an International Conference (Amsterdam, The Netherlands, 1993). 1994   ISBN 0-7923-2667-9

*Published on behalf of the *Société Universitaire Européenne de Recherches Financières* (SUERF), consisting the lectures given at Colloquia, organized and directed by SUERF.

Kluwer Academic Publishers – Dordrecht / Boston / London